Tales from Colombia

*The Deeds and Misdeeds of 41
Peace Corps Volunteers Who Answered
President Kennedy's Call to Serve*

GARY DEAN PETERSON

Paulary Publishing

Fruit Heights, Utah

Grateful acknowledgement is made to the
members of
Colombia '64 who supplied material for this book.

ISBN-13: 978-0-615-45747-5

Cover Design by Amanda Hackmeister

Manufactured in the United States of America

Paulary Publishing
973 So. Valley View Drive
Fruit Heights, Utah 84037
http://garydeanpeterson.com

Contents

GLOSSARY

acción communal	community action	*granja*	agricultural extension farm
AID	Agency for International Development (U.S.)	*guadua*	largest species of bamboo
Amerindian	Native American	ICA	International Cooperation Administration – predecessor to AID
ASWAC	American Studies, World Affairs and Communism	*Incaparina*	high protein dietary supplement made from cotton seed and corn
Cafeteros	Federation of Coffee Growers (Colombian)	*junta*	governing body
campesino	rural person, farmer	*Llanos*	tropical grass plains stretching from eastern Colombia into Venezuela
campo	rural area		
Carabinero	mounted national police	mestizo	person of mixed blood
CARE	Cooperative for American Relief Everywhere	*nucleo*	central school, usually with five grades - supports four to six satellite schools having only two grades
casetas	open air tents or buildings used for dances	*panela*	partially refined sugar from sugar cane, similar to brown sugar
Castellano	pure Spanish, Castilian Spanish		
CIA	Central Intelligence Agency	PCV	Peace Corps Volunteer
Colombia '64	Colombia FAO/PINA-ETV/UPT 1964	PINA	*Programa Intregrado de Nutrición Aplicada*
cordillera	mountains, mountain range	*pollo*	chicken
corrida de toros	bull fight	RPCV	Return Peace Corps Volunteer
cumbia	a Latin dance	*selva*	jungle, forest
ETV	educational television	*Semana Santa*	Easter week
FAO	Food and Agriculture Organization (UN)	*teple*	Colombian musical instrument similar to a guitar
FARC	Revolutionary Armed Forces of Colombia	*tienda*	small store
		UNICEF	United Nations Children's Fund
fique (cabulla)	plant with long leathery leaves containing a fiber similar to hemp	*vereda*	rural community
		Violencia	Colombian civil war during the late 1940s and 1950s
		yuca	manioc, cassava

COLOMBIA
WITH DEPARTMENTS
AND TERRITORIES
IN 1965

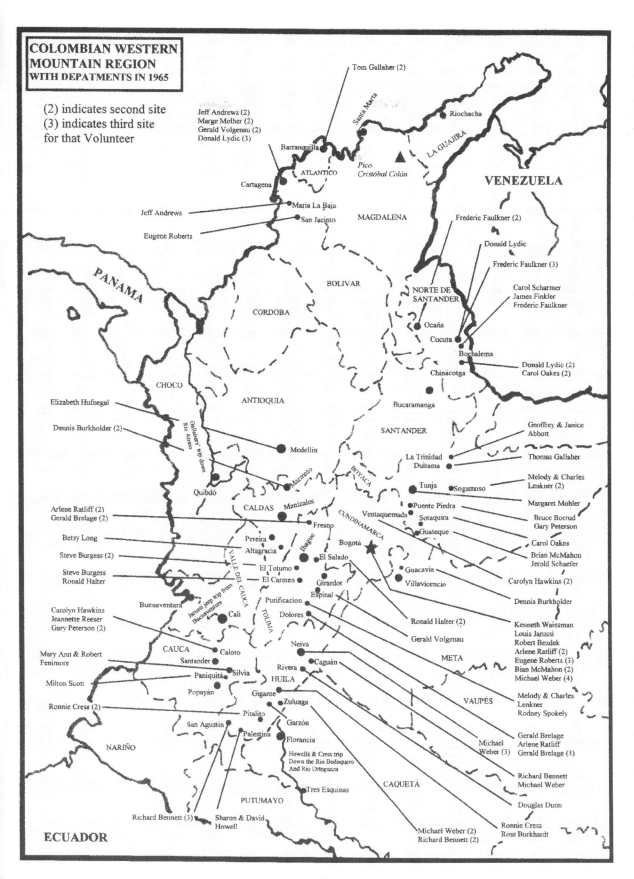

COLOMBIAN WESTERN MOUNTAIN REGION WITH DEPATMENTS IN 1965

(2) indicates second site
(3) indicates third site
for that Volunteer

Tom Gallaher (2)

Jeff Andrews (2)
Marge Molher (2)
Gerald Volgenau (2)
Donald Lydic (3)

Riochacha

Santa Marta

LA GUAJIRA

Barranquilla

VENEZUELA

Pico
Cristóbal Colón

ATLANTICO

Cartagena

Maria La Baja

Jeff Andrews

San Jacinto

MAGDALENA

Frederic Faulkner (2)

Eugene Roberts

Donald Lydic

Frederic Faulkner (3)

PANAMA

BOLIVAR

CORDOBA

NORTE DE
SANTANDER

Carol Scharmer
James Finkler
Frederic Faulkner

Ocaña

Cucuta

Bochalema

Donald Lydic (2)
Carol Oakes (2)

Chinácotga

CHOCO

Elizabeth Hufnegal

Dennis Burkholder (2)

ANTIOQUIA

Bucaramanga

Medellin

Gallaher's trip down Rio Atrato

SANTANDER

Geoffrey & Janice
Abbott

La Trinidad
Duitama

Thomas Gallaher

Quibdó

Marmato

BOYACA

Tunja

Sogamoso

Melody & Charles
Lenkner (2)

Arlene Ratliff (2)
Gerald Brelage (2)

CALDAS

Manizales

Puente Piedra

Margaret Mohler

Fresno

CUNDINAMARCA

Ventaquemada

Sotaquira

Bruce Borrud
Gary Peterson

Betsy Long

Pereira

Guateque

Carol Oakes

Steve Burgess (2)

Altagracia

Bogotá

Brian McMahon
Jerold Schaefer

Steve Burgess
Ronald Halter

VALLE DEL CAUCA

El Totumo
El Carmen

Ibague

El Salado

Guacavia

Carolyn Hawkins (2)

Girardot

Villavicencio

Dennis Burkholder

Buenaventura

Jarussi jeep trip from Buenaventura

Purificacion

Espinal

Carolyn Hawkins
Jeannette Reeser
Gary Peterson (2)

Cali

TOLIMA

Dolores

Ronald Halter (2)

Gerald Volgenau

META

Kenneth Waissman
Louis Jarussi
Robert Bezdek
Arlene Ratliff (2)
Eugene Roberts (3)
Bian McMahon (2)
Michael Weber (4)

Mary Ann & Robert
Fenimore

CAUCA

Caloto

Neiva

Caguán

Santander

Rivera

Milton Scott

Paniquitá

Silvia

HUILA

VAUPÉS

Popayán

Gigante

Zuluaga

Melody & Charles
Lenkner
Rodney Spokely

Ronnie Cress (2)

Pitalito

Garzón

San Agustin

Palestina

Florancia

Michael
Weber (3)

Gerald Brelage
Arlene Ratliff
Gerald Brelage (3)

NARIÑO

Howells & Cress trip
Down the Rio Bodoquero
And Rio Orteguaza

CAQUETÁ

Richard Bennett
Michael Weber

Douglas Dunn

Tres Esquinas

Richard Bennett (3)

PUTUMAYO

Sharon & David
Howell

Michael Weber (2)
Richard Bennett (2)

Ronnie Cress
Ross Burkhardt

ECUADOR

Caribbean Sea

ATLANTIC OCEAN

PANAMA

Cartagena

Panama City

VENEZUELA

COL OMBIA

Bogotá

GUYANA

SURINAM

FRENCH GUIANA

Popayan

Pasto

Quito

ECUADOR

Guayaquil

Tumbas

Amazon River

Manaus

Belém

Fortaleza

PERU

Leticia

AMAZON BASIN

B R A Z I L

Recife

Machu Pichu

Lima

Cusco

La Paz

BOLIVIA

Santa Cruz

Savador/Bahia

Brasilia

Lake Titicaca

PARAGUAY

Belo Horizonte

CHILE

ARGENTINA

Rio de Janeiro

Portillo

Valparaíso

Santiago

Carlos de Bariloche

PAMPAS

Buenos Aires

URUGUAY

Montevideao

ATLANTIC OCEAN

PACIFIC OCEAN

PATAGONIA

Tierra del Fuego

South America
Trips by Volunteers

+ + + · Author's trip to Machu Pichu (Chap. 15)

– – – · Trips home through Central America
(Chap. 19)

╫ ╫ ╫ · Long & Hawkins trip (Chap.19)

PREFACE

High in the Spring Mountains of Nevada, almost 8,000 feet above sweltering, smog obscured Las Vegas, a small band of stout hearted adventurers prepared to ascend the heights of Mount Charleston. Though it was mid summer (August 5, 2007) the air at this altitude was cool and clear. A soft breeze drifted down Kyle Canyon rustling the needles of the pine trees that stood tall among the towering granite formations.

The climb would not be trivial, another thousand feet to the summit of Cathedral Rock, but this group was accustomed to difficulties and hardship, even danger. In age, they were remarkably homogeneous, about 64, give or take a couple of years. The men were generally fit and ready for this endeavor although under golf hats and baseball caps the hair tended toward gray or white, or might be lacking altogether. The women were no less capable for that had always been the understanding in this fraternity, that each member was expected to carry his or her own weight and be ready and able to assist another. This was, after all, <u>Colombia FAO/PINA-ETV/UPT 1964</u>, trained at the University of Nebraska, tested in Puerto Rico and seasoned in the dense jungles, rugged mountains, deep valleys and tropical plains of Colombia, South America.

As they wound their way up the trail, many used walking sticks; others carried copious quantities of water. The grade was steep, but between puffs for air, words were exchanged, news of recent events and reminiscence of time spent on other mountain tops in another land. The pace was, perhaps, a bit slower and the rest stops more frequent than they would have been 43 years earlier, but the indomitable spirit, determination, and love of adventure were still present. This certainly was, and still is, a most remarkable group of people.

The peak was attained by mid afternoon and the stalwart crew began their decent after a short rest. They arrived at the lodge leg weary and willing to admit the years had taken their toll. Yet the twinkle in the eye and infectious enthusiasm had not been extinguished by the years and trials of life. In spirit, at least, they retained every bit of their youthful exuberance for exotic places and new experiences, a love of life and its surprises.

Not everyone from the original group was present of course. A foursome had opted for a round of golf instead of the mountain trek. One RPCV (Returned Peace Corps Volunteer) and his wife arrived late and used the time to check in. Another had sent word from Zambia he wouldn't be able to attend. Others were tied up with business or family commitments. Three members had dropped out of sight and even the group's retired FBI agent had not been able to track down his missing comrades. Two others had passed away over the years, one killed in a tragic airplane crash, ironically, in the mountains of Colombia. Still, those present were the representatives of a diverse group, made up of teachers, veterinarians, college professors, business people, engineers, a bank executive, the FBI agent and even a Broadway producer.

As the group dined on a Colombian cuisine of *ajiaco Bogotáno, frijoles* and *carneasada,* stories were passed along, tales of hair raising bus rides, reprisal killings, all night parties, poisonous snakes and dreaded parasites, rescuing imperiled missionaries, Amazon jungle adventures, death on high mountain glaciers, brutal jails and a heroic midnight ride.

Though certainly older and maybe a bit wiser, these adventurers were not so different from the young idealists that had congregated at the University of Nebraska some two score and three years earlier. The distinction was that now they shared the memories of their Colombian experience, whereas, in 1964, they had had almost nothing in common.

They came from every corner of the country and from every level of society, sixty-four innocents, imbued with President Kennedy's philosophy of fighting the Cold War by lifting others up from poverty so they could become self-reliant and cease to be targets for communist propaganda. With Fidel Castro exporting his brand of Marxism from his island citadel and Che Guevara fomenting revolution on the South American continent itself, the United States had sent an army of such volunteers (over 600 strong at the time) into Colombia.

Here then, is the story of two years in the lives of this group of Peace Corps Volunteers and how the experience affected their lives. It is also the story of two countries, one struggling with the long term consequences of the Cold War and about to become mired in an Asian conflict, a bloody side show of that war. The other appeared to finally be on the verge of breaking out of economic and cultural stagnation, ready, at last, to make real progress toward attaining the potential of a talented people and a fertile land. Inevitably, this account also involves the story of the Peace Corps itself, still an evolving concept in 1964 when these young idealists answered President Kennedy's call and boarded aircraft for the trip to Lincoln, Nebraska.

INTRODUCTION
(Reminiscence of a Colombia '64 Volunteer)

Looking back, it is remarkable how little I knew of the world in the spring of 1964, a time when I was trying to wrap up my undergraduate classes at the University of Kansas. As the world was changing in remarkable ways, so too would my life. Sitting in the hill country of eastern Kansas, I really had little conception of the world. I knew that the barbershop in downtown Lawrence had only recently been integrated and lots of civil rights marches and sit-ins had been going on down South. President Kennedy was dead. Vice President Lyndon Johnson took over the office and he looked like a shoo-in to be elected to a four-year term in the fall.

America had yet to enter into full combat in Vietnam. I knew that U.S. military advisors were there. And I could only presume that they were there, well, *advising*. As for Vietnam itself, wasn't it somewhere near Korea which was somewhere near Japan?

The Free Speech Movement had yet to hit Berkeley. No one knew what a hippie was, much less a Yippie. Tie-dye was not yet the fad. I went to classes wearing khaki pants, a white button-down shirt and loafers. When I got a haircut, I asked the barber for a Princeton cut.

As for things Latin, I knew that Fidel Castro was once a scrappy underdog battling against the evil Cuban dictator, Batista. Only a few years before, TV news programs portrayed him as a sort of guerilla hero that was holed up with his bearded band in the island's western mountains. But all that hero business jerked to a sudden halt after his fighters won the revolution and Castro announced that he was, of all things, a communist. Oops. The Red Menace. Now the newspapers portrayed him as a Caribbean bad guy who gave overlong speeches and, if Kennedy had not stood up to him, he would have planted Russian missiles right there just 90 miles from Florida. Che and his beret had yet to make the fronts of t-shirts.

As for South America, where I thought I might be headed, it was still pretty vague in my mind. It was that bubble topped continent in the lower half of the globe. Colombia was near the top. What I knew about it was precious little, beyond that it was spelled with two Os and not an O and a U. The capital was Bogotá. It once had a dictator. But didn't all those South American countries? It had rebels rooting around in the hills. Time Magazine said one of the rebel leaders was called *Tiro Fijo* which meant "Sure Shot." Great name for a bandit, I thought. Who could have guessed that old *Tiro* would still be around making the government crazy 40 years later.

I never gave a thought to drugs. Not from Colombia, not from anywhere. I think some of the arty kids on campus actually smoked marijuana. We're talking Kansas here, remember. But as a far as I knew, Colombia had nothing to do with reefer madness, much less cocaine.

I was just plugging along, going to classes. The only thing I was smoking was a pack of Winstons a day. When not in classes or drinking 3.2 beer with the guys, I was working as a director of a men's dorm and going on dates trying to cop a feel on Julie Nicolson who not only was great looking but along with some other fine attributes she had been to Mexico and could actually speak Spanish.

I knew about four words of Spanish – *Si, adios, señor, señorita* and *la cucaracha*. Maybe I knew a couple of others. It was not that I had spent a life entirely unexposed to the Spanish language. Some years back, *La Bamba* had been a big hit song. I had studied French in high school and college. I thought I understood it ... but I was wrong.

So there I was, a wide-eyed guy from Colorado Springs hanging out in Kansas. I was about to graduate with two degrees – one in journalism and the other in psychology. It had been my plan to go into advertising, say clever things, drink martinis and hang out on Madison Avenue. But after a few courses, I realized that I was not much interested in what advertising people actually did for a living. And a career of selling toothpaste seemed to be, well, rather shallow. With that thought at least partially resolved in my brain, I found myself with no clear options about what to do with the rest of my life.

And then, on a soft, sun-dappled afternoon, Sargent Shriver, the director of the still spanking-new Peace Corps, came on campus to speak. Shriver had a big jaw, a big smile and a sophisticated style that fit right in with the Kennedy clan. And what's more, he offered an intriguing possibility for my future – at least for the near term. Cool, I thought - or at least I think I thought that. But I'm not sure the word "cool" was used much then.

I filled out the forms. It made sense. I had nowhere else to go really. So why not go away, far away. South America seemed interesting, so I checked that option. It would be a great adventure. I figured I could learn a third (actually second) language. When I got out, the government would give me a $2,000 readjustment allowance. Hell, I could buy a new Volkswagen with $2,000. And finally, I could probably do some good. I liked the idea of doing something good.

I sent off the Peace Corps papers. I had hoped to hear something right away. But I didn't. As summer approached, I was on the phone with my mother (this time not asking for money). If I didn't have word from the Peace Corps, she did. The FBI had been nosing around the neighborhood, asking questions about me. The folks down the street apparently were saddened by the thought that I would likely end up in prison. After all, isn't that what FBI agent Efrem Zembalist, Jr. did on TV? send people to prison?

As it turned out, the feds missed the fact that I had stolen an airplane at the age of 15 (but that's another story). And the Peace Corps said I could join a training group headed for the University of Nebraska. The project: agricultural work. Nebraska? Agricultural work?

I am not sure what I had in mind about the Peace Corps, but it never included farm work. At that point, my farm skills included being able to positively differentiate between a horse and a cow. Lots of cowboy films helped with that. Also I dated a rodeo queen who was a barrel racer. But no matter my inexperience, South America beckoned. But first, before I'd ever get introduced to the notion of raising rabbits, the Peace Corps required a physical exam.

The nearest place to Lawrence, Kansas for an exam that met U.S. government standards was at an Air Force base 25 miles away at Topeka. When I showed up, the docs were completely charmed by the fact that I was applying to the Peace Corps. I was a first for them. They had checked the pulses and called for coughs from jet pilots, but not anyone who might be sent off to live in a grass shack in some forgotten corner of the world.

Normally a physical exam is a physical exam. One is much the same as another. But I do recall two things from that medical probing. One, the medics were intrigued with the discovery that I was red-green blind. They were getting into this whole Peace Corps thing. And they worried that like pilots, I might get washed out because of the color blindness. So they gave me what Peace Corps doctors later said was the most exhaustive eye exam they had ever seen. As it turned out, the Peace Corps cared not one whit if I could see reds just like most other people or not.

Second, I listened while the Air Force guys groused. Here they were sitting out in the middle of boring Kansas when what they really wanted was to do the jobs they had been trained to do. 'Sure hope we get into a war,' one said. 'It would help get a little rank around here.' Of course, that's a down side for a peacetime military, too few opportunities for promotion. But as we all know, you have to be careful what you wish for.

Then on a sunny day in September, I think, I boarded a plane in Colorado Springs, flew to Denver where I picked up a flight to Lincoln, Nebraska. I admit Lincoln seemed a peculiar choice: Why Cornhuskerville in the middle of the white-bread Plains States to get ready for a tour of duty in tropical South America? The Lincoln-bound plane was a prop job, comfortable for that era. Food wasn't bad. But the best part was I ended up sitting next to a pretty blonde, who turned out to be a model from Omaha which, as it turns out, is just down the road from Lincoln.

Julie was back at KU for her senior year and had quietly moved on. Apparently she figured that somebody who would just up and take off for South American was not all that good a prospect. I was sad to see her go. But later, in retrospect, I had to admit she had made a wise choice. At any rate this new girl, whose name I can no longer remember, seemed like a good person to help me recover from my Julie hangover.

Gerald Vogenau
Ann Arbor, September 2008

1
THE UNIVERSITY OF NEBRASKA
AND THE IDEALISTS WHO WOULD BE VOLUNTEERS

President John F. Kennedy was flying into Billings, Montana for a speech at the Yellowstone County Fairgrounds the announcement tacked to the Student Union bulletin board read. The article caused some stir among the students at Montana State University.

John Fitzgerald Kennedy seemed to connect with young people, and especially college students, in a way no other president had. There was his youth, good looks and charm, compelling oratory and, of course, his Peace Corps that was, if not wildly popular, at least widely discussed on campus.

Just that summer the first Peace Corps Volunteers had returned after their two years of service. These inaugural Volunteers were featured in news stories across the country and those from Montana were interviewed on local radio and television. Time Magazine published a cover story on the Peace Corps saying, "....it is possibly the greatest single success the Kennedy Administration has produced."[1] And here was the president, speaking within a few hours drive.

So five of us, all students, all members of the Phi Sigma Kappa fraternity at Montana State, piled into a car in the predawn hours and left Bozeman for the 150 mile drive to Billings. Though a bit groggy and tired, we were looking forward to the trip. It was an excuse to get out of town, check out the girls that might be at the gathering and maybe learn a little something about politics.

On the morning of September 25, 1963, we pulled into Billings with plenty of time to visit friends at Eastern Montana College and around town. Then, after a breakfast, it was out to the fairgrounds to be sure of a good seat.

The multi-car cavalcade arrived, that clear autumn morning, with a forest of little flags flying on the black limousines. So many people exited the cars it was impossible to tell which one was the president. But as the entourage mounted the stage, Kennedy's familiar form was obvious walking next to Mike Mansfield, senior senator from Montana. The crowd in the stands rose to its feet with applause and cheers.

As the introductions were being made, I remember there was a breeze and Kennedy kept running his hand through his tousled hair to keep it from becoming completely unruly.

The president's speech was mostly about recent legislation passed to protect wetlands, establish parks and reclamation projects, but a couple of sentences concerning the communist threat caught my attention, "....we are trying to assist the hundred-odd countries which are now independent to maintain their independence. We do that not only because we wish them to be free, but because it serves our own interests."[2] This, it seemed to me, was a direct reference to the Peace Corps.

After the speech, the motorcade exited the fairgrounds for the Billings airport and Air Force One. Our party regrouped and headed back to Bozeman. On the way, there was

---

[1] Time Magazine, *It Is Almost As Good As Its Intentions,* July 05, 1963,
http://www.time.com/time/printout/0,8816,875013,00.html.
[2] President Kennedy's Remarks at the Yellowstone County Fairgrounds, Billings, Montana, September 25, 1963, *Public Papers of the Presidents,* Kennedy, 1963, p. 724.

discussion about what we had witnessed, the president, the Peace Corps and returning Volunteers.

Two months later the young energetic President we had seen on that beautiful fall day was dead, mortally wounded by an assassin's bullet.

Of the five fraternity brothers who took that trip to Billings, two, Chuck Brome and I, would join the Peace Corps and serve in South America along with a third Phi Sig, Don Durga. We would be stationed in Colombia, Equator, and Bolivia, three different programs, but with the same Peace Corps goals.

Nearly a year after Air Force One departed the Billings International Airport, another large airplane settled out of the clear Montana sky and landing at the same Billings airport, one of many landing on that hot August day. This aircraft taxied to the terminal and the pilot cut power to the engines. One by one the four propellers slowed their rotation and stopped. The co-pilot slid open the side windshield next to him and waved to the man in coveralls who was chocking the plane's wheels. A stairway was rolled up to the door of the aircraft and the passengers began to deplane. No enclosed ramp providing air-conditioned passage from plane to terminal, there was only the portable stairway and a walk across the hot tarmac to the terminal doors.

Inside those terminal doors Louie Jarussi and his brother waited. Boarding was a simple matter in those days, no searches, no screening of carry-ons, no long lines. Family and friends were welcome to say their good-byes to departing passengers in the waiting area and wave to them as they walked out to the airplane. The atmosphere was more relaxed and less hurried than the process encountered today. It was still the age of innocence for the air traveler. D. B. Cooper's first ever hijacking-for-ransom was seven years in the future and 9-11 with its aftermath, the TSA, was half a life time away.

Louie shook hands with his brother, who had brought him to Billings from their small town of Joliet forty miles to the southwest, and walked out the terminal door drawn along by the line of passengers filing across the concourse and up the steps into the aircraft. Some of the passengers seemed excited and some slightly bored, but the six foot two inch, 210 pound, 20 year old was less sanguine.

Loui Jarussi

"I had never flown in an airplane before," he remembers, "and when I boarded the old four engine prop, I was scared it would not get off the ground. My brother was watching me get on the plane figuring he would never see me again. After several stops, we landed in Lincoln, Nebraska and when I stepped off the plane, I remember the oppressive humid wall of heat that hit me in the face and a strange smell in the air. As I recall, it was from all of the silage made from soy and corn grown in the area. I was away from Montana for the first time in my life and wasn't quite sure how to handle it."[3]

Jarussi was one of 64 trainees traveling to the University of Nebraska that day. They came from all over the United States, from Vermont to California and from Florida to Alaska. Most had grown up in rural areas, small towns, farms and ranches, but a number were from cities, even the biggest, New York, Houston, and Los Angeles. Their

---

[3] Louie Jarussi, personal email, 11 July 2008.

backgrounds and resumes were as varied as their origins, ranging from ranch hand, auto mechanic and waitress to seaman, farm manager, banker and advertising agent. About the only thing they had in common was that they had all submitted applications to the new people-to-people government outreach program called Peace Corps and had taken the qualification test, the first step in a screening process that would eventually determine which ones would become Volunteers. They had all received letters inviting them to train for the FAO-PINA[4] Colombia 1964 program at the University of Nebraska (ETV – Educational Television - was not part of the program at this point). The letter stipulated that this was an invitation to train only and there was no guarantee the recipient would actually become a Volunteer, a condition of acceptance that would soon be made painfully clear to each arrival.

Jerry Brelage climbed out of the car into the sweltering heat and stepped onto the University of Nebraska Ag Campus on the outskirts of Lincoln some two and a half miles from the main campus down town. Like all the would-be Volunteers arriving that day, his emotions ran high.

"I had no idea of what I was getting into," Jerry recalls. "That was the first time I had been in an airplane. I was a small town boy from Indiana. Just getting to Nebraska was the most exciting thing that had ever happened to me in my life."[5]

So why had Jerry come? Why had he made this decision to offer up two years of his life, placing his future in the hands of this new government agency? He certainly had other choices, or did he?

Jerry C. Brelage grew up on a dairy farm on the edge of Batesville, Indiana, a town of about 3,000 at the time, closer to Cincinnati, Ohio then Indianapolis, Indiana. He had completed three years of college at Ball State Teacher's College where he had played some soccer, about his only connection with South America, but one that would turn out to be a real asset in training and in Colombia. However, after three years of college, Jerry was out of money and lacked any real direction. He was looking for other opportunities.

It was a time of restlessness for this generation. The young people making their way to Lincoln, Nebraska were not of the later baby boom generation. These men and women were a product of WWII. A few were even born before the United States entered the war, but all would be considered war babies, beginning life at the time when Hitler was rolling across Europe and the Japanese were gobbling up Pacific islands, bombing and occupying American territory. Many could remember soldiers returning from that great war if not the war itself. They all certainly had a clear recollection of the Korean Conflict. That was the war of their youth. The first use, by the U.S., of jet combat aircraft, the Pusan Perimeter, Inchon Landing, Chongjin Reservoir, Heart Break Ridge, and Pork Chop Hill. Harry Truman and Dwight D. Eisenhower were the presidents of their formative years. The Korean War was followed by the relative peace of the late 1950's, television, trios, and Elvis. As this generation became politically conscious they were treated to a charismatic president, his beautiful wife and young family. Then they were shocked by the world's realities, Sputnik, the Cuban Missile Crisis and a presidential assassination.

---

[4] Food and Agriculture Organization (UN agency) – Progama Integrado de Nutrición Aplicada (Colombian agency) - organizations that were to support the group's work in Colombia.
[5] Jerry Brelage, personal email, July 1, 2008.

Having decided against going back to school Jerry mulled over his prospects, "I had taken the physical to be drafted by the army. I saw the advertisement on TV for the Peace Corps the end of June and that tests would be given in Cincinnati. I said that I would enlist in the Air force if I didn't hear from Peace Corps by September 1st. Of course I heard about the 1st week of August."[6]

The date Jerry was to leave for Nebraska turned out to be the day of his brother's wedding and he was in the wedding party. Jerry had to bring his traveling clothes and suit cases to the ceremony and while the wedding was finishing up, he was busy in the back of the church changing clothes. Jerry had a friend take him to the airport where he grabbed the plane for Chicago, then on to Omaha and finally Lincoln.

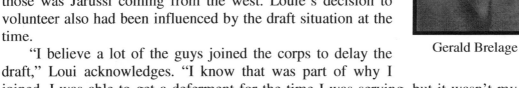

Once on campus, Brelage was directed to the Nebraska Center for Continuing Education, which became known to the trainees as the Kellogg Center, the name taken from the building's major donor. The center was located on the edge of the ag campus so it was out of the way of the school's regular students, but close enough so school facilities were available to the trainees.

Here Jerry met some of the other trainees who were arriving singly or in twos and threes from the airport. One of those was Jarussi coming from the west. Louie's decision to volunteer also had been influenced by the draft situation at the time.

Gerald Brelage

"I believe a lot of the guys joined the corps to delay the draft," Loui acknowledges. "I know that was part of why I joined. I was able to get a deferment for the time I was serving, but it wasn't my main reason for going. I was just out of options in Montana and wanted to try something different other than the military."[7]

The draft was on the minds of most young men at the time. It was the middle of the Cold War. The United States was not in a shooting war at the time, Korea was now a memory of the 50's and Vietnam, though lost by the French, had only military advisors from the U.S. There was the threat of nuclear annihilation, but the 50's hysteria of Civil Defense aircraft spotters, grade school drills of hiding under desks and basement bomb shelters had given way to a general *blasé* attitude about the potential for impending doom. In the vernacular of the times, "we had learned to live with the bomb." Of course, every so often the reality of the threat did intrude as in the case of the Cuban Missile Crisis of 1962. The Peace Corps service did not replace military service, however. If your draft board allowed you a deferment for as long as you served, upon your return your status immediately reverted to full eligibility.

Not all trainees were mindful of the draft, however. Besides the women and couples there was Tom Gallaher who had already served in the Merchant Marines and the Marine Corps. At six two and a lean 185 pounds, Tom was the epitome of what a Marine and seaman should be. With red hair, chiseled features, and robust physique, he looked like

[6] Jerry Brelage, personal email, July 6, 2008.
[7] Louie Jarussi, personal email to Gary Peterson, July 15, 2008

he should have been in a swashbuckler as either tough rogue or gallant sailor. While most of the group struggled through the daily exercises and mile run in tee-shirt, trunks and tennis shoes, Tom ran in combat boots and handled the push-ups and sit-ups with seeming ease. His heavy Bronx accent betrayed his New York origins where he had picked up a degree in English from Fordham University. At 25 he was one of the oldest members of the group to survive the selection process.

Folks joined the Peace Corps for a variety of reasons [Tom writes], some from a sense of adventure, some from idealism, some to avoid the draft, some to live and work in a foreign country, for most of us it was probably a combination of the above. For me it was a direct result of an experience I had when I was 17 or 18 and in India.

After I graduated from high school, I worked for a few years before I went to college as an able bodied seaman. "I shipped out," was the expression they used. I traveled all over the Far East, Japan, Thailand, China, India, the Middle East, Africa and Europe.

On my first trip to India, the ship's first port o' call was Bombay, now called Mumbai. We sailed from Karachi; it was a short trip, as I recall, less than 24 hours. We arrived at dawn and after we had docked the ship and had breakfast, it was my job to go aft to take down the flag (all ships when entering port are required to display a flag of their country of origin).

Arriving at the stern of the ship, I saw this skinny kid about my age eating out of the cans in which we stowed our garbage while we were in port. I will never forget the look on his face as long as I live.

How is it possible, I thought, that in the United States we have so much food that we store it in huge grain silos and here are people hungry enough to eat our garbage. How is this possible, for us to have so much and not share it with others who are in such need? Is he not a man and are we not all brothers? And yet there he was cringing like he expected me to kick him like some mange dog.

I motioned to him to follow me. I took him to our mess hall and fed him a proper breakfast. Later that afternoon, after I had finished work, I got all my money, went ashore and gave it all away to the people begging in the streets, women and emaciated little children, next to whom the poorest *campesino* (farmer, rural person) in Colombia would look prosperous.

Thomas Gallaher

So when I was in college and heard about President Kennedy starting the Peace Corps, my first thought was, that's great, its about time the U.S., the world's wealthiest nation, did something to alleviate the crushing burden of poverty and hunger that afflicts so many of the world's people, the ones that I had seen and experienced first hand in my travels in Asia and Africa.

However, by the time I was ready to graduate from college, I thought it would be a good idea to get my military service out of the way before I was drafted. So I enlisted in the Marine Corps – real smart move, what was I thinking?

After I got out of the Marine Corps, I went to work for an advertising agency Young & Rubicam. It just so happened that they were the agency that handled the advertising for the Peace Corps. Do you recall the ad with the tag line, "The Toughest Job You'll Ever Love?" That was a Y&R ad.

After a few months at Y&R, I applied to the Peace Corps and was accepted. I resigned from the firm, thus aborting a potentially lucrative career on Madison Ave. to pursue my dream.

In fact I specifically applied for an ag program, because I wanted to learn about farming. Yes, me, a boy from the streets of New York. I had this fantasy about being a farmer, living far from the concrete canyons of the city, being close to nature, sinking my fingers in the good rich earth. I thought the Peace Corps would teach me the skills necessary to become a farmer. Boy was I naive, but not as naive as the Peace Corps. Whatever let them think they could take a kid from the concrete jungle and make him into a farmer in four months, and a Spanish speaking one at that.

When the letter from Washington came, notifying me of my acceptance, I was jubilant. I had traveled all around the world, but I'd never been to Nebraska, so when I boarded the plane at La Guardia, I was excited and eager to be on my way.[8]

Gallaher's big city background and broad experience gave him a unique prospective on the group, but did not necessarily put him at ease or make him over confident.

My first impressions of Lincoln and our fellow PCVs (Peace Corps Volunteers) were, gosh, how young and wholesome they all look. Hope they don't think I'm too old.

Having grown up in New York City, I was happily surprised to see how open and friendly everyone was. I felt at last I had found the true Americans, the sturdy yeoman, farmers that had made this country the great nation it was, open handed, warm hearted, hearty folks, not at all like some of the attenuated city bred types I'd grown up with. This was the real America as I had imagined it would be.[9]

The other "old timer" in the group was Eugene Roberts, also 25, from Glenn Dale, Maryland, a varsity wrestler and graduate of Yale University, though probably more helpful in his Peace Corps job was his work in the Department of Animal Husbandry at Penn. State.

Other ivy leaguers were Fred Faulkner, 22, of Crawford, New Jersey, a graduate of Harvard University and Brian McMahon, 22, of Colorado Springs, Colorado who had attended Dartmouth Collage.

---

[8] Tom Gallaher, personal email, October 8, 2008.
[9] Ibid.

Another Coloradoan arriving at the campus was Ronnie Cress, graduate of Colorado State University. Of the 32 single trainees that would make it to Colombia as Volunteers, 8 would be women. These young ladies were trail blazers in their own right. In the early 60's it was still unusual to find women, especially young single women, venturing out on their own and here these young women were, embarking on a path that would place them in a foreign country, living and working in rural, and possibly remote, areas under rudimentary conditions. These women were pushing the envelope of what was permissible and in some cases going beyond what was socially acceptable. The early 60's were still a time of relative social conservatism. The feminist movement and the sexual revolution were in their infancy. Betty Friedan's *The Feminine Mystique* (published in 1963) had just become the handbook for the feminist, but the big name leaders of the cause were only beginning to emerge.

The young people arriving at the University of Nebraska Ag Campus were still bound by the social rules observed by their parents. The wild excesses of the counter culture revolution, called the hippy movement, the free and easy drugs, the uprooting of the youth and the casual attitude toward sex were yet in the future. To those flying into Lincoln, the precursors of the Cultural Revolution would have been known as beatniks. Woodstock was still four years away and Haight-Ashbury, San Francisco was just collecting its first residents of the Beat Generation. The VW busses that would one day travel the country packed with shaggy, unkempt social outcasts had not rolled off the assembly line yet.

The draft, of course, was not a factor in Ronnie's calculation to volunteer. Looking back over the decades she lays out her reasons:

> I entered the Peace Corps because I wanted to continue learning after I graduated from Colorado State University. I did not want, at that time, to continue my learning through a university, but through experience. In addition, I was very grateful that I had been born in the United States and had the opportunity to pay for my college education. I felt it was likely that in another country I would not have had that freedom or opportunity.
>
> My minor was in French so I wanted to go to Morocco. The Peace Corps wrote back and stated that I would be much more suited for the PINA group going to Colombia because of my experiences and that if I could learn to speak one language, I could learn another.
>
> When I told my mother that I was accepted to Colombia, she said, 'How wonderful, I didn't know that you had applied to Columbia University.' She was really disappointed that it was the Peace Corps in Colombia, S.A. and not the university.[10]

Ronnie Cress

Another trainee who wanted to give something back while extending his education through experience was Robert Bezdek, 22. Born in a Czech community north of Waco,

---

[10] Ronnilou Cress Kordick, personal email, 12 July 2008

Texas, Bob spoke Czech before he learned English. He and two sisters grew up in Corpus Christi where he attended Catholic schools through high school. To pay for this education, Robert worked at a grocery store beginning at age 13. Robert had never been outside the Texas-Louisiana area except for two summers of study at Manhattanville College north of New York. After high school it was on to seminary where Robert trained to become a priest.

"After four and a half years in the seminary, I left and finished my degree at St. Mary's University in San Antonio," Robert recalls. "Clearly, I recognized that my life was sheltered and I realized that I needed/wanted to live in another country and learn another language fluently."[11]

Robert Bezdek

Robert hoped to go to Thailand, but when the Colombia program was offered, he accepted as South America was his second choice.

"My interest in the Peace Corps and a stint in a Latin American country was that it would give me a broader view of life and help improve my limited Spanish. Moreover, I had a burning desire to travel. One of my major goals was to further my education through life experiences and then return to academic work..."[12] These objectives Robert would achieve and much more.

Wanting to give something back and helping others were motivations for most Volunteers. This was expressed by Betsy Long, of Roxboro, North Carolina, a graduate of Meredith College in home economics, a real plus for the work this group was to do. "I volunteered after President Kennedy was assassinated," she says. "I was raised in a family that always believed in helping others."[13]

And Jim Finkler, 22, of Milwaukee, Wisconsin, a graduate of Marquette University, proved that the trainees came from all political persuasions. "I joined the Peace Corps probably because I was a bit of a young idealist. I wanted to give something back for what I had received and for the opportunities I had access to at that time in my life. I might, however, have been the only Volunteer to vote for Barry Goldwater in 1964."[14]

The idealism expressed by Jim and others is perhaps illustrated most succinctly in the recollections of Bruce Borrud, 22, of Northridge, California. Bruce was born in, yes, Billings, Montana and raised in North Dakota where his father had a John Deere dealership. After the war, the family of five - Bruce had two brothers - moved to California where his mother taught elementary school. Bruce's older brother became a Lutheran pastor and ran a summer camp for youth in South Dakota. Bruce worked at these camps during summers as a counselor and finally as camp director for a camp in the Black Hills. Because of this experience he took an interest in teaching and switched to education his last two years at UCLA.

[11] Robert Bezdek, personal email, Sep. 25, 2008
[12] Robert Bezdek, personal email, Jul. 8, 2008
[13] Betsy Long Bucks, personal email, Jul. 9, 2008
[14] Jim Finkler, personal email, Aug. 4, 2008

"I was a college senior at UCLA when President Kennedy was assassinated in November of 1963. It was a traumatic time for me since I believed in Camelot and the message to 'ask not what your country can do for you, but what you can do for your country.' As a result, several of my friends and I at UCLA applied for the Peace Crops in early 1964. I was the only one of this group to either be accepted or pursue it. My first training offer was to work in community development in Africa with training to begin in June. I begged off since I had a summer job as a camp director in the Black Hills of South Dakota, but said I would consider a different assignment after the summer. Subsequently, they sent me the FAO/PINA program schedule to begin in September. I accepted with great anticipation and was pleased to be a part of our group in Nebraska."[15]

Bruce Borrud

Finally, there was a desire by some to change a way of life, a motivation best told by Ron Halter, 20, of Lima, Ohio, the only trainee with no college education to survive the deselecting process. He had attended thirteen different schools before graduating from high school. Family homes included one with a "two-holer" out house and long handled outdoor water pump. At least there was a garden and chicken coop out back which provided food for the family. Ron remembers vividly his reasons for applying to the Peace Corps. It was the first step leading to two years that would have a profound effect on the direction of his life.

When I graduated from high school I was disillusioned. Although I thought that I wanted to be an aerospace engineer, one trip to the University of Detroit's School of Engineering ended that dream. How was I going to pay for it?

Ronald Halter

Looking back, the main reason I joined the Peace Corps was not humanitarian, but to escape the lower socioeconomic-class life that I was doomed to be part of, given the history of my family. My younger brother ended up spending 30 years as a rubber worker at Goodyear. I was greasing cars and pumping gas for $57.00 a week (50 hours a week). I had no money to travel and see the world. Also, no one in my family had ever attended college or could envision why anyone would want to; therefore, the Peace Corps helped me to break out of rural Ohio and break the family mold."[16]

Then there was Gerry Volgenau from Colorado Springs who had just received his degree from a school on the plains of Kansas and was now headed for the plains of Nebraska.

---

[15] Bruce Borrud, personal email, Jul. 8, 2008
[16] Ronald Halter, personal email, Jul. 8, 2008

So I showed up at the University of Nebraska – or rather an aggie outpost of it – decked out in my white button-down shirt, my khaki pants and, I am sure, an unwavering expression of bewilderment.

At the outset, our group numbered more than 60, almost all recent college graduates. To my eye, most seemed better prepared and more confident than I felt. Some had just emerged from classy eastern schools like Dartmouth, Yale and Fordham. While some others of us hailed from schools in the hinterlands like, well, the University of Kansas.

Some certainly were more sophisticated. Ken Waissman, who seemed to tap dance in straight from Broadway, found this Hicksville largely devoid of what he'd known as civilization. "A hot night in Lincoln," he said, "is sitting in front of the Cornhusker Hotel and waiting for the other cab to come by."

In terms of agricultural knowledge, most of the group – unlike Ken, a couple of others and me -- seemed to have a pretty good handle on farm life. They had lived on farms and ranches, driven tractors, plowed fields, raised sheep for 4-H Clubs, planted everything from tomatoes to sorghum, mucked out stalls and even shoed horses.

Brian McMahon shone with a distinctly ranch land patina. He was a true cowboy. He wore a silver belt buckle that he'd actually won riding in a rodeo. For me, that was very cool. Like the old Willie Nelson song, "my heroes always were cowboys."

And there was the guy with movie star looks who caught every girl's eye ... and *ear* when he strummed his guitar and sang with a stunning falsetto.

The flashy education, the farming skills, a facility with Spanish, the insouciant confidence evinced by so many probably would have been more intimidating, except that everyone was so nice. So unpretentious. And I can only guess all these years later, they were probably as unsure about Peace Corps things as I was.

Gerald Volgenau

Also the staff kept reminding us that we were the cream of American youth, carefully hand-picked and so on. Ah, to be among the chosen few. I liked that. But hand picked? I knew about the FBI, but that hardly felt like a round of applause.[17]

As for me, Gary Peterson the author, my sense of excitement was palpable. After seeing President Kennedy in Billings, Montana, I had applied for the Peace Corps, then waited all summer for some response. Now here I was, entering training. In a way I was coming home. I was actually born in Lincoln February 19th, 1942 though my family moved to Montana before I was four years old. My father worked in Nebraska before the war, but holding a reserve commission in the army, he was activated following the Pearl Harbor attack. After the war we moved back to the family ranch thirty miles east of Great Falls where my brother and I grew up attending a one-room school house and a small

[17] Gerald Volgenau, personal email to Gary Peterson, Sep 22, 2008.

high school of some forty students. Both my parents taught in the local high schools on and off to help support the farm where we raised wheat and Hereford breeding stock.

Gary Peterson

I had spent that summer picking hay bails and building fence after my graduation from Montana State University and felt I was in good shape, but the heat combined with the humidity of eastern Nebraska was suffocating. Fortunately, the extreme heat only lasted a few days. The next three months were delightful as far as the weather was concerned, cool, mostly clear skies with the beautiful mid-western autumn foliage.

Most of the trainees were already there by the time I arrived, but I didn't have time to get to know anyone before we were called into a meeting where we met the program director Deon Axthelm. Carolyn Hawkins, from Hodgenville, Kentucky said he reminded her of her father and I think that we could all relate to that sentiment.[18] He did oversee the entire program, but took special interest in each individual trainee.

Sundays were mostly free time, but on this Sunday there was still moving in and setting up to do. We were in a dormitory setting with bunk beds and common shower-bathroom facilities, not spacious, but adequate. That evening we met the staff. Half this group was language instructors all from Latin America. There were a doctor, social studies professor and various teachers of agriculture, health and home economics.

Monday, August 31 we began the schedule that we would follow for the next two and a half months, rising at 6:00 AM, PE for an hour, breakfast at 7:30, then Spanish, social studies, lunch, Spanish, technical studies, dinner at 5:30 followed by more Spanish. Structured classes were over by 8:30, but by that time we were so tired there was only time to write some letters or maybe study a little. We did get Saturday night off and, of course, Sundays were free.

"The training was intense and sometimes grueling with long hours," Gallaher says of it, "but compared to Marine Corps boot camp, not too harsh. My one regret was that I didn't get to know everyone better."

There was little doubt but that Spanish was of overriding importance, with the emphasis on developing verbal skills; little time was spent on reading the language. Trainees who had had some Spanish moved along more rapidly, of course, and were placed in higher classes. The rest of us struggled trying to memorize enough words to string a sentence together. Carolyn Hawkins, the petite dark haired Kentuckian, was embarrassingly swift at picking up the language. She began in my beginner class, but quickly moved on to a more advanced section. Though a natural at languages, Carolyn very nearly dropped out of the program.

Carolyn Hawkins

Carolyn was born in a sharecropper's house - about seven miles from the Abraham Lincoln Historical Park, in Hodgenville, Kentucky - where there was no electricity and no running water.

---

[18] Carolyn Hawkins Denton, personal email, August 23, 2008.

There, she was surrounded by grandparents, uncles, aunts and cousins. Social events were holidays and birthdays with lots of family, and going to the Barren Run Baptist Church.

> Graduating from a Baptist college in Campbellsville, Kentucky in 1964, my liberal arts degree with an emphasis in sociology and economics, didn't seem to prepare me for anything special. Seeing a pamphlet on the library counter about Peace Corps intrigued me... "helping others help themselves." Being in the stage of my life when I was still rather idealistic, I completed the application. Much to my amazement and my family's, I was invited to training.[19]

Carolyn's first experience away from family was the trip to Nebraska; the separation was an emotionally strain. Like some others, her flight to Lincoln was her first ride on an airplane.

Carolyn relates, "Grandfather Hawkins died while I was in Nebraska and I had the difficult decision of whether to go home or stay. I stayed....probably would not have come back had I left."[20]

Spanish for most of the group was difficult and exhausting, perhaps the most difficult part of the training.

> I found Spanish language immersion the toughest part of the program [Gallaher says]. I would often skip lunch and instead do laps around the track because after 3 or 4 hours of intense focus in our language classes, the last thing I wanted was to sit around a table over lunch trying to speak even more Spanish. It made my head split. So I soon began to forgo lunch. My absence, however, did not go unnoticed.
>
> Before long I was asked to see the "dreaded shrinks." They wanted to know if my behavior indicated an inability on my part to relate to people or some more serious pathology which would not bode well for my success as a PCV. I responded that it was just too difficult, trying to eat lunch and simultaneously speak Spanish. I'd tried to, but it felt like my head would explode if I were to continue. Apparently my explanation satisfied them, because that was the last I heard about it.
>
> While I knew acquiring Spanish language facility was absolutely essential if I was to be successful as a PCV, it was a chore.[21]

The lunchtime training in Spanish was difficult for just about everyone and more than a few were in danger of going hungry because they could not come up with the words for pass the what ever. But there were exceptions, those who had a head start on the rest of us.

> Among the assembled numbers were people who actually had studied Spanish [Volgenau recalls]. They could speak in complete sentences, could

---

[19] Carolyn Hawkins Denton, email to Gary Peterson, Aug. 23, 2008.
[20] Ibid.
[21] Tom Gallaher, personal email, Oct. 9, 2008.

conjugate verbs. And – from the very beginning – they knew the words for *fork, knife, spoon* and *butter*. All this proficiency gave them a distinct edge at meals where we had language tables and the staff admonished us to speak only Spanish. Since even, "Pass the salt," was beyond my early skills, I pretty much kept my mouth shut, except for cramming bits of food into it. In fact, you probably could have coaxed a livelier conversation from the average Trappist monk.[22]

But gradually the language began to take shape in the trainee's minds. Tongues started to manage the rolling Rs and even the trill of the double Rs. Mouths became used to the Ñ and the "LL" pronounced like a "Y."

> In the four hours a day of Spanish, I stumbled along with the other beginners [says Vogenau]. I'd try to substitute French words for Spanish words I did not know. Or English with an O tacked onto the end. Or sometimes gibberish when my mouth refused to form actual words. No one was fooled.
>
> A squat, absolutely dear Peruvian woman instructor decided that my name in Spanish should not be *Geraldo*, which I could come close to pronouncing, but *Gerardo* with two *r*s both of which had to be trilled. Damn. Not only was I now eating saltless food, I could not even pronounce my own name. But I learned. And ultimately I was thankful to that sweet lady from the Andean highlands.[23]

Between the language labs, class room instruction by native speaking Latinos, practice sessions and the language tables at lunch time, over half our day was devoted to Spanish. Everything else had to be squeezed into the remainder of the day. First on the list was technical studies which at least moved us outside in the wonderful Nebraska fall air.

Technical studies was meant to train us in the skills we were to pass on to the Colombians. For the girls, this meant nutrition. Carolyn remembers, "making corned beef with the Noyes sisters (two of the instructors in home economics), planting gardens, killing chickens and rabbits, dressing them, and saving the hides of the rabbits."[24]

Both guys and gals participated in the gardening projects. A group bound for Bolivia was just finishing up training when we arrived. We overlapped a few days.[25] As part of their training, they had planted gardens which we harvested. Then we planted our own gardens. Seeds were laid out on raised beds, a requirement in some parts of Colombia with heavy rainfall. Not everyone was completely successful in this endeavor; some were just agriculturally challenged from the start. Tom Gallaher, the seaman/Marine had joined in part to learn about farming, but the art of agriculture takes time to master.

> What I really looked forward to was the ag part of the program, where I would learn to be (I thought) a farmer. Unfortunately, growing up in an apartment house in the Bronx and undergoing a few months training, however

---

[22] Gerald Volgenau, personal email to Gary Peterson, Sep 22, 2008.
[23] Ibid.
[24] Carolyn Hawkins Denton, email to Gary Peterson, Aug. 23, 2008.
[25] A female Volunteer from this group later died in a car accident in Bolivia.

intensive, does not a farmer make. I remember being paired with a kid from Nevada (he later washed out). I diligently tended our small garden plot. My partner, to tell the truth, was not a big help. I hoed, seeded, mulched; I did everything but sing to those seeds. Nothing seemed to help. Our garden plot looked so forlorn when compared to the riotous growth of vegetation covering the adjacent plots. One day in desperation and fear I would be sent home, I turned to my partner, "You gotta help me out here buddy, our plot looks like Death Valley."

My partner looked at me scornfully and said, "Hell, I'm a big Nevada wheat farmer, what do I know about growing some piss ant vegetables."[26]

Though Gallaher was having his problems with producing vegetation, other trainees with little farm experience were muddling through and getting things to grow. Vogenau was another non-farm trainee with little experience in growing things.

Afternoons the staff trained us in earthy things. We planted gardens. I did what I was told. I hoed and plunked down seeds. My hope for anything but weeds was small. But miraculously, a few weeks later actual sprouts appeared. They were green and everything.

The wry Gene Roberts, who became one of my best friends, took a picture of me and my harvest. He titled it "Man discovers the beet." In four words, he had equally captured my delight and my rookie gardener status.

We also raised rabbits, and I am afraid I became too much attached to them. I tried to block out any thoughts of their dark future. Certainly they were not destined for feature performances at Easter or even to pop from a magician's hat. We were talking protein, not pets.[27]

As intense as the Spanish training was, social studies and particularly communism received, if not as much attention in terms of time, even more in depth. ASWAC as the trainees called it, an acronym for American Studies, World Affairs and Communism, had a real emphasis on the last. We studied classical writings, techniques of revolution, appeal to underdeveloped areas, movements in Latin America, and communism versus democracy, a fairly thorough education on the subject. In some ways we were to be thrust

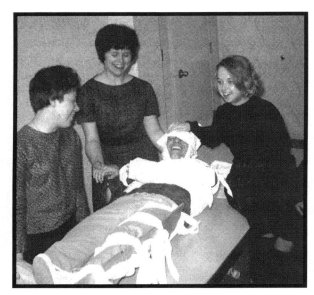

Ronnie Cress, Arlene Ratliff and Margaret Mohler practice splinting.

[26] Tom Gallaher, personal email, Oct. 9, 2008.
[27] Gerald Volgenau, personal email to Gary Peterson, Sep 22, 2008.

into the front lines of the Cold War and the government wanted us to be prepared.

On the lighter, or at least diverting, side, were the extra-curricular activities. First aid was delved into, not just the usual how to bandage a wound and perform CPR, but how to set bones, give shots, treat stomach problems, parasites and infections. If not trained medics, we had at least a nodding acquaintance with just about every possible malady and some idea of what to do about it.

There was "Deadly" Dudley, the Cuban self defense expert who taught us how to throw a man to the ground with a swift kick. He showed the girls how to defend themselves with items they might be carrying, like sticking a comb handle up an attacker's nose or piercing his windpipe with a nail file. We were not experts, I suppose, but maybe we picked up a few hints on how to defend ourselves if attacked.

Deadly had a sidekick with him as his assistant and demonstrator. This was his daughter who was a muscle-bound pint sized version of her dad. Bob Bezdek accepted a challenge to compete with this tough and obviously well conditioned young lady.

> Toward the end of the training sessions with us, he (Deadly that is) challenged the class to compete against his daughter in one-arm push-ups. Because I had short, stocky arms, the group in training shouted out my name and probably also Jarussi's. Hell, I bet Louie was behind my selection as push-up artist, for he had a delightfully mischievous personality - like encouraging me to smoke a cigar that exploded in my face one time.
>
> In any case, I was totally embarrassed to defeat the Cuban's daughter because he chewed her out so strongly that I took a sacred vow to never compete against a female in this type of challenge again, especially if she had an overly-muscular dad similar to this authoritarian guy.[28]

We were given a trip to Pioneer Village at Minden, Nebraska, a twenty acre museum with old sod and log buildings, steam tractors and threshing machines, not unlike the agricultural conditions we would find in Colombia. The staff gave us a list of items to check out, that might prove useful in South America like butter churns, foot powered sewing machines, an old cotton gin, bee smoker, old rat traps, and many other things. One item, a hand made rope bed frame and mattress, was actually constructed and used by Steve Burgess in Colombia.

There was a news sheet in Spanish put together by the trainees who were more proficient in language studies called, "El Hocicón." It was printed in the old purple dido machine style and contained little stories and inside jokes. Even some of us less accomplished language experts contributed small stories written after hours of piecing a few words together. The last page always had a list of vocabulary words for the week which we were supposed to master. But most of us were so busy trying to just learn to speak enough words to get through the program we didn't worry much about reading Spanish.

And there were outdoor activities of an uncomfortable, but interesting nature or so Gerry Vogenau remembers:

---

[28] Robert Bezdek, personal email, Oct 13, 2008.

Over a couple of afternoons, we learned about horses. Brian McMahon was the principle teacher. The Peace Corps' logic was: if we were going to live somewhere in the Colombian countryside, we might need to get from one rural place to another. And a horse was likely to be the best way. So it was deemed by those who got to deem such things that we learn how to pick a good horse from a not-so-good horse. Sort of like buying a used car, but you don't get to kick a horse in the hoof. Also, we were expected to master at least the rudiments of riding. All that I recall about the horse-choosing part was you need to get a horse with black hooves, not pale colored ones. Wan hooves apparently are weak hooves.

As for riding, I did fine. Not Clint Eastwood, mind you. But certainly acceptable. O.K. I admit it, I suffered one embarrassing moment. During a gallop across a grassy field I neck reined the horse for a left turn and leaned left. The horse – and I always thought horses were humorless – jerked right. Thud. I leaped up. "I'm O.K. I'm O.K," I said, sounding a bit ridiculous even to myself. No damage. The only bruised part was my fantasy about being the Durango Kid.

Also our group – because we joined in the early years, I guess – became test rats in the great Peace Corps laboratory. The agency honchos of course knew that we needed to speak a foreign language and have certain skills and background. These were givens. But they wanted to test other ideas. Would the rigors of Outward Bound training – sort of short-term Boy Scouts without the merit badges – make us better Volunteers? Would rabies shots (given in the stomach, I might add) help us survive if bitten by a bat or a dog whose mouth looked like a Crest commercial? Would having every wisdom tooth pulled avoid having a Colombian dentist pull them, no doubt with industrial size pliers?

One of the Outward Bound elements was to camp solo over night in the woods. Not so tough. The night was warm. No rain. The bad part for me was that I had seen the Peace Corps dentist the day before. In less than an hour, he had pulled all four of my wisdom teeth, two of which were impacted. I bled. And by nightfall in the woods, I was still bleeding through my stitches. So I dined on soft things, baked beans cooked right in the can by the campfire. It sounds a bit gory, but it wasn't at all.[29]

Ronnie Cress remembers the solo over night most vividly, "I could not believe it when they were handing out electric blankets for our sleeping bags. I knew, sometime or other, a psychologist would be walking around so I watched and waited. The minute I heard foot steps, I took the plug of the electric blanket and kept trying to jam it into a tree as if I was trying to find an electric socket."[30] Ronnie certainly had more guts than most of us. Playing with the shrinks, even if this was an obvious joke, seemed daring to the point of foolhardiness.

[Volgenau recollects that] underlying all of the training and experimentation were some ominous tensions. We learned that before being allowed to go to Colombia we all would have to somehow stay alive while floating in a

[29] Gerald Volgenau, personal email to Gary Peterson, Sep 22, 2008.
[30] Ronnilou Cress Kordick, personal email to Gary Peterson, July 12, 2008.

swimming pool with our hands and feet tied. This was part of the Outward Bound program. Word of this led to many *sotto voce* conversations in the group.

I certainly had some anxieties. Now, I can swim. Crawl, breast stroke, side stroke, butterfly, you name it. But this sounded like my next plane ride could be in a body bag. And the flight would not be going to Colombia.

This float-or-die exercise was called drown proofing. After all, the staff must have reasoned that the possibility lurked in our Latin future that one of us might be forced to survive for hours after leaping from a sinking ship. But more important – and the overriding tenant of Outward Bound – was to have us accomplish things that seemed impossible and, by succeeding, give us confidence to fight, as the Man from La Mancha said, other "unbeatable foes."

Ultimately, no one drowned. If high fives had been invented then, we would have been slapping all around.[31]

Ron Halter described the drown proofing final exam in a letter to his sister:

We were given 25 min. to do this – swim 2 lengths of the pool (a special drown proofing stroke) diving to a depth of about 4 ft, make a forward & a backward summersault, then dive to a depth of about 12 to 15 ft (the bottom) and pick up a little piece of rubber with your teeth then swim, under the water, half the length of the pool. May I add that all this time we had our hands tied behind our backs and we weren't allowed to touch the sides of the pool. This was the first test.

The next test lasted 90 min. under the same conditions, but all we had to do was stay afloat. Part of the time was with, hands & feet tied (30 min.), then with feet free and finally we made our pants (regular street pants) into a floatation device.[32]

In general, the girls did much better at this drown proofing with hands and feet tied than the guys who struggled to keep from settling to the bottom of the pool. Most of the women could float with little effort and keep at least their noses above water.

Other events were more pleasant. Jarussi recalls, "I remember that we were often invited to a special dorm that housed the nice girls who were studying home economics. They would put on meals and entertainment for us. I was just getting friendly with one of the coeds when we were sent to Puerto Rico."[33]

Not everyone made it to Puerto Rico of course. There were those that dropped out of their own accord and then there were those that were removed. The selection process began with the endless psychological tests and interviews with the psychiatrists. There were two psychologists and two psychiatrists on the staff and they seemed to be everywhere. One Saturday night several of us went to a movie; it was "Shot in the Dark" with Peter Sellers. We were just beginning to relax and enjoy ourselves when someone turned around and there about five rows behind us sat two of the "shrinks" and their

[31] Gerald Volgenau, personal email, Sep 22, 2008.
[32] Ibid.
[33] Louie Jarussi, personal email to Gary Peterson, July 11, 2008.

wives. Looking back now, I suppose it was just a coincidence, but no one believed that at the time.

If we were stressed or had any problems, we were encouraged to talk to one of these medical professionals; we were assured that they would help us through our difficulties. But nobody bought that for a moment. Rumors had it that a voluntary visit to their offices would mean a one way ticket home. Word was, two trainees had confided personnel troubles to the good doctors and were gone the next day. This was probably an exaggeration, but the general wariness of the "shrinks" was real.

The selection process was brutal and feared. Halter expresses his concern at the time in a letter to his sister, "So far we have traversed one selection board. At that time we lost some people and along with the people who left for personal and family problems we have 49 left out of our original 64. Next week is our other selection board and I think we will lose about 4 or 5 people (I hope I am not one)."[34]

Volgenau puts into words how we all felt:

As we soon learned, the psychologists held all the Drop Dead cards. More than the instructors of language, culture and farming stuff. More than the senior staff. Or at least it seemed that way. One word from a head doc and you were "deselected."

Interesting term: "de-selection." It wasn't in the dictionary then, and isn't now. It's one of those words made up by government officials, when straight-forward English fails to meet their purposes.

So Peace Corps trainees were never "fired" or "dumped." Nor were they "let go" or asked to "seek other opportunities" or even, as might have been appropriate, told "Adios." All of that was too harsh. Too politically incorrect in an age before *that* term had been invented. We were simply selected to not be among the select. Goodbye.

During the first two months or so we underwent two de-selection announcements before heading off to Puerto Rico. The first announcement seemed unnervingly capricious; the second, more of the same. In a number of cases, it made no sense to us. We had gotten to know these people well. We were side by side constantly – sweating, studying, sleeping, swimming, not drowning. Some were Spanish wizards. Others could make a hoe handle sprout daffodils. And yet, suddenly they were gone.

Interestingly, two or three de-selectees basically said, "To hell with your opinion. I can do this. And I'm going to." And they went to South or Central America on their own hooks. They taught English and worked at other projects. And they stayed, and stayed. Not just for months but in some cases for years. By their very actions, their answer to the psychologists was: "Shrink that."[35]

---

[34] Ronald Halter, Peace Corps trainee, to Joyce B. Scannell, his cousin of North Wales, PA, November 1964, Personal Files of Ronald Halter, Lenexa, KS.
[35] Gerald Volgenau, personal email, Sep. 22, 2008.

Janice Abbott

Amazingly, all four of the married couples survived even though we were warned at the outset that if one of a pair was deselected, the couple would leave. The married couples appeared to be a step ahead of the singles. For example, there were the Abbotts, Janice and Geoffrey, an attractive pair, quiet and competent. The Abbotts were from Greenwich, Connecticut and had both attended Allegheny College in Meadville, Pennsylvania. Like the other couples, they seemed to exude a self assurance the rest of us lacked. Maybe it was that they could confide and reinforce each other where we singles were on our own. I concluded that they were just more mature and they all seemed to sail through training with little effort. It was not until later that I understood they were having some of the same difficulties the rest of us were having.

I remember arriving in Lincoln for training [Geoffrey recalls], and for some reason, I guess because we came from the NY metro area, Deon Axthelm, the project director, thought we were Gallaher. We were the first married couple to arrive.

We were black listed almost immediately because the Nebraskans put us in the nearest housing to the Center, impressing upon us that if we didn't like it, we could try one of the other married couples' rooms they had arranged. We were not particularly pleased with their choice and took them up on their option to change quarters. That put us on the short list of "being too concerned with personal comfort" and therefore at risk of being unable to adjust to living in Colombia.[36]

Geoffrey Abbott

So the ten weeks of training in Nebraska came to an end. Of the 64 individuals that arrived on that hot, humid day in August, 42 survived to be given graduation certificates at a dinner the evening of November 20th. Each of us looked around the table. One more trainee would leave the program in Puerto Rico, but for the most part these were the members of our FOA/PINA (Colombia '64) group that would be going to Colombia.

All of the would-be Volunteers who set foot on the University of Nebraska agricultural campus back on the 29th of August had been picked to serve as agricultural, health and home economics extension agents, all that is except one. That singular individual was Kenneth Waissman, 24, from Pikesville, Maryland. Ken had a bachelor's degree from the University of Maryland and a masters from New York University. He had made Who's Who in Colleges and Universities in 1962. Ken was not in training for his experience or education in agriculture or health; he was there for his expertise in the field of educational television.

---

[36] Geoffrey Abbott, personal email, Aug. 18, 2009.

Through negotiations with the Colombian government, the U.S. State Department had agreed to field a team to support the fledgling in-school educational television system Colombia was trying to build. It seemed the ideal way to get modern, well developed, educational programming to the country's schools, especially rural schools that lacked top flight teachers and school equipment. Ken describes the series of events that led to the creation of a subgroup in the agricultural-health-home economics training group.

I was a graduate student at NYU's theater, film and TV division (The Tisch School) when Sargent Shriver came to the campus to speak about the Peace Corps. He talked about a special Peace Corps group in Bogotá, Colombia producing Educational Television (ETV) programs that were televised to approximately 500,000 children a day throughout the country. This appealed to me on many levels: the adventure of living and working in a foreign country; learning to speak a foreign language; the opportunity to produce and direct television shows right out of college and of course, the *pièce de resistance,* getting a draft deferment.

Kenneth Waissman

I was registered in my hometown, Baltimore and my draft board was run by Democrats, which meant they didn't draft return Peace Corps Volunteers.

I applied for the ETV group and by the end of June, I was told I had been accepted and would be leaving in August for the training. I had the required physicals, received my passport and was waiting for the notification. July came and went. August began and I still didn't hear anything. Finally, I called the Peace Corps office in Washington and was told that there had been a mix-up. The group I was supposed to train with had already begun and they forgot to inform me. They said it looked like they might begin a new ETV group at the beginning of the year and if that happened, I could be a part of it. This was very disappointing to say the least. Although there was the possibility of still going at a later date, what would I do in the interim? What about my deferment from the draft? Something told me to go over to Washington and speak to someone directly.

The person who headed up the 'Colombian Desk' at the Washington Peace Corps office was a tiny older lady with a salt and pepper Prince Valiant-styled hair cut. As we spoke, she recalled that there was an ETV station in Lincoln, Nebraska and since there was an agriculture group ready to begin training there at the University, if I was willing, she'd put me into that group and make arrangements for me to intern at the ETV station. Upon arriving in Bogotá, I'd be assigned to the ETV project at the 'Red Nacional' (the Colombian National Network.)

When I arrived in Lincoln, Dean Axthelm knew nothing about my supposed 'interning' at the UHF-ETV station nor did he have anything on record about my joining the ETV project upon arriving in Bogotá. He said he was sure he would hear something about it from Washington. A couple of weeks went by and there was still no word from Washington. Finally, I spoke to Axthelm again, saying that although I was developing a great camaraderie with the group, I had no intention of working in agriculture or horticulture or in anything that didn't come with a metropolitan skyline. I asked for a ticket back home. He asked me to be patient for a few more days.

I later found out that he not only informed Washington that I wanted to leave, but added that some others whose forte wasn't feeding rabbits or making fertilizer might follow. Using the fact that I had been brought to Lincoln on the pretext of interning at the ETV center as training for the Colombian ETV project, he petitioned them to set up an ETV sub-training group. Finally, word came that a Peace Corps trainer would be arriving to lead this new sub-group. Thus, Bob Bezdek, Tom Gallagher, Elizabeth Hufnagel, Lou Jarussi, Marge Mohler and Gerry Volgenau joined me in leaving the 'farm' for the glamorous world of television.

Within days, Judy Lavicka arrived in Lincoln to lead the newly formed ETV group. Her only qualification for this pioneering job was that she was "the 60's' First Ever Party Girl!" I remember her grand entrance into the cafeteria where we saw her for the first time, walking toward us, tossing back her long blond hair, sashaying in short shorts, cut low enough to show off her naval, and a white blouse tied into a halter. (Today it would all be done in slow motion!)

Our first impression of her panned out. She had absolutely no idea what she was doing. A bureaucratic selection with no logical basis. However, she winged it very well and off we went down the Yellow Brick Road to the land of *Televisión Educativa.*[37]

Thanks to the initiative of Mr. Axthelm and Ken the ETV sub-group was organized. Gerry describes how the ETV section was constituted and some of their training:

Our very small group – only six of us – would train to work in an educational television program for Colombia's primary schools. The first TV group, Colombia 13, had started the project about a year or so before. Colombian educators – in coordination with Volunteers – designed the academics, Math, Science, Language Arts, Music and so on. The TV classes were all designed to fit into the regular national academic program. In Bogotá, Volunteers trained directors and producers and on-screen teachers. Out in the various departments (equivalent to states in the United States), other Volunteers worked with teachers in the schools on how best to use this electronic teaching aid.

I had never studied teaching. At KU, the standing joke was that co-eds only had one answer to the question: "What's your major? Elementary Ed."
Education was something that women did. This was an era before anyone had even imagined something called a glass ceiling. For me, working in the schools with teachers seemed doable. Certainly more so than vegetable gardening. After all, I had spent most of my life inside classrooms. I felt confident that I knew a thing or two about them. As it turned out, what I knew was less than what I had imagined.

---

[37] Ken Waissman, personal email, Aug. 8, 2010.

So this subgroup came together. Ken Waissman, Mr. Broadway, had already been destined for the Bogotá studios. Joining him (and me) were Marge Mohler, who actually had studied education and Tom Gallaher, the big and irrepressible New Yorker who had graduated from Fordham University, Elizabeth Hufnagel, who had studied mathematics at Syracuse, and Louie Jarussi and Bob Bezdek as TV technicians.

The state of Nebraska already boasted an ongoing education television program for its public schools. We studied that. We visited one-room schools in the Nebraska field because it was thought that they might be similar to what we would find in Colombia. They were not, particularly.

We talked to grade school teachers. We entertained their students. We gave them names in Spanish and called the cutest little girl "Angelita" and taught them Spanish words that we had just learned ourselves. Basically it was fun.

In the final days before we left for Puerto Rico, the trainees put on a show about our training that was largely written and completely produced and directed by Ken Waissman. Very funny, very clever. It included a black-out routine where the room was darkened and someone in a chorus on stage would shine a flashlight on his own face and recite a smart-alecky line, usually an inside joke. And Ken also put together a boffo routine where the cast of trainees sang send-up lyrics to the "Guys and Dolls" Broadway tune of "I've got a horse right here. His name is Paul Revere."[38]

Like Gerry, Marge Mohler, of Ann Arbor, Michigan, a graduate of Eastern Michigan University was not unhappy to be asked to join the ETV team:

Margaret Mohler

I must have been the queen of the naïve as I had no clue regarding training. I expected the Spanish classes, but the phys ed part was one big pain. I have never been athletic and found all that running to be torture. I did excel at drown proofing as I floated vertically with my nose out of water. Lucky me. I never suspected there was something called de-selection or sessions with psychiatrists.

When Peace Corps invited me to training, I was so excited I never questioned whether I would be suited for nutrition work. I couldn't cook much except chocolate chip cookies. I didn't think I could ask Peace Corps to find a group better suited to my skills. When the staff at Lincoln asked some of our group to switch to ETV, I was thrilled.[39]

Tom Gallaher was another urbanite that had been brought into this bunch, most of whom had at least a nodding acquaintance with rural America. His attempts at raising a garden Colombian style were not going so well and he was afraid of being deselected.

---

[38] Gerald Volgenau, personal email, Sep 22, 2008.
[39] Margaret Mohler, personal email to Gary Peterson, Jul. 17, 2008

I was called in to see our program director, Deon Axthelm.

"Sit down Tom," he says. "I've been watching you and I've come to a decision. I'm afraid that if we send you to Colombia, you could set back the progress of Colombian agriculture a hundred years. We do, however, have another program that I would like you to think about, 'ETV,' and he gave me an opportunity to sign up. And that's how I left the farm and became a TV mogul.[40]

While the rest of the ETV subgroup trained with Waissman, Bezdek and Jarussi were channeled into a different path, that of working with the actual TV sets. Loui adjusted to the change in direction readily enough.

"When I was put into the ETV technical training I remember working with a local television shop, climbing all over houses and roofs in Lincoln installing televisions, antennas and the connections that were used at that time. I also remember getting the crap shocked out of me many times learning to repair those old tube type TV sets. They put out a lot of voltage and you had to ground them before working on them."[41]

With the twelve weeks of training and selection boards behind them, Colombia '64 looked forward to the next phase of training. After being in a totally controlled environment for nearly three months, Ron Halter reveals his feelings about the prospect of some freedom in a letter to his sister. "We will be leaving on Nov. 21 at 2:00 pm and flying directly to New York City where we will spend the night at the Wellington Hotel (55th & 7 Ave.). The next morning we fly out to Puerto Rico for 4 weeks, one week working with an ag extension worker and one week on our own, then two weeks in "Outward Bound" camps. I am really looking forward to this."[42]

Perhaps the most surprised trainee among those going to Puerto Rico was Dennis Burkholder of Rock Lake, North Dakota. He was undoubtedly the first of the group to send in his application to join what was then a fledgling experiment.

In the spring of 1962, a 19 year old Dennis sat in his Freshman Honors English classroom at the North Dakota School of Forestry at Bottineau Junior College located just 20 miles from the Canadian border. The day's assignment was a research paper due in one week.

Six days later he began his "extensive" research on his chosen topic: The Peace Corps. Frankly, there wasn't much data to research in those early days and the resulting paper was a little too short and needed some padding. His old maid instructor was inclined to be emotional and sensitive. So Dennis decided that penning a poem would be just the thing to save him from the dreaded "D."

Dennis Burkholder

"*I love my country, my home and this land*

[40] Tom Gallaher, personal email, Oct. 9, 2008.

[41] Louie Jarussi, personal email, Jul. 11, 2008

[42] Ronald Halter, Peace Corps trainee, to Joyce B. Scannell, his cousin of North Wales, PA, November 1964, Personal Files of Ronald Halter, Lenexa, KS.

No other country, so great and so grand.
Freedom for everyone - 'tis not just a dream
In the US of A, the country supreme."

The drivel served its purpose and earned the author a B-. Good enough. Unpredictably, it also planted a seed of interest in Burkholder and he sent in an application to join the Peace Corps. Not surprisingly, it went unanswered.

Two years and three college transfers later an invitation to join a group training for Agriculture and Nutrition to serve in Colombia, S.A. arrived in the mail. Dennis had given up on ever hearing anything on his application, but now here it was, an acceptance. Well, why not?

Dennis arrived in Lincoln, studied Spanish, drown proofed, ran around the tractor testing track, played four square, self-defended *a la* Deadly Dudley's CIA inspired kill with one well placed ashtray delivered to the nose in a hard upward thrust, and kept up with ASWAC well enough to evade the preliminary rounds of the dreaded de-selection process. The death squad of psychologists and psychiatrists hadn't noticed any of his mental deficiencies. With just Puerto Rico training and one more de-selection remaining, he had survived Nebraska.[43]

---

[43] Dennis Burholder, personal email to Gary Peterson, Oct. 7, 2008.

2

THE EVOLVING PEACE CORPS

Forty-two young Americans were on their way to Puerto Rico for the last phase of Peace Corps training before heading to Colombia. While they were in Nebraska, the question of who would be the next president of the United States had been debated. Both candidates expressed faith in the young Peace Corps. Senator Barry Goldwater said, "at first I thought it would advance work for a group of beatniks, but this is not so.....I have been impressed....I'll back it all the way."[1] And President Johnson voiced his advocacy:

> The nations of the world want our young people. The peoples of the world need our young people. And surely a nation rich in goods and ideas can provide young people.[2]

With limited access to the usual means of communication, television and radio, members of Colombia '64 followed the campaign and election as best they could. Though day to day events of the campaign season were obscured, some of the significant headlined highlights were picked up by the trainees:

> At the same time that we were fully focused on training [Volgenau recalls] the world was moving on. The presidential race was in full cry. The Democrat was President Lyndon Johnson, Kennedy's successor after the assassination. The Republican candidate was the arch conservative Sen. Barry Goldwater, of Arizona.
>
> In any campaign, typically one moment or incident stands out. The photo of Adlai Stevenson in a barber's chair with a hole in his shoe. The Kennedy-Nixon debates with Nixon looking unshaven. Sometimes, an election turned on it; sometimes not. But they were memorable.
>
> In 1964, it was a TV ad. And if it did not turn the election, it severely bent it. It ran only once on September 7. With birds chirping in the background, a pretty little girl stands in a field of flowers, slowly picking the petals of a daisy. As she tugs each one, she counts. "One, two ..." she repeats some and puts others out of order because she is so very young. At petal number nine, an ominous male voice sounds. It too is counting. Not daisy petals, but a countdown for a missile launch. Eight, seven, six ... The girl's eyes turn to the sky, the camera zooms in on the pupil of her eye and soon the whole screen is dark. At zero, the blackness is replaced by a flash, an explosion and the distinctive mushroom cloud.
>
> As a firestorm rages, you hear Lyndon Johnson's Texas twang:
> "These are the stakes! To make a world in which all of God's children can live, or to go into the dark. We must either love each other, or we must die."
>
> An announcer's voice comes on: "Vote for President Johnson November 3rd. The stakes are too high for you to stay at home."

---

[1] "Peace Corps Growing As fourth Year Starts," *Peace Corps News,* Fall, 1964, Vol.2, No. 3, p. 1.
[2] Ibid.

Earlier it seems that Goldwater had made some imprudent remarks about using nuclear weapons in Vietnam. Of course the election was more complex, but Goldwater's goose was cooked. Johnson won the vote before we left Nebraska.[3]

In the New Year President Lyndon Johnson would appoint his Vice-President, Hubert Humphrey, the new chairman of the Peace Corps Advisory Council. Humphrey observed, "The Peace Corps has been a living monument to the idealism, skill, and devotion of American youth, and serves as an example of humanitarianism for all the world."[4] This appointment must have been particularly gratifying to Humphrey; he would be working with an organization for which he had fought long and hard.

Hubert H. Humphrey
*38th Vice President
of the United States*

But there was another underlying dimension to the support for this new style of foreign aid. In just the four weeks the Colombia '64 Volunteers would spend in Puerto Rico, France would perform an underground nuclear test at Ecker, Algeria. The U.S. would test a much larger device in the Pacific and another in Nevada. America's Lockheed SR-71 spy aircraft would set a new world's record for a jet plane, 3,500 kilometers per hour. The Cold War, and its competition for the hearts and minds of the world's people, was everywhere evident. And the outcome of this struggle was not a foregone conclusion.

Following WWII, the communist Soviet Union had built an empire stretching from Eastern Europe to the Bering Straight. China had gone communist along with North Korea. The British had managed to turn back the communist tide in Malaya, but just barely. The United States had led an alliance that had saved South Korea, but at the cost of over 54,000 American lives. The French had pulled out of the fight in Indo-China. And most recently, Fidel Castro had declared his country, Cuba, for communism, providing his client, the Soviet Union, with an outpost not 90 miles from the United States. The island nation also became a center for exporting communism to all parts of Latin America. Communism was on the march.

At the same time America's prestige abroad seemed to be in decline. Self-criticizing books like The Lonely Crowd, The Affluent Society, The End of Ideology, Foreign Aid: Our Tragic Experiment, and especially the Ugly American by Eugene Burdick, convinced many of U.S. impotence. The term "Ugly American" became the metaphor for Americans abroad who were seen as being loud, obnoxious and out of touch with the local populations. U.S. businessmen, diplomats and particularly tourists were viewed in this light. Unlike the very successful Marshal Plan, foreign aid was represented as just millions and billions of dollars poured into the pockets of despots and tyrants who used the money to keep their populations oppressed. Clearly, Americans thought, some new

---

[3] Gerald Volgenau, personal email, Sep. 22, 2008.
[4] "HHH Heads PC Council; Meeting Set," *Peace Corps News,* Spring, 1965, Vol. 2, No. 4, p. 1.

approach was needed. Many saw a Peace Corps style program as at least part of the answer.

America, of course, has a long history of overseas grass roots philanthropic organizations. The earliest were religious in nature. Christian evangelists not only preached to the peoples of Africa, Asia and the Pacific, but they built schools, taught trades, and trained doctors and nurses. This tradition was carried into the twentieth century by such organizations as the Catholic Relief Services, the American Jewish Joint Distribution Committee, the National Lutheran Council, the World Council of Churches, and Church World Services among others. By 1961 there were 33,000 American missionaries serving overseas.[5]

There were also non-religious outreach programs like the International Development Placement Association which provided an avenue for American college graduates to teach and do community development in underdeveloped countries in the early 1950s. Medical International Cooperation Organization (MEDICO), founded by Dr. Tom Dooley, built and staffed hospitals in Southeast Asia. Dooley became something of a folk hero, the American Albert Schweitzer, living and working among the people. To the young idealist he was the antithesis of the Ugly American.

Other agencies established overseas programs of assistance including the American Red Cross, the Cooperative for American Relief Everywhere (CARE), the National 4-H Club Foundation, Project Hope, Volunteers for International Development and the African-American Institute.

But the organization that was truly the closest to a prototype Peace Corps was the International Voluntary Services (IVS). Founded in 1953, IVS was nondenominational and accepted college graduates for two year assignments to work at a grass-roots level in foreign lands. Volunteers were trained or selected for a specific skill and were paid just a subsistence allowance during their period of service. Only about two hundred young Americans had traveled and worked in foreign countries through IVS, but the model had proven itself.

Other countries had established Peace Corps style programs, Australia's Volunteer Graduate Association, West Germany's Council for Development Aid, Holland's Bureau for International Technical Assistance, and the British, Voluntary Service Overseas (VSO). Most of these were supported by a combination of government and private financing. Often they did admirable work, but on a small scale. Members of the U.S. Colombia FAO/PINA-ETV/UPT 1964 group (Colombia '64) would have contact with some of these organizations in South America.

The seeds that would eventually grow to become the Peace Corps were planted by two U.S. Congressmen, Henry Reuss (Democrat, Representative from Wisconsin) and Hubert Humphrey (Democrat, Senator from Minnesota). Reuss had traveled to Southeast Asia in 1957 investigating how U.S. tax money was being spent. He was dissatisfied with the American government programs of the time, but in his travels he had discovered a UNESCO team of a few teachers from the United States and other countries. These young people were working with local villages to establish schools. Reuss was so impressed by the effectiveness of their work, he began a campaign to organize what he

---

[5] Gerard T. Rice, The Bold Experiment, (Notre Dame, Indiana: University of Notre Dame Press, 1985), p. 2.

called a "Point Four Youth Corps," upon his return. In January 1960, he introduced H.R. 9638 calling for a study of his proposed Youth Corps.

While Reuss was pushing his idea in the House of Representatives, Hubert Humphery was working on a similar plan in the Senate. He had proposed the idea in speeches on several college campuses and had received a warm reception. In the spring of 1960, he introduced Senate S. 3675 which called for creation of a program to send, "young men to assist the peoples of the underdeveloped areas of the world to combat poverty, disease, illiteracy and hunger."[6] The bill used the name, "Peace Corps."

Though Reuss and Humphery had some support from noted public figures such as General James Gavin, Chester Bowles, William O. Douglas, James Reston, Senator Jacob Javits and others, progress was slow. The real turning point came during the fall presidential campaign of 1960.

Senator Javits had urged the Republican candidate Richard Nixon to look into the idea, but Nixon rejected his proposal. The democratic contender, John Kennedy, on the other hand, was more receptive. As part of his criticism of the Eisenhower administration's foreign policy, he was looking for an antidote to the Soviet Union's infiltration of the developing world with teachers, doctors and technicians advancing the communist cause at the grass roots level.

Early in the primaries when Kennedy was competing against Humphrey for the Democratic nomination, Humphrey had scored points on college campuses with his pledge to create a Peace Corps as outlined in his bill. Although by July Kennedy had secured the nomination, beating out Humphrey, he did take note.

In the Kennedy-Nixon televised debate on October 13, Nixon accused the Democratic party of being the war party, noting that the U.S. had become involved in wars while Wilson (WWI), FDR (WWII), and Truman (Korean War) were presidents.

This accusation may have been on Kennedy's mind when later that night he flew to Ann Arbor, Michigan. At 2:00 AM in the morning an exhausted John Kennedy arrived at the University of Michigan campus to find some ten thousand students waiting for him. Surprised by the magnitude of this reception and with no prepared speech, he began an extemporaneous address:

> I want to express my thanks to you, as a graduate of Michigan of the East, Harvard University.
>
> I come here tonight delighted to have the opportunity to say one or two words about this campaign that is coming into the last three weeks.
>
> How many of you who are going to be doctors, are willing to spend your days in Ghana? Technicians or engineers, how many of you are willing to work in the Foreign Service and spend your lives traveling around the world? On your willingness to do that, not merely to serve one year or two years in the service, but on your willingness to contribute part of your life to this country, I think will depend the answer whether a free society can compete. I think it can! And I

---

[6] Gerard T. Rice, *The Bold Experiment*, (Notre Dame, Indiana: University of Notre Dame Press, 1985), p. 11.

think Americans are willing to contribute. But the effort must be far greater than we have ever made in the past.[7]

The response was wildly enthusiastic. That early morning exchange in the student union building at the University of Michigan made a deep impression on both the candidate and the students.

At Ann Arbor several students organized the Americans Committed to World Responsibility which held meetings to discuss the idea of developing a Youth Corps program. A petition requesting such an organization be established was signed by over a thousand students.

On November 2, one week before the 1960 election, candidate Kennedy gave a speech at the San Francisco Cow Palace. As part of that address, before some forty thousand people, Kennedy referred to the positive reception his suggestion to serve had received at the University of Michigan and called for a new government program:

> There is not enough money in all America to relieve the misery of the underdeveloped world in a giant and endless soup kitchen. But there is enough know-how and enough knowledgeable people to help those nations help themselves. I therefore propose that our inadequate efforts in this area be supplemented by a Peace Corps of talented young men willing and able to serve their country in this fashion for three years as an alternative to peace-time selective service – well-qualified through rigorous standards; well-trained in the language, skills, and customs they will need to know.[8]

The next day the New York Times' headlines read: "Kennedy Favors U.S. 'Peace Corps' to Work Abroad."[9] The news media across America picked up the theme and candidate Nixon was forced to make a counter proposal, that if elected he would, "increase the effectiveness of our recruiting programs for service abroad, provide more accurate training facilities for those going abroad, and provide improved incentives for making a career out of such service."[10] On January 20, 1961, President John Kennedy gave his inaugural address which included the now familiar, "Ask not what your country can do for you – ask what you can do for your country," line. The next day he telephoned his brother-in-law, Robert Sargent Shriver asking him to oversee a task force to look into how a Peace Corps might be organized. An idea was finally about to blossom into something tangible. Shriver fit into the Kennedy camp easily, though the Kennedys considered him a bit too liberal. A Yale educated lawyer, his career had been in business, education (Chicago Board of Education) and government. Kennedy had tapped him to head his search for, "the best and brightest," to fill out his administration. Before that task was even completed he was being called to flesh out this idea of a Peace Corps.

---

[7] Peace Corps Online, *Remarks of Senator John Kennedy at the University of Michigan proposing creation of the Peace Corps – Octorber14, 1960,*
http://peacecorpsonline.org/messages/messages/2629/2044326.html (10 Aug. 2007).

[8] Gerard T. Rice, The Bold Experiment, (Notre Dame, Indiana: University of Notre Dame Press, 1985), p. 15.

[9] Ibid.

[10] Gerard T. Rice, The Bold Experiment, (Notre Dame, Indiana: University of Notre Dame Press, 1985), p. 16.

Shriver's first recruit was Harris Wofford, a 34 year old law professor at Notre Dame. He and Shriver had become friends while Wofford was Kennedy's campaign advisor on civil rights issues. Shriver and Wofford set up shop in a suite in the Mayflower Hotel in Washington D.C. and preceded to interview people on their ideas of what a Peace Corps ought to look like and how it should function. They plowed through a mountain of reports including a study from the International Cooperation Administration (ICA) of the State Department. There were many ideas amongst all this data, but no consensus and nothing that Shriver and Wofford found striking.

Meanwhile, President Kennedy kept the pressure on by including mention of his efforts to form a National Peace Corps in his state of the Union address on January 30th. And he called for a report from Shriver on progress by the end of February. Shriver and Wofford were floundering in a sea of ideas, but with little solid evidence on possibilities of success or an over all architecture. Shriver had scheduled the first Task Force meeting for the morning of February 6th, but as the date approached he still had no concrete plan.

Sargent Shriver with President Kennedy in the Rose Garden.
Courtesy of the Peace Corps Digital Library

Unbeknownst to Shriver, help was on the way. While Shriver, Wofford and now Gordon Boyce struggled to develop some kind of cohesive plan, two officials of the Far Eastern division of ICA were working on a plan of their own. Warren W. Wiggins, deputy director of Far Eastern operations, was unhappy with what he had seen in U.S. overseas programs and especially government officials. Still in his 30s, Wiggins had helped administer the Marshal Plan, had served as U.S. economic advisor to the Philippians and been director of the American aid program to Bolivia.

His collaborator was twenty-six year old William Josephson, Far Eastern regional counsel for ICA. Both had been inspired by the idea of a Peace Corps type organization and had worked out an outline for such a program. They laid out their plan in a paper entitled, "The Towering Task." To try and get their paper into Shriver's hands, the pair sent copies to the ICA group working on the study to be forwarded to Shriver, another to the White House and a third directly to Wofford. Shriver finally did obtain a copy and sat down late Sunday night (February 5th) to review it. As he read the paper he became more and more intrigued. First the study covered the thinking and proposals suggested up to that time:

> Most of the academic and other institutional approaches to the opportunity of the National Peace Corps suggest tentative pilot projects, involving small numbers of people and consequently a limited political, economic and psychological impact. This cautious approach is proposed by many because of the clear possibility of a fiasco the organization and administration of a large number of Americans working on a variety of programs and projects in many countries with varying cultures and needs undeniably is an extremely complex and difficult undertaking. It is the prevailing view that if a great many Americans are scattered abroad and if significant numbers of them fail either in their own eyes or in the eyes of the recipient peoples, or if large numbers of the Americans have severe health, emotional or other problems, the resulting criticism will extend far beyond the project, *per se*.
>
> Thus, one course of action is becoming clear and apparently has the support of most people expressing an opinion: Proceed cautiously, start with small pilot projects, don't make mistakes, limit the program to 1,000 or 2,000 for a beginning (some say a few hundred)....[11]

Then the paper examined the problems with this approach:

> The first major difficulty with most of the thinking that has been expressed to date (as summarized in Part I above) is that if the overall program is launched at the 1,000 or 2,000-youth level, it will be more likely to fail in the absolute sense than at a level, say, five or ten times greater. Generally speaking, such small numbers won't be significant enough in the recipient countries to get the governmental and institutional attention it needs. Exceptions can, of course, be found, but it is believed that they will be rare. Sending 100 students to a Latin American country won't be important enough to get presidential support from that country. Active support from a Minister of Agriculture, Health or Education would be surprising as a general rule. And if the country needed to get legislative or financial support, it might not be forthcoming. However, 1,000, or 5,000 Americans, working on something important in a single country, would merit considerably more political, administrative and financial support. One hundred youths engaged in Agricultural work of some sort in Brazil might pass by unnoticed, except for the problems involved, but 5,000 American youths helping to build Brasilia might warrant the full attention and support of the President of Brazil himself.[12]

---

[11] Warren Wiggins, *A Towering Task,* http://peacecorpsonline.org/messages/messages/2629/2109015.html
[12] Ibid.

Finally, the report made a stunning proposal:

> The purpose of this paper is to advocate consideration of a "quantum jump" in the thinking and programming considering the National Peace Corps. Its postulate is that America ought to consider initiating the program with several thousand Americans participating in the first 12 to 18 months – say, 5,000 to 10,000. The ultimate level of manpower to be utilized in this program will, of course, depend upon its initial success and difficulties. However, the potential of this program is great and it may prove to be the case that it should be at the 30,000, the 50,000 or possibly even at the 100,000 level.[13]

Then the paper advocated an aggressive approach toward implementing the plan:

> The Executive Branch should decide that the Peace Corps will be launched in calendar year 1961 and at a level sufficiently large to: 1) Assure maximum chance of success; 2) demonstrate that major activities can be undertaken in particular countries; 3) test the wisdom of a variety of types of approaches and activities. Thus, it is believed that in February President Kennedy should decide that, even in advance of legislation and formal administrative structure, the Peace Corps will be launched with a major Presidential statement or speech, that a call for volunteers will be thus issued, that preparatory work for a series of specific pilot projects will begin, that screening of applicant will be under way, that to the extent necessary appropriate contracts will be negotiated and that selected foreign governments will be contacted.[14]

Shriver was captivated. This was bold, decisive and called for action that would require a crash program, just the approach he could buy into. He telegraphed Wiggins inviting him to his Task Force meeting the next morning. "The midnight ride of Warren Wiggins," is one of the legends in Peace Corps annals. Wiggins and Josephson were introduced to the group. Copies of *The Towering Task* were passed out. The spirit and general outline of the paper would become the philosophy of the Kennedy Administration's Peace Corps.

To get things moving, in accordance with the plan, the Task Force decided to push for an Executive Order rather than wait for legislation that might delay the process a whole year. That could come later.

On February 24th Shriver delivered his report to President Kennedy. The report called for:

1. $12 million be allotted from the Mutual Security Act contingence fund.
2. The new organization should be in the State Department, but separate from ICA.
3. The Peace Corps be lean in terms of bureaucracy and agile, able to experiment and adjust.
4. Immediate establishment of a Peace Corps by Executive Order.
5. Actual operation was left open, whether through existing private organizations, with colleges and universities through contractual arrangements

---

[13] Warren Wiggins, *A Towering Task,* http://peacecorpsonline.org/messages/messages/2629/2109015.html.
[14] Ibid.

with other government agencies, through the UN and other international organizations and finally, the Peace Corps itself could administer some programs.

6. Volunteers would be deferred, but not exempt from the draft.
7. Though it was assumed most volunteers would be college graduates, all able-bodied American citizens over eighteen would be eligible.
8. Applicants would have to pass written and oral tests.
9. Training would be a priority, especially language, and colleges and universities would be used where feasible.
10. Volunteers would receive a subsistence allowance while in the field, equivalent to counterparts in the host country, and a modest readjustment allowance upon successful termination of service.
11. The goal was 2,000 Volunteers in the field by year end.

On March 1, 1961, President Kennedy issued Executive Order #10924 establishing the Peace Corps as a new agency within the State Department. Upon the signing he remarked:

> I have today signed an Executive Order providing for the establishment of a Peace Corps on a temporary pilot basis. I am also sending to Congress a message proposing authorization of a permanent Peace Corps. This Corps will be a pool of trained American men and women sent overseas by the U.S. Government or through private institutions and organizations to help foreign countries meet their urgent needs for skilled manpower.[15]

Now the organization had to be built. The ball was rolling, but it would have to be pushed, mostly up hill.

Shriver presented the President with a list of highly qualified people for the position of Peace Corps director. Kennedy rejected them all in favor of his bother-in-law. Shriver protested that there were others more qualified and there was the nepotism factor that would be brought up during conformation. Kennedy insisted on Shriver and noted that since the organization was operating under executive order no confirmation was required. Shriver acceded to Kennedy's demands to head the organization, but insisted he be confirmed as he would have to face the Senate after an authorization bill was passed anyway.

Sargent Shriver was appointed the first Peace Corps Director March 4, 1961. He was confirmed by the Senate on March 21st. The nepotism charge was never an issue.

Next Shriver went on a talent hunt, this time for his own organization. Several people from the Task Force stayed on including Wiggins, Josephson, Boyce and Wofford. He obtained John D. Young from the National Aeronautics and Space Administration (NASA), who had been instrumental in creating that agency. Young pushed for a lean organization unencumbered by multiple levels of management and bureaucracy, just what Shriver wanted. Shriver surrounded himself with a mix of

---

[15] Peace Corps On Line, *Keeping Kennedy's Promise,*
http://peacecorpsonline.org/messages/messages/2629/2044326.html.

professional bureaucrats, insiders who knew the ropes and outsiders from business and academia to provide freshness and spontaneity.

Bill Moyers, age twenty-six was one of Vice President Johnson's key aides and the main liaison between Kennedy and Johnson. His efforts to be moved over to the Peace Corps were resisted by both staffs, but finally, he was allowed to follow his druthers.

The next battle was in keeping the Peace Corps as an autonomous program. Kennedy had proposed a reorganization of all foreign assistance programs, including ICA, Food for Peace and the Development Loan Fund, that they be consolidated under one unit to be called the Agency for International Development (AID). It was naturally presumed by most State Department officials and Congressmen that the Peace Corps belonged there also. Legislation creating AID could also be used to create the Peace Corps and the President seemed agreeable.

Shriver, Josephson and Wiggins were horrified at the prospect of having the Peace Corps absorbed by this new giant bureaucracy. They felt it was essential for the integrity of the organization they envisioned that it be a separate unit directly under the State Department with close ties to the President. Shriver received some support from Dean Rusk, Secretary of State and Chester Bowles, Under Secretary of State, but the committee within the department that was working on the proposed foreign aid package was unmoved. Shriver needed the President's support, but Kennedy was occupied with the Bay of Pigs fiasco and its aftermath. To make matters worse, Shriver had been ordered by Kennedy to take a trip to determine what countries might be interested in hosting Peace Corps Volunteers.

As events approached a climax, Shriver, now in New Delhi, sent a cable to Wiggins telling him to ask Vice President Johnson to intercede for them. Bill Moyers was assigned the task of approaching Johnson. In a meeting with LBJ, Moyers, Wiggins and Josephson argued that the Peace Corps, as a part of AID, would lose its independence compromising its unique appeal to young people, and entangle it in the usual bureaucratic red tape. Johnson agreed and arranged a meeting with the President set for May 1st. In this meeting Johnson was able to convince Kennedy of the importance of an independent Peace Corps. The result was a memorandum to Dean Rusk on May 2nd from Ralph Dungan, chair of the meeting which was to decide the fate of the Peace Corps, that said:

> This is to inform you that yesterday evening the President, in consultation with the Vice-President, decided that the Peace Corps should be organized as a semi-autonomous unit within the Department of State and that the Director of the Corps would have an Assistant Secretary status and would report directly to the Secretary of State.[16]

Peace Corps autonomy had been preserved.

By May Shriver's trip abroad had netted invitations from eight countries with requests for 3,000 Volunteers. Thousands of Volunteer applications had been received and were being reviewed. In June President Kennedy announced he had requests from over twenty-four countries. In July the first Peace Corps projects were announced, Ghana, Tanzania, Colombia, the Philippines, Chile and St. Lucia. Over five thousand

---

[16] Gerard T. Rice, *The Bold Experiment*, (Notre Dame, Indiana: University of Notre Dame Press, 1985), p. 65.

applicants had taken the entrance tests and the first selectees would soon be training in Puerto Rico.

The program was moving, but there was still the matter of congressional funding. Republican Senate Minority Leader Everett Dirksen advised that the Peace Corps should have its own bill in order to speed the legislative process. On June 1, 1961 Hubert Humphery introduced Senate bill S. 2000 to establish the Peace Corps. Shriver personally lobbied 363 members of congress in an intensive campaign to win approval.[17]

As the bill moved along through committee, the Peace Corps made sure there was at least one Volunteer from each state and by August many states had colleges and universities involved in training programs. The bill passed the Senate on August 25, 1961 by voice vote and the House by a vote of 288 to 97. It authorized a $30 million budget for the first year, $10 million less than requested. The act laid out the purpose of the Peace Corps in Section 2:

> To promote world peace and friendship by making available to interested countries Americans who will:
> 1. Help the people of these countries meet their needs for trained manpower.
> 2. Help promote a better understanding of the American people on the part of the peoples served; and
> 3. Help promote a better understanding of other peoples on the part of the American people.[18]

The act's passage was just in time because Volunteers were already leaving for the first two programs. First to arrive were the 51 young Americans who stepped off the airplane at the Accra airport in Ghana on August 30, 1961. President Kwane Nkrumah had a need for English teachers. While the country had many local and tribal tongues, English was the common language of the country's secondary and higher education systems and there were just not enough native English teachers. Nkrumah was concerned about the Peace Corps being used by the CIA to infiltrate his country, but finally decided to take the chance.

The first group of Peace Corps Volunteers to arrive in country disembarked from the airplane and as part of the welcoming ceremony sang the Ghanan national anthem in Twi. The effect was electric and could not have made a more positive impression on the people and dignitaries of the host country.

Within a few days the Volunteers had spread out across Ghana and on September 12, 1961, Tom Livingston of Wood Dale, Illinois became the first Peace Corps Volunteer to begin his assignment when he started teaching English in a secondary school in Dodowa, Ghana.[19]

A day after the Ghanan Volunteers arrived in country, thirty-five Americans landed in Tanganyika.[20] This program was actually the pilot project for the Peace Corps and had

---

[17] Gerard T. Rice, *The Bold Experiment*, (Notre Dame, Indiana: University of Notre Dame Press, 1985), p. 79.
[18] University of Nebraska, *Syllabus for Peace Corps Training Program*, August 29, 1964 – November 21, 1964.
[19] Gerard T. Rice, The Bold Experiment, (Notre Dame, Indiana: University of Notre Dame Press, 1985), p. 201.
[20] Tanganyika would become the independent nation of Tanzania on December 28, 1961.

been carefully selected. Tanganyika was receptive to the idea of the Peace Corps and had a need. This country of nine million people, the size of Texas, Louisiana and Arkansas combined had only eight hundred miles of paved roads. The soon to be independent nation had an economy that was being strangled by its inadequate infrastructure. With a geography that ranged from Mount Kilimanjaro, 19,340 feet above sea level to Lake Tanganyika, the world's second deepest lake and included rain forests and the Serengeti Plains, the task would be daunting.

Fifty-six candidates entered training at Texas Western College at El Paso. This group was made up of surveyors, geologists and civil engineers. They received refresher courses in their disciplines and intensive training in Swahili, the most widely spoken language among the 120 tribes of the country.[21]

As the celebrated first Peace Corps program, the group was flown to New York to visit the UN and then to Washington D.C. to meet President Kennedy. Finally, on August 31, 1961, they reached Tanganyika, a day later than the Ghana group.

Once in country, the Volunteers found plenty to do. They designed a network of roads throughout the country. They worked on water lines, harbors, airports and laid out entire towns. However, once Tanzania became independent, there was a cut back in money for roads and other construction projects. Much of the design work accomplished by the Volunteers was never used.

Also, since the Americans were constantly on the move, few close bonds were formed between Volunteers and Tanzanians. They did not become part of the communities, they were just there doing a job. Two of the three purposes of the Peace Corps, as stated in the Peace Corps act were not being met by this approach. Warren Wiggins determined the Tanganyika experience would not be repeated.

Shortly after the Tanzanian training was announced, President Kennedy told the nation that sixty-four Volunteers would be sent to Colombia to work in rural areas to improve farming practices, aid in rural construction and public sanitation. The President commented on that May 16th day:

Warren Wiggins with President Kennedy

---

[21] "Candidates for Tanganyika Project Will Begin Training End of June," *Peace Corps News,* Vol. 1, No. 1, June 1961, p. 3.

I am particularly pleased that the second project will be in Latin America because of the many ties of mutual respect and mutual ideals which bind us together as brother republics in this traditionally free and democratic hemisphere.[22]

Unlike the Ghanan and Tanzanian groups, these candidates were to be generalists, preferably with rural backgrounds. They were to receive two months of training at an American University and another month in-country before fanning out across Colombia. Once in the field they would be working with Colombian counterparts in community development programs sponsored by CARE and Colombian Department of Community Development. The emphasis on community development by the Colombian government was a response to the country's recent *Violencia*, a period of civil strife that had torn the country apart (see Append. III). This first group of Peace Corps Volunteers to Colombia would be part of the country's efforts to recover from the internal divisiveness and destruction, and help move the people toward peace and prosperity. They would be the pioneers paving the way for Colombia '64 which would arrive three years later.

An aftermath of the Violencia was an upsurge of communist and Marxist subversive groups in Colombia. Some of these were supported directly or indirectly by Cuba, sometimes through other Latin American organizations. The threat of another country in the Western Hemisphere going communist was real.

Adjustments were made after the first few programs had been in the field for a time, though the central tenants of a tightly controlled, small, non-bureaucratic and flexible organization were rigorously adhered to. Under Wiggins's guidance, Peace Corps moved away from using U.S. sponsored private relief organizations as vehicles to operate in the field and concentrated on Peace Corps run programs.

Training, on the other hand, was almost entirely turned over to educational institutions. U.S. colleges and universities were contracted to conduct the training. Each institution would develop its own program which meant there was a constant flow of new ideas and methods to learn from. Academia shared information, but each school had the prerogative to try new things. This supplied a certain renewed vitality to the organization over the years.

Shriver encouraged staff members to serve in the field in administrative positions and not just stay in Washington. He created a department of evaluation to check on country programs for effectiveness, weaknesses and inefficiencies.

A serious irritation to the Peace Corps was the constant accusations that the organization was just a front for the Central Intelligence Agency (CIA). This was a repetitive theme of Russian, Chinese and Cuban propaganda. Shriver received assurances from the President and the head of CIA that no attempt would ever be made to infiltrate the Peace Corps. This agreement was known in the Corps as "The Treaty." In addition, no Volunteer was to work for the CIA for ten years after service in the Corps.

Though Shriver was scrupulously careful to exclude any espionage from occurring through the Peace Corps, there was no doubt that the Corps was a tool in America's struggle in the Cold War. In September 1961, Shriver informed Kennedy that 280 Colombian students were returning to their country after a three month educational trip to

---

[22] "President Announces Second Peace Corps Project," *Peace Corps News*, Vol. 1, No. 1, June 1961, p. 2.

the Soviet Union.[23] Shriver used this information to push for a concentrated effort in Colombia. By January 1964, over six hundred Volunteers were serving in the country, more than in any other single nation.[24] Programs ranged from literacy-teaching, development of co-operatives for the marketing of products, agricultural extension work, pre and post natal care to organizing communities for self help projects.

The Peace Corps of 1964 had grown to 5,300 Volunteers in 46 countries with an annual budget of $96 million.[25] [26] Sargent Shriver was still director, but had also been named to head President Johnson's War on Poverty program. Fortunately, Warren Wiggins had retained his position as associate director for Program Development and Operations. The Peace Corps was in Africa, Latin America, the Near East and Far East with the heaviest concentration in Latin America. By late 1964 there were over 4,300 candidates in training in the United States, Puerto Rico and the Virgin Islands.[27] Forty-two of those would-be Volunteers, the members of Colombia '64, were winging their way to Puerto Rico to prepare for eventual service in Colombia.

[23] Gerard T. Rice, The Bold Experiment, (Notre Dame, Indiana: University of Notre Dame Press, 1985), p. 264.

[24] Gerard T. Rice, The Bold Experiment, (Notre Dame, Indiana: University of Notre Dame Press, 1985), p. 187.

[25] "Corps Now in 46 Countries," Peace Corps News, Fall, 1964, Vol. 2, No. 3, p. 2.

[26] Gerard T. Rice, The Bold Experiment, (Notre Dame, Indiana: University of Notre Dame Press, 1985), p. 88.

[27] "Corps Now in 46 Countries," Peace Corps News, Fall, 1964, Vol. 2, No. 3, p. 2.

3

PUERTO RICO – AN INTRODUCTION TO THINGS LATIN

Our training at the University of Nebraska had ended. With mixed feelings we said farewell to staff and teachers who had shepherded us through the first three months of training, and boarded the airplane for New York City. It was November 21, 1964, the next day would be the first anniversary of President John F. Kennedy's assassination. On the airplane, Bruce Borrud commandeered the aircraft intercom and read a telegram from Sergeant Shriver to all Volunteers recalling and commemorating that day.

We overnighted in the big city and did our best to take in as much of the Big Apple's night life as possible in one evening. This was facilitated by Ken Waissman who was anxious to show us "his town." The next morning we assembled at the airport for the flight to Puerto Rico.

On Sunday, November 22nd we checked into the Hotel Normandea on the sea shore in San Juan. For a day, at least, we could feel like tourists. After the cold temperatures of

Betsy Long, Tom Gallaher, Jeanette Reeser and Ken Waissman find
some time to play tourist on a beach in Puerto Rico.

Nebraska and New York City, the mid 80s, tropical humidity, and white sandy beaches certainly helped create that feeling. To Gerry Volgenau,

> Puerto Rico was still America, although it was far more Latin than Anglo-Saxon, more Catholic than Anglican, more rum than Bourbon. Puerto Rico was steamy days where the sun seemed to glow through finely etched glass and nights wore softness that lay on your cheek like a cat's fur. It was martinis in

tourist bars and *ron y coca* in the *barrio,* eruptive politics about, "is we is or is we ain't part of the United States."

It was painted toenails at pool side in luxury hotels, cut-off jeans on public beaches, single-light-bulb shacks in garbage-strewn neighborhoods and farm towns where homes have cement floors. It was cement walls that seemed to sweat and murals dripping in tropical reds, yellows and greens.

It was America and Spain and Africa. It was *arroz con pollo* and *una whaper* at *Burga Kin.* And it was a vibrant people who mostly went about daily life never quite earning enough money to be able to wash the dirt from under their fingernails – real people, hard-working people. Puerto Rico sat one notch down the American ladder and one step up the South American *escalera.*[1]

No sooner had we arrived than the orientation meetings began. There were instructions on how to conduct ourselves, the health hazards of the island and introductions to the new people we would be working with, but by late afternoon we were given some freedom to explore on our own or enjoy the white sands and blue-green salt water. Three of us decided to head for the old part of the city and visit the great fortress which has guarded the city for centuries.

San Juan is a modern, bustling city with a population, at that time, of about 400,000 people out of an island peopled by 2 million souls. It is located on the north side of the island just to the east of center. Adjoining the west side of the city is San Juan Harbor. Stretching around and enclosing the north perimeter of the harbor is San Juan Island, an islet connected to San Juan proper, and the rest of Puerto Rico, by bridges and a causeway at its southeastern tip.

The elongated islet, about two miles by a half mile, is the site of the old colonial San Juan. Our hotel, Normandia, was located on the eastern shore of this small island surrounded by parkways, other hotels and modern buildings. But the western half of the islet contains the historic structures of old San Juan, the colonial city, now a tourist town featuring narrow streets, souvenir shops and Spanish colonial architecture. The old town is protected by walls and fortifications, San Cristobal and La Fortaleza, once a formidable stronghold and still the governor's palace today. Beyond all this at the tip of the islet sits El Morro, the citadel guarding the entrance to the harbor. This massive structure once served as the eastern anchor of Spain's Caribbean empire protecting the gold plate fleets before they left for the dangerous voyage across the Atlantic with the gold, silver and jewels of the Americas that made Spain the richest nation in Europe and paid for her wars and expanding empire. It was this great fortification that the three of us had decided to investigate.

Because it was already late, we grabbed a taxi for the short hop to the fort bypassing Old San Juan, San Cristobal and the other fortifications along the way. The taxi dropped us at the east end of the parade area, a large open lawn that separates Old San Juan from the fort. In colonial times this open area provided a clear field of fire for artillery and musketeers stationed in El Morro firing back toward the land side. As we crossed the green lawns, the true immensity and extent of this edifice became apparent to us.

Castillo de San Felipe del Morro (Fort Saint Philip on the Headland), the fort's full name, lays on a promontory jutting out into the sea. Along this peninsula runs a thick

---

[1] Gerald Volgenau, personal email, Sep. 22, 2008.

stone wall which also extends across the land side completely enclosing the fort. The top of this wall is wide enough to allow for the maneuvering of cannon. Along the summit of the wall is a palisade with the characteristic notches to protect musketeers and artillerymen.

Inside this massive outer wall are open areas for maneuvering cannon, supplies and troops. This series of courtyards and roadways rings the inner wall that rises vertically to over 140 feet above the sea which lies at the base of the outer wall. Slots dot this inner wall allowing musketeers to cover the courtyards and take aim at attackers coming over the outer wall. The top of the inner wall is designed with watch towers and turrets to mount cannon and protect soldiers firing shoulder weapons. The sheer size of this massive stone structure is overpowering.

Ramparts of El Morro

We didn't have much time before the fort would be closing so we roamed the ramparts and hurried along the stone staircases leading from one level to another as fast as we could. After spending some time at one of the look-out stations that hang out over the walls, we discovered a circular stone stairway enclosed in a vertical shaft that plunged from the top of the fort down into the very bowels of the massive structure. Descending these stone steps that spiraled downward in the dark was scary, but just what we imagined we might find in this gothic citadel.

At the bottom we found ourselves among a series of large rooms with huge, thick, plank double doors on the courtyard side. These were cannon rooms where the Spanish mounted artillery at the lowest level for a clear line of fire across the entrance of the harbor. Each room had two or three gun ports, several feet in length, built into the massive walls like small rectangular tunnels bored through the thick rock breastworks. It was easy to imagine cannon rolled up to the openings in the wall ready to fire at some marauding vessel trying to gain entrance to the harbor.

Lacking any kind of good sense, we took turns crawling through these gun ports so we could get a good look at the outside of the ramparts and the harbor. At the base of the wall we observed there were several feet of sand and rock between the water's edge and the parapet, enough room, we decided, for a path along the base of the wall.

Exhibiting even less sound judgment, one by one we crawled through the gun port and hung by our finger tips from the outside of the opening. Letting go, we slid down the not quite vertical wall to the narrow piece of ground at the base of the fortress.

It would be a simple matter, we thought, to walk around the fort on this strip of land between breastwork and ocean back to the land side and regain the entrance. What we did not count on was how complete the old Spanish defenses were.

Once outside, there was no way of climbing the wall back to the gun port. The Spanish had constructed the bulwark so it was quite smooth, impossible to climb. But we had our little beach of fifteen or twenty feet, though we found as we walked clockwise along the wall, it actually narrowed here and there to five or six feet. This was a bit disconcerting.

When we reached the north side of the fort where we expected to be able to walk back onto the island, we found a wall, quite insurmountable, extending from El Morro back along the island's perimeter toward Old San Juan. This was part of a defensive parapet that, at one time, had encircled the entire islet protecting the old colonial town. Between Old San Juan and modern San Juan the wall had been removed, but next to the fort, it was still intact. How far the breastwork extended we did not know.

The second thing we discovered was that the tide was coming in, another circumstance we land-lubbers had not taken into account. Our narrow bit of beach was shrinking rapidly and waves were beginning to lap at our feet.

Our formally casual stroll now became much more hurried as we raced along the narrowing beach searching for a way back onto the island. At one point we had to climb over a rock ridge that protruded out into the sea. Climbing down off the ledge we were back on the beach knee deep in sea water and soaked to the waist from the

The walls of El Morro

occasional wave. The situation was becoming desperate and I began to imagine the headlines, "Peace Corps Volunteers Swept Out to Sea."

To make matters worse, the relatively smooth beach had given way to wet slippery rocks that we were now forced to climb over. Moss and lichen made for poor footing and slimy handholds. The low sandy beaches were now small lagoons that we had to wade through hoping that we could cross without being met by a monstrous wave. Even the little waves were now reaching chest high. Panic was setting in.

Fortunately, before the waves crashing down on us swelled to something over our heads, we found a gate in the wall that led into a cemetery. We scrambled through the arched opening, never so glad to be three living beings, though we were among hundreds of dead.

We found ourselves in a forest of stone tombs, crosses and effigies laid out in rectangular bocks with pathways between like a miniature city. This was Cementerio de San Juan, the final resting place of early colonial war veterans, 18th and 19th Century citizens of Old San Juan, and other defenders of the old Spanish Empire. Picking our way through the maze of ancient tombstones, covered crypts, and memorial statuary, we finally made our way back to the green between El Morro and Old San Juan.

Looking back at the massive fortress we had a new appreciation for its defensive capabilities. It had defended this Spanish outpost for over 400 years from Carib, Dutch, French and English attack and had been breached only once. And now it had the further distinction of having defeated three adventurous young Americans, though we were certainly less formidable than previous attackers and our intentions far less nefarious.

Puerto Rico was discovered by Europeans on November 19, 1493 by Christopher Columbus on his second voyage to the "Indies." Among his crew was one Juan Ponce de León who would return in 1508 with 50 men to conquer the island

Puerto Rico became the corner stone of the Spanish Caribbean Empire. Even before El Morro was built, the islanders, both Spanish and native Arawaks were battling the Caribs. These fierce, war-like Indians originated in the Guiana lowlands of mainland South America and had already spread along the coasts of Venezuela and Colombia. Their progress was halted by the Puerto Ricans, rescuing the rest of the islands of the Caribbean from these invaders.

To defend the island and protect the gold shipments passing through the port on the way to Europe, the Spanish continually added to the island's fortifications, culminating with La Fortaleza in 1533 and El Morro in 1595. The construction

Sentinel of the Spanish Caribbean Empire

was none too soon, for immediately the French began raiding the coastal settlements. Next came Sir Francis Drake who tried an artillery duel with El Morro and lost. The Earl of Cumberland led 18 ships and 10,000 men in an assault from the land side and actually breached the walls of El Morro with heavy siege guns only to be defeated by a plague that decimated his army. The Dutch of the Dutch West India Company under General Boudewijn Henderikszoon laid siege to El Morro, but couldn't penetrate the stronghold. And finally the citadel was tested one last time, during the Napoleonic Wars, by English. Lieutenant General Sir Ralph Abercromby who led an attack that was thrown back by an army of 20,000 Puerto Ricans reinforced with 300 French soldiers from Haiti. Through all this El Morro remained in Spanish hands, the stronghold protecting the Spanish plate fleets.

It was not until United States Army troops landed on Puerto Rico during the Spanish American War that the island was successfully invaded. By the Treaty of Paris (1898) Puerto Rico was ceded to the U.S.

The Volunteers of Colombia '64 found an island of bustling cities and busy roads, a mix of American initiative to improve and the Latin ability to enjoy life, a beautiful green island fringed with white sandy beaches and a blue-green sea, a land blessed with a charming people, friendly and generous.

Our schedule was to be a week working with Puerto Rican Agricultural Extension and Home Demonstration Agents, a second week working on community relations assignments and visiting small rural farms, then two weeks at Camp Radley, one of two Peace Corps camps in the mountains of Puerto Rico. Bright and early Monday morning (Nov. 23, 1964) we were given the names of the towns we would be staying in, a contact in the town and $100 for two weeks living expenses.

Ron Halter was assigned to Fajardo, a small town on the east coast. He found a long distance cab – we were not allowed to drive while in Puerto Rico – and headed east from San Juan. He took up residence at a boarding house and quickly learned the difference between the Castilian Spanish we had been taught in Nebraska and the Caribbean tongue of the island. Still, he was able to get along at the *Servicio de Extension Agricola* for the first week.

The second week Ron visited fishing boats, attended Mass in a "backwoods" area and toured sugar cane farms. He rounded out the week with a PTA meeting and Thanksgiving with a civilian employee of the nearby U.S. Naval base and his family.[2]

While Ron went east, I (your author) was assigned to the west coast, to the town of Aguadilla, the local that claimed to be the site of Columbus's landing on Puerto Rico. I roomed with a family and ate at a restaurant in the town. I shadowed the agricultural extension agent for a week, taking several trips into the *campo* (rural areas), which was very informative. I learned about tropical agriculture from actual farmers and I learned how they grew their crops. The second week, I visited, factories, docks, town officials, anyone and anywhere that I could practice Spanish. I even attended a baseball game at Ramey Air Force Base where a local team played a team from Mayagüez. I was surprised to find major league players on both sides. Apparently, they played in Puerto Rico in the off season to stay in shape. After two weeks of relative low pressure and unstructured time, it was load up for the Peace Corps camps.

---

[2] Ronald Halter, Peace Corps trainee, letter to Joyce B. Scannell, his cousin of North Wales, PA, November 28, 1964, Personal Files of Ronald Halter, Lenexa, KS.

During this two week introduction to things Latin, not everyone had been banished to the outback. Bruce Borrud relates:

I was assigned to an ag extension office in San Juan for those first two weeks. The closest fellow Volunteer to me was Betsy (Long) who was on the outskirts of town. We'd meet on weekends and do things together. Thanks Betsy for being an English speaking *compadre* during that time. I shared a room ($1 a night) with a Cuban refugee who spoke no English. He was an older man who slept most of the time. I was told he had had some wealth in Cuba, but was forced to flee after the Castro revolution.

I came down with a nasty cold and the local food didn't sit with me well. I'd have to say that I was experiencing culture shock for the first time. I was glad when the group reunited at Camp Radley.[3]

While the ag and home economics people were getting some idea of what tropical agriculture and Latin society was all about, the ETV subgroup was off on its own adventures. Gerry Volgenau remembers the group's activities that included a rather sobering revelation concerning circumstances the group would soon encounter:

Once again, our group was divided – Ag people over here, ETV people over there. Over a period of about a month, our ETV group would try to learn from some pros at the Rio Piedras campus of the University of Puerto Rico in San Juan, spend a week living with a family somewhere on the island and end up near the sea coast town of Arecibo for a final shot of Outward Bound training.

In San Juan and beyond, we really had to start using Spanish. And no one ever said anything like the textbook stories of Juan and Marie going to the movies. We learned local jargon. *Guagua* meant bus. I remember one toddler with his tiny hand gripping his mother's finger at a bus stop, repeating "Gua-gua-gua-gua." It sounded like baby talk to me too. Clerks did not say "*Buenos dias*,' they said *"a sus ordenes."* Easier was "*Una Coca.*" In Caribbean style, the words in Puerto Rico came fast with whole letters often disappearing entirely. "*Como esta tu?"* instead of *Como estas tu?"* At times it did not seem the locals were speaking in sentences, but just one very, very long word.

I remember the university where the salt air seemed to make the walls ooze with moisture. And it all smelled a bit salty, like a harbor after the tide had gone out.

I only remember one instructor. She was the head of instructional television for all of Puerto Rico. A handsome and smartly-dressed woman, she told of the time she went to Bogotá to interview for the job as head of the country's educational TV programming.

"I remember going to the opera one night in Bogotá," she said. "We were dressed in evening clothes, suits and ties and long dresses. And as we came out, there were children on the street - begging. Some had distorted arms and legs. And scabs. Some were just dirty faced babies in dirty diapers. Every one shivered in the chilly high mountain darkness.

---

[3] Bruce Borrud, personal email to Gary Peterson, Oct. 29, 2008.

"And as I walked to the hotel," she said. "I could see where these children were sleeping. In doorways, under newspapers. Three or four together. Out on the grassy traffic medians with trucks rumbling by."

"I cried myself to sleep that night. And the next night, and the next. I could not bear it. I had to turn the job down."

The director's story impressed me. So, I thought, that was what was yet to come.

My week of living with a family was in the small town of Morovis in the center of the island. They spoke nothing but Spanish. Meals were like a return to my first weeks in Lincoln at the language tables. I was somewhat less of a mute. I could now say, "Pass the salt."

Afterwards, our ETV minigroup joined the ag people at a camp near Arecibo for a final round of Outward Bound training.[4]

Robert Bezdek also makes reference to the *directora* in a summary of the ETV group's activities he recorded shortly after rejoining the rest of the trainees at Camp Radley:

Expecting nothing short of chaos on arriving at Puerto Rico, we ETV'ers were surprised to meet a woman so well organized that we petitioned Peace Corps headquarters for an extra two weeks of training with her. Doctor Viera, Assistant Director of WIPR ETV station and a graduate of the University of Texas - she has an amazingly long list of titles and accomplishments - introduced us to everyone from the top echelon down to the janitor, requesting all of them to contribute to our training whatever was theirs to give.

The first week we became familiar with the station organization and equipment, personnel, programs, and studied in any department we wished. The following week, under the direction of Señor Ramirez, the utilization group visited schools in the metropolitan area as well as some outside the city. The *technicos,* followed the previous week's schedule, studying under the assistant engineer at the station, Señor Perez.

As the agricultural extension and home economics group "publicoed" their way to Camp Radley, Marge (Mohler) and Lisa (Hufnagle) journeyed to Florida (Puerto Rico) at the foot of mighty (Mount) Yunque, for field training. Likewise, Tomás (Gallaher) stormed Corozal, and Geraldo (Volgenau) livened up Morovis. Luis (Jarussi) and Roberto (Bezdek) battled Rio Piedras traffic to specialize in television repair under the tutelage of Señor Rivera, Director of the Audio Visual Department. We were sent to various parts of the island on repair missions. Taking advantage of an ideal situation, Ken Wassiman remained working in his bailiwick at the station.

In retrospect, we profited much from our extended training. Today, good-byes will be said and sincere thanks will be expressed as we prepare for our camp visit. In addition to special thinks to those already mentioned, we ETV'ers would like to express our gratitude to the Peace Corps *jefes* for the two extra

---

[4] Gerald Volgenau, personal email to Gary Peterson, Sep. 22, 2008.

weeks of training, to the personnel at WIPR and to the many devoted to Puerto Rican education.[5]

Tom Gallaher's first assignment was also in San Juan where he had some time to play tourist and learn something about a different approach to people:

The first part of our training in Puerto Rico consisted of working at Puerto Rico's main television broadcast studios in Rio Pierdas, just outside San Juan. We were put up in a rather posh beach front hotel about ten minutes walk from Old San Juan. My roommate was Louie Jarussi and it was there that I really got to know him. Louie was very friendly and outgoing, always with a big smile. The people at the T.V studio loved him. His Spanish, as I recall, was a lot better than mine.

One afternoon after finishing up at the studio I went back to the hotel. Louie was either already in the room when I arrived, or arrived a short time later. Anyway, we both decided to go for a swim. We swam out to a raft that was stationed about fifty yards offshore. When we hauled out of the water there was a guy lying on the raft sunning himself. He didn't acknowledge me after I climbed aboard and since I was from N.Y., I didn't acknowledge him figuring he wanted to be left alone.

When Louie climbed up, however, he addressed the guy, "Hi, I'm Louie Jarussi."

NO RESPONSE.

"This is my first time in Puerto Rico isn't this water great?"

MONOSYLABIC GRUNT in response.

Louie however doesn't give up, "I 'm from Montana, where are you from?

One word reply, "NEW YORK."

Pointing to me, Louie continues, "My friend here's from N.Y."

Another MONOSYLABIC GRUNT."

"Are you down here on vacation ?" Louie inquires.

He gets another GRUNT in response.

I would have long since given up on trying to get a response from this guy if I had even tried in the first place, but not Louie.

"We're Peace Corps Volunteers, down here on a training program."

Well that finally got a response. The guy sat up and introduced himself. Turns out he's a detective in the NYPD down in San Juan on vacation and he asks us to be his guests for dinner and meet his wife. We had a great time. And I learned an important lesson, that most people are friendly and want to be engaged. That may not seem like much of an insight but in my neighborhood in the Bronx when I was growing up, the mantra was MYOB, mind your own business.

During the second part of the program we were sent out to various sites scattered around the island to be immersed in a Spanish language environment. I was sent to a small mountain town Corozal. I stayed with a family with two daughters. It was there that I learned that roosters do not necessarily crow at

---

[5] Robert Bezdek, "ETV'ers," article in El Hocicon, Dam P.R. Issue, p. 5.

dawn; they crow any damn time they please. I remember thinking my first night, as I tossed around in bed, " What the ** #!!!#**&# is going on here I'm going to have to strangle that thing." Lucky for me, two days later the town celebrated its *Fiesta Patronales* and as a special treat we had roasted chicken for dinner, after that there was no more crowing.[6]

Separating our group was necessary for training purposes, but the ETV people resented missing out on the Outward Bound program and they eventually decided to do something about it. Ken Waissman was, of course, right in the middle of the mini-rebellion.

The majority of the group went to the Outward Bound Camp while the seven of us in the ETV group went to San Juan and the ETV center there. I asked our Peace Corps representative in San Juan if we could join the rest of our group at Outward Bound for our last weekend in Puerto Rico. The answer came back negative. The Outward Bound camp wasn't authorized to have us. Hell with that, I thought, and persuaded everyone that the seven of us should hire two taxis, drive across the island and show up late Friday evening. Once there, I doubted the head of the Outward Bound Camp would risk our safety by turning us away. I was right. They took us in and we reunited with the rest of the group, spending our final weekend in Puerto Rico at Outward Bound, repelling off the dam, rock climbing and mainly just having a blast.[7]

By the time the ETV subgroup joined us, the ag/home econ folks were just finishing up our training at Camp Radley. There had been plenty of Spanish instruction, camp clean up and even construction projects, PE of course, but there were adventures to experience also, rock climbing and trekking.

The beautiful island of Puerto Rico lies between Hispaniola (Haiti and Dominican Republic) to the west and the Virgin Islands to the east. The north coast of the island faces the Atlantic Ocean and the south shore borders the Caribbean Sea. Puerto Rico's coastal low lands are verdant, dotted with white sandy beaches. Inland, a series of mountain ranges provide a raised backbone for the island.

While sugar cane and other tropical crops are grown in the lowlands, it is the mountain sides and valleys that produce the prized Puerto Rican coffee picked from small trees or bushes grown in the shade of towering orange trees.

The mean temperature along the coasts varies from about 74.5 degrees Fahrenheit during November-April to about 80 degrees during May-October. In the mountains temperatures run 5 to 10 degrees cooler.

There is no true rainy season but usually more rain falls between May and December than during the rest of the year. In the Caribbean National Forest on Mt. Yunque rainfalls amount to 300 inches a year. The Lajas Valley in the southwest, on the other hand, has a desert-like climate. In the coastal areas the

---

[6] Tom Gallaher, personal email to Gary Peterson, 10 Oct. 2008.
[7] Ken Waissman, personal email to Gary Peterson, 20 Aug. 2010.

rain usually comes in sudden brief showers immediately followed by bright sunshine. Raincoats and umbrellas are seldom used.

Puerto Rico has a great variety of plant life. Palm trees and mangrove flourish along the seacoast, bamboo in great clumps along the roads and streams. Flamboyant and African tulip trees, bougainvillea, hibiscus, poinsettias, a distinctive golden trumpet, the *canario*, and scores of other plants splash vivid color against the predominantly green and brown landscape. The rain forest on El Yanque is a jungle of tropical and sub-tropical trees and plants – giant ferns, orchids and trailing vines. All year round, everywhere, flowers bloom.[8]

It is in the mountains of Puerto Rico that the Peace Corps had established two training camps.

Camp Crozier was open in September, 1961, on the site of a U.S. department of Agriculture recreation area, built in the late 30's. An existing stone and concrete building was converted into the administrative center. The other buildings are wooden 'casetas' that sleep 10-12 trainees, a language laboratory housing electronic equipment for the use of tapes, mess hall, classroom and staff quarters. The 45' X 75' instructional swimming pool is also located at Crozier.

Camp Radley, which was opened in July, 1962, is three miles from Crozier. It has the same facilities as Crozier, with the exception of the pool and language lab. Each camp has a maximum capacity of 110 trainees at a time.

It was here Colombia '64 was immersed in the Outward Bound training that they had been introduced to in Nebraska, a program originated by the British as a means of toughening up their youth.

Philosophy: A great deal is being asked of the men and women who volunteer to give two years of their lives to the work of the Peace Corps. There is no assurance of personal reward beyond the satisfaction which comes from rising to a challenge, and it is quite possible that two years of difficult work will produced few tangible results. On the other hand, frustration and hardship

Bruce Borrud surveying Camp Radley.

[8] Office of the Commonwealth of Puerto Rico, *Puerto Rico*, June 1962, p. 7.

are certain to be constant companions. It is therefore essential that before embarking on such an assignment, the Volunteer must have a realistic assessment of his own capacity, his goals, and his endurance in the face of continued challenge.

Every individual has certain limits beyond which he does not readily push himself. Many of these limits are natural and sensible. Others are irrationally derived from force of habit and lack of realism rather than from actual physical barriers. It is this second category of limitations which the camp experience, based on the British 'Outward Bound' training, is designed to help the Volunteer understand and overcome. In so doing, the camp staff seeks to encourage confidence and staying power in the Volunteer, as well as an "esprit de corps" which will transcend the long miles of separation once the Volunteers are on the job in a foreign land.[9]

The ag subgroup of Colombia '64 arrived at Camp Radley and settled in. Before dawn on Monday we were up for our three mile run to Camp Crozier where the swimming pool was located. After a short dip, it was back to home base. Carol Oakes, from Rexford, New York, a small town in the Mohawk Valley just north of Schenectady, recalls, "running down the hill – how many miles was it – every morning and then back up the hill to do sit-ups and push-ups. Now my memory wants to say we had to do 100 of each (boy were we tough), but was it more like 50 of each? Then trying to get off the ground to climb a stupid rope suspended from somewhere."[10]

Sandwiched between, Spanish, chores and work sessions was the rock climbing described in our group news sheet now printed with an actual mimeograph machine:

Repelling and rock climbing were not for the faint of heart.

Our first day at the rocks entailed a practice session on the slopes of the camp on the art of yelling commands, rope tying, falling…and belaying. After this we were taught to repel. We were next taken to the dam in order to practice our repelling. As we stood there with our knees quivering, we thought for sure that it was a 200 or 300 foot drop. After we had all finished the descent (which turned out to be a lot of fun) we

[9] The Peace Corps Training Camps in Puerto Rico, Peace Corps publication, Description of camps and training distributed to trainees at the camps Crozier and Radley.
[10] Carol Oakes Ford, personal email, Oct. 8, 2008.

were ready for a second try. We are now waiting our third session which I understand is a 90 foot challenge.[11]

The "90 foot challenge" turned out to be a day of climbing some of the island's real shear cliffs. Each of us was given the opportunity to scale the easiest climb and if successful, we were allowed to move on to the next hardest. Interestingly, it wasn't the big and strong that excelled at this sport, or even the tall and lean. Rather, it was the small and wiry. Carol Scharmer of Baltimore, Maryland scrambling up the Book Rock Face with what seemed surprising ease. It was a climb the other girls and even most of the boys could not master.

The overall champion of the group, however, was Rodney Spokely, 21, of Nielsville, Minnesota. His dazzling performance certainly was not due to a life of practice. Nielsville is in the Red River Valley of the north where the water flows the wrong way – north – and the land is so flat farmers cut ditches in the fields so the rain water will drain off.

At five nine, Rodney was the shortest guy in the group, but his abilities in navigating those cliff faces were truly amazing. He and Carol could find hand holds where no one else could and were able to pull themselves up and over ledges that defeated other climber's best efforts. The rest of us pulled and stretched, hung on and teetered, slipped and fell; some strong men were reduced to tears of frustration. Making it to the top of even a relatively simple climb was especially rewarding. It was a bruising and often frustrating day, but everyone agreed it was a great outing.

Finally, there were the treks, first a series of afternoon and evening hikes during which we learned to follow terrain maps, read a compass and live off the land – seeds, roots, berries, and giant tree snails (*escargot* anyone?). We were all very thankful oranges were in season.

The finale was a four day event in which we were dropped off in groups of threes and fours with the challenge of finding our way back to camp in four days. We were given a map and one meal.

One group of our girls started at Lago Garzas some 30 miles from camp by road, which we were not supposed to use, or 20 miles across the Cordillera Central and some very rough country. Carol Oakes, one of that group remembers, "being dropped off with maps that were

Jerry Schaefer, Jeannette Reeser and others
ready for another trek.

[11] Fred Faulkner and Ronnie Cress Kordick, "Rock Climbing," article in El Hocicon, Dam P.R. Issue, p. 5.

incorrect, but we were still expected to find our way back to camp. I was with Betsy Long and Arlene Ratliff. I know the first night out we stayed in the top of a coffee bean storage shed. We thought we would be safe, but during the night little bugs started crawling out of the coffee beans piled up on the floor. Yuk."[12]

One night, just at dusk, they came upon a house of some size with a well kept yard. It almost looked out of place in the rugged mountains. The discovery proved to be a stroke of luck for the hungry, dirty young women. The family treated the trainees with the greatest kindness, "letting us sleep in beds and we got to shower and eat a great meal."[13]

By contrast, the last night the group found only a small house of a very poor family built up off the ground on stilts. The area under the house was used for storage. The trainees passed the night on the ground in that storage area. Most of the houses in the back country wore bright paint applied just for the Christmas season, a tradition in rural Puerto Rico. But this house exhibited only weathered boards on its shabby exterior.

"We felt so sorry for this little family that when we left the next morning, we left our blankets for them to use."[14]

As for me, Gary Peterson, having survived a close call at El Morro, I thought I was ready for anything. I was in a group of three that was dropped off not too far from Carol Oake's group, on the slopes of Monte Guilarté, a 1200 foot peak north of Ponce (named after Ponce de León), the major city on the island's south coast. Again, it was only about

Michael Weber

a 20 mile hike over rugged terrain to get back to camp. In my team were Charles Lenkner and Mike Weber. Chuck was one of the married guys in our group, age 23, a graduate of the University of California at Davis. He had been on the staff of a scout camp in his college days, so I thought, here was an enthusiastic outdoorsman. But he proved to be a very lay back, take advantage of opportunities kind of guy. Mike Weber, on the other hand, was more like me, be prepared and stay ahead of events was our approach. Mike, age 20, had attended Southern Illinois University and had worked as an engineer technician, farm hand and carpenter's apprentice. Now 20 miles is not a long distance to cover in four days even given the mountainous terrain and time we would have to spend foraging for food. As we tramped through jungle growth and over mountain tops, Mike and I were constantly on the lookout for edible plants and those tree snails. Chuck was also looking for food sources, but they tended to be more of the rural *tienda* (country store) or school lunch program sort.

When Mike and I suggest it was getting late and was time to set up camp, Charles would just chuckle and say, "Let's go a bit further. I'm sure we'll find something more comfortable." And we always did.

We did camp out one night and fixed our one provided meal, and that was under the protection of a bridge. The other two nights we slept in a screened in porch and the back room of a store. We ate at a school (government provided hot lunch program) in the

---

[12] Carol Oakes Ford, personal email to Gary Peterson, Oct.8, 2008.
[13] Ibid.
[14] Ibid.

middle of the mountains, at tiendas a couple of times, with a family once and with a construction crew which donated parts of their lunch in return for our story and some laughs. We arrived back in camp on December 20th, dirty and smelly, but otherwise in good shape.

One trek produced a story of sacrifice - for the good of the team. Bruce Borrud tells of his group coming to a shallow stream they would have to cross. Now we had all been warned about the parasites that infested these tropical creeks and the four hikers, Bruce, Richard Bennett, Brian McMahon and Ross Burkhart were all looking for a way to avoid getting wet and possibly contracting some dreaded parasitic disease. There was no bridge in the vicinity and the stream was too wide to vault, but gradually, three of the group began to size up Ross. Burkhart, who's Spanish nickname was *Gigante* (Giant) stood over 6 feet 5 inches and could stride across the little creek in just a few steps.

Bruce describes the eventual solution arrived at by his group, "After some discussion we determined that Gigante (being the largest) would carry the other three across, one at a time on his back. Thus, he would be the only one exposed to this potential hazard. After crossing he was carefully dried off, possibly even with alcohol we had in a first aid kit. In the spirit of the Peace Corps, Gigante sacrifice himself for the greater good."[15]

It is true that on our 3 day cross country hike Ross Burkhardt carried each of us [Rich Bennett writes], his three trail mates, across a wide stream on his back. It seemed logical that exposure to the schistosomiasis parasite in the water should be limited to one instead of all four and he was, after all, "El Gigante". He is a great human being. In the end, even Gigante escaped the dreaded parasite.[16]

The most brutal trek, however, was the one embarked upon by a group dropped off in the Toro Negro National Forest about 35 miles from camp. This was truly wilderness country, in the heart of the Cordillera Central with actual jungle to penetrate. Steve Burgess (Sublette, Kansas), Don Lydic of Farnam, Nebraska, Jeff Andrews from Morriston, Florida, and Doug Dunn of Osceola, Nebraska had to deal with challenges above and beyond anything the rest of us had to confront.

They began their trek full of confidence with a

A tienda (small store) in the Puerto Rican back country.

[15] Bruce Borrud, personal email to Gary Peterson, Oct. 29, 2008.
[16] Richard Bennett, personal email, May 6, 2009.

canteen of water, a machete, a meal, two compasses and a map of the area. But they hadn't walked more than a couple of hundred yards when they discovered the trail didn't match the map. A closer look at the map showed it was of 1940 vintage, totally out of date. They tried to make use of it by orienting themselves with landmarks shown on the map, but even this didn't work. Finally they just struck out on a trail that seemed to be going in the right direction. After wondering around all day, they came to some buildings and found a shack to sleep in for the night. They were so tired they didn't eat that night. Also, they thought they better conserve their food until they emerged from this wilderness.

The next day it was more of the same, trails that turned in the wrong direction or just petered out. After wondering around for three hours without making any discernable progress, they decided to take a compass heading north and strike out on their own. Without a trail, they had to hack their way through the jungle and underbrush with the one machete they had been given, lead man cutting his way through. Hours later they came to a steep slope, but at least it was clear of trees and brush. They slid down this 150 foot drop on their backs, picking up scrapes and imbedded thorns.

At the bottom of the slope they found themselves in a canyon with steep cliffs on both sides. They had progressed from being lost in a jungle to being trapped in a blind canyon. There was little they could do but follow this sheer sided alley until they could climb out. Hours later they found a cleft in the canyon wall and were able to climb out. Completely lost as far as the map was concerned, the group decided to rely on their compass. They took a heading and struck out in a northerly direction. Finally, after a day and a half of this kind of travel, they intersected a road. Following this welcome sign of civilization, the weary guys found a farm house where they were invited to sleep in the hog shed. At least it was warm and dry. They ate their can of beans and curled up next to the pigs for a reasonably good night's sleep.

They made good time the next day and slept on a concrete school balcony that night. The next morning they were off to a good start, but found their way blocked by a lake (probably Lago Camaonillas). However, a little searching turned up a ferry that took them to within five miles of camp Radley. They celebrated by eating the last of their rations and walking triumphantly into camp.

Later the trek director told the group that they had been given the hardest route as a test to see how they would handle the challenges. Apparently they passed as all four made it to Colombia.

The ETV folks had missed out on the wilderness treks, but they did arrive in time for some of the events at the camp.

We got to do some of the fun stuff [Vogenau relates], like rappel off a 100-foot dam. It was simple. Just stand with your back to the abyss, hook up the ropes, then leap out backwards – like your life was not worth a *centavo* – and bounce your way down the dam face. It was so much fun that after my first rappel, I scrambled my way back to the top of the dam to do it all over again.

Later we went for a swim at the beach. Just for fun, a few decided to practice their drown proofing skills which basically involves trying to relax while leaving your face in the water and as the need arose – which it did with regularity – you swept your arms to the side with a breast stroke, raised your head and took another breath. Since you have little chance to look around during the breath taking, an off shore current swept several of us out to sea before we looked up to see that the figures on the beach now were quite tiny. As with the drown proofing in Nebraska, no one died.[17]

Our Puerto Rican experience came to an end on December 22nd. The next day we boarded the airplane in San Juan for the trip back to the states and Christmas with family and friends. As we settled into our seats for the take off, most of us just wanted some sleep, but one trainee, now a full fledged Volunteer, could only marvel at the series of events that had brought him this far:

Burkholder had gone through Nebraska training in awe of his fellow Volunteers some of whom came from prestigious universities from all around the country. Still amazed and dazed, he entered the Puerto Rican chapter of his adventure too dumb to be scared of Outward Bound training. Repelling on the face of a dam, cliff-climbing, drown-proofing in the Caribbean Sea, a four day survival hike from hell through the rain forest, intra camp runs in pre-dawn light, spending two weeks in Ponce all alone. He celebrated his 21st birthday and final selection in camp and didn't even notice the small earthquake that shook the shelter.

Unbelievably, he had been selected – or more correctly – not de-selected.
Now it was off to Colombia.

Ufda (North Dakotan).

Que estoy haciendo?(Spanish)[18]

---

[17] Gerald Volgenau, personal email to Gary Peterson, 22 Sep 2008.
[18] Dennis Burholder, personal email to Gary Peterson, 7 Oct. 2008.

4
COLOMBIA FINALLY – BOGOTÁ

On New Years Day 1965 the forty-one Volunteers of Colombia '64 flew into New York City from the cities, mountains and plains of the United States. After a short night of trying to get some sleep on terminal seats and benches, the blurry eyed youths again boarded an airplane, this time the destination was the country of Colombia. The long anticipated flight was very nearly straight south from New York to Bogotá as the two continents, North and South America, do not lie on a north-south line, but are shifted with respect to each other, South America being far to the east. Colombia, in the northwest corner of the continent lies directly south of the northeastern states, east of even Florida. Short hours later, the young Volunteers would finally arrive in country to begin the work they had trained for these last four months.

Bogotá - city of perpetual spring. Situated only five degrees north of the equator, but at 8,659 feet above sea level, the sunlight is bright and penetrating when it shines. But much of the time the city is protected by a light cloud cover and is refreshed with soft, cool breezes off the mountains. Even on a cloudy day it is not cold. Only when it rains or in the early morning hours is there a decided chill in the air.

High mountains around Bogotá provide a picturesque back drop for the city's modern high-rise office buildings and hotels. The central plaza of the city, the Plaza de

Bogotá as seen from the mountains at the edge of the city in 1965.

Bolívar, is surrounded by stately government buildings of marble and granite. The plaza is an open paved expanse where pigeons flock to receive the bread crumbs tossed by visiting tourists and scurrying government officials.

The city has a cosmopolitan, almost European, flavor. The Volunteers found a city of contrasts, from the up-to-date office buildings to the statuesque cathedrals, from the elegant opera and concert halls to the dilapidated houses of the city's *barrios* (slums). Bogotá boasts museums like the Museo de Oro, featuring the gold work of the country's ancient peoples, the Quimbaya, Muisca, Calima, Tolima, Darién, Sinú and Tairona (see Appendix I for a history of ancient Colombia).

As for restaurants, the range was nearly infinite. Colombian cuisine was fully represented from the coastal, tropical fare of plantains and manioc to the mountain's chicken and potatoes. But of more interest to the Volunteers was the variety of restaurants representing cultures from all over the world, Hungarian, French, Italian, Chinese, Japanese, Indonesian, the list goes on almost indefinitely.

Entertainment was like-wise abundant and varied. There were the museums, opera, theater, movies - from the inexpensive barrio movie houses to the modern upscale cinemas - and, of course, there are the bull fights, the *corrida de toros.*

Our introduction to Colombia was, then, this teaming, bustling city not so different from any large U.S. city, but with its own distinctive features. Tom Gallaher writes about his first impressions of the city from the viewpoint of a former Marine:

> Large numbers of young soldiers, seemingly at every street corner, held automatic rifles at the ready. The soldiers, their brown heavily Indio faces impassive and inscrutable under their helmets, seemed isolated and out of their element on the bustling sidewalks of Bogotá. I could imagine how easy it would be for one of these young kids, because that's what they really were, just kids, alone as he was, if he felt threatened either by an angry crowd or some action perceived as threatening his safety, to react in a less than positive way. It would take only a second to switch off the safety guard and squeeze of a few bursts. I was not reassured to observe that in some cases the safety guards were already off.[1]

We spent a week in Bogotá meeting the Colombian Peace Corps administration, the PINA *jefes* we would be working with and we attended part of the old ag/nutrition extension Peace Corps group's twelve month conference which was a bit of an eye opener. We learned something of their frustrations, successes and how to go about getting help from our Colombian counterparts.

So for a few days, whenever we could get away, we explored the city, investigating office buildings, hotels, restaurants, museums, the barrios and the entertainment. Very quickly we began to get a sense of what Colombia might be like, or at least its capital.

> From the very beginning, Bogotá struck me as old, stony cold and not quite dried [Vogenau recalls]. Everything seemed damp – sidewalks, the buildings, the short mustachioed men in their 1930s suits and women, broad faced and grim in their drab *ruanas.*

---

[1] Tom Gallaher, personal email to Gary Peterson, Oct. 21, 2008.

For those not familiar with the ruana, it is a blanket that has a small slit in the center for men to wear something like Clint Eastwood's serape in "A Fist Full of Dollars." For women, their often colorful ruanas have a slit from the center to one side and is draped around the shoulders like a shawl. Ruanas are a Colombian icon – as symbolic of the country as coffee or – nowadays – cocaine.

The city seemed dirty in a long, historical sense. In 1538, Spanish conquistadors plunged their way up from the coastal jungle to this Andean plateau at more than 8,600 feet (see Appendix II for a history of Spanish colonial Colombia). The Indians called it Bacatá (emphasis on the last syllable), which means tilled fields. The Spanish kept the ancient Chibcha name and added their own religious twist, calling it Santa Fe de Bacatá. Before long it was known as Bogotá (once again with an emphasis on the last syllable).

To my eye, the city still wore remnants of grime from when the Spaniards founded it 426 years before. The grouting never seemed to have been scrubbed; nor the creases in the stone facades. And Bogotá's greenery felt like an alien invasion – the grass, untrimmed on the traffic islands and in stretches of scraggly lawn or seeping up through sidewalk cracks.

Bogotá grasses were disturbingly greener than green, eerie in their luminescence. Here in the high country, these sproutings acted like a low-caste jungle without portfolio. If anything, the city grass struck me as fierce and unrelenting in its clawing growth.

With their drab formality and precise Spanish, Bogotános seemed generally stern with a hurried, incurious air of the oppressed. *"Mañana,"* is not an expression heard much in Bogotá. At first I thought this might be a get-it-done-now city. But the reality of Latin dawdling was indeed alive in its inactive way in Bogotá – just not the expression.

Plaza de Bolívar in central Bogotá with the perennial cloud cover.

La Septima (Seventh Avenue), as I remember, was the main shopping drag. And one morning, before Peace Corps leaders scattered our group across the countryside like corn bits to chickens, one of our group returned with fine news of a shopping discovery. She had found a wonderful place to buy ruanas.

"What was the name of the store?" she was quizzed.

"Almacen."

Jokes, of course, are never as funny when they are explained. But almacen is a general term that means department store. So we could take our pick, her shopping discovery could have been any one of scores of such stores.

Another day, a member of the group returned from an outing where she had met an important local official.

"I can't remember his name," she said, "but he was short, dark skinned with a moustache and wore a black double-breasted suit."

Like saying the store's name was almacen or department store, the new Volunteer had aptly described just about every man in Bogotá's downtown.

Bogotá, we learned, was famous for its pickpockets. The grab-and-run thieves often worked not just singly, but in pairs and/or in gangs. One to bump and distract the victim, on say a sidewalk or bus, another to slice open your pocket or purse, grab the goods and make a getaway.

I talked to one volunteer who got robbed while driving a Jeep through the downtown. When he made a left-turn hand signal, a thief in a crosswalk just snatched the watch right off his wrist.

Thievery was so bad, so over-the-top dreadful, that this urban vice sometimes morphed into legend. An outlaw mark of distinction for the city – sort of like mobsters in Chicago. Several times I heard Bogotános crow about a story of the U.S. Secret Service agents who came to check out city security in advance of a well publicized visit by Vice President Richard Nixon. The Secret Service agents stayed, according to the story, at the city's best hotel, the Tequendama. And on their first night in town, thieves sneaked in and looted all their rooms while the agents were out to dinner.

"How good are the thieves in Bogotá?" Went one quip: "They can steal your socks without taking off your shoes."[2]

And there were the street urchins referred to by Dr. Viera, the Puerto Rican ETV director. They were not so visible in the daytime, but seemed to come out at night to beg in the streets, especially near restaurants and places of entertainment. They were always young, not yet teenagers, on down to toddlers. They were invariably shabbily dressed with dirty faces and they solicited with scrawny outstretched arms. Many had orange tinted hair, open sores and distended bellies, obvious signs of malnutrition. Occasionally, a small group would even put on a little skit or hold up signs to attract attention. These little waifs were a manifestation of the city's poverty and were particularly disturbing to the Volunteers when there first arrived.

All this is not to say that everything in Bogotá was completely dreary [Vogenau continues]. And as the months of service plodded by, a few days in the city felt like a real vacation. On weekends, we joined the crowds that jostled in to see the bullfights. This blood on the sand was entertaining not only for those of us who had read Hemingway, but for every pickpocket on the city. Bump, jostle, grab and run.

---

[2] Gerald Volgenau, personal email to Gary Peterson, April 4, 2009.

Where to sit? *Sol? Sombra?* Or *Solysombra?* For those not up on *corrida* seating, Sol means sitting in a section where the sun broils you for the entire afternoon. The cheap seats. Bull fighting's bleachers. Sombra means shade, the expensive seats in the cool afternoon shadows. And solysombra is both sun and shade, medium priced seats.

Bogotá's restaurants were first rate. Most of us were unsophisticated enough to have never eaten Swiss *fondu*. We discovered it in Bogotá. Our favorite restaurant (or certainly mine) was the Balalaika where Colombian waiters dashed from table to table wearing red tunics straight out of Doctor Zhivago. The restaurant was run by a White Russian expat who, each evening, would step out of the kitchen and sing arias from his favorite operas.

No matter where we went, we drank lots of Club Colombia beer and Ron Viejo de Caldas and Ron Extra Viejo de Caldas and Ron Buc from Bucaramanga. Also, scotch was pretty easy to find, but bourbon, almost never. It should be pointed out that during those years, the booze was safer to drink than the water.

Recreational drugs had not yet really made the Colombian scene in a big way. No one yet had heard of Colombian Gold or cocaine cartels. Medellín was known not for crime bosses, but by its nickname: the city of eternal springtime.

Sometimes we made forays to Bogotá's San Andrecito, the city's center for black marketers where, for some amazingly low prices, you could pick up anything from cigarettes to 35 mm cameras to TV sets. TV sets, in those days, were a rarity in Colombia.

And Bogotá also had doughnuts. The national capital, to my knowledge was the only city in the entire country where you could buy an actual doughnut. In Medellín, you reportedly could find another U.S. style treat – peanut butter. These were savored treats that reminded one of home, bits of Gringolandia. And knowing where to find them was as common among Volunteers as the ability to conjugate *estar*.

In 1965, Bogotá had only one shop with doughnuts. It was hidden away on a back street. But more than a few Volunteers found their way to this bakery in search of a sugary taste of home. But understand, these baked goods were not Winchell's style raised doughnuts. Each one weighed about two pounds. And the effect on your stomach was something equivalent to gulping down a vulcanized tractor tire. But then, a taste of home sometimes requires sacrifice.[3]

Finally, there was the assignment of sites. One by one we were called in to meet with the Peace Corps representatives who told us where we were to be located. As was expected our group would be scattered all across the country. Most of us would be along the mountains of the Eastern Cordillera from the department of Huila in the south, through the cities of Bogotá and Tunja to Cúcuta near the Venezuelan border in the north. One contingent would be in the Tolima Department in the Upper Magdalena. Several sites were in the Cauca Valley and up into the Central Cordillera from south of Popayán to Medellín.

---

[3] Gerald Volgenau, personal email to Gary Peterson, April 4, 2009.

Jeff Andrews, from Morriston, Florida, a political science graduate of Florida State University, and Eugene Roberts drew sites near Cartagena on the Caribbean coast. Dennis Burkholder was assigned Villavicencio, Meta out on the Llanos. About the only areas of Colombia not covered by our group were the Pacific Coast, the far eastern Llanos territories and the jungles of the Amazon River basin, though even these areas would be visited by members of Colombia '64 traveling on business and vacations.

The last couple of days were spent being trained in the "Lubauk Method," a system for teaching adults to read and write. The Colombian government hoped we would be able to participate in the country's literacy program, an effort to teach all Colombians to read.

By the time we had completed the training, everyone was anxious to leave the capital and head for their sites. We said our farewells and boarded airplanes, trains, and buses. We would be out of touch for four months. By the time we again assembled for a conference, everyone would have scores of stories to share.

And so the FAO/PINA contingent of Colombia '64 departed the capital. As for the ETV subgroup, Louie Jarussi, Bob Bezdek and Ken Waissman would remain in Bogotá, but the rest would be scattered across the country along with the ag/nutrition people like seeds broadcast in the field. The hope was that some of that seed would fall on fertile ground, take root and produce tangible results.

But what of this country these young North Americans were about to spend two years of their lives in? What about the people they were going to come in contact with and the terrain with which they would have to contend? In training they had learned that Colombia is the only South American country with both Pacific and Caribbean coast lines. It also extends south to the Amazon River where its river port town of Leticia lays four degrees south latitude. Except for that arm of territory that reaches down to this great river, Colombia is situated between latitude 1° N and 11° N so the country as a whole is just north of the equator with terrain ranging from sea level to almost 20,000 feet. Its territory, some 440,000 square miles (a little larger than Texas and California combined), may be divided into the mountainous western one half and the eastern plains. Of Colombia's 16 million people (in 1964), about 0.02 percent lived in the eastern flat lands. The overwhelming majority resided in the mountainous western portion where the country's cities, industry, ports, infrastructure and markets were located.

These fundamental facts, the Volunteers had learned in the ASWAC classes in Nebraska. But in truth, they were about to discover a nation of immense diversity in people and geography, a world of breathtaking scenery, spectacular beauty, inspiring history and heroic achievements. They would come to understand this remarkable nation in a way few North Americans have.

Some would work in or visit those eastern plains, where broad rivers meandered for hundreds of miles eastward from the mountains until they reach either the Amazon flowing eastward to the Atlantic or the Orinoco running north toward the Caribbean Sea. The southern region of this flat land is part of the Amazon River Basin, the *selva,* an immense jungle, dense and forbidding, where rivers are the means of transportation. And it is along this profusion of waterways that most of the region's sparse population is located, scattered in the occasional villages that dot the river banks. Away from these ribbons of commerce, deep in the forested interior, there were still tribes of Indians untouched by civilization. Thus the population of this region is almost exclusively Amerindian.

To the north of the selva, stretches the Llanos, the great plains of northern South America running from the foothills of the Andes into western Venezuela. Like the pampas of Argentina and the Great Plains of the old west, this is cattle country. Counterpart to the *gaucho* and cowboy is the Colombian *llanero*. Careless and loose, fearless and tireless, these hardened horsemen can stay in the saddle from dawn to dusk or at least that is their reputation. The range they ride is a tropical grassland, treeless at the higher elevations, grass, brush and scrub trees in the low lands with islands of trees on high spots protected from the seasonal inundation. Steamy hot and humid during the rainy season, the prairie becomes almost impassible with flooded rivers and swampy low lands infested with the crocodile-like *cayman*, flesh devouring *piraña* and blood sucking leaches. Clouds of insects hover in the brush and tall grass awaiting the approach of mammalian prey upon which they can descend, stinging, biting and chewing.

The dry season is less humid, but still hot. Then water may be hard to find, confined to the rivers and streams where malaria carrying mosquitoes lurk. Grass becomes dry and much less palatable to the cattle and horses. Instead of mud, the llanero must contend with the clouds of dust raised by the cattle's cloven hooves and there is always the unrelenting heat.

Though cattle operations have existed in the Llanos for over two centuries, most of this tropical plain was still inhabited, in 1964, predominantly by indigenous peoples. This accounts for the population density of 0.95 persons per square mile, a large territory with few people. The jungle area to the south had even fewer people, less than 0.2 persons per square mile. Contrast this with the 104.7 population per square mile in the mountainous western portion of the country. It is in this western region that the country's inhabitance has always thrived.

The mountains are the northern end of the Andes which run along the west coast of South America from the southern tip of Chile to the Colombian-Ecuadorian border. Just north of this frontier, the Andes split into three ranges and run north-northeast through western Colombia tapering off as they approach the north coast. While there are some truly impressive peaks, Huila (17,700 feet), Tolima (18,400 feet), Ruiz (18,300 feet) and Santa Isabel (16,700 feet), all perpetually capped with snow, the three *cordilleras* are, in general, less lofty than the Andes of Ecuador and Peru. The Central and Eastern Cordilleras have a mean altitude of 9,000 feet above sea level and the Cordillera Occidental that hugs the Pacific coast is lower yet with a mean altitude of 6,000 feet. Also, unlike the western slope of the Andes further south, particularly of Peru, the mountains, valleys, and sometimes deep gorges that separate them, are abundant in luxurious vegetation. Except for the desert of La Guajira which, ironically, juts out into the Caribbean, but is cut off at the base by the mammoth 19,000 foot Pico Cristóbal Calón, all Colombia receives ample rain fall during the wet season and is, in general, verdant with a prodigious variety of plant life from the tops of its mountains to the coastal plains.

Though not as high as other parts of the Andes, the Colombian cordilleras are never-the-less, rugged and have always been an effective impediment to communication and transportation within the country. Passage from Honda, at the upper end of the navigable part of the Rio Magdalena, to Bogotá was difficult in the extreme in the early times.

Portage was by mule or on the backs of humans in colonial days. The paths across ravines and up the sides of mountains were too treacherous for any kind of wagon or even horses.

The trail from Bogotá eastward was only slightly less daunting. The passage of only 80 miles to Villavicencio, on the edge of the Llanos, drops from the capital's 8,700 feet to 1,200. Again the going was difficult in the extreme; horses could only be used during the dry season when conditions were most favorable. The trek was described by European visitors in those early days as a purgatory of discomfort and danger.

Thus, the cordilleras of Colombia have divided the western populous part of the country socially, politically and economically since pre-Columbian times into three zones. The northern coastal area has always had a significant population and is tied more closely to the Caribbean than the Colombian interior. The mountainous interior, where, in 1964, three-fifths of the country's population lived above the 3,300 foot level, is naturally divided into two zones. There is an eastern zone that includes the Eastern Cordilleras and upper Magdalena Valley and a western zone consisting of the Western and Central Cordilleras and the Cauca Valley between them. As transportation improved, parts of the Pacific west coast became closely tied to this region providing access to the outside world by sea. Until the early 1900s when rail lines began to break down some of the transportation barriers, the Rio Magdalena was the Colombian interior's main avenue to the outside world.

Even this waterway was not easily navigable as rivers were in other countries. The mouth of the Magdalena was so obstructed and hazardous to shipping that practical entrance to the river was well above its swampy estuary and was reached overland from Cartagena in colonial times, then Santa Marta in the early republic and finally Barranquilla. Progress along the river was slowed by sandbars and rapids with Honda the functional end of the line. Until the middle of the Nineteenth Century, transportation was by poled or paddled boats, making it a two month journey for a cargo vessel of any size.

These divisions within the country were intensified by the lack of a need for commerce outside one of these zones. The Caribbean north coast has always been able to trade over the water seaway more easily than with the country's interior. As for the mountainous interior, a range of agricultural products are available within each zone. Being close to the equator, seasonal effects experienced in the southern and northern latitudes are erased. There is only a wet season and a dry season with no significant temperature change. Climate differences are created by changes in elevation. High in the mountains farmers have grown potatoes for thousands of years. Since colonial times, sheep and goats are pastured on high plateaus. Further down grains are cultivated, *guinoa* in pre-Columbian times, wheat, barely and oats later. The lower slopes and high valleys are ideal for maize. And the tropical valleys and lower plains produce *yuca* (manioc), avocado, cocoa, tropical fruits and with the arrival of the Spanish, bananas, sugar and rice. So each zone was self-sufficient in obtaining a great variety of agricultural products including fish and later beef and mutton.

As diverse as the geography of this country was, its people were no less so. The coasts and western lowlands featured a black population with pure Amerindian blood in the veins of the high mountain people. Caucasians and Mestizos shuffling papers in the high rise office buildings of the big cities and there was a sprinkling of Asians scattered here and there throughout the country. In between the low and the high elevations, and scattered among the tall buildings of Colombia's villages and cities, there was every conceivable mixture of these races. If geographic variance is a hallmark of Colombia, equally characteristic is racial diversity.

So these forty-one young Americans were being dispersed across the mountains, valleys, forests and plains of this country just emerging from a devastating civil war, the Violencia, groping for solutions to the question of how to become a more active partner in the modern world. The reconstructed Colombian government's hope was that America's new Peace Corps would be part of the answer.

5

WHEN A GALLO IS ONLY A CHICKEN

In Bogotá Ron Halter and Steve Burgess were advised they would be site mates stationed in the Department of Tolima near the city of Ibagué. A glance at a map told them this was in the upper reaches of the Magdalena River Valley between the Eastern

Steve Burgess

and Central Cordilleras. It's an area where Paleo-Indian projectile points have been found and is just east of the Quimbaya gold region. It would probably be hot they decided, but after Steve's trek in Puerto Rican hell, he figured he could handle anything. It was a long bus ride up and over the mountains out of Bogotá, then the drop down into the Magdalena Valley to Ibagué. Once in the capital of Tolima, the two Volunteers began to experience the Peace Corps they had read about.

The town of El Carmen proved to be about an hours bus ride south of Ibagué. This "bus" was a multicolored, open air vehicle crammed with campesinos and their baggage. Along with boxes, crates, and suitcases, there were chickens, dogs, and a pig or two. In the heat and humidity of the Magdalena Valley, the open sides of the bus did provide good ventilation and undoubtedly reduced the assault on the two young Volunteer's nasal passages.

The city's pavement quickly turned to a gravel road and then to dirt. Every time the bus stopped, which was frequently, dust rolled in making for a very hot, smelly and dirty ride. Ron and Steve were relieved when they finally arrived at the village that was to be their site.

El Carmen was located in a wide valley with towering mountains on all sides. The village was small, about twenty houses, and poor, no electricity, no running water, not even outhouses. "All of the homes were constructed of bamboo frames filled in with adobe and painted with white wash that was mixed with a pesticide. The floors were usually dirt. The roofs were either thatched or corrugated metal."[1]

The two new arrivals were provided quarters in the town's school which at least had running water, though it had to be boiled before drinking. The school also had the town's only latrine, a blessing indeed.

Once settled, the first order of business was to become accepted by the townspeople. Though there was much curiosity on the part of the Colombians, communication was a problem. Both Steve and Ron were struggling with just the Spanish they had learned in training and in Puerto Rico. The villagers were patient, however, and little by little the two Volunteers became acquainted with the people of El Carmen. Even with their rudimentary language skills, they were able to ascertain the immediate needs of the community, many of which were obvious.

The poor conditions in the village were due to the lack of steady employment. The citizens subsisted on wages earned working in the coffee groves up on the mountain sides. The coffee tree or bush grows at a higher elevation then El Carmen. The plants

---

[1] Ron Halter, personal email to Gary Peterson, December 11, 2008.

have to be tended intermittently and then the beans are harvested, a labor intensive operation. But the work was seasonal and for months at a time the villagers would have no income. Thus, proper nutrition and health care had been seriously neglected. These were the areas Burgess and Halter would work on first. By the end of the first month Ron was able to report:

> As a matter of record, we now have two gardens going and have started a boy building a rabbit hutch, which should be finished tomorrow.
> The one garden is in very fine soil and it grew like it was shot out of a gun. But along came the ants and cut it down just as fast. We have re-seeded and are taking steps to subdue the ants. The other garden is in average soil and we are having average results.[2]

So the first of their problems were becoming evident, poor soil, lack of fertilizer, the many insects in this tropical climate and the demoralizing lack of sanitation facilities. And, of course, there was their language deficiency. If they were going to succeed, the two Volunteers had to make some kind of breakthrough with the villagers. Enter *el gallo*.

Gallos are fighting cocks. A little bigger than a Bantam, these roosters are bred for combat. Now, two chickens attacking each other would ordinarily be capable of doing only a minimal amount of bodily harm. Therefore, a sharp metal spur is attached to each leg of the gladiators making the aggressive little cocks potentially lethal. Two of these combatants are placed in a ring while the crowd around the ring places bets on their favorites. The fight continues until one rooster is dead, severely injured or just quits.

Cock fighting was a big sport around the El Carmen area, but few of the local compesinos had the money to purchase and maintain a real champion bird. However, our two gringos were presented with an opportunity to invest in a gallo whose sire had won twelve consecutive fights, a super star in the world of chicken fighting.

The two Volunteers thought this might be a good way to gain acceptance by the villagers if not outright hero status. So they purchased the bird for 50 pesos (about $4.50 U.S.) and christened it Son-of-a-bitch or SOB for short. Next they hired a man from the town, a reputed expert in cock fighting, to keep and train the gallo.

After a couple of weeks of training, a match was set with a gallo from a neighboring town. Steve and Ron put money on their champion hoping to recoup some of their investment while, "the campesinos of El Carmen went all out to bet on the gringo's cock."[3]

The fight started out well enough with SOB holding his own and even getting in a couple of good licks with his beak and spurs. It looked like the Volunteers and the town had themselves a winner as SOB pecked and slashed at his opponent. But then the other gallo suddenly flew into the air and nailed SOB in the neck with one of his metal spikes and the champion of El Carmen went down.

The villagers were devastated. Not only was their pride hurt, but they had just lost a good share of their grocery money for the coming months. The two sports *aficionados* were, themselves, out some $200 on the deal. But just when the prostrate chicken seemed

---

[2] Ron Halter, letter to Joyce Scanell, North Wales, Penn., Feb. 1, 1965, Personal Files of Ron Halter, Lenexa, KS.
[3] "SOB-STORY", article in El Hocicon, Colombia 2 de Enero, p.2.

on his way to fowl heaven, the trainer rushed in and flapped SOB's wings up and down, and then gave the unconscious bird a version of mouth to beak resuscitation. Finally, the trainer took a mouth full of *aguadiente* and sprayed a mist of the liquor into the rooster's face. He also applied ample amounts to the animal's wounds. Miraculously, SOB was brought back to life. The trainer took the injured bird home and nursed him back to health. Then he began to train SOB for the next event, all at the Volunteers' expense of course.

At the next tournament the villagers hoped to regain some of their losses and again bet heavily on their champion. This time SOB appeared to be a little less confident and only fought when he was cornered. In the process of sidestepping and weaving, one of his metal spurs broke off. Then the other spur came off. The unarmed gallo was then obliged to run for his life, ducking and dodging trying to find a hiding place away from his belligerent antagonist. The gringos finally pulled SOB from the ring. They were down another $200 and the town's people were despondent.

A couple of nights later as Steve and Ron were enjoying a quiet dinner, they discussed what had been gained and what had been lost in this adventure into the world of chicken fighting. They had been in this project with the community. They had suffered the same setbacks as the campesinos and therefore had won acceptance by the villagers. As for SOB, they concluded that, though a bit tough and stringy, he was certainly better as a main course than he ever was as a gallo.

Ron and Steve with their "champion" fighting cock, SOB.

While the events in the tale of SOB the gallo were unfolding, Burgess and Halter were making real progress in some other areas. Their early work to improve the villager's diets by introducing them to the cultivation of gardens had bogged down due to poor soil conditions and insects. They discussed these problems in a meeting with their PINA counterpart in Ibagué. Though substantially independent, the ag/nutrition extension Volunteers were under the nominal supervision of the local representatives of this government agency and were to have its support. The Colombian representative was usually located in the departmental capital, was often an M.D., and had, to varying degrees, access to Colombian government facilities and resources.

In the case of Tolima, this PINA official was Dr. Jaime Moncera who the Volunteers referred to simply, as Jaime. Jaime, it seems, had some pull, for a day after the meeting a truck arrived at El Carmen ready to haul manure to the gardens from a nearby ranch. The truck also carried 100 lbs. of insecticide. As a result Ron could brag a few weeks later, "needless to say our gardens are simply beautiful, and more gardens are springing up by the week."[4]

The next item and perhaps the most noxious problem to the Volunteers was the lack of latrines. This deficiency was the subject of the next meeting with Jaime. Not long after the consultation a government official showed up to survey the problem. Shortly thereafter, a truck loaded with concrete pre-fab latrines drove into town. These were "planted" near many of the town's homes. Each owner of a new sanitation facility was obliged to pay 50 pesos and dig a three meter hole over which the latrines were placed. Because the ground was so hard (compacted clay soil), this proved to be a greater obstacle to overcome than the 50 pesos, so not all homes were supplied with a facility. But Steve and Ron figured they would add to the number gradually and be able to get the rest installed before they left the site and this did indeed prove to be the case. By the time Steve and Ron left Colombia, all the homes in El Carmen were furnished with a latrine and the sanitation of the community was greatly improved.

Jaime (left) and owner of a prefabricated outhouse.

With gardens booming, the Volunteers needed someone to show the women how to prepare the vegetables, a chore neither of the male Volunteers had the background to deal with. So they appealed to Jaime and in no time a Colombian government nutritionist showed up to organize a mothers club. She then went on to teach the members of the club the basics in food preparation, cleanliness and sanitation.

Upon their arrival in El Carmen, Steve and Ron had been able to live in the school. "This was a one room school with a small living quarters. Steve and I slept side by side in a closet sized room. This was efficient. Steve had brought a Coleman lantern with him from the USA. We placed it on a small table between the collapsible cots we used as beds. This allowed us our only respite from our new environment, reading the books given to us by the Pease Corps. (Each site was provided with a collection of some 50 paperback books donated by book companies.) Then one day a school teacher appeared. She was about 50+ years old and needed a place to stay."[5] Fortunately for the two *Norte Americanos* there was one vacant house in the town. After arranging to rent the small structure, the two evicted Volunteers were moved in a couple of hours.

---

[4] Ron Halter, letter to Joyce Scanell, North Wales, Penn., April 7, 1965, Personal Files of Ron Halter, Lenexa, KS.

[5] Ron Halter, personal email to Gary Peterson, Dec. 11, 2008.

Given a little more room, Steve began thinking about a more substantial bed. He had observed that most of the people in the village slept on the floor on woven mats made from crushed and dried sugar cane stalks. Harkening back to a frontier bed he had seen at the Minden Pioneer Museum in Nebraska (USA), he had an idea. He took large sections of bamboo, one material in abundance in Tolima, and constructed a bed frame. For a mattress,

Steve reading by lantern light in their cramped residents.

he drilled holes in the bamboo and wove a rope in between the long sections of the frame creating a mattress. He demonstrated how to make the bed to an assembly of the villagers and some of them gave it a try. They could even lay their sugar cane mats on the ropes to make a still more comfortable sleeping surface. Steve would use this bamboo and rope bed for the rest of his stay in El Carmen.

Having become thoroughly integrated in the village and more confident in their language skills, the two Volunteers were ready to explore the rest of their site which included the surrounding area, the outlying *veredas* (communities). However, this remote part of the Tolima Department had few roads and little bus traffic. If Ron and Steve were going to visit the veredas, it would be on foot or horseback and walking was almost out of the question because of the distances involved. Fortunately, the site was authorized one horse by the Peace Corps so the Volunteers set about finding a trusty steed.

Tolima is home to one of the most famous breeds of horses in South America, the Paso Fino, which has a distinctive gait. Rodney Spokely, the closest PINA Volunteer from Colombia '64, advocated these horses. Located in Purificación, Rod had contact with some of the finest Paso Fino breeding farms in Colombia and had become an admirer of this breed. But the horses Steve and Ron found in the El Carmen area were not of the best quality and all Steve could think was, "what this country needed was a good Quarter Horse."[6] The El Carmen Volunteers located a gray Paso Fino mare that was for sale and, in spite of Steve's misgivings, made the purchase.

Though a farm boy from Ohio, Ron was born long after the horse-drawn implement days and had no experience with horses. Steve on the other hand turned out to be a real cowboy. He knew how to feed and care for the horse, and Ron stood mesmerized as Steve shod their new mount for the first time. With the horse, the two Volunteers were able to reach even the most remote areas around El Carmen.

---

[6] Steve Burgess, personal email to Gary Peterson, Mar. 2, 2009.

Steve was never enamored with the Paso Fino breed based on the performance of this horse, though he would make good use of it, even utilizing it as his primary means of transportation to a secondary site he later picked up. However, years later he would change is mind about the Paso Fino horses and become invested in the Colombian breed himself.

Steve and Ron had been in their site for only four months and things were moving along so well on the nutrition and sanitation front, they decided to attack problems at a higher level. Up to this point they had been working with the villagers on a one-to-one bases for the most part, but to succeed at any big projects, they needed to be able to deal with the town's people as a group and the villagers had to be able to act together to get things done. So Steve and Ron called a town meeting to organize a *junta* (community council). The Volunteers guided the assembly through the process of electing officials and the first project the new junta decided to tackle was electrification of the town. The Colombian government came through with 10,000 pesos for the project and the program was underway. This was real progress of a substantial nature and encouraged the two Volunteers to turn to other matters.

Among the subjects stressed in the training in Nebraska was personal health. The villagers of El Carmen, like much of the rural population of Colombia, did not appreciate the importance of a balanced diet nor did they have access to even basic medical attention. Even the Volunteers were troubled by some of the diseases and parasites that drained the stamina of the townspeople and could be terminal for the young, the old, and those already weakened by malnutrition or other diseases.

All Volunteers in the rural areas received a medical kit to take with them to their site. This was more than just a first aid kit; there was a variety of bandages and disinfectants of course, but also medicines for everything from dysentery to constipation. Most Volunteers in the tropical areas took airolin, a drug to suppress the symptoms of malaria. Ron also took an orange pill designed to counteract the effects of diarrhea especially dehydration. The pair generally ate with families in the village and were therefore exposed to some of the same unsanitary conditions as the rest of the townspeople. Ron had to get his bottle of 30 orange pills refilled every month or two. He had diarrhea almost daily during his time in El Carmen.

Steve and Ron also used items from their kits to treat some of people in the town. Word got around and soon they were inundated with health problems. They asked Jaime if he could find a nurse from the Public Health Office that could stop by and take care of the most urgent cases.

One Sunday Jaime rolled into El Carmen with 10 nurses, 4 doctors, 1 dentist, 3 clerks, 1 microscope tech. and a mobile x-ray unit, a veritable field hospital. The village's health problems were taken care of, at least temporarily.

To keep the health services rolling Ron began giving first aid classes at the school using books in Spanish he picked up in Ibagué. Steve, who had had two semesters of microbiology lab in college, applied for the loan of a microscope from a hospital laboratory in Ibagué. A condition of the loan, however, was that the Volunteers do a study for the lab on stool samples of the villagers. So both Volunteers began taking once a week classes at the Ibagué lab on collecting and analyzing stool samples.

Finally, there were the individual students the Volunteers were working with. Steve was instructing six young people on the use of a typewriter, while Ron was spending hours with a villager teaching him to read and write, part of the Colombian adult literacy program.

In terms of entertainment, El Carmen offered very little. There was the occasional saint's day or festival with some dancing and lots of drinking, but not much else. However, not so far away was the town of Rovia which had electricity and, more importantly, a movie theater. Steve and Ron worked to maintain some contact with the priest in the town and when there, they would attend the theater. Most movies in Colombia were American with a sprinkling of European and Mexican offerings.

It was a struggle to keep up with the German or French movies, having to depend mostly on the Spanish subtitles, but an American movie was another matter. While the Colombians labored to follow the plot, the Volunteers could relax and enjoy the presentation. On one visit Steve and Ron happened on the American movie, The Rounders with Glen Ford. Steve relates, "this was a funny movie and I laughed my head off, but the Colombians, because they had to read the subtitles, missed out on the humor. They all turned around and looked at the crazy gringos who, they were sure, had lost their minds."[7]

After a whirlwind of activity the first few months in El Carmen, things began to slow down for the two Volunteers. In early May they traveled to Bogotá for the group's first conference. Returning, they found little progress had been made on projects in their absence. "All the men had left for the hills to pick coffee and the only people that were left were the old, who can't work, the real young who don't want to work, and of course, the drunks."[8]

The first junta installed with so much promise had never functioned properly and the electrification project did not get off the ground. A new junta was elected. "The new junta turned out to be just as bad, if not worse, than the old one."[9] So the electrification project languished.

Perhaps even more discouraging for the two Volunteers was their dysfunctional breeding program. In the first weeks after arriving at El Carmen they had obtained several rabbits from a *granja* (agricultural extension farm) outside Ibagué. These were distributed to families willing to build hutches and feed them. To the Volunteer's consternation, none of these pairs had produced a single batch of offspring. The families that had spent time nurturing and caring for the rabbits were starting to give up on them. It would surely not be long before the breeding stock would begin showing up on dinner tables.

Still there were the successes, the medical care, the latrines and the gardens were doing great. Vegetables were now being grown not only by villagers, but gardens had spread outside of town into the *campo*. And language was no longer a barrier. Both Volunteers could now carry on a conversation without straining to catch even the gist of the exchange. Responses came easily in Spanish or as the Colombians liked to say *Castellano* (Castilian Spanish, pure Spanish).

Not long after the conference, Ron Halter was moved to a new site. This was a result of conversations at the four month group conference and was not unusual. Many of the

---

[7] Steve Burgess, personal email to Gary Peterson, Dec. 7, 2008.

[8] Ron Halter, letter to Joyce Scanell, North Wales, Penn., May 14, 1965, Personal Files of Ron Halter, Lenexa, KS.

[9] Ibid

Volunteers were moved after the first few months. Often a Volunteer, after working as part of a pair, having picked up the language and some self confidence, wanted to strike out on his, or her, own. This way both Volunteers could run their own programs. There was probably some ego involved in these moves, but also individualism and a genuine desire to spread the work out, affecting as many people as possible.

Ron's new town was El Salado about 30 minutes by car due east of Ibagué. The town of some 2,500 was larger than El Carmen, but at an elevation of 3,000 feet, still quite warm. Big haciendas in the area raised rice, coffee, cattle and chickens commercially, but most of the campesinos who worked for the large land owners, did have their own small plots of land (a half acre or so) to use for their own purposes. These were used to grow sugar cane, *yuca* (manioc) and plantain for the family's use and to sell.

Another difference Ron discovered between his old site and this new town was the public observance of funerals. Where the inhabitance of El Carmen were few and somewhat scattered, funerals were very private affairs, but in El Salado with a denser population and the one cemetery, it was hard to miss the sullen processions. These were especially disturbing to Ron when the occasion marked the end of a child's life.

> It was like the cold hand of death swept through the town. Once or twice a week, there was a small family procession that was led by the father of a child who had died in the night. On his shoulder he carried a small box, often not much larger than a shoe box. This was a way of life and almost commonplace for the Colombians. But I never got used to it.[10]

The Volunteers were told in training that 40% of the deaths in Colombia were among children less than five years old. Many of the illnesses of the young and very young were the result of inadequate nutrition, thus the emphasis by the Colombian government on gardens and small livestock that could be raised by families. These needs were evident at El Salado no less than in El Carmen.

Ron went to work to carry out his plans for his new site:

> The following are the projects that I have and/or hope to have in the coming months:
> 1. One 4-S club[11], thirty members.
> 2. Demonstration gardens in the *Puesto de Salude* (Heath Clinic) and the school.
> 3. Reorganization of the junta......in order to get the priest out of the presidency.
> 4. A school lunch program, for the new term, using CARE.[12]

In November Ron reported:

---

[10] Ron Halter, personal email to Gary Peterson, Dec, 11, 2008.

[11] Corresponding to the American 4-H – *Salud*(Health), *Servicio*(Service), *Sentmientos*(Feeling) *y Saber*(To know) instead of Head, Heart, Health and Hands.

[12] Ron Halter, letter to Joyce Scanell, North Wales, Penn., Sep. 3, 1965, Personal Files of Ron Halter, Lenexa, KS.

1. The 4-S club is coming along just fine. Although I have lost a few members, the ones that I do have are doing a good job. Membership is now at 17.
    a. Gardens – So far, of the 17 members, I have just 8 who have gardens planted. If it ever stops raining, I will get the other 9 planted, but as it stands now it could be a month before that happens.
    b. Rabbits – I have started raising rabbits for later distribution to the members of the 4-S club. Classes will start next week on the care and feeding of rabbits. The rabbits I obtained from Bruce (Borrud) went to a family that I think is very progressive and will not need indoctrination first.
2. Outlying veredas – I took a trip to three of the local veredas to see if I could possibly do anything in them and it doesn't look good. Most of the houses are very widely dispersed and hard to get to. One thing that pleased me very much was that I knew most of the people that I met out there, if not by name I at least knew their faces, but all of them knew me and called me by name.
3. Counterpart – There is a boy in El Salado who, of his own accord, has been helping me with my gardens and has really shown an interest in the 4-S club. He is working part time with a tailor but is not making much money. I am hoping that with constant contact with the two government agencies (Min. & Sec. of Ag.) he might get a job and then in the future, when I leave, he will be able to take over what I have started.
4. *Accion Comunal* – As far as the junta goes I believe it is almost hopeless. Although the priest did resign the post of president, he still controls the junta and just last week the new president resigned because of it.[13]

As in El Carmen, to get any big projects accomplished, a concerted effort by the community as a whole was required. The Colombian government encouraged the organization of juntas to galvanize and organize such efforts. This program was called *Accion Comunal.* These juntas could be very effective, but in the case of El Salado, the junta was run by a person not respected in the community. This was the local priest.

In rural Colombia the village priest was invariably an important person. If the town had other professional or wealthy citizens, doctors, lawyers, businessmen, etcetera, than the priest might concern himself with just the spiritual needs of the community. But if he was the sole educated individual, he often assumed, by default, the roll of community leader. The Colombia '64 PINA Volunteers worked with these men sometimes on a daily basis and generally with good results. These were clergymen who had the best interests of their charges at heart and were often the driving force behind community improvements. And perhaps that was the case with the priest of El Salado.

However, this priest had lost the respect of the people of his parish. He had become the town joke. Although he was bright, affable and intelligent, it was common knowledge he had fathered two children with a girl who worked as his administrative assistant. He also condoned if not actively participated in the importation of prostitutes for the town's annual *fiesta*. This character flaw cost him his standing in the community, made him an ineffective leader, and was particularly galling to Ron who was himself Roman Catholic.

[13] Ron Halter, "Pease Corps/ Colombia Volunteer's Activity Report," Oct. 1 to Nov. 1, 1965, Site: El Salado.

Halter's efforts to find a strong leader who could unite and energize the community were not successful and this was one area where little progress was made. However, on other fronts, there was substantial movement. By the end of the year Ron had two 4-S clubs going. The clubs took trips to two different experimental farms which built enthusiasm among the members.

Ron had built a relationship with not only the PINA *jefe*, but also three Colombians in the Ministry of Agriculture in Ibagué. This gave him access to government resources and hopefully would mean continued interest by the government in the town's problems.

But gardens had not been a success in the area. The clay soil required a great deal of attention and work to grow the vegetables, and the campecinos were just not willing to put forth the effort.

Rabbits looked more promising and could become an important protein source for the people. Ron had obtained some breeding stock from Bruce Borrud in Boyacá (five does and a buck) with which to start a program. The main problem was to get the campecinos to keep the hutches clean and fumigated as tropical diseases were a constant threat. An advantage to the rabbits was that the Colombians were used to roasting, boiling, or frying meat and readily adapted to its consumption.

Of even more promise were chicken projects. "With the backing of the Minesterio de Agricultura I have been able to get some chicken projects going. Chickens are very popular here. Two breeds are widely used. They are the Road Island Red and the Leghorn."[14] Chickens required less care than the rabbits, didn't have as many health issues and were generally just turned loose to forage for themselves. And the local population was accustomed to the preparation and consumption of *pollo*. However, it took about a year to get a chicken to eating size this way and the meat was as tough as shoe leather. It had to be boiled for a long period of time to make it palatable.

Ron convinced one of his 4-S clubs to try a chicken project using commercial methods. They purchased 100 chicks from the PINA *granja* in Ibagué and vaccinated them. The chicks were raised in one room of the house that Ron was renting. Commercial chicken feed was purchased in Ibagué and used to supplement whatever the fowl could scrounge on their own. In a few months the club had broilers ready to eat. "The Colombians were flabbergasted. They had never seen chickens so large. Having raised them in only a few months was even more unbelievable. Campesinos came from miles around just to see for themselves and stood in amazement."[15]

However, a problem developed when the town's people tried to cook the chickens. Using their usual method of incessant boiling, the meat virtually disintegrated. The overcooking produced a watery paste punctuated with clean, white bones.

Ron consulted with Steve for a way to deal with this new problem. His old partner suggested Ron try selling the chickens commercially. Ron and his club members were able to market their chickens to restaurants in Ibagué and to a Presbyterian mission on the outskirts of the city. The money earned was used as seed money to encourage individuals to start their own projects. The 4-S club, now solvent, elected its own leaders and treasurer and continued to function after Ron left the site.

Another program Ron looked into was bee keeping.

---

[14] Ron Halter, Pease Corps Site Final Report – El Salado, no date, p. 2.
[15] Ron Halter, personal email to Gary Peterson, Dec. 11, 2008.

Bees in this area could be a great project. Honey is not produced and bottled on any commercial basis, although there is a market. A bottle of honey will sell for at least $8.00. The initial investment is about $300.00. One bee hive will produce about 60 bottles a year, therefore you can buy your hive and still make some money all in the first year.

I was all set to start this project on a big scale. I have sent 13 young boys (members of my 4-S club) to a bee workshop sponsored by the Cafeteros. I had received the OK on an 80,000.00 peso loan from the Caja Agraria. But now I have only three months left and it would be foolish to start it and then leave, dumping all this on a new Volunteer. But it will be here ready for him to start when he arrives.[16]

Meanwhile, Steve had also been investigating further opportunities. Work in El Carmen had about peaked. Many gardens were producing, some chicken projects were prospering and nearly every home in the village had a latrine. Sanitation, medicine and nutrition had improved, but the big projects were going nowhere. The electrification project that had started so optimistically, had ground to a halt. The junta could not get organized in any meaningful way. The president would get drunk before a meeting to work up the courage to stand before the members and the meeting would devolve into chaos. There seemed to be no one who could pull the townspeople together and no drive among them to really improve their conditions especially when it would require some real sacrifice.

As Steve visited the outlaying veredas, he came across a town that seemed much more progressive. This was El Totumo, about five miles to the north of El Carmen, easily accessed on horseback. After a few visits, Steve began to work with the residents of this town on gardens and the people were very receptive. His garden projects flourished to the point one campesino wanted to go commercial. Steve helped him build his garden into a tomato farm and he was able to sell his produce at markets in town and then in the surrounding area and eventually in Ibagué. This venture was so successful that the farmer was still in business ten years later when Steve visited the town on a return trip to Colombia.

With this kind of interest, Steve decided to move to El Totumo and commute back to El Carmen instead of the other way around. He financed another campesino in a project to raise broilers. Starting with 50 chicks, the farmer fed and took care of the fowl and sold them both in town and to markets in Ibagué. He expanded and was still in business when Steve left. Later others would take his example and begin chicken farms in and around the town.

Another project Burgess helped with was the school expansion. El Totumo's school, at the time of his arrival, held first, second and third grades. The town wanted to add fourth and fifth, but there just wasn't room. Steve helped organize the town through the junta, which met for this specific purpose, into a community work party. Bricks made of mud with cement mixed in were manufactured. Then the construction of an additional room was begun. This room was made large enough to house the two additional grades. It was one of the really successful community projects in the area.

---

[16] Ron Halter, Pease Corps Site Final Report – El Salado, no date, p. 3.

There was one other town endeavor begun before Steve left El Totumo. This was an enterprise to supply the town with running water. Years earlier, a dam had been constructed in the mountains above El Totumo to provide the town with a potable water supply, but the project had faltered. No water line had ever been laid. Partly this was for lack of money and partly for lack of an organized effort by the town itself.

However, one day, about six months before Burgess was due to leave Colombia, he received word that there was another gringo living in town. Steve doubted the story, but investigated none the less and found that indeed there was a Norte Americano that had just moved in. He worked for the Bavarian Brewing Company which had a brewery in Ibagué. The company was in the process of building hog farms in association with their breweries as a way of utilizing the waste products of the breweries. El Totumo had been selected as the site for one of these swine feed lots. But the project needed water and lots of it, first to build the facility and then to water the animals.

As a Volunteer, you learn to take advantage of opportunities whenever they appear, so Steve consulted with the town's leaders and they agreed to a proposal. "If the Bavarian Brewing Company would provide the money, El Totumo would come up with the labor force to complete the water line from the mountain dam to the town."[17] The project was well under way when Steve left and he was assured of its success because both the citizens of El Totumo and the brewing company were behind it. And sure enough when he returned ten years later the town had its running water.

As with Steve Burgess's water project, it was often the case that a Volunteer who began a major project did not get to see the final outcome. So, one particular experience was especially gratifying to Ron Halter in the days just before he left Colombia. This project concerned a school at the end of a rugged mountain trail outside El Salado:

> Toward the end of my tour, I was invited to visit a small village high in the mountains north of my site. The village was the cultural center of numerous coffee growers. I wasn't invited to discuss chickens, rabbits, gardens or any other project that I had been involved in. The villagers wanted to show me the school they had been trying to complete for the past two years. They imposed a village tax on everything that was bought or sold in the village. With the money, they had made a good start, but at the current rate, only their grandchildren would be able to use it. They asked for my help in interceding with the US Embassy. They had been told by the Cafeteros (the union of coffee growers) that the USA could help. I was impressed with their efforts. I met with a representative of the Cafeteros who provided records of what had been spent and what was needed. With records in hand, I went to the US Embassy in Bogotá. Sure enough, there was a special ambassador's fund that was established to help projects like the one I proposed. The funds were disbursed and the school was finished.

> Once the school had been completed, a special *fiesta* was scheduled within the mountain village. A US Foreign Service Officer from Washington DC and his wife were the US Ambassador's special representatives. Also, the US Embassy official with whom I had coordinated on the project came with his wife. We all met at a tienda near the base of the mountains outside of El Salado.

---

[17] Steve Burgess, telephone conversation with Gary Peterson, Feb. 23, 2009.

The villagers had pre-positioned horses and mules for us to ride to the village. The villagers were ready for us when we arrived. A huge pot of *arroz con pollo* (rice with chicken) was being cooked on an open fire in front of the school. Also, a quartet was playing *teples* (a Colombian folk instrument similar to a guitar), and singing Colombian folk songs. Speeches were made by the villagers, the USA officials, and representatives of the Cafeteros. A great day was had by all.[18]

As with many of the PINA Volunteers, Steve and Ron started small, working with gardens, rabbits, chickens and latrines, in an effort to improve the nutrition and sanitation of individual families. These were the skills they had been taught in Nebraska. But once established, Volunteers invariably became involved in larger enterprises, commercial agricultural operations, school and aqueduct construction projects, programs that effected whole communities.

Perhaps this talent and resourcefulness was what Warren Wiggins had in mind when he insisted on recruiting generalists as the second generation of Volunteers. He must have believed that young Americans could affect change through their own initiative and entrepreneurial spirit. Placed in a foreign environment, they would none the less, recognize the problems facing the people they were working with and find solutions. Ron Halter and Steve Burgess had demonstrated that Wiggins's faith in the American spirit was well founded.

---

[18] Ron Halter, personal email to Gary Peterson, Dec. 11, 2008.

6
NUCLEOS, BOMBS, BANDITS AND ROMANCE

As the Colombia '64 Volunteers departed Bogotá for their various sites, one couple was left behind. Melody Lenkner had developed a severe case of bronchitis upon arriving in the city, so she and her husband, Charles, were held back. This was Charlie who had

been part of my team on the great outback trek in Puerto Rico. As I noted in that story, Charlie was cool and lay-back, the epitome of the picture I had of a Californian, tall, self-confident and amiable. He was a graduate of the University of California, Davis where he had majored in agricultural education. Because the department had a variety of foreign students, it was easy to pick up courses in tropical crops which looked good on his Peace Corps submission.

Melody, with that beautiful, infectious smile that would light up a room, was outgoing and engaging. She had also attended Davis where the two had met. This couple was a natural for the Colombian program.

Their assignment of Purificación in southern Tolima was a bit of a surprise. We had been told in training in Nebraska that southern Tolima and Huila would probably be off limits due to bandit activity left over from the Violencia. Never-the-less,

Melody Lenkner

several people in our group were assigned to both these departments. As the others left for their sites, Melody coughed, wheezed and suffered through the next few days staying at the Cordillera Hotel receiving treatment from Dr. Gifford, the resident Peace Corps doctor. Within five days the good doctor had Melody's symptoms under control and the Lenkners boarded a plane for Ibagué.

From Ibagué, the Lenkners caught a bus for Purificación, fifty miles to the south. The town, of about 5,000 inhabitance in 1965, sat astride highway 40 running north and south just west of the Magdalena River. Its altitude of 550 feet above sea level and its location at 3 degrees, 51 minutes north insured a climate of oppressive heat, dusty in the dry season and stifling humid in the rainy months. The proximity of the Magdalena guaranteed an abundance of six legged fauna.

Purificación was on a hill overlooking the Magdalena River [Charlie remembers], that was the older part of town. There were lovely big trees that offered shade near the old and pretty church. Along other roads, there was less shade, fewer trees, but newer stores. They were masonry and had living quarters on the second floor; many were still under construction.[1]

Charles Lenkner

---

[1] Charlie Lenkner, personal email, April 1, 2009.

The area surrounding the town, particularly on the west side of the river, was dominated by large estates producing rice, cotton and cattle. Providing labor for the *estancias* was a mestizo population living in the town or "squatting" on small plots of land nearby which they used to raise food for their families with any surplus sold at the weekly market.

To educate the children of these families, the Colombian government had established a school system in the area consisting of a central school called a *nucleo* and four satellite schools scattered around the area. Each satellite school had teachers and facilities for first and second grades.

The nucleo was the heart of the system with not only the first two grades, but class rooms for grades three through five as well. Besides teachers the nucleo had a nurse, a nutritionist, an agriculturist and an adult literacy expert. There was some dormitory space, kitchen and cafeteria facilities. Ideally children would attend the satellite schools for two years then transfer to the nucleo to complete their elementary education, even boarding at the nucleo if commuting was not feasible.

The nucleo system was developed by the Colombian government as part of the campaign to end the Violencia that had devastated Colombia during the 1950s. They were located in areas where violence and bandit groups were still a problem. This meant rural areas, usually in or close to mountainous regions, primarily in the southern parts of the country. Often Army or Mounted National Police (*Carabinero*) units would be concentrated in the same areas.

This nucleo was located five miles from the town of Purificación, on the east side of the river not far from where the land began to slope upward marking the parameter of the Magdalena Valley. Faculty and staff lived in the facility itself. All the educators and experts took their meals at the nucleo's cafeteria.

The school had a Chevy van, Suburban vehicle for transportation and a driver was on staff [Charlie writes]. Basically the school was built as a rectangular structure with a court/school yard in the middle, not unlike an old frontier fort. The main entrance, double doors, was centered in the west wall. The buildings around the court yard housed several large bedrooms, one became ours. The staff agronomist and his wife, the school nurse, had a bedroom next to ours and further on there were a nurse's office and other bedrooms for the teachers. To one side of the yard and a mini plaza, were some classrooms. On the south end were the kitchen and dining/lunch room. There were more extensive grounds outside the nucleo with a basketball hoop and backboard.

The school had a cow or two which the driver would hobble and milk. They built a kiosk while we were there as well as a demonstration garden. There was a developed source of water where you could climb down into a cistern and take a bath from water spilling out of a pipe higher up.

It was very hot and it was dry during our stay. We tried to boil and keep a supply of drinking water in a covered kettle. Most of the food served from the nucleo kitchen was soup. We drank lots of *gaseosas* (soda pop) trying to stay hydrated.[2]

---

[2] Charlie Lenkner, personal email to Gary Peterson, Apr. 1, 2009.

As has been noted, the nucleo system was a tool in the government's war against bandits and terrorism, after effects of the Violencia. The aftermath of that violent period was never far from the Lenkner's thoughts. Reminders were everywhere.

When you traveled by bus in Tolima, you wanted to be damn sure and have your Peace Corps-Colombian ID card on your person, readily at hand [Charlie remembers]. Buses were stopped and folks taken off and checked. It was at this time I first read or heard on the radio that a bus was stopped down toward Pasto and, presumably, leftist guerillas took four nuns off and shot them. That was, my first awareness of the continued civil war that morphed into what now remains of the FARC insurrection which the press pegs as about 45 years in duration.

There was a revolutionary leftist priest Camillo Torres who was shot down in the jungle while we were in country.

When we cleaned out the closet in our room so we could move in, I remember finding a magazine with pictures of corpses from the Violencia with the "*corbata*" effect. Folks were killed and then their throats slit and their tongues pulled down and out, kind'a like a necktie. Tolima and Huila were among the last departments to be "pacified". No one talked about it, but fear remained.

Every night the van was pulled up close to the main door, in a blocking position. Then the doors were closed and locked. Essentially every one of the metal folding chairs the school had were stacked against the doors, well out into the hall - the "alarm." The nurse and *agranamo* (agriculturalist) had a child and had hired a local girl to help take care of her. That girl slept on a reed mat outside their door as alarm #2. Their door was the next one down from ours, closest to the chairs.[3]

The teachers and other employees at the nucleo were more on edge than the local population. They felt they were particular targets of the bandits because they represented the government in the area. Tensions would ease for a while only to be rekindled when there was a killing or kidnapping somewhere in the region.

Volunteers who were stationed at nucleos worked under different circumstances than independent Volunteers like Steve Burgess and Ron Halter. Instead of developing their own projects, the Volunteers in nucleos were integrated into the nucleo's program. Here they were paired with a counterpart from the nucleo's staff. The two were to reinforce each other, "an info exchange and stimulus deal."[4] But the North American, "get to it and get it done," attitude didn't always mesh with the Colombian, "in it for the long haul," approach. "Mainly what we lacked was a program or program goals. I'm sure the agranamo was trained adequate for the job. I don't think that there was any stepping on toes, but I didn't know for sure how he really felt or where he wanted to take his work."[5]

Some of the staff at the nucleo were of particular interest to the Lenkners. "One of the teachers was an Afro-Colombian from El Choco (one of the most primitive departments in Colombia). I wouldn't say he was the token black in the government

[3] Charlie Lenkner, personal email to Gary Peterson, Apr. 1, 2009.
[4] Charlie Lenkner, personal email to Gary Peterson, Apr. 2, 2009.
[5] Ibid.

program, but he was one part of the edge of change. He was the only African-Colombian in the area. He was a very nice and pleasant fellow. We enjoyed the interaction and we learned something about his very wild part of the country."[6] [7]

Outside the nucleo was a land not totally foreign to the two Californians, but with Colombian peculiarities. After settling in at the nucleo, there were plenty of opportunities for trips in the vicinity of the nucleo. They visited some of the large ranches where Charlie observed cattle raising Colombian style:

> There were some very nice horses and some *corrientes* (type of cattle), small but useful. Depending upon the weight of the critter (bigger when crossed with Brahmas) multiple *jinetes* (horsemen) would rope it with their twisted leather lassos and dally, pulling different directions to control the animal.
>
> This is where I saw the traditional forked tree stump buried in the middle of the corral. Roped or haltered animals could be pulled up for treatment by passing the lead rope thru the fork and then tying off.[8]

The Lenkners observed, "folks traveled on the river, the Magdalena, mainly using dugouts. They used nets to cast for fish. The nets had weights on the edges and some were made of copper. These were to protect against or pacify 'The *Muan*,' some river god or spirit."

And there were parties where,

> ….the folks danced the *cumbia* and other local dances. We went once to a money raising carnival or fiesta at a nearby school, or community center. We had a good time till beer and other libation facilitated a fight. Vocalizations and actions indicated two men were becoming pretty agitated. One had the ever present machete out and he was swinging it in a threatening manner. The other guy was making do with a machete case for defense.
>
> I wasn't prepared for a blood feud, so I went looking for a big stick. The one I found was a chunk of bamboo, about 10-12 feet long and 4-6 inches in diameter. The sight of the crazy gringo with the tree seemed to help the two antagonists get over it.
>
> Besides machetes, most of these gents, especially if they came on horseback, carried quirts. The body or handle of same was pretty much flat, made of a heavy bar of steel decorated with plastic braid wrapped around it. This was another nasty weapon employed in fights.[9]

Trips to town were frequent and usually interesting though the Lenkners never were completely comfortable in this urban setting.

---

[6] Two Volunteers from Colombia 64 would visit The Choco a few months later (see Chap. 11).
[7] Charlie Lenkner, personal email to Gary Peterson, Apr. 2, 2009.
[8] Ibid.
[9] Ibid.

On one occasion it was market day in Purificación, but the folks in town seemed a bit edgy. I think the area was pretty conservative; maybe they thought we were commie pinkos.

We got along by tending to business and not looking around or turning around at shouts etc. Melody did once and was pretty much grossed out, but she would never tell me what she saw. She did learn to not get suckered in again.

I remember watching a dog urinate on a bare foot and leg of a guy there in the dust. The dog wet him down pretty good before he caught on - maybe he thought it was spilled beer.[10]

And there were the long, hot and dusty trips to Ibagué. "The capital city seemed pleasant enough. We went there on several occasions and ate at a place the Volunteers seemed to favor. Every time I got sick on *beefsteak a caballo* (steak with a fried egg on it). Melody never did.[11]

While Charlie worked with the agranamo, Melody collaborated with the nutritionist and the nurse and had her own unique experiences. The nurse, in particular, "left her with some lasting impressions."[12]

"I went out one night with the nurse, the driver and Charlie, for ballast, to a successful birthing in the campo," Melody writes. Another time, "I was in attendance for a crude, but successful treatment of an abscessed wound on a fellow's arm. The procedure was performed with a few instruments, mostly improvised, like a razor blade scalpel, no anesthetic, maybe soap as the substitute for an antiseptic, no topical wound medicine and no antibiotic, not even oral."[13]

On another occasion, "there was a student with a laceration that needed stitches. Pretty much the same drill; add dull needle and probably not official sutures and lemon juice, including seeds, as antiseptic rinse."[14]

The Lenkner's stay in Purificación was of short duration. Where Melody had had her problems in Bogotá with respiratory diseases, now it was Charlie who found he had a reaction to the flora of this tropical climate.

Allergies are part of my make up and I seldom had a break while at the nucleo. I was down to about my early high school weight. We needed a different climate or location.

Our leader in Ibagué was Dave Myron. He agreed to come out and look things over for a possible site change, maybe up the hill and out of the dust.

I rode with him in the green Jeep and we went up and to the east. The elevation made things cooler and moister in short order, but there were other complications. I didn't see any women out and about. Certain intersections had sandbagged machinegun emplacements manned by the army and there were troops on duty in many places along the way.

Several small towns we passed through, looked like movie sets. The

[10] Charlie Lenkner, personal email to Gary Peterson, Apr. 2, 2009.
[11] Ibid.
[12] Ibid.
[13] Melody Lenkner, personal email to Gary Peterson, Apr. 3, 2009.
[14] Ibid.

fronts of the buildings were still up and in place even if sagging, but the middles and backs had been burned and/or blasted - gone entirely. We stopped briefly and went into a chicken fighting ring and watched the effects of different fighting spurs. There wasn't any eye contact. We left well before dark.[15]

Charlie's allergies would not permit him to stay in Purificación and the adjoining high country was just too dangerous for even the intrepid. Peace Corps finally decided to remove the Lenkners to a mountain site with an entirely different climate. The new site would be Sogamoso, the old temple site of the Chibcha nation, high in the Cordillera Oriental north of Bogotá.[16]

The Lenkners would be replaced in Purificación by a member of Colombia '64 just then arriving in country. Rodney Spokely had been convalescing at home in Neilsville, Minnesota. While in training in Puerto Rico, Rodney had developed a cyst on his tailbone that required some minor surgery. At home over Christmas the tumor was lanced and the morbid matter drained. However, he was not allowed to leave for Colombia until the wound ceased to excrete fluid and was completely healed. So, two months after the rest of his group had reached Colombia, Spokely flew into Bogotá, the last of the FAO-PINA/ETV Volunteers to arrive in country. In the capital Rod was assigned to the nucleo site just vacated by the Lenkners. It seemed logical in a perverse Peace Corps sort of way, if allergies and the heat were too much for Californians, why not send a Norwegian from Minnesota.

After a series of bus rides, Spokely found himself in the steamy, verdant plain that formed the Magdalena Valley assigned to the nucleo just vacated by the Lenkners. Aside from the heat, Rodney decided the site showed some promise. There was a town of some size nearby and the nucleo did provide life's essentials, bed, board and a roof for protection from sun and rain. He found the co-workers congenial and the transportation adequate. However, the climate and the almost constant irritation of insects (particularly mosquitoes), spiders, snakes and even alligators, or more correctly, South American cayman, were things that would require getting used to.

Rodney Spokely

Spokely worked closely with the agriculturalist in the nucleo teaching classes and working on projects. He was also part of the team that visited the satellite schools augmenting class work and the teacher's lessons. Each day of the week the team visited a different school spending Friday at the nucleo.

After a few weeks of these visits, Rod began to take stock of the condition of children in the schools. One of the situations he observed was the range in the level of health of these kids. Some were apparently in good physical condition, but many were suffering from abnormalities associated with poor nutrition. This was an area being addressed by the nucleo's nutritionists, but that would

---

[15] Charlie Lenkner, personal email to Gary Peterson, April 2, 2009.
[16] See Chapter 10.

be a long term solution of training the families to provide more nutritional meals. Rodney thought the problem could be helped fairy quickly by instituting a school lunch program in the satellite schools.

Exploring the possibilities, Spokely found there was no provision or resources in the government's nucleo system for this additional expense. He approached the PINA agency that was supposed to support the group and received the same answer. Finally, he made contact with CARE (Cooperative for Assistance and Relief Everywhere) which showed some interest in the project. Enlisting the aid of the nucleo staff, Rod pursued efforts to use CARE resources to construct and run a school lunch program for all four satellite schools. By the time he left Purificación, Spokely had reached his goal. He had an operating program that provided a hot nutritious meal for every child in all four schools.

Besides teaching classes and promoting nutrition programs, Rod worked with the agriculturalist on projects in the nucleo. Bees, goats, and various vegetables and grains were being raised on an experimental basis. One thing that had not been tried, however, was a fish pond.

The small, shallow reservoirs were a big item in the mountains. The Colombian government and Peace Corps Volunteers were quite active in promoting these trout ponds at altitudes as high as 10,000 feet where the sun's unfiltered rays provided an abundance of energy for the growth of fish food. If it worked at high altitudes, why not give it a try down here at 500 feet?

Spokely convinced the nucleo director and the agriculturalist to try an experiment. A shallow bed was dredged out next to the nucleo and filled with water. Instead of trout, warm water fish were planted, bass and catfish. The young minnows seemed to be doing fine as moss and algae grew supplying plenty of feed. Then one morning one of the staff members burst into the dining room where Rodney and the agriculturalist were having breakfast.

"*Caimán, caimán,*" the exited man yelled, "*esta comiendo la piscada.*"

Sure enough, when Rod and the agriculturalist got to the pond, they found a five foot cayman swimming lazily among the newly planted minnows. The prehistoric carnivore had found a home, complete with moss to hide in and plenty of little munchies. Now a five foot cayman with its gaping jaws and long teeth designed for ripping flesh is not an animal to toy with. So the nucleo director summoned a staff member with a rifle and the cayman was dispatched before it could do very much harm. The fishpond experiment had survived the predator's intrusion.

Several months after the cayman incident word reached the Tolima Volunteers that several girls from a Peace Corps Health Group would be coming to the department. Actually, progress of these trainees had been closely monitored all along as Brian McMahon, the Colorado cowboy, had a sister in the class. Since Colombia '64, like most Peace Corps groups, was heavily weighted toward the male side, the arrival of an all female company was anticipated with some eagerness and there was a great deal of speculation as to where they would be stationed. In the end, the Volunteers of the Health Group went to two departments, Boyacá and Tolima. Two of the girls from this group were assigned to Purificación. Rodney and the two girls would become fast friends; Rod would even attend one of the girl's weddings a few years later. But the two female health Volunteers were based in the town, while Rod worked at the nucleo, so their relationship was one of social visits and not so much work related.

Spokely's experiences were on the fringes of the violent area of southern Tolima. Further south the Violencia had not been quelled nearly as successfully as two other Colombia '64 Volunteers discovered. Upstream of Purificació on the Magdalena River, Jerry Brelage and Arlene Ratliff were also assigned to a nucleo. Their introduction to Tolima was anything, but comforting. A six hour bus ride from Bogotá left Brelage and Ratliff stranded in the small town (some 2000 inhabitance in 1965) of Dolores still fifteen miles short of their destination, the Nucleo Escolar de San Jose. They were informed there was no bus to the nucleo, the only way to get there was by Jeep or on foot. But the two Volunteers had all their belongings with them, too much baggage to carry that far "*a pie*" (on foot).

However, the pair was undaunted. After the Nebraska training and the Puerto Rican experience they were used to quandaries. After all, this was the Brelage from Batesville, Indiana who had slipped out of the back of his brother's wedding party to catch the plane to Lincoln four months earlier. Arlene, from San Jose, California, a graduate of California Polytechnic College in San Jose, looked around at the tropical landscape and guessed her former hobbies of snow and water skiing were not going to be indulged in for a couple of years. But her third passion, that of reading, would not only be a great comfort, it would prove invaluable in her work in Colombia.

Arlene Ratliff

While the two Volunteers were still taking stock of the situation, a Jeep from the nucleo pulled up with a welcoming committee. The relieved pair was picked up along with their baggage and transported to the facility where they expected to spend the next twenty months.

Nucleo Escolar de San Jose was in extreme south-eastern Tolima, a region where the aftermath of the Violencia was still evident and banditry still a major problem. This was the reason for the nucleo and it was the justification for a strong contingent of the military in the area.

Dolores itself contained an army unit and a headquarters. Smaller army detachments were scattered around the region in posts with attached barracks. One of these posts was located very near the nucleo. Though probably necessary to contain the violence and control the outlaw bandit groups still operating in the area, particularly higher in the mountains, the army was not popular with the local population. The citizens of Dolores were Liberals and no doubt supported, at least tacitly, bandit elements representing that party. The next town down the road favored the Conservative Party which also had guerilla groups in the region and so the conflict simmered, tensions remained and cooperation between the towns was nonexistent.

The commandant, a captain stationed in Dolores, was particularly despised by the local citizenry. It seems he had been posted there as a lieutenant during the latter stages of the Violencia when the army was cracking down on the guerillas. This lieutenant, now captain, had been responsible for the deaths of several people in the area. Whether these were guerillas, or supporters of the guerillas, or just innocents who were caught in the crossfire is, perhaps, impossible to know at this point, but the acts had gained him undying animosity among the locals.

With the pressure of the army, the bandits still holding out were reduced to stealing a few head of cattle, an occasional raid on a coffee plantation and a kidnapping or two for ransom. Though the Violencia was over, the remnants of that civil war were still a threat and presented a danger to the teachers and staff at the nucleo.

The nucleo itself was well organized and well run. Like its counterpart at Purificación, it had classes for five grades and served four satellite schools in nearby communities. The nucleo had demonstration gardens, rabbits and chickens. It even had running water and electricity provided by its own generator which ran for an hour after dark. Then it was candlelight only.

The two Volunteers had their own rooms and ate at the nucleo cafeteria. Arlene worked at the nucleo with the nutritionists and health workers most of the time, while Jerry was part of the team that visited the satellite schools and communities.

The first three days of the week the team, consisting of Jerry, another *agricultor,* a *nutriciónista* (some times this would be Arlene), a nurse and a manual arts teacher, traveled to the outlying schools. The furthest of these was an hour and a half on horseback. On Thursdays, the team, including Arlene, would make the trip to the Dolores school by truck, a welcome change.

On Fridays the team and Volunteers stayed at the nucleo where Jerry taught, "ag, English, and some P.E."[17] Arlene was occupied with teaching nutrition, health and assisted in the English classes.

On Saturdays Jerry and Arlene would make the trip to the market in Dolores. This free-wheeling, open air celebration of the free market system based on barter attracted much of the town's population and many from the surrounding communities. It provided a chance for the Volunteers to meet people on their own without the presents of their nucleo counterparts. Here they could make acquaintances that would serve them well when they encountered these people in the course of official duties.

Before long, work at the nucleo began to settle into a certain routine. The Volunteer's Spanish was improving to the point they were able to make a real contribution to the classes and many of their ideas for improvements were even being considered by the nucleo staff. Except for the interminable mosquitoes and oppressive heat, the situation at the nucleo was just becoming comfortable when the Volunteers received a message from Ibagué. "Peace Corps asked us to come into Ibagué to review our first impressions and meet some of the jefes in the capital."[18]

As requested, Arlene and Jerry went to Dolores in the afternoon so they could catch an early bus to Ibagué, about a four hour trip. In Dolores they ran across the army captain who informed them he was going to Ibagué the next day and invited them to ride with him and avoid the uncomfortable bus trip. However, he was not planning to leave until 10:00 AM and the Volunteers wanted to arrive in the city early for meetings so they politely declined even though it would mean a long ride on crowded busses.

The next morning Jerry and Arlene caught their bus in the early morning hours and made it to Tolima's capital in time to meet with Peace Corps officials and some of the Colombian government agency heads. By evening both Volunteers were exhausted and

---

[17] Jerry Brelage, personal email to Gary Peterson, Oct.13, 2008.
[18] Ibid.

turned in early. The following morning the Americans from Dolores were up having breakfast when they picked up a newspaper to catch up on world and local events. There, at the top of the front page the headlines blared: "Army Captain and Four Soldiers Killed by Road Mine." The captain, long hated by the local population, had finally been dealt with. The perpetrators had used a road side bomb, an instrument of destruction that would become known forty years later and half a world away as an IED (Improvised Explosive Device).

Arlene and Jerry were shaken. What if they had accepted the captain's invitation, would they now be part of the headline? Would the bombers have carried out their execution, or would they have spared the gringos and missed the opportunity to even old scores? It was indeed disconcerting to think about.

In any case the murders were enough to convince Peace Corps that Dolores was too dangerous for Volunteers. Arlene and Jerry were pulled out of the Nucleo de San Jose and sent to another nucleo, Los Guyabos near Fresno in northern Tolima. It proved to be a precipitous move accomplished without adequate preparation. The nucleo was not ready to accommodate the Volunteers into their program nor did the staff adjust very well to their presents or take advantage of their abilities.

After a discouraging few months, both Volunteers applied for transfers. Arlene Ratliff was shifted to Bogotá to work directly with PINA officials and planners in writing nutrition classes. Jerry expressed his desire to go back to the nucleo at Dolores. Peace Corps official had real reservations about a return. They were now worried about the kidnappings occurring in that region – the bandits were increasingly pursuing this new source of revenue. Jerry was informed that if he were captured and held for money, the Peace Corps would not pay a ransom - this was United States government policy. In spite of the warning and conditions of his return, Jerry insisted and was finally granted his request to go back to the Nucleo de San Jose.

Upon his arrival in Dolores, Jerry was welcomed warmly by old friends and colleagues. He once again took up his position at the nucleo and resumed his place on the team that visited the outlaying schools, and generally the work went well. Chicken and rabbit projects didn't catch on - the rabbits, especially, seemed to be susceptible to a variety of tropical diseases - but the demonstration gardens at the nucleo were a big success. Over a hundred garden projects were developed in the communities the nucleo served.

Though his Spanish was now much improved and he was making gradual progress in promoting some of his ideas, Jerry wanted specific projects he could call his own. He felt he needed to be recognized for what he might do independent of the nucleo staff. He was gaining some recognition from the communities he worked in, but the process was slow and haphazard. What he needed was some kind of event that would gain a bit of notoriety, something that would set him apart from the other nucleo teachers and staff. The opportunity came, not in the course of his teaching or even through his association with people at the market, but through sports, and, ironically, at the expense of the Colombian Army.

Soccer, of course, is a very popular sport in Colombia. Soccer fields exist anywhere there is enough flat, open space to play. There were school teams in the Dolores vicinity as well as adult teams. One team was made up of nucleo staff members along with a few locals from the area. Jerry took an interest in this team having played the game back in the United States. However, he quickly discovered his footwork was not in the same league with these Colombians who had been playing since childhood. But, because he was good at handling the ball with his hands, skills picked up in football and basketball, he made an exceptional goalie. So Jerry was adopted into the team as they prepared for their next game.

The soldiers stationed around Dolores also had a team which was only too eager to show the local campesinos how the game was really played. A match was arranged and the stands were filled with spectators cheering on the home team against the not very popular Army team which had only a few dozen fans.

As play began it become obvious the two teams were evenly matched except for a ringer the army had recruited. He was very good, far and away the best player on the field. As the game progressed, the star of the Army team was the difference. Gradually, the Army began to pull ahead and the crowed was becoming silent and subdued. Once again the Army had the upper hand as it did in all things pertaining to the community.

Then, "sometime during the first half the Army star broke free and was dribbling the ball toward me at the goal. Usually Colombian players play a finesse game without much physical contact."[19] They are shifty and skilled in handling the ball with their feet; speed and craftiness are their stock-in-trade.

> As the Army guy dribbled toward me, I moved to intercept him. I scooped up the ball, but did not stop. A step later I slammed into him and literally leveled the Army's star player. He weighed about 130 pounds and at the time I was about 190 and in good shape. The contact for me was minor because of my size and being accustomed to contact from football, but he was carried from the game. The people from the communities loved it. They really enjoyed seeing this ringer get hurt. We even won the game. Over a year later when I left, the town's people were still talking about it and it gave me real status in the community.[20]

So Jerry became known as the Norte Americano, distinct and separate from the rest of the nucleo staff. With his new found celebrity, Jerry promoted some new ideas. He started a strawberry project with plants he obtained from the Fenimores (one of the married couples of the Colombia '64 group) in Silvia, Cauca. This turned out to be a great success with several families not only growing their own strawberries, but selling them at the market in Dolores.

He worked closely with the young, enthusiastic agricultural expert at the nucleo, spending hours brainstorming with him on innovations and new ways to improve the economy and lives of the people in the area. "I think I was a motivator for him to start and implement new things."[21] Jerry would be best man at the agranamo's wedding before he left the site.

Because Jerry was teaching English at the nucleo, the director was able to apply for and get permission to start the first year of *colegio* (high school) at the facility. This was a

---

[19] Jerry Brelage, personal email to Gary Peterson, Oct.14, 2008

[20] Ibid.

[21] Jerry Brelage, personal email to Gary Peterson, Mar. 25, 2009.

remarkable achievement for a rural school and provided an unusual opportunity for the children of the area.

Volunteers of various groups living in the same department would commonly gather at the home of a Volunteer living in town. In Cauca, this was the leader's house in Popayán. In Boyacá, it was the leader's place in Tunja. In Tolima it was Lila Goldfinch's apartment in Ibagué.

"Lila was an instructor of English teachers," Jerry Brelage relates. "There were three Volunteers in the apartment, two girls and a guy. When we first arrived, there we stayed and partied a lot at their apartment in Ibagué."[22]

"She often hosted impromptu gatherings that permitted all of us to unwind, share experiences, *speak in English,* and share photos taken in our sites."[23] These social events were mostly male affairs as the number of girls available was so limited. The arrival of the all girl Health Group made a significant change in gatherings. Jerry says, "the quality of our parties increased tremendously."[24]

One of these parties was especially memorable for Ron Halter and Steve Burgess.

One night, we were all gathered at Lila Goldfinch's apartment [Ron writes]. It was around my 21st birthday. Now that it was legal for me to drink, Steve decided to challenge me to a drinking contest. We started throwing back shots of aguardiente. By the end of the evening, Steve (an experienced frat guy from K State) was under the table and I was declared the winner (dubious honor).

On my way back to our hotel, I saw the soldiers being delivered to the town square near the cathedral. I didn't know what to think. I did my best to make myself invisible, and continued to the hotel. When I woke the next day, I had to ask others if I had had a bad dream. I felt relieved to know that it was a short term security measure for the national election. Since then, Steve and I have often chuckled about that night.[25]

Something similar happened to me on a bus ride at about that same time [Jerry Brelage recalls]. Due to the still remaining violence in southern Tolima we were usually stopped twice on our way to Ibagué. I was going to Ibagué right before that election. We were stopped and everyone was removed from the bus and all our luggage was searched. I had just purchased a nice leather piece of luggage for short trips and one of the soldiers broke the zipper. It must have been well into the second year and my Spanish was pretty good. I cut loose with every cuss word I knew at the soldier. There were about 10 soldiers with rifles standing around and I heard click, click, click as they took off the safeties on their guns. I just said you could do anything you want with the luggage and backed off. I realized that they were really concerned about weapons being smuggled into Ibagué.[26]

---

[22] Jerry Brelage, Personal email, Apr.8, 2009.

[23] Ron Halter, Personal email to Jerry Brelage and Steve Burgess, Apr. 8, 2009.

[24] Jerry Brelage, Personal email, Mar. 23, 2009.

[25] Ron Halter, Personal email to Jerry Brelage and Steve Burgess, Apr. 6, 2009.

[26] Jerry Brelage, Personal email to Ron Halter & Steve Burgess, Apr. 6, 2009.

Traveling by bus, you could get stopped anywhere in Colombia, but it was more frequent in Tolima, especially southern Tolima where there was more violence. These stop and search incidents were a little unnerving. Usually such affairs were conducted by the Army or National Police in uniforms, but sometimes you weren't sure who it was that was holding up the bus, even if they were in uniform.

I took a trip to see Rodney and another to see Jerry and Arlene [Ron Halter reports]. It was on the trip to see Jerry and Arlene, that the bus I was on had to slow down to ford a shallow, slow moving stream. Immediately upon crossing, about 10 armed men in soldier uniforms stopped the bus. We were ordered to exit the bus. I became very concerned, were these really soldiers or bandits in soldier's uniforms?

Jerry had reported that a Colombian army officer had been assassinated near his site and the thought crossed my mind that I could be next. At 6' 3", blue eyes and light brown hair, I literally stood head and shoulders above the rest of the passengers. The leader of those who stopped us approached me first, looked at my identification, and politely asked me to stand to the side. He then began to examine, interrogate, and occasionally search the remaining passengers with much less deference than he had shown me. I guess we all passed muster, because we were permitted to continue our trip.[27]

In fact, Peace Corps Volunteers were often treated with respect above that of other *Norte Americanos* and Colombians. Local Colombians made a distinction between tourists, either Colombian, European or from the United States and Volunteers. This was especially true in the rural areas as Ron remembers.

I can't recall ever having a cross word with a Colombian in Tolima! As I think about it, I find that to be quite remarkable. Also, most of the Colombians I met in Tolima were polite, respectful, and when they realized that I was with the Cuerpo de Paz, they often showed deference.

I can recall entering a tienda to buy this or that. Upon striking up a conversation with the attendant/owner, it was obvious that I was not a tourist and the conversation often turned to the Peace Corps. Subsequently, the price of the item was lowered without bartering. This happened more often than not. I came to realize that, at least in Tolima, there was a price for a tourist, a lower price for a Colombian, and an even lower price for a Peace Corps Volunteer (PCV). I can't explain it. I can only surmise that we, as PCVs, developed a reputation that was appreciated and respected.

I can recall conversations that started out with the Colombian asking me "...what are you here to exploit?" When I explained my purpose in Colombia, they often looked puzzled, as though they could not understand my answer, but they never again challenged my presence.[28]

[27] Ron Halter, personal email to Gary Peterson, Apr. 5, 2009.
[28] Ibid.

Between the towns Ron Halter and Steve Burgess worked in just south of Ibagué and the nucleos in southern Tolima lay the town of Espinal at the junction of the highway to Bogotá. Here, within sight of the Magdallena River, the Colombian government had selected several schools for the initiation of their Educational Television Program. Gerald Volgenau would be the ETV Volunteer from Colombia '64 working on the operation in this corner of the world.

Espinal was not a city, but it was big enough to be called a town. It had a big cathedral (of course), a small hospital, tiendas on the corners, a post office and three or four paved roads, not counting the highway which passed through on its way to Ibague, the departmental capital. The other roads were no more than pale dust.

My actual work site was in the city of Girardot, which moldered by the Magdalena River about 10 miles away from Espinal by chicken bus. I was supposed to look after the city's primary schools where previous Peace Corps Volunteers had already placed TV sets, some 20 schools – some right in the urban downtown, others sprayed out the city's fringes.

This commuting arrangement from Espinal to Girardot apparently was set up so I could live near, and learn from, two Volunteers already living in Espinal. One Volunteer was a blond California dude, with surfer good looks and an easy manner. He usually hung out with the local young bucks, played "Pa Todo El Ano" the guitar and soon bought himself a pet monkey. He named the monkey Mijo, a common shorthand for *mi hijo* (my son). As I recall, his job was to develop physical education programs for the schools.

The second Volunteer was Patricia Hill, a pretty, endlessly cheerful Volunteer from Florida with Irish freckles and shoulder-length hair the color of honey poured through sunlight. If one word were to describe her – although one would really never do – it would be vivacious. I guess I have always been a sucker for vivacity.

I know, I know. You already have guessed where this is heading. The three of us ate meals – breakfasts and dinners – at the patio table of Señora Rodriguez and her two children in their 20s. One offspring was a rather sulky man, Umberto, who became sulkier after he failed to seduce Senorita Patricia. The other offspring was a beautiful and joyous daughter, Maria Isabel, whose coy charms brought Colombian and European swains from as far away as Bogotá.

As you might imagine, eating breakfast and dinner together each day, going on outings and such, one thing did lead to another for Pat and me. It was in some ways like a shipboard romance. We headed off for a few days and raucous nights at the big festival *foklorico* in Ibagué.

When Easter break came, we headed off together for a vacation of sun, sand and warm Caribbean waters in the resort town of Santa Marta. We joined the CARE rep, John Rucker, based in Ibagué for a vacation jaunt down near Neiva. There we stayed in a rustic resort back in the hills – run, by my best guess, by a former Nazi on the lam. There we went horse-back riding in the hills. It all seemed like storybook stuff. Very romantic. And a constant series of school vacations made getting away easy. Hardly a month went by when we weren't celebrating some saint's day with a *puente* (bridge) that created a four-day weekend.

By the time the summer months showed up, we were engaged. Pat, who had come to the country two years before with Colombia 13, agreed to extend her service for an extra year. The actual wedding was scheduled to take place the following fall.

Meanwhile I was trying to manage my schools in Girardot. About a month or so on site, I discovered a problem at one of the downtown schools. As per the agreement to getting a TV set and the appropriate materials for ETV, this school was required to set aside a classroom to be used for the TV classes. This TV room faced a walled-in, dirt court yard where, during lunch break, the kids would pace up and down memorizing their lessons (all elementary education in Colombia was based on rote learning), play games and eat their lunches.

As it turned out, half of the designated TV room was filled with shelving that held the city's archives – records of all sorts of transactions, agreements and contracts and detailed histories of each of the city's departments. Almost every document carried the blue imprint of the city's official stamp and the signature of some bureaucrat.

Fitting both the archives and the TV class in the same room initially was no problem. The kids still had plenty of room to sit on the floor and watch the televised class. But as weeks slipped by, the students tended to do what kids do – that is, get into everything. All too soon, all the city archives were tumbled onto the floor, creating an inland sea of white paper. And with the constant coming and going of TV classes, this ocean of officialdom was soon crumpled, torn and covered with small, very dirty footprints.

Clearly this was not good.

So I went to visit the city official in charge of the district's schools. His title was *Jefe del Grupo* or group leader. He was a classic bureaucrat. In Colombia they are called *corbatas* (wearers of neckties). This one was frankly fat and sweaty in a white *guiabara* shirt – domineering over people below him, obsequious to those above.

"Look," I said. "We have to do something. All these papers on the classroom floor do not make for a good learning environment. What's more, these are the city archives, for heaven's sake. Shouldn't they be protected? Doesn't anyone care about the city records. Don't you think someone from the city ought to clean up that mess."

The Jefe del Grupo mopped sweat beads from his forehead and then from the glistening gully at the base of his throat.

"Absolutely," he said. "It's very important. I'll take care of it."

The white-shirted acolytes near his desk nodded with approval. I nodded with approval.

"How long do you think it might take to clean up this mess?" I asked.

"Two weeks" He said this with assurance.

His acolytes nodded again. I said, "OK" and left.

Two weeks passed. And then three, when I returned to his office.

"You know," I said, "those papers are still there."

"*No es culpa mia,*" he said. It's not my fault. It was a phrase I would hear many times during my months on Colombia. This was a sort of "mañana attitude" with a time extension for Colombian lassitude.

"But it will be done," he said.

"When?"

"Two weeks."

Versions of this same verbal dance replayed themselves several more times. It was the "*mañana*" attitude with an additional 13 days. Still the papers lay on the floor getting more torn, more crumpled and dirtier.

All this began to feel like a test of wills – the *jefe*'s and mine. In my mind, the whole matter had evolved into a question of principle that went beyond a classroom wallowing in neglected documents. In retrospect, I can tell you with some assurance; this was not a good attitude to take on.

So after a while, I'd had enough. But by this time I had developed a plan. It was a rash plan, but it might work. Back in the official's office, I asked the same question again and the jefe, once again, promised: Two weeks."

"O.K.," I said, "but if the papers are not out of that classroom in two weeks, I am going to go in there with a shovel, pitch them all into the courtyard." At that point, I brandished an even rasher threat. "And I'm going to burn them."

The jefe, whose shirt that afternoon was marked with half moons of sweat at the armpits, laughed out loud. Imagine that, the Gringo kid says he's going to burn the city archives. His stomach jiggled with amusement. As did his jowls. He chuckled. His acolytes giggled. I left with a shrug.

One week passed and then two. And yes, the archives still swamped the floor. So on a sweltering afternoon, I set out to keep my word. With the help of two workers that had been loaned to me by a friend who ran a patient drug factory next door, we went into the classroom with shovels and brooms. Two hours later the floor was clean. The paper sea which had been inside had been converted to a sullen scrap heap in the patio where the occasional breeze would send paper escapees scurrying away across the dirt.

After all my shoveling, I was as grimy as the papers. Dust stuck to my sweat-soaked shirt. I had been swearing under my breath in English. But the job was done, the point was made.

Completely exhausted, I got on a bus and went back to Espinal to take a shower and eat dinner. Frankly, I was more than a little nervous about this whole escapade. But I also was feeling a bit self righteous. But then that night the worst possible thing happened. It rained. Not just a little rain, a lot of rain. A gulley washer, a toad choker. A slam bang thunderstorm. It took little to imagine the city's paper archives steadily melting into a soggy mass right in the middle of that school yard. No longer documents in a dirty, but salvageable pile, but a gelatinous mound of cellulose.

And who had put our city's documents there? Who was responsible for that giant gelatinous glob? Gerardo. The *Cuerpo de Paz*. The *estados unense*. The gringo.

And who was most certainly going to be the object of an official complaint to the U.S. embassy? And who, for the sake of diplomatic equanimity, was likely to be shipped out on the next Avianca flight to Miami?

Despite my night long prayers, the next morning arrived on schedule. There would be no avoiding the consequences of recklessness. I would have to board that bus for Girardot. The music surely was playing there. And I would have to face it.

The morning was sour, grey and drizzly. The bus refused to break down. Once in Girardot, I forced myself to walk to the school. I wanted nothing more than to be invisible. At the school, I hesitated at the corner of the high wall that surrounded the patio and then – with no small sense of dread – I peered inside.

I was astounded. What I saw was nothing. The patio was empty. No document mountain. Not a single scrap of paper. Nothing but a yard of tawny dirt.

My mind raced. What could have happened? Had the janitor burned everything? Was some Houdini act afoot?

I walked over to the TV classroom. It was dark. The kids were in their home rooms. No session was on the air. But the TV room was not empty. There splayed out on the floor were all the thousands of documents I had shoveled out the day before. It almost seemed like a time warp. Yesterday never happened. I never came with a shovel. The city archives were never tossed out into the dirt.

I never did learn exactly what happened, how or who pitched that mass of paper back into the classroom. And frankly, I did not ask. I figured I had dodged one bullet, it made little sense to jumping in front of another.

Days later I ran into the jefe del grupo. I did not mention the archives; neither did he. About a month later, I visited the school only to discover that the TV classroom floor was clean. No papers. The documents, which somehow, had magically moved back into the classroom, now had magically moved away. I was told that the city's precious documents had been transferred to another building, maybe not with a shovel this time.

At any rate, I would not be going home prematurely.[29]

---

[29] Gerald Volgenau, personal email to Gary Peterson, April 6, 2009.

7
HUILA – WHERE ALL THINGS BEGIN

While the Volunteers in Tolima were contending with poor sanitation, less than *bravo* gallos, bandits, government papers, even the army, seven other members of Colombia '64 found themselves still further up the Magdalena River in the department of Huila. This was the other department that was to be off limits, the Volunteers were told in training, because of the residual effects of the Violencia.

Huila might be termed the department of beginnings. It is in Huila that the mighty Magdalena River has its source near the juncture of the Cordillera Central and the Cordillera Occidental. Here in the southwest corner of Huila, the Magdalena begins its nearly one thousand mile journey to the sea, transiting virtually the whole of the western mountainous one-third of Colombia from south to north, the main water artery of Colombia's interior. It is in Huila that the central and eastern mountain ranges diverge, running north, providing habitation for the majority of the country's population. And here in Huila is where San Agustin is located, an archeological site devoted to one of the most ancient cultures in, not only Colombia, but all of South America. Huila encompasses, then, the origin of so much that is Colombia.

Toward the northern end of this department is located its capital, Neiva, situated along the Magdalena River. An hour south of Neiva, Doug Dunn from Osceola, Nebraska, survivor of the Puerto Rican trek through hell, was stationed in the town of Rivera. Further to the south, and thus further up steam, Ross Burkhardt of North Bennington, Vermont and Ronnie Cress of Pueblo, Colorado found themselves in the town of Gigante.

Burkhardt was the tallest member of the group and the trainee who ferried others across the stream in Puerto Rico. At six feet, five inches, he would find that he literally towered over the average Colombian. Because of his height, he had acquired the nickname Gigante (Giant) in training and thus, apparently, this logical and well thought out selection of site assignment. Burkhardt's partner in Gigante was Ronnie Cress, the same trainee who had had the gall to tweak the sensibilities of the Nebraskan shrinks. Still further south, at Zuluaga were Mike Weber of Tuscola, Illinois and his companion Rich Bennett of Modesto, California, who had often entertained us in training with his guitar playing.

To the south of Mike and Rich were Sharon and David Howell of Gallien, Michigan. The couple was stationed in Palestina, less than 70 miles from the fountainhead of the Magdalena River and within 20 miles of the stone artifacts at San Agustin. These were seven members of Colombia '64 about as far up Colombia's giant creek as you could get.

Burkhardt and Cress took stock of their town. Gigante was a hot and dusty village of about 2,600 people in 1965, on the banks of the Magdalena River. The town was especially proud of its brand new fire department. The firemen even had uniforms, an innovation that helped greatly in recruitment.

The first order of business, for the two Volunteers, was to find accommodations. Ross found a place to stay with two community action Volunteers that had been in town for over a year. Their abode was an old store front on main street, not spacious, but it did have electricity and running water, though not potable. As was the case in most of

Colombia, except the big cities, you drank untreated water at your own risk, water that might harbor amebas, worms, and various other aquatic livestock.

The two seasoned Volunteers did get Ross off to a quick start in terms of contacts with the local population. "I was able to establish a few projects in town, but mostly I worked in the surrounding veredas."[1] To begin with, "the projects" consisted of family gardens, and sanitation improvements. But quickly, Ross recognized the ubiquitous problem of lack of dietary protein. Rabbits seemed a possible solution, so Ross conducted a search for some breeding stock and located several pairs available from Colombia '64 Volunteers in Norte de Santander. Here was a chance to obtain some rabbits and visit a few old friends from training. Ross flew up to the Venezuelan border and acquired several of the fuzzy, long eared hoppers. On the way back, he stopped over in Bogotá and spent the night at the Peace Corps hang out, The Pit, a sort of flop house for Volunteers, cheap, but relatively clean.

Ross had been carrying his breeding stock in cardboard boxes which worked all right as long as they were traveling, keeping the rabbits off balance. But once the boxes were stationary, the contents started looking for food. The furry vegetarians quickly gnawed through the cardboard and began searching the premises for green stuff to eat. Before long there was a screech from a female Volunteer who thought her bed was being invaded by a rat. The commotion only served to upset the rabbits which scooted for cover, alarming other residents of the facility until a local uproar turned into general bedlam throughout the facility with blankets, pillows, Volunteers and rabbits flying in every direction.

Ross Burkhardt

Ross spent the rest of the night corralling the little critters with the help of a not too appreciative bunch of blurry eyed Volunteers. With almost no sleep, Ross made it to the bus the next morning for the long trip to Gigante. It had been a bit of a harrowing experience, but the venture paid off. Rabbits were added to chickens as a protein source for the families of the communities Ross was working in.

With rabbits, chickens and garden projects moving along, Ross was making real progress. Next, he petitioned for and received the help of a Colombian nutritionist who he worked with closely to teach the *madres* (mothers) of the communities how to prepare the vegetables and meat to provide more nutritious meals for their families.

Burkhardt was pleased with his early successes in the field of nutrition, but the real breakthrough occurred when the two *accion comunal* Volunteers left at the end of their tour. Ross's former room mates were replaced by two Colombian agricultural extension agents. This exchange proved to be a boon to his Spanish facilitation and he was introduced to, not just nutrition projects, but agricultural programs where the fundamental economics of communities could be changed. Families were encouraged and supported in growing crops they could sell, elevating them up and out of a merely subsistence existence.

Ross's success in Huila was amplified because of the two Colombians he was fortunate to have as site mates and co-workers. At the same time he assisted the

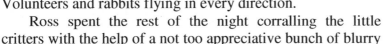

---

[1] Ross Burkhardt, telephone interview, Nov. 11, 2009.

agricultural extension agents with contacts and American know how. And there was the other objective of the Peace Corps, which was to develop person to person relationships. Ross would stay in contact with his two Colombian counterparts for many years after his return to the United States.

Ronnie Cress arrived in Gigante full of enthusiasm and ambition. She felt her background, education and training had all come together for her contribution to this work. Born in Westcliffe, Colorado, an old mining town about 7,000 feet above sea level in the Colorado Rockies, Ronnie was raised on a fox ranch where she cleaned chicken houses, fed pigs, milked cows, weeded the garden, staked hay and sheered sheep in addition to taking care of the foxes. She had a bachelor degree from Colorado State University and a masters degree in educational administration from Northern Colorado University.

However, like most Colombia '64 Volunteers, Ronnie was apprehensive about her limited Spanish and how to make even living arrangements. Fortunately, she became acquainted with and was adopted by the Perdomo family.

Señora Perdomo insisted Ronnie take up residence across the street so the family could keep a watchful eye on her. Though Ronnie did not know it until much later, the Perdomos always had a family member or trusted friend somewhere in the area or tagging along wherever she went, especially when she took trips into the campo. Bandits being a problem in the area, the family was making sure that their *gringa* would be safe.

The Perdomo family owned a tienda in Gigante and would be considered upper middle class in this Colombian town. Ronnie's house was small, but adequate for one person. She ate many of her meals at the Perdomos, a nice arrangement, but one that would lead to a problem. Ronnie began to gain weight. This was a universal complaint of female Volunteers in rural Colombia. The campo diet, high in starches, seemed to have opposite effects on the sexes. The girls all gained weight, while the guys all lost pounds.

This weight gain was fine with the Colombians as they like their women a little on the "*gordita*" side and the Perdomos thought Ronnie was underweight and thus underfed. But the trend in heft was unacceptable to Ronnie. To make matters worse, she broke her arm.

On a trip to Nieva for a departmental conference, Ronnie, along with Dave and Shari Howell, were running for a bus stop to intercept a departing vehicle, when Ronnie slipped and fell, jamming her arm into the street surface. She pulled herself up out of the mud all right, but her left forearm was an inch shorter than it had been and she was in excruciating pain.

Dave and Sharon rushed her to the hospital where she was given enough pain killer to get her through the night and then she was flown to Bogotá. After a flight that included a 2 ½ hour delay, not bad for local Colombian airlines, Ronnie arrived at the capital and met with Dr. Gifford. He took her to a Colombian doctor with X-ray equipment who found that both wrist bones of her left wrist were fractured. Ronnie's wrist was pinned and put in a cast.

Back in Gigante, Ronnie found she was much less mobile and now the Perdomo family insisted she eat with them even more and sent breakfast over to be sure she wasn't starving. All this was just too much for Cress. She just had to make a change. She began cooking her own meals in order to gain some kind of control over her diet. There may have been some hurt feelings over this, but the Perdomos never let it interfere with their friendship or their concern for their little gringa.

In fact, to facilitate Ronnie's self maintenance, the Perdomos insisted she use a gas stove though it seemed out of place in her "little hut."[2]

Then one afternoon as Ronnie was preparing dinner, the stove burst into flames. Ronnie jumped back from the fire and grabbed a container of salt she had on the counter. She tossed what salt she had onto the flames which did help some, but she just didn't have enough to put out the fire completely.

Meanwhile, word spread throughout the town that the gringa's house was on fire. The volunteer fire department was alerted, but before going to the emergency, the firemen had to stop at their homes and don their uniforms. "Finally they came, all fancied up in their uniforms with buckets of water."[3] By this time Ronnie had run out of salt and the fire was beginning to spread, threatening to engulf the kitchen. The firemen threw their buckets of water on the fire. "This, of course, only served to spread the fire throughout the house."[4] Just as it began to look like Ronnie's home would become a smoldering cinder, the fire started to die down. Enough water to cool the fire along with some shovels of dirt had turned the tide. "In the end, the fire was put out," Ronnie concludes, "and I had to chuckle about the firemen and their uniforms. Fortunately, I was able to dump the gas stove for a wood one."[5]

In spite of a kitchen fire and broken wrist, Ronnie was working hard on projects in and around Gigante. Unlike the male Volunteers of Colombia '64 who generally started on the agricultural side, Ronnie's approach was to work on nutrition through mother's

Family outside a typical guadua framed, mud dab home.

clubs which first had to be organized. After three months on site, she could report to the PINA office in Neiva some success in organizing three woman's clubs in veredas near the town.

In Rioloro, she had been able to hold three meetings with attendance varying depending on the level of violence on the day of a meeting. Ronnie did even better in the vereda of Gran Via. Here she met with 15 to 20 women to talk about nutrition and particularly Incaparina (see footnote).[6]

[2] Ronnilou Cress-Kordick, personal email, April 21, 2009.
[3] Ibid.
[4] Ibid.
[5] Ibid.
[6] Incaparina was a protein-rich dietary supplement developed by the Institute of Nutrition of Central America and Panama (INCAP). It was derived from cotton-seed flower and corn, and costs much less than

There was enough interest that she was invited to work with the women individually in their homes on the preparation and use of the product.

Ronnie also organized clubs in Ver Cruz and an area adjacent to Rioloro. In Potrerillos, she taught classes in the school and supplied the teachers with materials on nutrition to reinforce the instruction. Using the school as a base, she, "planned to begin a 4-S club and a woman's club."[7]

She thought she could get a woman's club started in another vereda, Cahaya, within a couple of months. But it was in Trés Esquines that she really scored. Here she was able to work with a *mejoradora* (home economics agent), Concha Maurrique, who was already established in the area. Together Concha and Ronnie developed a woman's club with eleven members where they gave classes on Incaparina and nutrition. They had a 4-S club with twenty *niñas* and *niños* attending regularly. And it was here Ronnie saw the first tangible fruits of her labors.

Ronnie with a family out in a vereda.

Thank the heavens above, I have finally seen some results from my work. In February I gave a talk on Incaparina to a club. Four months later the mejoradora and I were making visits in the campo and one mother was feeding her six month old child Incaparina. You certainly can tell the difference. The children in the campo, in general, aren't playful and very seldom smile, but this one jumps on your lap, laughs and, the mother said, very seldom cries. It is common practice, in the campo, to feed the children *panela* (partially refined sugar made from sugar cane similar to brown sugar) and water.[8]

As for her town of Gigante, Ronnie hit upon a novel idea which she wrote home about.

Listen, I would like to start a sports club here, but I need some help. This is the plan. There are many girls my age who are doing nothing, but staying in the house (see footnote).[9] If I could get them organized through a sports club

---

milk or dehydrated milk products. The Colombian government through PINA was promoting the supplement as a major weapon against protein malnutrition.

[7] Ronnilou Cress-Kordick, "PINA Informe de Gigante," El 28 Marzo 1965.

[8] Ronnie Cress to Mrs. Cecile Cress, Pueblo, Colorado, Jul. 4, 1965, Personal Files of Ronnilou Cress-Kordick, Las Vegas, Nev.

[9] A common situation for young women in Colombia waiting to get married.

103

(basketball or volleyball) and start them working together, then in time, maybe I can give them classes in nutrition and each one of them could do the work that I am doing now. But I need sports equipment which you can purchase as a kit through CARE and have sent to me in Colombia.[10]

While her family in the U.S. took the responsibility of lining up the sports kit, Ronnie organized the young women in the town. The project proved an example of international people to people service initiated by a Peace Corps member. In the report to PINA in July, Ronnie noted the sports club in Gigante and women's clubs in six veredas.

Besides work, there were amusements, like fiesta in Neiva, an annual event. Ronnie anticipated a pretty big party, but it turned out to be above and beyond her expectations.

Mother, I just passed the five most *sabroso* (delightful) days of my life. It's impossible to explain without being in the middle of it. The Fiesta de San Pedro (*Bambuco*) in Neiva. There were queens from all the departments. Bull fights, dancing, parades for five days. I barely slept.[11]

But there were also threatening and disheartening aspects of the country which Ronnie discovered on a trip back to Bogotá to have her wrist looked after. This was a side of Colombia she had not encountered before.

"Outside the governor's office in Neiva there were people screaming, 'Yankee go home,'" Ronnie wrote. "They burned the American flag, and it was even worse in Bogotá. But at my site I have seen none of that."[12]

Visiting another Volunteer's site was often a special occasion for both the traveler and the host. The visiting PCV was able to see new country, learn how other Volunteers lived and what work they were doing, and the visitor was always entertained and fussed over. The hosts had the opportunity to show off their site, their work, living conditions and the people they worked with.

So it was with some excitement that Ronnie made arrangements to visit two Volunteers from Colombia '64 to pick up an item she needed. In the course of her work, Ronnie decided it would be helpful to have a projector. She learned two Volunteers from her group had just what she required.

The keepers of the projector were Rich Bennett and Mike Weber who resided south of Gigante about three to four hours by bus. Ronnie rode the bus south to Garzón, then caught another bus heading east up into the mountains. However, after about 40 minutes, the bus stopped and dropped everyone off in the middle of nowhere.

So I had to walk the rest of the way, 2 ½ hours, through creeks up to my knees, with a suitcase in one hand and a sack of groceries in the other. I had to

---

[10] Ronnie Cress to Mrs. Cecile Cress, Pueblo, Colorado, May 16, 1965, Personal Files of Ronnilou Cress-Kordick, Las Vegas, Nev.

[11] Ronnie Cress to Mrs. Cecile Cress, Pueblo, Colorado, Jul. 4, 1965, Personal Files of Ronnilou Cress-Kordick, Las Vegas, Nev.

[12] Ronnie Cress to Mrs. Cecile Cress, Pueblo, Colorado, Jun. 8, 1965, Personal Files of Ronnilou Cress-Kordick, Las Vegas, Nev.

laugh at myself. I looked so ridiculous. I'd been soaked by the rain so my hair was long and stringy, my ruana was about to fall off. My dress was soaked and dirty. And as I'd meet campesinos, they were scared to death because, a *señorita* never goes out by herself and then to see something like me in my condition straggling down the road. But I finally arrived, and the guys were so sweet and glad to see me that it was worth it a million times over.[13]

Rich and Mike's town was up in the mountains and much cooler than the sites along the Magdalena. "They have the nicest place," Ronnie observed, "it was just on old *guadua* (see footnote)[14] house and they have made all their furniture out of guadua and plywood. They are very neat and their house has lots of personality."[15]

The next morning Rich took Ronnie on a horseback tour of some of the veredas they worked in and to a *finka* (farm) high in the mountains. That evening she treated the boys to a real American dessert.

> Last night was great [Ronnie later wrote]. I made a pie which they appreciated very much – butterscotch & banana cream. The crust – that was something else – I had no flour or lard. So I used what they had on hand, oatmeal, honey, eggs, sugar and salt. We had no oven, so we took the skillet, put a pressure cooker rack on the bottom, sat the pie pan on top of that and put on the lid. Our make-shift oven turned out a pretty fair pie. They liked it and that's all that counts. They've been eating good old campo food, *platano, arepas, papas* and *sancocho* – gets pretty tiring.

Surprises from the states were always welcomed by the Volunteers. Sometimes it was something as mundane as just a package.

"Guess what I found waiting for me when I came home from work? – a beat up *cosa* (thing) with brown paper that looked as if it had been run through a sugar cane crushing machine. But the outside didn't matter at all. Inside was this little box containing a bunch of delightful little goodies. There was a pink comb and wonderful little pins to put in my curlers. I had lost almost all of mine. Also, some real strong American hairpins."[16]

Volunteers were given thirty days of vacation each year and were expected to use this time to get out of their sites and visit other parts of Colombia and South America. No trips to the states were allowed. This time was meant to broaden the Volunteer's knowledge of Latin America and its people. Ronnie used her first vacation to visit some remote and wild country, the tributaries of the Putumayo River. This was once rubber

---

[13] Ronnie Cress to Mrs. Cecile Cress, Pueblo, Colorado, Apr. 11, 1965, Personal Files of Ronnilou Cress-Kordick, Las Vegas, Nev.

[14] Guadua (Guadua angustifolia) is the largest species of bamboo and can grow to a foot or more in diameter. It is native to South America and used extensively in construction.

[15] Ronnie Cress to Mrs. Cecile Cress, Pueblo, Colorado, Apr. 11, 1965, Personal Files of Ronnilou Cress-Kordick, Las Vegas, Nev.

[16] Ronnie Cress to Mrs. Cecile Cress, Pueblo, Colorado, Aug. 6, 1965, Personal Files of Ronnilou Cress-Kordick, Las Vegas, Nev.

country and would later be the domain of FARC and other drug/revolutionary bands. But in 1965, this was just untamed jungle.

Oh, what a week, interesting, hard, fun and beautiful [Ronnie wrote of this trip]. Five of us (Ron, Marge, the Howells and I) took a trip to the Territory of Caquetá, to the capital, Florence. It is an eight hour bus ride from Gigante with roads that are little more than mountain cow trails. Terrible, deep, sharp and dangerous.[17]

We arrived in Florence about 10:30, tired, hungry, dirty and as usual, no money. Where to stay? Eat?? Ah, a hotel off the plaza. The manager told us a night's stay was 45 pesos. We hadn't seen 45 pesos since we left the land of dollars. "Impossible Señor." Thank God he took pity and gave us a room and breakfast the next morning.

The next day we left for Puerto Laro. The only place on the bus available was on the gasoline tanks along with the coffee sacks. So we loaded up like another sack of coffee and off we went with boxes jammed in our ribs, cans falling on our hats and potatoes on top of our feet. But we arrived whole as usual.

At Puerto Laro there were boats waiting, but they started at $50 each. We negotiated the price down to $25. We grabbed a can of cookies and off we went in a canoe to Trés Esquinas. The river was wide and smooth, very full. The sun shined bright and we were happy little sailors looking forward to an interesting trip. Night came and the moon was bright and it sparkled on the water as we sang our boating songs.[18]

There are no buses or roads to Trés Esquinas (which is located at the fork of the Rio Caquitá and Rio Bodoquero). Canoes and airplanes are the only means of transportation.

We stopped at one of the campo houses that are few and far between. It smelled like rats and looked worse. A woman went around in back of the house and killed a chicken for our supper. That night we slept in the boat.

The landscape is beautiful; it is all jungle on both sides of the river with trees and brush right down to the river's edge. The river was very high and quite wide, but has little current.[19]

We arrived in Trés Esquinas just passed noon. The first thing we saw was a "cafeteria." Oh, what a heavenly sight. We dashed in and found a big room full of tables, unpainted, a months worth of garbage on the floor and the food – oh yes - in the corner there were crackers and stale candy bars. That was our cafeteria.

We looked over the town – what town? There was only an Air Force Base – *no mas*. With no food and no place to stay, we looked for a way out. There was a plane that left at 1:30 and if we didn't take it we wouldn't get out until Friday. So we hopped on and ended our short time in hell.

---

[17] Ronnie Cress to Mrs. Cecile Cress, Pueblo, Colorado, Jun. 26, 1965, Personal Files of Ronnilou Cress-Kordick, Las Vegas, Nev.

[18] Ronnie Cress, "Journal of Colombia," no date, personal files of Ronnilou Cress-Kordick.

[19] Ronnie Cress to Mrs. Cecile Cress, Pueblo, Colorado, Jun. 26, 1965, Personal Files of Ronnilou Cress-Kordick, Las Vegas, Nev.

Back in Florence we went to the Plaza Hotel and had a huge dinner of sirloin steak, the most appreciated and delicious meal in all Colombia or so it seemed to us. The manager offered us a room for the night again.

They have a lot of monkeys in Florence. We ran into some Americans buying monkeys from the campesinos for 35 pesos ($1.85). They will sell them in the states for $200 each. Can you imagine? They also have what they call *tigres* – little cats that look like tigers, very darling.

That night the Volunteers from Florence took Marge and me to visit "whore town." It was really sad. Each girl had her own room where they stayed along with their kids. We stayed out till 6:00 A.M. and left at 7:00 on the bus, another 8 hours to get home.[20]

During the trip to Caquetá, the Howells pressed Ronnie to consider helping them with work further south. Finally, after returning to Gigante, Ronnie consented to a trip to take a look at Pitalito as a possible site relocation.

The town looked really promising, but Ronnie confessed, "I would hate to leave Gigante in some ways and in other ways I would like to move."[21]

Things were moving along better than at any other time since she arrived. It would be a hard choice to leave. One group of girls was especially endearing to Ronnie, but their party very nearly ended in a tragedy.

My 4-S club girls in Rioloro are little dolls. Yesterday we went on a *paseo* (outing, party) to the river. The girls went swimming. One girl swam out too far and the current was pulling her so she couldn't get to shore. I dove in, very unsure of myself, but with the hope that the drown proofing or something from training would help me. I was able to get her out thanks to God. But it seemed like an eternity before we were pulled to safety.[22]

Ronnie, in a dress, demonstrating how to plant a garden to school children.

[20] Ronnie Cress, "Journal of Colombia," Aug. 11, 1965, personal files of Ronnilou Cress-Kordick.
[21] Ronnie Cress to Mrs. Cecile Cress, Pueblo, Colorado, Jun. 26, 1965, Personal Files of Ronnilou Cress-Kordick, Las Vegas, Nev.
[22] Ibid.

During this time Ronnie also volunteered to help out with a conference in some small towns in central Huila. She gave two one-hour presentations in three different villages in three days. The subject was health and to help her keep the people's interest she developed a play with paper mache puppets. "I made a glass of *leche* (milk) puppet, a rabbit puppet, lettuce, carrot, orange, a *platano* and Incaparina. I painted faces on them and called them Senorita Leche (milk), Senor Conejo (rabbit) etc. The title of the play was <u>Bienvenida de Incaparina</u>."[23] It was a hit. So much so that Ronnie was encouraged to perfect it and send it to the Colombian Institute of Nutrition.

Finally, Ronnie did make the move to Pitalito, but she had some qualms about the living arrangements. "Pitalito is the center for all nine southern Huila Volunteers. They all come in once a week at least and stay. So we needed a large house. The house Ron has is huge, like a hotel which I think, with a maid and all, will be all right to live in together because all of the Volunteers will be coming and going."[24] It was, after all, a time before the sexual revolution and sensibilities of propriety still mattered.

With shelter arranged, Ronnie sized up her new work site:

> Pitalito, Huila is located six hours south of Neiva. It is the center of the Municipio of Pitalito. The town itself has a population of 10,000, electricity, sewage system, water, a health center, a hospital, a normal school, and four public schools.
>
> The municipio is in large part mountainous. The people are mestizo mainly. They have a very favorable attitude toward Volunteers. The homes are made of guadua and plaster and in the town there are indoor sanitation facilities. Their diet is the regular Colombian diet of *platano, yuca*, rice and corn.[25]

Ronnie had begun working with government, civic entities and individuals in Pitalito much as she had in Gigante. As in Gigante, she found this slow going and only minimally productive. Just as with her play, <u>Bienvanida de Incaprina</u>, and the work with Colombian teachers, nurses, majoradoras and nutritionists in Gigante, she discovered she could reach many more people by training the educators, government specialists and local officials, than trying to reach those in need herself. This switch in tactics was started in Gigante, but came to fruition in Pitalito where there was more opportunity to work with the "teachers." The culmination of this program was "a course on nutrition that was taught by PINA and Salud Publica to all the teachers in the municipio."[26]

This course was the real key to getting the teachers and public officials involved. School was adjourned for a week while these classes were conducted.

> I made a guide of the nutrition course and presented it to PINA along with the plans for the course [Ronnie relates]. I asked them if they would program the course and coordinate with Salud Publica and the Secretary of Education to give

[23] Ronnie Cress to Mrs. Cecile Cress, Pueblo, Colorado, Jun. 26, 1965, Personal Files of Ronnilou Cress-Kordick, Las Vegas, Nev.

[24] Ronnie Cress, "Journal of Colombia," no date, personal files of Ronnilou Cress-Kordick.

[25] Ronnie Lou Cress, "Home Economics Questionaire for Information Booklet," Jul. 19, 1966.

[26] Ibid.

the course. We received permission from the Secretary of Education to give the course May 23-29. The Director and Nutritionist of PINA, in coordination with the Salud Pulblica nurse and Puesto de Salud director of Pitalito, taught the course, directing all the classes with a few exceptions which were given by Richard Bennett and myself. The course was attended by sixty teachers (one teacher representing each of the 60 schools). The teachers from the rural areas provided their own board and room by staying with friends and relatives in Pitalito. Due to the fact that PINA is low on funds, the demonstration materials used in the course were paid for by the Drugeria del Puesto de Salud of Pitalito and PINA furnished the educational materials given to the teachers.[27]

Conducting this course with the cooperation of PINA and Salud de Publica was quite a coup and a real turning point in Ronnie's efforts to build a self sustaining nutrition program in southern Huila.

Christmas was a grand commemoration which the Colombians celebrated from the first of December to January 6th, the Day of Epiphany (Three Wiseman Day). This provided plenty of holiday time for the Volunteers.

Christmas night several Volunteers came in and we invited some Colombians [Ronnie wrote]. The Colombian custom is to open presents on Christmas night, have a big family gathering and dinner. They say the *Niño de Dios* brings gifts.

The next day five of us left for Cali for the *feria.* We took a taxi because of the difficulty in getting seats on the bus and, supposedly, it would be a shorter ride which turned out to be a joke since the taxi had three flat tires. We left at 4:00 A.M and arrived at 9:00 P.M.

We were in Cali from the 26th to the 31st. When we arrived, we went through cultural shock. The city is large, with lights flickering everywhere, clean factories and a lovely climate. It is similar to any large American city. We went to the bullfights almost every day which is very exciting. There were many Volunteers there and many parties. How I made it with no sleep I don't know.

From there, we flew to Bogotá on the 31st and spent New Years Eve in one of the nicest places in Bogotá, the Balalaika, which was a small Russian place. There were parties all over, but we couldn't afford any of them and we hadn't reserved any place to stay since we were leaving at 4:00 A.M. on a plane to Leticia. So we ate and then played bridge until 4:00 in the morning.

We went out to the airport completely worn out. It had been several nights without sleep. However, the flight was postponed until the next day. We went back to Bogotá on an Avianca (the airlines) bus - one of the funniest rides I think I ever had. The engine must have been in bad shape because it backfired like a bomb every time it took off. Plus it had no brakes and three broken windows. We nearly froze in the early morning cold. We told the driver that if the airplane was in the same shape, we thanked God it didn't take off. Avianca put us up in the President Hotel and that night we went to "My Fair Lady."

---

[27] Ronnie Lou Cress, "Site Report Cuerpo de Paz, Pitalito, Huila," no date, Personal Files of Ronnilou Cress-Kordick, Las Vegas, Nev.

The next day we left for Leticia.[28]

What a welcome we received when we arrived in the jungle town. We stepped off the plane into a musty, damp, hot, humid climate to find Jeff Andrews (a Colombia '64 Volunteer) trying to find a plane out of Leticia. His safari had been a failure and he just wanted to get back to his site.

We couldn't find a way into town so we walked the humid half mile imagining ourselves stuck in a swampy, shanty town with alligator meat to eat for the next month. The only hotel available was 80 pesos a night. At that rate I had enough money to sleep half a night. But for a place to wash our sweaty bodies, we'd pay anything. Having checked in, I took off my musty clothes and dashed for the shower, flipped it on and .....no water. *Que mas*!! 80 pesos and no water.

Mike (far right), Ronnie (next) and friends with an Amazon pet.

But there was a life saver in Leticia Mike (also known as Mike the Greek), an American living in Leticia where he captures and buys animals to sell in European and U.S. markets. He offered to let us live in one of his buildings and sleep in hammocks.

The next day we went out on the Amazon in canoes to spear alligators for meat. We stopped at an Indian village where we bought necklaces. The Indians do almost no farming and raise no animals. Meat is brought in from Bogotá. But they do have lots of fish.

We went on to Benjamin, a village on the Peruvian side of the river. Then we went back into some lakes off the Amazon. The water was very warm and crystal clear with pink porpoises jumping to gasp a breath of air.

We paddled on back into the jungle. The noises and sounds of the jungle were indescribable. The distinct vegetation – water lilies were growing with their shadows magnifying their perky, carefree leaves. The ants attacked us from every tree we got close to. Back in the lakes we went swimming - clothes and all. What a way to wash ones cares away on the equator. Shivering, but happy, we canoed back to Leticia.

That night, we left at eight to shoot alligators. The night was a little biting, but clear. The romantic waves danced on the Amazon. We went back into the

---

[28] Ronnie Cress to Mrs. Cecile Cress, Pueblo, Colorado, Feb. 4, 1966, Personal Files of Ronnilou Cress-Kordick, Las Vegas, Nev.

lakes again, the jungle noises were wonderful. They sent a delightful chill up my spine. We stayed out till three o'clock in the morning. The hunt was quite unsuccessful as far as the alligators went because we only shot a few small ones, but as far as the sounds, smells, and sights, it was worth every minute. We ate alligator meat the next day which was very much like chicken, but lighter. Delicious.[29]

We flew back to Bogotá the next day and at 7:00 P.M. we climbed aboard a taxi to Neiva. The road had been closed at night because of bandits, but the driver said it was all right now. We had driven only about 20 miles when the taxi driver told us that bandits had robbed a taxi that afternoon at 5:00 P.M. and killed one of the passengers. He said there was one town that was especially dangerous and that from there until Neiva, we would be in danger.

Well, we were about 5 minutes out of this town when we came to some big logs the bandits had put across the road to stop traffic. The taxi driver just stepped on it and drove right over the logs. But five miles down the road, the accelerator linkage broke. So there we were in the middle of bandit country waiting for the car to be fixed. The driver finally repaired it and we made it to Neiva. We were exhausted from fright and lack of sleep.[30]

The last few weeks Ronnie could revel in some of the successes and achievements of her work in Colombia. These were rewards for her time and effort; there had been tangible and intangible accomplishments.

I went to Criolla today. Each child was so precious, every one had brought me a bag of fruit (oranges, papaya, *caruba*, bananas, etc.) until the table was full! I couldn't even think of carrying all of them, so I had to take one or two from each bag. So darling.

Today I went to Bretania. The whole junta showed up to plant a garden. It is about a half hour by bus and an hour by horse. I arrived early and talked with the teacher while she prepared the meal. She is a dear! Freckles, sparkling eyes and enthusiasm. They provided me with a beautiful white horse. All my cares were lifted on that muddy, but delightful trail. That evening I walked on the road gathering wild flowers until the bus came.

My work has been a real joy – hard – but satisfying. Mr. Horan, Peace Corps Director of Colombia, called me to Bogotá June 6 to see if I could arrange with the Colombians to present the teacher classes in other sites. The teachers are so enthused and are using my material in their programs.[31]

Ronnie Cress's tenure had indeed gone well. She had accomplished her goal of developing a system in which the Colombian's would be teaching Colombians, multiplying her efforts and creating a nutrition program that would carry on after she left.

[29] Ronnie Cress, "Journal of Colombia," no date, personal files of Ronnilou Cress-Kordick.
[30] Ronnie Cress to Mrs. Cecile Cress, Pueblo, Colorado, Feb. 4, 1966, Personal Files of Ronnilou Cress-Kordick, Las Vegas, Nev.
[31] Ronnie Cress, "Journal of Colombia," Jul. 20, 1966, personal files of Ronnilou Cress-Kordick.

David Howell

The two Volunteers who had encouraged Ronnie to move to Pitalito, were David and Sharon Howell. The couple were themselves located further south, in fact their town, Palestina, was the most southerly of any Colombian 64 site in the country.

David was a graduate of Michigan State University and had worked on farms, in nurseries and even been a 4-H leader. Sharon had a B.A. from Kalamazoo College where she had played basketball and field hockey; she was, therefore, well equipped for the physical demands of training and the Colombian campo life.

Palestina, the Howell's site, was a small town with a population of some 700 people in 1964. It was in the mountains high above the Magdalena Valley at an altitude of 5,000 feet, located near the Rio Guaropa, a tributary of the Magdalena. The elevation meant a cooler climate; the average year round temperature being 70° F.

The people also differed here as compared to almost anywhere else in Colombia. It was an immigrant population of campesinos who had moved in from various parts of Colombia to try and better their lives. These settlers owned their own land, from a few hectares to large land holders of a hundred hectares or more. Thus the Howells were working with people who were progressive and open to new ideas. Gardens, for instance were readily accepted.

Sharon Howell

Home gardens are very feasible in our area [the Howells reported]. The climate is well suited to this type of program. Also, many of the people, being from other parts of Colombia, have had some contact with vegetables, but have just lacked a source of seeds. There are some gardens already here and these have served as good demonstration tools. Also, because of the nutrition courses given to teachers in the *municipio* by PINA, interest is increasing among the teachers and spreading to families who didn't really understand the importance before. A Colombian who backs what the gringos say about nutrition, makes it much more convincing. Some teachers are planning to require each student to have a home garden which will be graded.

Since our first month or so, people have come to us for help, rather than us having to look for interested families. They generally know how to prepare the land and use manure if available, thus needing help mainly with how to make *eras* (raised beds) and to plant seeds in rows.

We are now working directly with 60 some families, and indirectly with again that many, who have started gardens from the examples of others or our *granja*. They need the most encouragement during the dry season.[32]

---

[32] David and Sharon Howell, Information for Information Booklet, 1966.

Gardens were a success story and would help in the nutrition area. But, as with most of Colombia, the lack of protein in the diet was a major problem. Rabbits were a potential solution to the protein problem, but bunnies had not done well in other parts of Huila because of the heat and diseases. However, at this altitude, even rabbits were a good prospect.

> The people in this area are receptive to rabbits. The Cafeteros had started some rabbit programs, but without much instruction, so the hutches were poorly made and the rabbits cared for poorly. The demand is high, and people like the meat.
>
> We have 6 female and 3 macho rabbits (just had several females stolen – so now we need more). We trade with people who already have rabbits that are related. We get people started and then they pay back with ½ of the first litter. If they want to buy a pair, we sell them for 20 pesos (in the campo, they sell for double that).[33]

A more familiar solution to the protein problem was chickens, if the people would care for the poultry and not just let the chickens run loose.

> We buy 100 chickens in Neiva, raise them in Palestina with a heat lamp and then sell them at one month. We encourage the use of concentrate, with some success. Two projects have the chickens in *gallineros* (chicken coops), with others having the chickens fenced in.
>
> We also sell fertilized eggs, with fairly good results, depending on how carefully the people are in transporting the eggs.
>
> The people prefer Rhode Islands; they think they are more disease resistant. Leghorns are also available.
>
> We have received additional help from the PINA nutrition course for teachers given in the Municipio of Pitalito (organized by Ronnie Cress). This is having an excellent effect on the attitudes of the people we work with. We now have counterparts in the veredas, the teachers, who have a great influence on the people.[34]

All in all, the Howells had discovered a "far country," one with a new population, here to improve their lives and the prospects of their families. These were progressive people, the kind of citizens that could move a community, a department, even a country forward.

The two Volunteers Ronnie visited to pick up the projector also had successful ventures in Colombia though their introduction to Colombia was anything but promising. Fresh from training and the Bogotá orientation, Richard Bennett and Michael Weber originally landed in the town of Caguán after an hour ride from Neiva in a hot, dust, open air bus.

---

[33] David and Sharon Howell, Information for Information Booklet, 1966.
[34] Ibid.

Caguán is just southeast of Neiva, still in the Magdalena valley, but away from the river and its life giving moisture. Here water was at a premium and conserved for essential use only.

Rich and Mike found a place to live and began exploring the possibilities of their new surroundings. While they tried to ingratiate themselves with the local population, the village padre and town officials, the two Volunteers went to work doing what they had been taught to do, plant a demonstration garden. The priest seized upon this use of the town's precious water as an almost immoral act and publicly branded them as communists.

Richard Bennett

In spite of this rather inauspicious start, Mike and Rich tried to convince the campesinos, towns people, government officials, even the padre as to the benefits of better nutrition, but all their efforts fell on deaf ears. The local population was truly living on the edge of starvation due to the lack of water. They were so busy just eking out an existence; they had no time to consider gardens, rabbits or other programs that might improve their subsistence livelihood. And the severe shortage of water hampered every effort to establish any kind of agricultural project. It's hard to grow things without water in a hot, dry climate.

After two months, Mike and Rich decided they were just not going to make any progress at this location. The priest continued to rail against them undermining any attempt to promote better conditions for the people and they had found no support amongst the town officials. Despairing of ever gaining a foothold in the town, they were considering applying for a transfer when events decided the issue for them. "Some of Tiro-Fijos group of guerrillas - or so it was said - shot up little Caguán one night and Peace Corps quickly found a new site further south in Huila for Rich and Mike"[35]

Again bandits had intervened to force Peace Corps to move Volunteers from their original site. Unlike the situation with Brelage and Ratliff, however, this move would prove to be for the best. Richard says of this second site, "There was plenty of water and the local people were quite open to the notion of growing things they could eat."[36]

Zuluaga was about mid way between Gigante and Garzón, but to the east, up in the mountains. Michael would remain here for the duration of his tour and extend for a third year to manage the government agricultural nursery in Neiva. Richard, on the other hand, stayed only long enough to hone his Spanish skills and learn how to be effective in promoting agricultural projects. He then applied for another transfer, this time even further up the valley to near the source of the great river, the town of San Agustin. "It was an interesting place in that large stone statues and other stone carvings had been made by pre-Columbian inhabitants of that area (see Append. I) and the Colombian government had created an archeological park for visitors and scholars."[37]

[35] Mike Weber, personal email, June 24, 2009.
[36] Richard Bennett, personal email, May 6, 2009.
[37] Ibid

It was here that Richard found a location where he could apply his talents and experience. Though raised in California, Richard came from a farm background well suited to the variety of agricultural endeavors found in Colombia.

> I was raised on a 110 acre farm in Oakdale, CA where we grew almonds and Thompson Seedless grapes. Twenty acres or so was pastureland, so we had animals…like the horse I loved to ride and the cow I hated to milk, along with chickens, sheep and pigs, lots of pigs. The swine operation began as an FFA (Future Farmers of America) project with one sow and grew to the point that its profits helped put me through UC Berkeley in the early '60s.
>
> As was true for many males in the Vietnam war era my draft board was right on my tail after college graduation, so the choice of service was either the "war corps" or the Peace Corps. Next stop… Nebraska.[38]

Richard's new site, high in the mountains, remote, and right in the middle of one of the most important archeological areas in South America proved to be an area ready for progressive ideas. Here there were people ready to listen to programs that could better the their lives and living condition including a unique addition to the Peace Corps repertoire, oranges.

Richard demonstrating the fine points of gardening to Huila teachers.

San Agustin had abundant water and receptive inhabitants and I began to do what we had been sent to do, utilizing school gardens at 5 or 6 campo schools to

---

[38] Richard Bennett, personal email, May 6, 2009.

stimulate interest among local residents in growing vegetables on their own plots. The young assistant priest attached to the church in San Agustin was very progressive and together we would visit outlying barrios where he would tell the people who gathered for his blessings to listen to what I was teaching about nutrition and vegetable gardens, which gave a huge boost to my credibility.

Consistent with the nutritional goals of our program, I also had a rabbit breeding program and an orange tree planting program, with the trees coming from the Colombian government nursery near Neiva. I would like to think that today there are dozens of orange trees growing throughout the area providing nutrition to a generation of campesinos that weren't even born when I was there. I hope they saved some of the rabbits for breeding.[39]

This new site would be Richard's home for the remainder of his time in Colombia and it was here he had many of those experiences that still stand out in his memory, his horse, visitors and vacations.

My horse, an albino, was appropriately named "Gringo" by its previous owner. Like many in our group, I had grown up with a horse, but not one like Gringo. The "Caballo de Paso" horses, sometimes called "paso fino", with their single-footed trot, were a revelation. They were great trail horses, ideal for moving through rough terrain at a ground eating pace while not jarring their rider to pieces. I have such fond memories of riding Gringo for hours over mountain trails, sometimes up to his belly in mud, full of stamina and willing to take me wherever I needed to go. One picture postcard moment I will never forget…returning on my horse from a day working in the campo, I stopped at dusk on a hill above town, wood smoke from cooking fires curling over the red tile roofs of this white washed pueblo nestled in a valley in the Andes mountains. I would love to see it again.

Because of the stone artifacts and its status as an archeological site, a few hardy tourists braved the seven hour bus ride from the nearest airport to come to San Agustin. Since the arrival of any "gringo" aroused interest in this isolated pueblo, they were frequently directed from the bus terminal to my doorstep, especially if their Spanish skills did not include asking directions to the *parque arqueologico.*" Many were young, traveling on a shoe string, so the *casa del Cuerpo de Paz* at times resembled a youth hostel. I was happy to feed and house the travelers in exchange for their company and their world perspectives.

Thanksgiving...Ronnie Cress had the idea of inviting all the Volunteers in Huila and some of their Colombian friends to a Thanksgiving banquet to be held in San Agustin.[40]

As Ronnie put it, "No, Thanksgiving was not a regular day – do you think Americans would pass that day as any other when we have received so much and I believe we even realize it to a fuller extent down here."[41]

---

[39] Richard Bennett, personal email, May 6, 2009.
[40] Ibid.

Almost all 25 volunteers in Huila attended. Ronnie oversaw the production of 3 roasted turkeys, 5 roasted chickens (all in wood fired beehive ovens normally used for baking bread), stuffing, mashed potatoes and gravy, peas, and pumpkin and cherry pies. A gaggle of Colombian girls were our guests and provided partners for the dancing after dinner. A couple of Volunteers had befriended some diplomatic corps members and obtained 6 bottles of whiskey and a case of rum so the party had a sophisticated tone. Each Volunteer chipped in 60 pesos ($4.00) to cover expenses. High living indeed. The meal was a great success and it provided an excuse for Volunteers to make the long journey to the archeological park.

Several people rented horses from townspeople and rode to the source of the Magdalena River, the main river of Colombia which flows all the way to Barranquilla and the Caribbean Sea.[42]

Vacations were a chance to get away and explore other parts of Colombia or even other parts of South America.

One year Bruce Borrud, Jeanette Reeser and I headed south along the coast, passing through Ecuador, Peru and Bolivia [Richard writes]. We happened to arrive in La Paz during Carnaval, when all forms of transportation stopped for several days, and we were getting edgy about getting back to Colombia on time. So, instead of retracing our route along the coast we decided to head directly north toward Colombia but found that there really were no organized means of transportation to get us there.[43]

Departing from the conventional means of transportation in South America can get you in trouble fast. Sometimes it is better to stick to the tried and true rather than improvise. Rich, Jeanette and Bruce, in trying to get to Colombia quickly, were about to place themselves in a position where they would be lucky to get home at all.

We flew north to the Bolivian border [Richard recalls] and when we got off the plane and asked how to cross into Brazil we were told to each get on the back of one of many motor bikes gathered at the dirt airfield and in a cloud of dust zoomed off down a dirt road, across a rickety bridge, and were dumped off at another dirt airfield... in Brazil.

Unfortunately, a plane only came to this place three times a week, so we spent the night in a miserable "hotel" near the field and waited for the next plane. When it arrived the next day the pilot told us the plane was full and we could not board. It was a grim threesome watching the DC 3 rev up its engines in preparation for takeoff. Then, at the last minute, the captain waived out of his window for us to get on. There were indeed no seats left on the aircraft.....we flew standing up in the aisle like commuters on a bus.

---

[41] Ronnie Cress to Mrs. Cecile Cress, Pueblo, Colorado, Nov. 30, 1965, Personal Files of Ronnilou Cress-Kordick, Las Vegas, Nev.
[42] Richard Bennett, personal email, Jun. 25, 2009
[43] Ibid.

We landed on another dirt field that was so muddy the passenger windows at the rear of the plane were suddenly opaque with mud when the rear wheel settled onto the field. Again we were left standing at an airstrip with no idea where to go next until a small boy led us down to a nearby river, a tributary of the Amazon. We sat there for a while until a dugout canoe with an ancient outboard putted up and asked if we needed a lift. After a relatively short ride on the river we pulled up to a dock at Leticia, Colombia...we had at least made it back into the country.

Leticia was a rough place with mud for streets and lots of bars. (To think there were other Volunteers that actually went to Leticia on purpose.) I recall we spent at least 2 nights there waiting for an airplane that never came, and finally hitched a ride on a Colombian Air Force DC 3 that was flying dried fish out of Leticia to markets in Bogotá. We actually sat on bales of dried fish since the plane was not configured for passengers on what was a long, smelly ride. Only Peace Corps Volunteers would consider that a vacation.[44]

Back in his site Rich explored ways of bettering his living conditions. This included cleaning house and cooking. The obvious answer was a maid, but as with all things Colombian, this had its drawbacks.

I got so tired of eating yuca I could have screamed. Yuca soup flavored with cilantro followed by fried yuca and perhaps a little tough chicken or beef if you were lucky was my common meal of the day. Ronnie Cress, very kindly spent a couple of days at my site soon after I got there and taught the maid I had hired to cook about 5 meals, including something like Salisbury steak and chili.

The maid, Diosalina, was a real mountain gal who pounded my clothes with a rock, ironed them with an iron heated by wood coals, shopped and cooked my meals and kept the house clean. Since she had only me to take care of, she spent her free time spinning hemp into twine and weaving shopping bags which she sold in town. I think that when I left she had saved enough from the (I'm sure) generous salary the dumb gringo paid her plus her bag making business to purchase a plot of land high in the hills and become part of the land owning class. I still can't stand the smell of cilantro.[45]

While Richard was toiling away in San Agustín, Mike Weber was having his share of equine problems tracing back to the pair's original site.

In early 1965 when Rich and Mike were first stationed together in El Caguán, one of the first orders of the day was to spend some of the Peace Corps settling-in allowance to buy a couple of horses so the two could gain mobility in their agricultural extension work. Rich chose an older but much smoother riding, caballo de paso (like a Tennessee Walker). But it was also very much a want-a-be stallion and fence runner, which is at the root of this memorable

---

[44] Richard Bennett, personal email, Jun. 25, 2009.
[45] Ibid.

transformation story. Mike bought a younger *lleuga* that turned out to be a great work horse but was not nearly so smooth to ride as Rich's *macho*.[46]

The move to Zuluaga included the Volunteer's horses, however, "after a few weeks of working in the little town of "el inspección de Zuluaga", Peace Corps found another site for Rich, but his horse was not needed. So Mike ended up with two horses."[47]

Mike on one of his horses.

After some time it became clear that Rich's horse was the clear winner for the part of the Peace Corps job that required weekend riding around the plaza with local farmers and other friends. You could just not beat a *caballo de paso* for this business of riding around town and stopping for some of the local firewater with your friends. But there were costs that came with this luxury. Rich's macho still mostly wanted to run the fence lines and chase female horses, so much so that it was impossible to keep this beautiful animal healthy. So Mike sought out the services of a local expert in castrating old male horses. A deal for this risky operation was struck and payment would be only after a healthy and fat animal was delivered.

This worked. Mike had many wonderful weekends riding in style until one of his local Colombian friends convinced him to sell this wonderful specimen of a horse to him so his wife could have the pleasure of riding in such luxury. The only problem was that at the time Mike's friend could not come up with the money.

Fast foreward about 2 years to when Mike was now stationed in the capital city of Huila, Neiva and about to move to Bogotá to start a third year of service working as a Volunteer leader with the Peace Corps and National Institute of Nutrition Office. Since this debt among friends was still outstanding and needed to be resolved before leaving Huila, Mike paid a visit back to Zuluaga, driving the GAZ Russian jeep that the Institute of Nutrition had acquired to add to the mobility of Mike's own horse.

Upon arrival at the farmer's house outside of Zuluaga, Mike learned that his friend was still without cash for liquidating the debt. But the farmer did have a nice fat pig of about 80 kilos running around in the yard. This was the perfect solution: a deal was struck and in the wink of an eye the handsome pig was tied up and in the back of the GAZ, bouncing down the mountain towards Garzón. After some tough bargaining at a couple of *carnicerias* (butcher shops) around

---

[46] Mike Weber, personal email, Jun. 24, 2009.
[47] Ibid.

the Plaza in Garzón, Mike found a very willing buyer, this time trading for cash. But it did not escape notice. The town was much amused upon seeing this funny gringo driving a Russian Jeep selling a pig that was tied up in the back as payment for a second generation horse meat debt.[48]

Just down the road apiece from Caguán, Richard and Michael's first site near Neiva, another Colombia '64 volunteer was stationed. This was Doug Dunn, one of the survivors of the trek in Puerto Rican hell and a native of Nebraska. In fact he had gone to school and graduated from that same campus where the Peace Corps training was accomplished.

Douglas Dunn

Richard Bennett recalls paying Doug a call in the early days soon after their arrival in the Magdalena Valley: "Mike and I rode our horses from Caguán to Rivera once to visit Doug. The day we visited was shortly after there had been a "rebel" attack on someone on the Rivera vicinity and there was talk of moving Doug out."[49]

In spite of the bandit problems, Doug stayed in Rivera and eventually settled on a poultry program as the best way to mitigate the lack of protein in the people's diets. Later he was able to use this project as the basis for his master's thesis at Cornell University. Drawing from that thesis, Doug describes his work in Huila and provides some statistics to amplify the anecdotal information on our work in Colombia.

Program Background: Prior to 1957, most nutrition programs were of an emergency nature, designed to bring food relief to countries during periods of abnormal hardship. It was realized that greater efforts were necessary if widespread nutritional problems in developing countries, especially in rural areas and among children, were to be alleviated. A new approach, "applied nutrition," was outlined in 1957 by UNICEF to help rural people improve their nutritional and economic status through foods which they themselves could produce.

The PINA program had been established in Huila in 1964, largely on paper, just prior to my arrival. Staff included a part-time director, who was a medical doctor, a full-time degreed nutritionist, an accountant, several nutrition aides and, most significant, a secretary, Esperanza, whom I will discuss later. In Huila we decided to initiate an "applied nutrition" program of small-scale family poultry projects. The native diet would be improved through the consumption of eggs produced, and family income could be augmented through the sale of surplus eggs. Chicken and eggs were already a favorite high protein food in the native diet. Since poultry raising was already a traditional enterprise, we felt that small-scale family poultry projects would be more enthusiastically accepted by the rural campesino farmer than other enterprises being considered.

A small distribution-demonstration farm (granja) was established. Through this farm baby chicks, flown in by commercial airfreight from a hatchery in

[48] Mike Weber, personal email, Jun. 24, 2009.
[49] Richard Bennett, personal email to Gary Peterson, May 8, 2009.

Cali, were grown to six weeks of age, when artificial heat was no longer needed. The starter chicks were to be distributed at cost plus 5% to rural families through Peace Corps Volunteers and *Nucleo Escolar* teachers. Sex-Link, a very handsome dual-purpose breed, a cross between a Plymouth Rock and a Rhode Island Red that produced a popular brown egg, was selected.

The following requirements were to be made of project participants: (1) An animal tight chicken hutch was to be constructed, ready to receive the chicks at the time of delivery. The chicks would be maintained at all times within the hutch. Local building materials could be used. (2) A commercially produced balanced concentrate was to be fed. Neighborhood tiendas started carrying the poultry concentrate, for sale by bag or pound. (3) A strict follow-up program of vaccination, worming and general sanitation would be followed. (4) Upon laying, a portion of the eggs produced would be consumed by the participating family to better their own nutrition. With help from PINA staff, I prepared a pamphlet, "*Proyectos Avicolas*," that explained in a simple manner the practices to be followed. It was the custom to let native chickens run loose and fend for themselves. It would be the task of the Extension Agents/Peace Corps Volunteers to demonstrate the value of improved breeds and modern management practices.

While I was directly involved in the development of this program at the state level, I lived in the rural community/municipality of Rivera (an hour from Neiva). In the early months, my Spanish was horrible. I made arrangements to hold weekly agricultural classes with the fourth and fifth graders at local schools. (Elementary school only went through the fifth grade.) One of those schools was a Nucleo Escolar, a rural school complex several miles out of town. The Nucleo Escolar schools were constructed and operated by the national Ministry of Education as an outreach program in areas of previous political unrest. Each week I would prepare a simple talk and conduct demonstrations on gardening, nutrition, etc. With my language disability, I found it easier talking with kids than adults. As the first batch of 600 chicks was to arrive at the granja in Neiva in the summer of 1966, I started promoting the poultry program in Rivera. My fourth and fifth grade students became my biggest allies. It was the classic example of reaching adults through their kids. There was initial reluctance to the idea of keeping chickens penned up and of feeding poultry concentrate rather than table scraps. The boys were insistent that things would be done as *Senior Duglas* taught. Finally, 15-20 fathers consented, most for only five chickens, the minimum number I would sell them. Creative chicken houses were soon under construction, using locally grown bamboo, palm branches and other native materials. They were beautiful.

The chicks finally arrived (July, 1966), transported to the schools by the PINA accountant in the program's Russian-made jeep. The handsome black and white Sex-Link chicks were the immediate status symbol of the community. Eight weeks later, when we had the second batch of chicks ready, many of the father/sons were already lining up to expand, from five to 10 or 15. And their hesitant neighbors were now on board. Word of the Rivera experience soon spread to other communities in the state, and the PINA poultry program was off with a cluck. At the end of my Peace Corps service in August, 1967, there were 96 poultry projects in the Rivera area.

Program Impact: Between July, 1966 when the program was started and September, 1968 when I wrote my master's thesis, 16,000 chicks had been distributed state-wide. Aside from wages, the PINA granja in Neiva had operated within the original 17,000 peso "rotating fund." As of September, 1968, the "rotating fund" had grown to 23,000 pesos as a result of the 5% mark-up on sales over the two-year period. A fair-sized operation had been accomplished with a very small initial investment.

In August, 1967 before I left for graduate school, I did a survey of 33 of the 96 projects in Rivera to document feed costs, sanitation practices, financing, mortality, eggs produced, eggs consumed, marketing practices and other project characteristics. Based on these findings, I was able to convince my major professor in the Department of Agricultural Economics at Cornell to send me back to Colombia for three months for a more intensive study. I collected data on 117 projects located in six different municipalities in the state of Huila. At my request, project participants loyally kept a one-month diary (record sheet) that included feed consumption, egg production, egg consumption and egg sales.

Three-fourths of the projects were of 25 birds or less. Many started with five chicks and then grew to their current size over a 12 to 18 month period. The projects surveyed had experienced only a 1.2% monthly mortality rate. Only 6% of the projects surveyed had <u>not</u> constructed adequate housing. The average cost of raising a chick to maturity (from 6 to 22 weeks) was 34.38 pesos ($2.12 U.S.). This included the 12.50 pesos paid for the 6-week old chick. Among the adult hens in the project, the average number of eggs laid per day was 0.655. 82% of the eggs produced were sold; 19% were consumed in the home. These statistics compared very favorably with commercial poultry farms in Colombia and the United States.

Average egg consumption among project participants was 18.6 eggs per month per family member. Compare that number with 3.5, the per-capita egg consumption in Huila according to a nutrition survey of families conducted in 1964. This represented a five-fold increase in egg consumption, a significant nutritional impact.

One of the larger chicken coops.

Average gross income among the projects was 3.53 pesos per month per hen. This compared with the average wage received by a farm laborer of 20.00 pesos per day. The poultry projects had increased family income by an average of 25%. The market value of a hen ranged from 27.00 to 40.00 pesos, higher during major religious holidays. At that price, participants could terminate their projects at any time and recoup their costs.

Now back to Esperanza and the rest of the chicken story. I was immediately attracted to Esperanza, the PINA secretary. Any reference to the two of us caused her to blush. This would generate more references, especially from Senor Cano, the program accountant, and so the relationship started.

Family henhouse with young attendants.

Dr. Dusan, the PINA director, loved staff outings. When I was in Neiva we would often go out in the evening to a favorite country-side restaurant known for its golden baked chicken. The group would include Maria, the nutritionist, Chata, the nutrition aide, Dr. Dusan, other Peace Corps Volunteers if they were in town, and Esperanza. The restaurant had a tiled outdoor eating area, under the stars, with a juke box of traditional favorites. I was much quicker at picking up the *cumbia* dance rhythm than I was at learning the Spanish language. And Esperanza was a good partner. Since the other Peace Corps Volunteers seemed reluctant to get out on the dance floor, I had a definite advantage. Dr. Dusan had two musician friends who would often accompany us on weekend picnics to the country. The two played guitars and had wonderful harmony. They would sing *"Espumas Que Se Va,"* a nostalgic tale of life using the metaphor of foam floating along on the currents of the Magdalena River by local composer Jose Villamil, in a way that put a lump in my throat.

Esperanza had two sisters and her mother would allow the four of us to go out to local parties unchaperoned. As young men would corner the "gringo" in a criticism of American foreign policy, Esperanza and her sisters would rescue me back to the dance floor.

Postscript: My Peace Corps service was one of the most transforming experiences of my life. It provided me a valuable world view and empathy for others. I eventually picked up the singsong Spanish and expressions of the Huila countryside well enough that at the end of my service, Huila Governor Max Duque Palma signed a proclamation naming me an official *"opita,"* the term used to describe the country folk of the southern Magdalena Rivera area. I was fortunate to have had very visible program accomplishments. I have many photographs of bamboo chicken coops with my fourth and fifth graders and their families, with chickens in hand, smiling with pride. Then there was the PINA staff and my wonderful neighbors in Rivera.

The Colombian people were so good to me. When I returned to the United States, Esperanza gave me a liquor bottle with *"Tratado Para Nostalgia"* printed on the label. I could use a good shot right now.[50]

[50] Douglas Dunn, Small-Scale Family Poultry Projects in Huila, Cololmbia, May 8, 2009.

8
BOYACÁ
MOUNTAINS, AN ANCIENT SOCIETY AND LIFELONG FRIENDS

Collecting the stories for this book has prompted me to reflect on my own participation in this Colombian adventure. My experience was different than the Volunteers of Huila and Tolima. Unlike those scattered along the Magdalena River, I was sent to the mountains of the Eastern Cordillera.

The high mountain plateau that once sustained the Chibcha Empire was to be my new home for the next twenty months. I could hardly have been more pleased. As a bit of a history buff I thought I was most fortunate. I was being sent to the area of one of the great ancient Mezzo-American civilizations, the country where the Conquistadors had defeated the Muisca armies and where Simón Bolívar had beaten the Spanish to gain South American independence from Spain. For a history junky this was pure nirvana. Little did I realize, the same could be said for just about any part of Colombia.

I remember clearly my first impressions of the Colombian countryside north of Bogotá. We were on a bus traveling from Bogotá to Tunja, from the southern capital of the old Chibcha Empire to the northern capital. The scenery was truly magnificent; I was always struck by it every time I took this journey. The road, for the most part, was along the sides of mountains with steep terrain or cliffs above and the same below the road so the view on the down hill side of the vehicle was unobstructed. From the windows of the bus you were looking down onto mountainsides and valleys, a panorama in shades of greens, blue-greens, tans, browns and yellows. In the forground were colorful wild flowers of pink, blue and yellow. Below the road were fields, pastures, gullies, little forests and even towns, some close and others far in the distance. Wispy white clouds

Easter flowers along the highway in Boyacá.

floated below down in the valleys, like puffs of cotton, suspended above hillsides and ravines. You could trace their shadows as they darkened a field or a village and then rushed on changing shape as they followed the varying terrain. It was almost magical.

Traveling on another bus, Tom Gallaher was also heading north, but he ran into some difficulties, because of his language inadequacies, the type of tribulations we all encountered especially in those early months.

After I had purchased my ticket and boarded the bus [Tom relates] I selected an empty seat and sat down. A half hour or so after leaving the bus terminal, the driver's assistant, the conductor if you will - a young boy who looked to be no older than 12 *anos* - came up and unleashed a unintelligible burst of Spanish. I understood not a word, but by his pantomime I could tell he wanted me to get out of my seat. I could see no reason to move and refused to do so. I showed him the ticket I had purchased which was clear evidence that I was entitled to go to Duitama, my destination. I thought he was trying to get me off the bus. Finally, after several minutes, he gave up, shrugged his shoulders and walked away. A few months later when I was more fluent in Spanish, I came to realize that I had been sitting in a section reserved for pregnant woman and he had been asking me move to another section. Spanish – 2, PCV – 0, but things would improve[1]

Ventaquemada - church on one side of the palaza, government buildings on the other.

Tom's experience was not unique. The language barrier was something we all suffered with those first few weeks in country. Fortunately, I was paired with Bruce Borrud whose Spanish was much better than mine. So I figured he would be able to understand what people were trying to say to us, giving me time to master the language. Bruce recounts those first few days in Colombia when he did most of the talking.

---

[1] Tom Gallaher, personal email, Oct. 21, 2008.

We were assigned to Ventaquemada, about 75 miles north of Bogotá. We then spent two days in Tunja for orientation before going to Ventaquemada.

Ventaquemada (Burnt Store), named after some historical fire event, was a town on the main highway between Bogotá and Tunja. It was a small town of perhaps 500 souls built in the Spanish style of a central square with the church on one side and government buildings on the other. We lived in the Puesta de Salud (health center) for about a week until housing was found for us about three miles north of town. We were to work in three veredas with the local farmers to improve the family nutritional level. Since we were at about 10,000 ft. elevation our families grew potatoes for the most part and that was their basic diet. As a result, we were told, infant mortality rate was 50% for our area.

My recollections are that we initially spent a lot of time walking around introducing ourselves to the locals by saying something to the effect- "*Somos miembros del Cuerpo de Paz de Los Estados Unidos*" (We are members of the Peace Corps of the United States).

One memory from our time in Ventaquemada was our initial meeting with the local padre. He was the one who had requested Peace Corps help for his community, so we met with him first. We were ushered into his quarters with our Peace Corps leader. We were seated at a fine table and served a shot glass of whiskey. Since the padre swallowed his welcoming glass with one swallow, I followed suit. Wow, just about knocked my socks off since I wasn't much of a drinker. I remember continuing our introductions with tears streaming down my face.

Since we were invited to come by the padre, we were readily accepted by the community. In fact, we were introduced to the community by the padre the first Sunday we were there.[2]

Besides Padre Rico, we met the town nurse while we were staying in the Puesto de Salud. She lived at the Puesto and we thought this early acquaintance would work to our advantage since she might be very useful in helping us with health and nutrition programs in our veredas. Her assistance, however, would turn out to be anything but steadfast.

Within a couple of weeks we were able to move from Ventaquemada to the veredas where we were to work.

Our housing was secured in a house in Puente Piedra (Stone Bridge) [Bruce relates]. Formerly, the room we were given was a tienda on the highway, but with the new highway located a half mile to the west, it had been

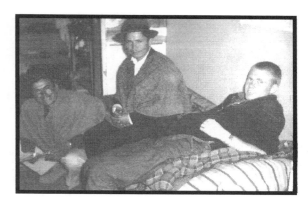

At home, I am visiting with men from the vereda in their typical hat, suit jacket, and ruana.

___

[2] Bruce Borrud, personal email, Jan. 17, 2009.

closed. It consisted of two rooms about 8' by 20'. It was part of a hacienda that was occupied by a caretaker family.

We finally moved into our house about January 20th and then had to furnish our two rooms. Mostly two beds, bookcase, lantern, gas Coleman type stove, and a few food items. We had no electricity or running water in our rooms.[3]

We not only worked in the campo, we were living in a vereda outside of town. The people in the area were mestizo to pure Amerindian. They were probably more progressive then people in the warmer climates which would be an asset in our work.

Their homes were more substantial than houses in the lower valleys. Old houses were of adobe bricks, but new homes were built of concrete block with a layer of plaster on the outside and then painted. Even brick was beginning to be used for new homes.

"Our assignment was the veredas of Puente Piedra, Supata, and Montoya, potato country at an elevation ranging from 9,000 to 12,000 feet. Most farms in these veredas consisted of just a few acres of potatoes, corn, and *habas* (beans) with some pasture for sheep and cows. There were two seasons, wet and dry, with occasional frost any time of the year."[4]

Bruce refereeing a girls basketball game.

"The first week was spent getting acquainted, playing basketball with the kids and refereing games. We played *tejo* (something like horse shoes except played with a steel disc and a powder charge that gives a good report when you hit the target) with the adults."[5] With the help of Padre Rico's introductions and our own socializing, we started to get to know the families in our veredas. Then it was time to get to work on gardens.

We began by putting up a big seed catalog poster by our front door and in our best Nebraskan Spanish said, "*Peda aqui para ayuda y semillas para su huerta casera-GRATIS,*" (Inquire here for help and seeds for your home garden – FREE) or something to that affect. Slowly people started showing up and we began the garden process. We had a demonstration garden at our house which did fine but in this cooler climate it took quite a while to grow a crop. We could grow very large *repollos* (cabbages)

[3] Bruce Borrud, personal email, Jan. 17, 2009.
[4] Bruce Borrud, personal email, Jul. 9, 2009.
[5] Gary Peterson, "Now On Peace Corps Job," *The River Press,* Feb. 15, 1965, p.8.

but it took the better part of a year. We probably started at least 30 gardens including a large school garden in just the first few weeks.[6]

Next we met with the local junta to determine what the people saw as their most immediate needs. Padre Rico facilitated the meeting held at the vereda school. Dr. Cortez, the PINA director for Boyacá, was there and gave a speech promoting a school lunch program, one of his priorities.

The junta decided that the biggest problem for the people was lack of water. There was a water source further up the mountain, but an aqueduct was needed to transport the water to the vereda. A means had to be found to raise the money to build the aqueduct.[7]

On my way to a garden with curious people following.

A second item, less pressing, was reforestation. Most of the native trees had long since been cut for firewood and building materials. There were a few stands of planted eucalyptus around. More were needed.

So our time was divided between the aqueduct project (which meant working with the junta), gardens and the school lunch program. The aqueduct and junta were particularly difficult as Dr. Cortez and Padre Rico were only available for the kick-off meeting, the rest was left up to us with our limited Spanish. Working one on one with gardens proved much more successful and this form of family agriculture boomed. The school lunch program was more difficult because we had to deal with teachers, parents and find the resources for food and building materials.

Securing materials meant trips to Tunja which was always a welcome adventure. There wasn't much for entertainment in Ventaquemada, but in Tunja there were movies, restaurants and a couple of great pastry shops that we visited on every trip to the departmental capital.

On one particular buying trip, the taxi driver we were using to haul our wood, wire and other building materials from place to place informed us we were spending too much money eating at the ordinary restaurants and he insisted we eat lunch with him at his regular haunt.

Against our better judgment we allowed him to take us on a drive into some back alleys we had no idea even existed in Tunja. As the street narrowed and the walls closed in, to the point that the taxi just had room to move down the alley, Bruce and I began trying to come up with an excuse as to why we had to get back to the center of town. But

---

[6] Gary Peterson, "Now On Peace Corps Job," *The River Press,* Feb. 15, 1965, p.8.
[7] Ibid

it was too late, the driver stopped outside this hole in the wall that turned out to be both dark and dingy.

The place was no doubt filthy, but it was too dark to tell. There were no menus; apparently you ate whatever was prepared that day. In the dim light of a smoky lamp flame, we were served *chicharrónes* (rice fried crisp), *morcilla* (blood sausage – just what it sounds like), and boiled potatoes all washed down with *chicha* (a beer made by chewing corn and spitting the masticated pulp into a vat where it is allowed to ferment). Our cabby seemed quite pleased with his meal and even had a second plate, at our expense as I remember. Bruce and I had all we could do to choke down the first serving. It was inexpensive and we did manage to keep food down, but we were glad to get out of the place.

Bruce and I fully expected to be retching our guts out for the next few days. However, we suffered no ill effects from the meal. Still, we avoided that cab from then on and stuck to Tunja's conventional restaurants and pastry shops.

On another trip we visited Puente de Boyacá where the pivotal Battle of Boyacá was fought, the battle that turned the tide of revolution in favor of Bolívar and the South Americans (see Append. II). There were no signs or monuments, just the stone bridge around which the battle had occurred. We tried to imagine the placement of troops for both sides, but didn't have a lot to go on. It was a beautiful site with shrubs and trees

Puente de Boyaca in 1965, the site of the Battle of Boyaca.

along walkways, a pleasant little park, and maybe that is as it should be.

More and more people were requesting help with gardens. The vegetables were being used in soups or stews. Some families even experimented with vegetables not ordinarily grown at this altitude. The cool temperatures were great for the cabbage family, cauliflower, and broccoli, but many other vegetables, like peppers, cucumbers and melons, would not grow at all. One señor tried growing various varieties of tomatoes. He figured if he could get some to produce, he could sell them for a good price. This willingness to experiment demonstrated the resourcefulness of these people. If you gave them an idea, many were ready to invest time and even money to try and better themselves economically.

With our garden projects blossoming in all three veredas, we tried to branch out into other areas, latrines, 4-S clubs, mother's clubs and the school lunch program. The key was the school and getting the nurse's cooperation. So we arranged a big day of vaccinations and demonstrations where we planned to push the school lunch program.

We had arranged a demonstration of Incaparina for the mothers and vaccinations for the children. We arrived at the school at 8:30 in the morning and had everything set up. The mothers started coming a little before 9:00, the time set for the demo. By 9:30 we had about 50 mothers and still no nurse. By 10:00 we had 80 mothers at the school and still no nurse. Bruce and I were going crazy. Finally, a little after 10:00 I left for Ventaquemada. Bruce and one of the teachers were going to try and stall.

I caught the bus, then walked to the Puesto de Salud and found the nurse standing around talking to the dentist who had come to town that day. She was quite undisturbed by the fact we had 80 people waiting for her. The dentist gave us a ride back to Puente Piedra. We arrived about 11:00. Bruce and the teacher had done a great job of stalling. They had talked about Incaparina, passed out the pamphlets we had, read through the recipes for this protein supplement. Then they started explaining the school lunch program, pointing out what would be built, where and ended by collecting the money for the program. This teacher should have been an actor or a politician. He has really cooperated with us and gone to a lot of work on this school lunch program. He collected a total of 330 pesos. That's enough money for 33 kids.

The nurse divided the mothers into groups of 8 for classes on Incaparina. She then vaccinated the kids that were there, about 20.

After the near disaster, we ate lunch at Señor Ferrero's (the junta president) along with the teachers. It rained while we ate, the first real rain since we arrived. We have had a couple of frosts which have raised heck with our gardens. Frost can occur anytime of year at this altitude. After an hour rest at the house we went back to the school and helped work on the pump for the well.[8]

Meanwhile, we were also trying to better our own conditions. We rigged up a shower, a barrel painted black with a shower head on the bottom that we hoisted up on the wall out in back of the hacienda. A bright sunny day, which was the norm, gave us a reasonably warm shower that night. We also set up a battery operated radio and found a

---

[8] Gary Peterson, *Colombian Diary* – Feb. 16, 1965.

Patio inside our hacienda

station in the Netherlands Antilles that broadcasted in English for an hour every night. Tuning into this station one night, we listened to Winston Churchill's funeral.

I remember the first reports of Marines landing in Vietnam to guard the ports. This didn't seem to be a big deal and we weren't too concerned until the scattered units ballooned to a full division. Then we began to think, "wait a minute, this could get completely out of hand."

The hacienda we were staying in was, in its day, probably a real show piece. It consists of several buildings attached end to end forming a ring of buildings around a courtyard with a planter in the middle. At one time it had had running water, with bathrooms, showers, and electric lights powered by its own generator. The water came from a pipe connected to a water tank up in the mountainside which provided water and water pressure. This had been a self contained, mansion, but all was now run down and in disrepair. About the only thing that still worked was the generator.

Besides the two rooms we occupied, the rest of the hacienda was used by the family that oversaw the farm for the owner. There was a mother, two small girls and four boys. There was apparently a father, but we never saw him. The oldest boy would fire up the generator for an hour at night – sometimes – it was pretty irregular, so we depended mostly on candle light and a gas lantern.

With gardens moving along fairly well and progress being made on the lunch program, we decided to tackle the protein problem. There was the Incaparina, but we were pretty helpless when it came to preparing meals with the stuff, so we opted for rabbits. After some searching, we picked up nine rabbits in Tunja from a Peace Corps couple that was going states side. We built rabbit pens and within a month we had bunnies. Problem was, the people were not used to bunnies, so we needed a means of teaching them how to serve rabbit, fried, baked or even hasenpfeffer. A mother's club was the obvious answer, but we were not making much progress organizing clubs with the unenthusiastic cooperation we were getting from the nurse. We tried to get Dr. Cortez to apply some pressure. He tried, but even his intervention didn't help much.

Sporadic progress was made on the community aqueduct. "The engineer was out and said they were about ready to construct the tanks and lay pipe for the aqueduct."[9] But

---

[9] Gary Peterson, *Colombian Diary,* Mar. 15, 1965.

then long stretches of time would pass without any meaningful advancement. It was all very frustrating.

Latrines went better. "I went to the Salud Pulica (Public Health) again and this time Dr. Cortez went with me. Well, the man is supposed to be out next Thursday with 10 latrines and 2 doors to fix the school's latrines."[10] Outhouses were not uncommon in our veredas, but not every home had one. Our objective was 100% coverage. Slowly we made progress in that direction.

In spite of progress in many areas, the critical program of *Clube de Ama Casa* (Mother's Club) was just going nowhere. Bruce and I organized several get togethers and the nurse even showed up for a few and actually laid out a schedule for weekly meetings. Then she missed a couple, so we tried to keep them going.

Bruce and the little family in front of "our" hacienda.

I went to the Mother's Club meeting today prepared to give a class on gardens, but low and behold, the nurse showed and ahead of time. I couldn't believe it. She gave a class on how to take measurements for making a blouse. One poor woman who couldn't count or read numbers was asked to demonstrate. She could not begin to carry out the task and was embarrassed. I felt so sorry for her. But the nurse seems to have no compassion or sensitivity about these things.[11]

Then the nurse missed the next two meetings. Frustrated, Bruce and I talked to Dr. Cortez who seemed at a loss as to how to motivate the nurse. He did suggest we might use a mejoradora from his office in Tunja. We discussed this as a solution, but decided bus schedules were too undependable and the distance too great to make this feasible. We needed another answer.

A solution evolved during our first group conference. After four months in country, Colombia '64 finally had its get together, a month late. All the Volunteers except for two departments gathered in Bogotá then left by chartered bus for Melgar, a resort town between Bogotá and Ibagué down in the hot country.

---

[10] Gary Peterson, *Colombian Diary*, Feb. 25, 1965.
[11] Ibid.

We stayed in a true tourist hotel frequented by rich *Bogotános*. There were meetings mornings and afternoons, but plenty of time to indulge in the Olympic sized swimming pool and the pool side bar. The food was wonderful and the chance to exchange war stories memorable.

There was a U.S. military unit staying there at the same time. I believe they were in country to train the Colombian army in tank tactics. Good guys and we got along with them famously.

There were also a few PCVs from other groups there vacationing. One of these "tourists," a gal, challenged some of the guys in our group to a swimming race. Her confidence raised suspicions and a probing inquiry. Finally one of her friends fessed up that this gal had won a bronze medal in the 1964 Olympics.

Betsy at poolside in Melgar.

Now that there was full disclosure as to the capabilities of this ringer, our side insisted on evening the odds. She would have to race against four guys in relay – one length for each of our guys and four lengths for the ace. Seemed only fair.

In spite of our conniving, the natator won easily, coasting effortlessly the last few yards.

Carol Oakes remembers the party vividly and some of the innovations our group was capable of on these types of special occasions:

Can anyone forget Melgar? And Frankie (one of the Spanish instructors from training) joined us for a wild party. What a time we had there – on some of the stories I plead the fifth. There was the water skiing in the pool on foot which consisted of holding on to a rope being pulled by other people running alongside the pool – I have a picture of Jerry Schaffer being one of the victims; – floating the furniture in the pool so we would have some-thing to

Margaret taking a stroll at the resort in Melgar.

134

hold our drinks. I also re-member Carol Tobash (Scharmer) and I going to the local tienda to get cases of Coca Cola to mix with the rum for Cuba Libres – we borrowed a wheel barrow to carry everything back to the hotel.[12]

After two days of resort living, it was back to Bogotá for more meetings and a visit to the Rockefeller agricultural experiment farms. It was during these meetings in Bogotá that the possibility of a site change involving Boyacá and Cauca was discussed. With the problems we were having trying to keep the mother's clubs in our veredas running, thanks to the uncooperative nurse, a PCV nutritionist could be the answer. Meanwhile, the district superintendent for southwestern Colombia wanted a male agricultural Volunteer at a *nucleo* in Caloto where there were now two girls from our group. It was agreed I would trade places with one of the girls.

So on May 18, 1965 after four and a half months in Boyacá I boarded a bus for Bogotá, the first leg in a journey to a totally different world, the kind of dichotomy possible only in Colombia, a country of not just variation, but extreme diversity. I was going from the high mountains of the Eastern Cordilleras to the lowland heat of the Cauca Valley, a different climate and a different population.

The bus I happened to catch that morning was a very modern Greyhound style bus, unusual on our mountain byways. Most of the busses we rode in the high country were similar to an American school bus, same hard bench seats, same windows that slide up and down, even the folding front door. It was on one of these mountain busses, a few weeks earlier, that I had the scariest ride of my life.

We were traveling south along this mountain highway so there were steep hillsides and cliffs on the right and a sheer drop off of thousands of feet on the left. It was a narrow two lane highway, though oiled, with traffic traveling in both directions.

We were moving along at a good clip when another bus passed us going at, what I thought was, an insane speed for this kind of road. Several passengers on our bus spoke up asking the driver why he let that *pendejo* (stupid one) pass him - how shameful. Of course, no self-respecting Colombian bus driver is going to let that kind of challenge go unanswered. After all, his *machismo* had just been called into question.

So our bus driver speeds up catches the other bus and passes him on an outside curve where he could not possibly see what was coming down the road. The passengers cheered and I began wishing the vehicle had come with seatbelts.

Now the other bus driver wasn't about to be humiliated in such a fashion and he crept

Bus depot in Tunja

[12] Carol Ford, personal email, Jun 30, 2009.

135

back up behind our bus waiting for a little open road so he could further aggravate an already out of control situation. Sure enough, we hit a straight stretch and he pulled out to make his run. Both busses stayed side by side for a while until the other bus pulled ahead a half mile down the road. It was obvious our bus did not have the engine power the other bus had.

Amazingly, no one on the bus, except me, seemed to be the slightest bit concerned about a real disaster in the making. I had visions of our bus colliding with another bus, or truck, leaving bodies strewn along the highway for half a mile.

Instead our driver was getting a razzing from his passengers. But the old boy still had a couple of tricks up his sleeve. He dropped back a little and waited. I can only suppose he had driven this highway a thousand times and knew every corner and turn in the road. He waited until we were going downhill and were approaching an inside curve, then he gunned his engine and shot down the road. I held my breath and eyed the back emergency door calculating how long it would take me to get to the door and out the back of the bus as it sailed off the road and over the edge of the cliff. I didn't figure I had much of a chance of making it.

Our driver caught the other bus right on the turn and he pulled to the inside just as we rounded that curve and came up on an absolutely blind outside curve where he could not see more than a few yards down the road. Thanks to the downhill run and the inside turn, he had the advantage over the other driver. He cut inside the other bus and swerved back in front, passing him before the outside curve. I told myself he would have abandoned the maneuver if he had seen another vehicle heading our way. But I'm not sure he had the time, and certainly not the inclination.

Once ahead, our driver made sure the other bus never had a chance to regain the lead. He swerved into the other lane if there was an attempt to pass. We turned off at Ventaquemada and the other bus sailed on down the road. As we rolled into town the passengers cheered and waved anything they had handy. Several men offered to stand the driver to a beer or two at the local pub. I needed something a bit stronger than a beer. That was the most exciting bus ride I ever had and one I never wish to repeat.

The school bus type vehicles operated in the high country. In the low lands, where I was headed, the closed in buses gave way to an open-air version, no doors, no windows, but usually lots of color. The paint schemes and decorations might be garish, bright or theme oriented, but were invariably imaginative and individualistic.

There were also trains if you weren't in a hurry. Train tracks often paralleled valley roads, but climbed their own routes through the mountains. These were steam-engine trains like the one Bruce and I road to Bogotá a time or two when the busses weren't running.

> You wouldn't believe this train [I wrote at the time], just like something out of the old west, wooden seats, the door at one end of the car kept flying open, banging and making a terrible racket. The bathroom was little more than a hole in the floor. It didn't have glass windows, just a kind of wooden shutter that you could pull down.[13]

These trains stopped at every town and road crossing.

---

[13] Gary Peterson, *Colombian Diary,* Feb. 17, 1965.

While I traveled west to the Cauca Valley, Carolyn Hawkins was making her way east to the high country of the Boyacá mountains.

This was quite a transition from the tropics to 9,000 feet in elevation. I lived in the health clinic until my apartment was finished, which an advance on my rent helped to complete. My accommodations were quite luxurious compared to Bruce's and other Volunteers. I had a bedroom and a separate kitchen on the upper level of the Mendes family home. The bathroom was shared with another boarder. The doorbell was the family dog, Chitan. The security system, along with the dog, was the concrete wall with broken glass chards mortared in at the top. There was running cold water which was rationed as well as the lights. Taking those cold showers was always a torture, but at least there was a bathroom. Of course, to purify the water, boiling was necessary or adding the (what were those tablets called?).

Not having an English speaking roommate certainly facilitated the learning of the language. When you hear Spanish the first thing in the morning and the last thing at night, it sticks with you.

Shopping for groceries meant a trip to Tunja by bus with the locals taking their wares to market. It was about a half-hour trip and would be something like our farmer's markets in the states. Learning to barter was a fun project. There were no plastic bags or paper sacks, just woven bags. These people were already living "green", but things may have changed since 1965.[14]

Market in Tunja.

While Carolyn was settling in, Bruce continued working on projects he and I had started, such as the school lunch program.

Gary and I had collected some initial seed money to build an outdoor covered kitchen area where food could be prepared. We put down a concrete base, built a brick fireplace, and put a roof over the area. Our plans were to receive food from Caritas and provide lunch each day. It took months, but we did receive our first shipment of food. Then things fell apart. Something happened at the port where the food was off-loaded and no more

---

[14] Carolyn Hawkins Denton, "Memories of Caloto, Valle de Cauca and Ventaquemada, Boyaca," Jul. 13, 2009.

Bruce tending the rabbits.

food was delivered. We felt bad for the folks who had invested in this project so we distributed the 800 pounds of food we had received to the stakeholders.[15]

Bruce and I had started raising rabbits at our house. Though it was slow going while I was there, after I left this enterprise really took off.

Rabbits were a hit [Bruce recalls] and I probably had somewhere in the neighborhood of a dozen projects. Generally the hutches were made of wood and chicken wire and a couple levels high. After a few months most of the smaller cages were filled with an average of 15-20 rabbits.

One enterprising farmer built his cages on the ground and would let his rabbits out each day to graze in a chicken wire enclosed yard. At night he'd return them to their cages. The only problem was catching them at the end of the day.

And then I ran into Silvino Munoz. He actually lived in another vereda closer to Ventaquemada but he was interested. He wanted a garden and then he wanted rabbits. We built both projects. Then he wanted a more secure income source and we began a chicken project. He sold his one cow and built a chicken house that was really nicer than his own home. He had electricity since he lived along the highway so he could provide heat for chicks. 200 Rhode Island Red layers arrived and he began his project. During one visit he told me that he was receiving 110 eggs a day on average from his chickens.

Silvino was a leader in his vereda and became a lifelong friend to me and my family. After I left Colombia, we exchanged Christmas cards for the next 40 years. He sent a picture of his family and I sent one of mine. He moved to Tunja and left the farm when he was in his 70's and moved in with his daughter. She wrote his Christmas letters the past ten years. He died at 94 about two years ago. The family has kept up the tradition and we still exchange cards at Christmas. Carolyn became a steadfast friend too and even hosted his granddaughter in her home as an exchange student in high school. This was one of the best examples of the Peace Corps developing a people to people approach.[16]

A friend from Ventaquemada, who now lives in Tunja, and I have been maintaining correspondence for 43 years [Carolyn Hawkins writes in her memoirs]. I had offered to sponsor her daughter to come to the U.S. to experience one year of school here, but she was not financially able, being a

---

[15] Bruce Borrud, personal email, Jul. 9, 2009.
[16] Ibid.

single parent. But she asked if her niece could come. So the school year 2005-06 we had Carolina Munoz Bernal living with us and attending high school.[17]

Another wonderful friend [Bruce continues] was Luis Eduardo Moreno. He lived high up on the paramo-higher country where it was cold. He completed a garden and rabbit project. And we developed two fish tanks at his home.

In 1976 I returned to Colombia with my wife Kathy to show her around. Unannounced we hiked up to the Paramo to see Luis Eduardo since I had spent lots of time at his farm. We had exchanged cards as well over the years, but he wasn't aware of our arrival. We ran into him at a tienda on the way up the mountain and he led us to his home.

Upon arriving, he ushered us into his living room and sat us down for a *"tinto."* On one of the living room walls was a framed enlarged picture of our family. He had taken one of our Christmas pictures and had his son enlarged it (he worked in a photo studio) for framing. People to people once again. Don Luis passed away in the 1980's.[18]

The fish tanks Bruce speaks of were started after I left Boyacá. This was another source of protein, but more than that, they were small commercial projects that could produce real revenue for the operator.

Somewhere along the way I heard that fish were available to distribute from the fish hatchery at Lake Tota near Sogamoso [Bruce explains]. So I gathered information on the building of fish tanks and the care of fish. I had a number of farmers who already had man-made ponds for their animals and several others that were willing to construct them. One farmer even built a small house near his outlying ponds so that a caretaker could live there and protect the lake from predators. In all I believe we had seven ponds and some 16,000 fingerlings (trout I believe) were delivered or we picked them up at Lake Tota.[19]

And finally there were two projects, the aqueduct and reforestation, that just never got off the ground while I was in Boyacá even though they were two of the desires expressed at our very first junta meeting.

Probably the greatest need in our area was a reliable water source in the dry months [Bruce reflects]. For almost six months there was little to no rain. Kids left school each day to walk to the *quebrada* (stream) and haul up buckets of water for the family to use. This was probably a four mile round trip plus hauling uphill 10-20 pounds of water.

Engineers from Tunja had designed a plan to capture the water on the paramo and send it down by galvanized pipe to the vereda homes. However, the government had no money to do this. I traveled to Bogotá several times with

---

[17] Carolyn Hawkins Denton, "Memories of Caloto, Valle de Cauca and Ventaquemada, Boyaca," Jul. 13, 2009.

[18] Bruce Borrud, personal email, Jul. 9, 2009.

[19] Ibid.

vereda leaders and we went with the engineering plans to seek help from the Alianza Para El Progreso.

Fortunately, I worked with an embassy fellow named Jaime Manzano (an American) who was sympathetic to our cause. We requested 50,000 pesos for this project ($2000-$3000) at the time. We needed to build a concrete collection tank and install two miles of galvanized pipe to 125 homes. About a month before I left Colombia in July 1966 we received approval. The men in the vereda would do all the work and when I left trenching was underway and the collection tank had been built. Each home scheduled to receive water would have a single spigot come to the edge of their property so it was not an indoor plumbing project by any means.

Reforestation was another need, one of those expressed in one of the first meetings we had with the vereda juntas. We requested 2000 trees from the government and distributed them to families who could plant them. 1200 were eucalyptus and over 600 were pine trees. They went quickly.

As I look over my daily diary I realize again that the Peace Corps was established to change lives for the better. It had that impact on me and I believe the folks of Puente Piedra, Supata, and Montoya knew that an American cared enough for their welfare to spend two years of his life living and working with them.[20]

After all our problems with the nurse in Venaquemada, by the time Carolyn got there, she had been replaced and the new nurse seemed much more mature and responsible.

The public health nurse and her son and daughter became my closest friends, other than Bruce [Carolyn writes]. This nurse, Eva, had a patient ready to go into labor and put me to work getting things set up. What an exciting experience. This was this woman's fifth child. The couple was so appreciative and showered us with fresh eggs and other produce as a way of payment. The doctor, who traveled from Bogotá once a month to the clinic, found all was taken care of very well. There was a female dentist from Bogotá who also visited the clinic monthly.

Bruce and I would get together at least on the weekends and I would try out my culinary skills on him. We shared a horse, Paso Doble, to use for our treks into the campo (I didn't use him much). Bruce did a lot with nutrition using his chicken projects, fish stocking of lakes and school gardens while I taught mothers how to use these products for more nutritious meals.

The young people were always pleading that I teach them English which we were encouraged not to do, but I yielded. It turned out to be way too many in the class room to be very effective. There was another kind of teaching which I enjoyed doing which was the Laubach method for teaching a Colombian how to read and write his own language.

---

[20] Bruce Borrud, personal email, Jul. 9, 2009.

When the central plaza was remodeled, Bruce and I contributed to have a bench there with the plaque noting it was donated by Peace Corps. So if you go to Ventaquemada in Boyacá some day, see if it is still there.

The "padre" in the village urged me to partake in the mass as a sign that we are all brothers and sisters. Of course, coming from the Southern Baptist tradition, this was very awkward for me. It seemed so odd to me that the men were on one side of the church and the women on another. As in most villages, the cathedral was the largest structure in town. One of the families there asked me to be their daughter's "*madrina*" and that was quite a festive day and entailed a lot of food preparation.

Bruce was fortunate to have a visit from his parents and we did some traveling together to see other points of interest, i.e. Lenguasaque where there was a "ruana" co-op. I came back with several of these Colombian panchos.

For Christmas, I went with my nurse friend, Eva, to visit her family on the coast in a little town called Aracataca. That is, as it turns out, the home town of the acclaimed Colombian author Gabriel Garcia Marquez. While there, she took me to see Santa Marta and the beach. Beautiful.[21]

South of Bruce and Carolyn's site at Ventquemada, on toward Bogotá, two other male Volunteers from our group were stationed. These were Brian McMahon, the Colorado cowboy and Dartmouth alum, and Jerold Schaefer of Neenah, Wisconsin. Jerry was a graduate of the University of Wisconsin in, what else, dairy and foods industries. Though dairy cows were somewhat scarce in the mountains of Boyacá, the agricultural background would serve Jerry well.

Jerold Schaefer

I was assigned to Guateque with Brian [Jerry writes]. Guateque was a small town in Boyacá of around 4000 population. It was about a 4 hour bus ride from Bogotá in an area called Valle de Tenza. It's on a road leading to the Llanos but still in the mountains.

Brian and I were lucky to have the backing of the Padre in Guateque, unlike some other Volunteers. He invited us to dinner the first night in town, probably to check us out, and announced on the church speakers the next day that we were from the *Corpo de Paz* and that we were there to help improve their lives. This would prove to be quite a task since our Spanish was rotten (Brian's better than mine) and none of us really knew where to start.

We eventually moved out of town to our exact site which was an hour walk from town towards the river. A new school had been built after the old school was damaged in an earthquake. The back wall had a large crack and was considered unstable. Since this was the only unoccupied building in the area we decided to move in. After some major repairs, the one room school became a

[21] Carolyn Hawkins Denton, "Memories of Caloto, Valle de Cauca and Ventaquemada, Boyaca," Jul. 13, 2009.

decent home. With the new school nearby, we had easy access to the students to start some "4H" programs.

Our main projects were planting gardens and raising rabbits and chickens. I think the most success was in the raising and distribution of rabbits to the school kids. As time went on and after we moved into the town, we once had a total of between 60 to 70 rabbits in cages in our back yard. Since it was much easier to work with the kids, we would help them build rabbit cages at their homes and then provide them with a pair of rabbits. Instructions on feeding and caring was easy. Getting them to kill and eat the cute bunnies was more difficult.

After about 3 months, we found that most of our time was being consumed in cooking, washing and taking care of our daily needs. So, we hired a local woman to cook and wash our clothes. Rosa stayed with us for the whole two years and, in fact, continued on with the next generation of Volunteers that eventually replaced us.

After 6 months we moved back into Guataque and rented a house along with two Colombians from the Public Health Dept - Vincent and Juan. At this point we became more involved in organizing groups and helped built two aqueducts to provide water to a school. We helped another group obtain assistance from PINA and constructed a community kitchen at another school.

Vincent, who I mentioned above, became a life long friend. After the Peace Corps he came to the States and lived with my family in Wisconsin for 6 months. Later, he attended the University of Southern Illinois to study English for 6 months. He then returned to Colombia and eventually opened 5 retail athletic shoe stores and put 4 kids through college.

Brian stayed in Guateque for about a year and then moved to Bogotá due to an asthmatic condition. He finished out his time working on various agriculture programs in Bogotá.

A large man-made reservoir has been built since I left Guateque and the area has apparently become a resort location. I was sent to Colombia in 2000 by my company but was unable to visit my old site due to the campo violence at that time. Too many kidnappings and I was not sure who would have paid the ransom money.[22]

Brian McMahon

Denny Burkholder relates a few experiences he had with Brian and some of his cow punching antics.

Brian was part of a whole bunch of crazy memories for me. One was the Christmas bullfight in some little town up north where they had several medium sized steers for the local macho toreador wannabes to fight. It was kind of pathetic, so Brian (braced with ample hops) gimps into the arena, stares down a steer and grabs it *a la* cowboy mode and throws it to the ground. The crow did not appreciate the fine rodeo style steer wrestling demonstration and booed because he spoiled their fun. I laughed 'til beer spewed out of my nose.

---

[22] Jerold Schaefer, personal email, Jun. 15, 2009.

Brian really was a cowboy and knew how to handle animals. He was the only guy who ever made my horse behave.[23]

Arriving in 1966 among the health girls, discussed in various chapters, was Brian's sister, Maureen. The brother and sister were both in the same department, Boyacá, though they didn't often meet. Still this was another first for the Peace Corps and it was part of our group's legacy.

Brian and I were the only brother/sister team sent to the same country [Maureen remembers]. We overlapped my first year in Sogamoso and Brian's second year in Guateque. We did meet up occasionally, usually in Bogotá on weekends and went to some great PC parties. I can remember dancing the night away to the Rolling Stones and "Satisfaction." We also went to see "Cat Ballou" (the cowboy spoof-movie with Lee Marvin) which, of course, was sub-titled in Spanish. Having hailed from Colorado, Brian and I roared with laughter at all the American jokes, which obviously suffered in the translation, because more often than not, we were the only two laughing out loud in an otherwise silent movie theater.[24]

Southern Boyacá was, indeed, an interesting part of Colombia. The people, the descendants of the ancient Chibchas, were generally industrious and welcoming, though more taciturn than the inhabitance of the lower valleys and coasts. Still, when among friends, they were as warm and congenial as any people anywhere.

The Congressional act that created the Peace Corps stated two of the three purposes of the organization were to promote understanding between the U.S. and the country served. Here in the high mountains of Boyacá lifelong friendships were formed between citizens of the two countries. Certainly the people to people part of Peace Corps work was a success here in these eastern mountains of Colombia.

---

[23] Dennis Burkholder, personal email to Jim Finkler, Jan. 29, 2009.
[24] Maureen McMahon Hibbott, personal email, Aug. 10, 2009.

9
NORTHERN BOYACÁ AND EAST INTO THE LLANOS

North of Tunja, the capital of Boyacá, the department spreads eastward out onto the Llanos. Still in the mountains, but not far from the great plains of Colombia were two couples from Colombia '64. These were the Lenkners who had removed from Purifacacion, Tolima to Sogamoso, Boyacá and Janice and Geoffrey Abbott stationed at La Trinidad. The Abbotts, from Greenwich, Connecticut, had been the first married couple to arrive in Lincoln and had earned the suspicion of the shrinks because they asked for a change in dormitory rooms.

We survived the training in Nebraska and Puerto Rico to find ourselves in the mountains of Colombia [Geoffrey writes]. As for our vereda, La Trinidad, outside Duitama in Boyacá, I remember that we did a lot of walking. The bus to the market in Duitama ran only twice a week, so any other time we needed to get to the main highway, or into town, we walked. I remember the figure 7 - whether it was 7 kilometers or 7 miles I am not sure. All I know is that for 12 pesos, if we had it, we could get a taxi from the market to our house on the plaza in La Trinidad. The problem was, with no way to contact said taxi service from La T., we had no alternative except the bus or walk the 7 to get from La T. to town.

When we took the taxi, we often had the same driver, who for some reason thought we were French. When the woman Colombian Peace Corps Director happened to get that same driver to take her from Duitama to La Trinidad for her annual tour or site review, she became confused when she asked if he knew where the Americanos lived. She wondered if she was going to the right place when he said he knew where the French people lived.

We relied a great deal upon the three women ETV PCVs in Duitama, Jeannie, Judy and Elaine, the tall Texan. They were our best guides: giving us a place to crash when in Duitama, feeding us, providing social contact with other Volunteers, counseling for culture shock, and just being good friends…visiting us in La Trinidad for gatherings, providing the rum (was that Ron Negro?).

Our house on the plaza in La Trinidad had been started as a tienda by our landlord, Don Jose De Los Angeles Avendano, or Lara for short. Somehow we worked out his finishing the upstairs as living quarters by paying, 18 months rent in advance. It worked out well, and with some kitchen cabinets and living room table work, we managed a workable home. A lending library worked well; nutrition classes on cooking and baking with a bit of Incaparina thrown in, rabbits in the back and we were set.

There was no running water, so daily trips to the river were in order. We did have electricity at times, even 110 volts upon occasion… enabling us to sneak in a small refrigerator, which we put upstairs in a bedroom where our helpful local "maid" Zenaida was not invited. How that refrigerator survived while suffering power failures and low voltage half the time, I never figured out.

Janice and I considered our area well developed, with one farmer up the river well ensconced with Purina feeds which supplied his large egg farm. Others grew garlic, potatoes, corn, etc. We introduced rabbits to a minor degree and generally interacted with the locals, but felt we were somewhat superfluous. Our site review/recommendation at our departure was that a replacement was in no way necessary. As is customary with bureaucracies, our evaluation was ignored, and we heard sometime later that replacement PCVs had been sent to La Trinidad.[1]

To the east of Duitama, not far from the boundary of the Cordillera Oriental where Boyacá drops precipitously down onto the Llanos, was the ancient town of Sogamoso, the old religious center of the Chibcha nation. The Lenkners were stationed in a village just outside Sogamoso, Firavitoba, after their initial posting at Purificación, Tolima. Charlie describes their new situation.

We were tickled to be in our new site. By that time orientation was small potatoes. Bought a mattress and bunked in a room in the Puesto de Salud, complete with a picture of JFK. There was water and a flush toilet. Hog heaven! We arranged to take our meals at a "hotel" on the corner of the municipal square, as opposed to the church square. It was owned and run by Don Gabriel and Doña Lola, both white haired and diminutive, prototype grandparents, having the patient calm natures that come to some with advanced age. It was at their table we became hooked on *changua* and learned to get along with odd chicken parts and bits of sheep hide in that delicious soup.

In short order, we found a house with a tall brick wall topped with roof tiles that ran between the front room and the detached kitchen. The other room was our bedroom. Both rooms were joined on the front by a nice covered porch walkway. Under the instruction of neighbor kids we made mud "plaster" and replastered the walls.

Firavitoba had municipal water and electricity and both functioned reliably. We had the common square tank, *alberca*, with a faucet where we laundered ourselves more than clothes. We hired a single mother for the laundry, soup for Oso (our dog) and house sitting if we were away.

Fleas, not mosquitoes, were the problem in the cold country. We went through many plastic puffer bottles of Peace Corps supplied benzene hexacloride, flea powder. And of course any bus ride was a reinfection opportunity. It was a small price to pay for the convenience of a trusted house sitter.

Not being used to or adept at the back streets and alley elimination mode of the region and as a demonstration, we hoped, it was not too long before we obtained one of the government model modular out-houses on site and erected. I do not recall ours having a door as sold (at a nominal fee). That was minor. The seat being the edge of an upended cement culvert, we didn't camp or read there, quick in and out. But it saved the trek down the street to the flusher at the Puesto.[2]

[1] Geoffrey Abbott, personal email, Aug. 18, 2009.
[2] Charlie Lenkner, personal email, Aug. 18, 2009.

Once settled, the Lenkners took note of their new surroundings. The geography and sociology were completely different than the Magdalena Valley they just came from.

What I'll call the Sogamoso Valley had some interesting common and unique aspects that were part of the Colombian picture [Charlie observes]. There were holdings of good valley land as well as hillside farm land which some campesinos owned. There were a few tractors, but it seemed most of it was farmed the *puro* campesino way – plow and oxen. Not all was tilled as there was pasture as well. Kikuyu grass from African Kenya was holding much of it together and limiting the erosion after centuries of use.

Constant grazing by small ruminants and equines, over the years, had had a negative effect on the hills. But I think it was not as great as firewood extraction. It was down to cutting brush with eucalyptus trees filling in where they would grow, generally the lower elevations. Reforestation would have been a viable program anywhere the government funding and infrastructure was available.

Around Firavitoba the valley grazing supported traditional dairy enterprises. There were some good sized, and in good flesh, Holsteins as well as a dual purpose breed of Normandy cattle, *Normandos*.

"Plowing" was done by the campesinos with wooden framed plows and oxen yoked by a head yoke. That is a stout timber shaped and then lashed to the horns of the animals so propulsion was mostly thru the neck. The critters being used by poor folks were dairy or dairy cross. They plowed with heads thrown back, noses up.

Tilling the soil with oxen using the horn yoke.

A project pending, which we left to our replacements, was the attempt to convert to a version of a pioneer ox yoke where the animals pushed into it with the their shoulders and body vs neck and vertebrae. Ox goading could get pretty serious, we hoped the conversion would help stop some of the suffering and the bawling.

A less involved outreach was getting a campesino to try a new wheat variety available from the *Caja Agropicaria*. The traditional custom was to save part of the crop for seed. Maybe not all bad because, if it lived to produce seed-wheat it must be adapted, but the government backed plant-breeder-developed seed was likely to have some advantages.

I made a deal with a cooperative and a progressive compesino to buy the seed if he would use it and then pay me back from income from the harvest. He put it on a parcel of valley land, seeded well and in proper quantity and obtained a great stand with an estimated yield of four times the usual production. We were about out of there so I didn't collect on the advance. I'd had my reward and he'd exhibited much initiative and resourcefulness. I hope that there was a demonstration effect as his neighbors passed by.[3]

Besides agriculture, the Lenkner's new area had some industry. This was a unique aspect of their site, producing a class of people distinct from the campesino farmers. Interestingly, these factory workers were not receptive to the Volunteer's ideas as Charlie recalls.

Impacting at least Sogamoso, Duitama, Firavitoba and Isa was the "French" steel mill at Belencito. A part of the rural population had access to good industrial jobs. The men from Firavitoba who worked there were observably different than those without that opportunity. They had nice suits for dress up, wrist watches, ten speed bikes and transistor radios. They were not much interested in our Peace Corps work and may have been a bit resentful. They were certainly suspicious of our motives. Partially they may have been not only economically empowered, but knew or cared more about our place and actions internationally. They were among those assuming we had CIA connections.

As far as economic development, the wages from Belencito had a limited multiplier effect because their money was not being spread much beyond the noted consumer items. They seemed not to have been motivated regarding increased consumerism with respect to homes, spouses and offspring.[4]

In spite of having an industrial plant in the vicinity, Firavitoba and, for that matter Sogamoso, conformed to the usual patterns of Colombian rural society which included the ever present open air market.

Sogamoso like Duitama and other larger towns had a grand weekly market served by market busses from the villages [Charlie remembers]. Volunteers loved it. Not only could we grocery shop, but we visited with other Volunteers and the vendors that followed the circuit.

The woman selling wooden spoons, bowls & baskets was on the ornery side. It seemed that a beer was her idea of a snack but she was strong. If you didn't buy her a beer or purchase something from her or even if you did she liked to pinch male Volunteer's bottoms. She could easily bring tears to your eyes, felt like vice-grips, not just hard working thumb and index finger.

The vendors looked out for us. If they saw pickpockets working the crowd they would casually scratch their cheek using all four fingers when they had

[3] Charlie Lenkner, personal email, Aug. 18, 2009.
[4] Ibid.

your eye. I think they wanted to make sure they got our money and not the thief. We did eat well.[5]

Couples made particularly good teams for the work we were to be doing in Colombia. While Charlie labored on the agricultural side, Melody tackled the nutritional and food preparation needs, especially the ever present protein deficiency.

Incaparina was our assignment [Melody writes], so being dutiful, we got little bags of the stuff and began to ponder how to get the word out. The need was obvious. I still have a vivid memory of one mother's little "*patojito*" languishing in her arms, his sparse little hair barely covering his scalp and his distended tummy sticking out below his grimy t-shirt. He was one for whom Incaparina was too late.

The first time I opened up a bag of the precious Incaparina, the smell of the flour was enough to knock my socks off, the taste being the only rival to the smell. How in the world do you peddle this disgusting stuff to a culture that is not only nutritionally naive, but certainly doesn't cook from recipes?

Well, I gathered up a group of women, lectured them on the importance of protein while demonstrating how to make cookies from Incaparina in my little electric skillet. I did find that if you added enough sugar and oil you could cover the taste, kind of like zucchini bread. Working with women one on one was more successful and I have very strong memories of going into the little homes where they cooked over an open fire, resulting in the smell of smoke permeated the inside of the house, those who dwelt within and any visitor who came near.

I tried other recipes with Incaparina including pancakes. One mom did take my lecture to heart and the evidence of the power of protein soon began to show in her toddler who became a chunky version of his former self.

We took long treks to distant veredas on our horses spreading the word about rabbits, gardens and nutrition, especially the need to eat your own eggs and chickens.....shouldn't be too much of a cultural switch, right? That's what we thought, until a young mother, looking older than dirt, explained to me that she could sell an egg and buy a pound of rice, which would go a lot further to feed her family than one egg. Oh, right I hadn't thought of that.

As we visited, we were always welcome and always offered a meal, most of which consisted of large bowls of unseasoned boiled potatoes. I eventually got to where I could finish half a bowl without having my throat close unmercifully around the dry food. The thing that would take the cake, though, is when after having consumed this meal, and we were getting ready to take our leave, they would inevitably grace us with a gift of a basket of eggs, their week's savings and all the protein that we had been lecturing them about was going home with us.[6]

Market day made a big impression on Melody just as it had on Charlie. And she also remembers the lady with the iron grip that liked to pinch the gringos.

---

[5] Charlie Lenkner, personal email, Aug. 18, 2009.
[6] Melody Lenkner, personal email, Aug. 21, 2009.

148

I loved the market and everything that went with Market Day from the ride on the bus to get there, all the jostling of folks getting on the bus with their goods and the chickens cackling on top of the bus, to the beautiful *muchilas* that we brought to carry our goods home in. The colors of the market were astounding almost as colorful as the vendors, one in particular stands out. She was a buxom lady with a round body dressed in faded black with a hat to match. Her only jewels being the wide toothless smile that she always greeted us with and her chubby fingers with which she routinely pinched Charlie's butt. In addition to the beautiful and colorful woven blankets and carefully crafted gleaming pottery, the array of vegetables also created a blaze of color.

Market day in Boyaca.

Then there was the great "fast food" that we could purchase while there. My absolute favorite was a lovely greasy sack of little tiny potatoes that had been boiled in that good tasting *manteca* (oil or lard) that they sold.

The need for soaking our vegetables in iodine became readily apparent when I watched a young boy stand on a container of beautiful red tomatoes and pee on the container of equally beautiful red tomatoes right next to it, enough to gag a maggot.

149

While I'm on the topic of iodine, when we first arrived in country we were pretty dutiful about the iodine thing. Once out in a distant vereda, we were served up a delicious looking fruit drink, into which, while the family wasn't looking, we slipped our iodine. When everyone returned to the table, all eyes were on our drinks which were turning a lovely purple color.

Others have mentioned the trips to the Crem Helado for our fix of American style food, but I don't remember anyone mentioning the big warnings that we had from Peace Corps headquarters about how laden the food was with fecal material. This, of course, did not deter us. We were more than happy to indulge in "fecal splits" with every trip to Bogotá. Maybe it was this or maybe it was the fact that our due diligence with the iodine faded as time went on that resulted in a good case of worms that was identified upon my arrival in the States.[7]

With time in country, came a familiarity and an understanding of this society with customs so different from those in the United States. There were some real cultural eye openers for Melody.

I came to realize all the implications of the term "machismo." We realized that Charlie would never make it into the "in" crowd when all of the attempts of the Colombian men failed to get him to visit the whore houses with them and then to top that off, he had been married for a year, and there were no resulting offspring! Macho points - 0. Every time a Colombian male would state that his wife was married, but he wasn't, my hair would stand on end, although I tried to keep my face from reflecting that.

The real corker, though, was when the women began to cotton to the fact that here we had been married for over a year, and there were no babies. Quietly a couple of women sidled up to me to ask why that was. I shared with them the miracle of birth control pills, which I could buy over the counter at the local pharmacy, horse pills they were. It's a wonder I didn't develop some kind of horrible cancer from them, the dosage of estrogen being about 100 times what birth control pills eventually came to contain.

At any rate, I told them that they too could partake of this great breakthrough, but then recanted when I remembered that of course it was against their religion, what was I thinking? The women gave me a puzzled look, what was I talking about? They didn't know it was against their religion. All of their babies were the result of their husband's need to demonstrate his machismo. I spent a lot of time gritting my teeth, but was happy to share at any point in time exactly how to go about purchasing those horse pills.

Our town in Boyacá, Firavitoba, was very small. It was mostly a town square dominated by a Catholic church that was twice the size of the square, actually the size of a football field, that had been under construction since forever. My other teeth gritter was when I learned that the campesinos in their rags, eating their rice and potatoes, were tithing to pave the church with marble. It wasn't as galling to them, however, as the most common comment was that "this life is nothing but a valley of tears", their hopes being pinned on the next life.

---

[7] Melody Lenkner, personal email, Aug. 21, 2009.

On a happier note, the best thing about the culture was the wonderful music and the dances. We captured the music on 45 rpm discs that we brought home, but there is no way we could capture the dances. As opposed to the U.S. where dances are limited to age groups and little ones never come to a dance, it was a free for all in Colombia - little babies and old grammas and grandpas hopped around among the *jovens* (young people) with sheer joy.

The fiestas in the town square were a delight, too. I remember one such fiesta where the opening event was to be the sound of milk shooting into an empty bucket from a large milk cow. As the resident celebrity, I was offered the honor of accomplishing the task. Easy enough, the cow's teats were dripping milk. I grandly sat in the milking position, forgetting that I was a frank city girl, and began pulling on the teats waiting for the sound of the milk shooting into the bucket. Nothing. I pulled some more. Nothing. I pulled some more. Nothing. The crowd was beginning to become restless, when red in the face, I gave up the task and passed it on to much more capable hands.[8]

As in every society, Colombia had its share of the mentally unstable. Perhaps many that should have been treated were never discovered; they just dissolved into the lowest element covering their problem with alcohol. But occasionally people with mental problems did get help and sometimes Volunteers were part of the solution.

In those days it seems that Colombia dealt with the nonviolently insane by leaving them at liberty to sleep and lounge in parks [Charlie observes]. One of our young friends, a kid about sixth grade to junior high, had a father who had a nervous breakdown. His physical health was already compromised. We called around and I ended up taking him up to the state mental hospital in Tunja on the bus. He was discharged fairly soon and had been helped, in my judgment.[9]

Aside from the work, the fiestas and an incidental embarrassing moment, the Lenkners did enjoy the holidays, Christmas, bullfights (country style), and an incident with a local gent expressing his machismo.

In most matters of community life it appeared that the higher authority was ecclesiastical [Charlie writes]. Certainly the major church holidays or days marking special events and times saw large turn outs of all ages with banners, displays, pageants and short parades. It was meaningful and important to the people and the people were important to us, and the events were spectacular.

Christmas time was a nice season with occasional frosts and clear cold nights. We cut a small juniper tree from a too thick planting up the canyon near the water works (near where you could sometimes pick black berries, *moras*) and we decorated it with small native pottery figures, bird whistles and such. Powerful skyrockets of native manufacture were part of the fun as they were at other times as well. Something I enjoyed were the homemade hot air

---

[8] Melody Lenkner, personal email, Aug. 21, 2009.
[9] Charlie Lenkner, personal email, August 18, 2009.

balloons launched with small fires in the baskets. Surprisingly, I don't remember any related house or brush fires.

Popular bull fights involved any male with a horse or ruana wishing to taunt young bulls from the llanos country. Generally, it worked pretty well with an occasional run down and bashing, but no one was hauled off to the hospital.

The bulls were turned in 3-4 at a time. Not always did the matador get attacked by the bull he was tempting. Often due to infusions of beer, the matadors were a bit relaxed as well as not real swift a foot. I remember one *audante* (daring one) from a market who was loud and active and eager. *Fira! Isa! Siga! Sube! Dele dele!* He was focused on one bull and lurching toward it with his beer bottle in a hip pocket when he was targeted by a critter from behind. Bulls eye, right below the belt, "head center." I can still see the kid's torso as it was whip-lashed by the *toro*. Limber didn't save him all together. He was still limping when it came time for us to go home. Loading spuds up the back ladder of the bus was much slower and harder for him.

Don Jose ran a nice tienda & bakery out of a corner brick building that included the family home. He was polite, smart and interesting. He turned out great hearty whole wheat rolls called *morgoyas*. They were our choice for bread with our meals, good any time of day. Our relationship was familiar, conversational, not chummy. We enjoyed it and his product.

His tienda served beer and pop as beverages. It was like others in as much as you might see several horses outside with their tie ropes (often incorporated into the bridle) leading inside where their riders stood around enjoying a beer, or several, and visiting, beer in one hand and tie rope in the other. His tienda did not have the partially screened (head to knees) urinal in the corner as some did.

I'd had egg, raw, in my beer in other places but had not had it there. I don't remember how they got that egg neatly into the bottle. It did slide down the hatch about as slick as it did from the shell, as I recall.

One day we were in there waiting for the bread to come out of the oven, it was taking a spell and we were in no hurry. We were visiting, I had a beer and Melody had something else. She was at the counter visiting and I had sat down on a bench back against the front wall in a bit of a shadow. I had on my usual outer garment, a dark ruana and brown snapbrim Stetson.

In came a local, since removed to Bogotá. He spotted the redheaded gringa, by herself. The urbanite could not believe his great good fortune. He entered into the discussion with gusto, *mucho gusto* (pleased to meet you), and pretty much proceeded to take over the chatter. Don Jose let him gush until he was way over his head and then he introduced Don Carlos in the corner. I unfolded, stood up, walked over and shook his clammy hand at about the level of my belt.

When we were leaving Fira we said good-by to Don Jose. He wished us well and said we had lived with them with dignity. Good enough, I thought.[10]

Tejo was played about everywhere in Boyacá, though never, it seemed, anywhere else in the country. Two or four players were set up like horseshoes except instead of a stake there was a stone. On the stone was placed a paper capsule containing gun powder.

---

[10] Charlie Lenkner, personal email, August 18, 2009.

The players tossed metal discs instead of horseshoes. Scoring was similar to horseshoes, the closes disc got the points, but the prize was when a disc hit the capsule and exploded the gunpowder. "I think it is horseshoes with sparks and noise, maybe we should introduce it in this country."[11]

And there was always basketball, popular everywhere in Colombia, but particularly in the mountains where it replaced soccer as the preferred team sport. Soccer fields were scarce in the high country because what flat land there was, was used for growing crops. So Colombians were often very good at basketball, as was demonstrated in a game in Tunja. Charlie describes the contest.

> As for the basketball game on Thanksgiving '65 in Tunja, between the Volunteers and the National Police (N.P.) barracks, I still think Borrud masterminded the deal. We got snookered about as slick as the boys in Melgar were taken in by the lady swimmer. Now the fact that the "game" came in the afternoon of Thanksgiving, not long after all the turkeys came out of the oven may have just been chance, but I personally think it was set up that way by the sneaky National Police Commandant.
>
> So, we had the 10,000 ft. elevation, stuffed guts and there was the fact that the cops were plum serious, averaged 6' 5" and up, were in shape and skilled. I think all Colombians with NBA potential were "inducted" into the NP. Now in Fira, Isa and Sogamoso we did not see officers of this stature out guarding the streets.
>
> Despite the fact that we "had them beat" with our fine set of turkey-stuffed cheerleaders it was kind'a downhill once we walked into the gymnasium, fine hardwood floor, bleachers, gathering crowd and all.
>
> It looked like a long shot for us as the National's took the floor for their warm up drills. There was their stature, their ability, their very serious demeanor, maybe the silky, colorful uniforms added something in addition to the depth of their bench. Our old sweat-shirts and cutoff jeans seemed immediately out of place. I suppose no one even noticed the number 007 one of us sported.
>
> The game turned out about as you might expect. We were very gracious in defeat, good sports. The game was competitive if very one-sided and respectful, no rough stuff. That backwards over the head shot I took near the top of the key was not a wise-guy thing really. For one thing it was unexpected and came as close to going in as any of my best, more conventional attempts.
>
> Months later, as fate would have it, the last familiar face I would see as I was leaving Colombia was that of the N.P. Commandant from Tunja. It was the Commandant that collected the 300 pesos leaving the country tax. I'm sure he was sorry to see us go. And likewise on our part we were sadly nostalgic.[12]

Bruce Borrud, the accused instigator, remembers the game also. "Sounds about right to me. I know we were soundly defeated by the locals and of course the crowd was with

[11] Charlie Lenkner, Personal email, August 20, 2009
[12] Charlie Lenkner, personal email, Aug. 16, 2009.

them. I believe it was a charity event to raise money for a local group. Charlie's version is thoroughly sanctioned by number 007."[13]

Many of the stories, fables and novels of Colombia are set in the great expanses of eastern plains, the Llanos. The Lenkners, as with so many were drawn to this mysterious section of Colombia though their first contact was the result of a rather unpleasant incident.

I suppose the Llanos is much like any other frontier or interface with the unknown, it makes us curious, portends romance and adventure [Charlie muses]. All by way of saying I was curious about this wild and wide open expanse of Colombia.

After we had sized up our site a bit, it seemed like travel to the veredas (there may have been up to 14 of them) was in order. I collected one unused Peace Corps caballo and bought another good horse. The man we obtained her from was a nice friendly *hacindado* of above average means. He owned valley land, had milk cows and *Paseos* (breed of Colombian horse), liked basketball and had given us a dog of perhaps collie linage back a few generations. The dog was just a pup, fat and furry and full of good humor. We named him Oso. He was kind of a village fixture when grown. One old grandma friend would recite a poem, "*Oso, oso de donde venice*...(Oso, Oso, where do you come from…)" when they crossed paths.

While still a pup but gaining size, Oso was set upon by a larger dog that turned out to be rabid. Folks came running and told us he had been attacked, but the rabid bite was yet to be figured out. The attacker was, however, dispatched by a town marshal twosome team and thrown in a pasture kitty corner from our rented house. Probably because of our friendship with the Puesto de Salude nurse and her municipal employed husband, and a push by me, the head was in fact submitted for diagnosis.

We didn't wait for results however. Having heard descriptions of the sick dog's behavior and appearance we had already decided to throw ourselves on the mercies of Dr. Gifford & company. We had looked our dog over very carefully for damage after the incident and probably had our hands in the other dog's saliva.

Peace Corps Bogotá said to get our fannies in a taxi and come in. Then we would still follow directions - it was early in our PC tour. In we went. We began receiving the injections (ten in the stomach) and were provided with the remainder of the series to be given by our friend the nurse. Getting back to our site was not going to be easy, as coincidently, the teachers and university students were out on strike and were blocking the roads heading north.

Peace Corps HQ devised an alternative plan, an end run or end pass, flight. We motored to Villavicencio to spend the night so we could catch the trans-Llanos flight to Sogamoso.

We and the vaccine were there to board the tried and true DC-3 bright and early the next AM. It carried passengers and freight, generally more of the latter.

---

[13] Bruce Borrud, personal email to Charlie Lenkner, Aug. 17, 2009.

It swung the big eastern arc out over the Llanos landing at Maní, Yopal, Pore and then Tame in Arauca and back southwest to Sogamoso.

Our flight was during the dry season, but we could certainly see the extensive, open, unpopulated nature of the Llanos country and the wet season stream courses and the forested islands of high ground that stuck up when the rest was flooded. The soil we observed on the edges of the runways was, at least on the top, like decomposed granite. It was able to support grass, lots of grass, but that seemed to grow in bunches or clumps with space between plants. The leaves seemed to almost shine or sparkle with what I took to be high silicate content.

In Sogamoso we got lucky and picked up a cab with eucalyptus branches tied to the front bumper to sweep nails and other puncturing devises from the student afflicted roads. This cab ride set me up for the next Llanos or near Llanos trip. Our driver was from Bluefields, Nicaragua and spoke English as well as Spanish. He was a savvy fellow and we enjoyed visiting with him when we were in Sogamoso. Once when we were talking, he invited me to come down to Yopal to his get-away house or cabin for a look-see and rest. I think it was maybe between Pajarito & Zapatosa. In any case it was in the last of the foothills overlooking the Llanos.

We needed another vehicle to make it work so my friend could stay on after I had to head back to the site. So our PC Volunteer Leader said he'd drive and we could regard the trip as a new sight survey. We went down following our friend.

I saw the work of a vampire bat on a foal and a calf, kind of a saucer shaped lesion on the neck used to bare capillaries and other vessels so the bat can lick up blood released. And we used the dilution technique, a garden hose, to save a horse from excessive application of organophosphate pesticide. This was at the near roadside house of a friend of his who lived far enough down the road, off the *paramo,* that climate and flora & fauna were tropical.

Closer to the Llanos things were drier than our first stop. Our friend had two horses and a mule waiting for us where the trail to his cabin took off from the road. They were nice animals. I got to ride the mule, a first for me and definitely the caddy class critter for that country and that ride. I was back up to near normal weight by then and the mule never missed a step nor broke a sweat and was very responsive.

The cabin was not large but big enough and comfortable for our purposes. It had a nice front porch that looked out over the Llanos, big screen TV you didn't need. It was very peaceful there. I liked to watch the African cattle egrets coming in to roost in the evening.

I appreciated our friend's introduction to his refuge and his sharing. When it came time to move on, we rode comfortably out to the green Jeep wagon.

Before heading home we drove out to the flats where there was a small town and some stores, kind of a cross roads. We noticed that some of the residents had a pallor, a yellowish tint that indicated their word for malaria, *palidismo.* It was part of the deal when living there.

We bought a whole stalk of ripe and ripening bananas for very little with the peso being at 20:1 for our dollar. What a deal, of course you had to have a Jeep to haul them out. We did a 180 and headed back for the tops of the mountains.

There were military units based in Sogamoso. The Lenkners had come into contact with the Army back in Tolima, but the troops in Sogamoso were different and Charlie took notice.

I liked the mule packed mountain artillery unit in Sogamoso better than the troops in the machinegun nests in Tolima peering out like ground squirrels. When they turned out for formation or dress parade it was worth seeing. The mules were nicely matched, "uniform" and well trained, well mannered. The mountain howitzers and mortars were well packed for transport. The troops looked good in their uniforms or fatigues, helmets or caps it all looked like US style stuff. The head officer was Pattonesque, jophers & Eisenhower jacket; don't recall any pearl handled revolver off hand, however.[14]

All Volunteers had to deal with government officials both Colombian and U.S. Often these people could be very helpful and even crucial to the success of projects. But sometimes they were little more than an annoyance. Charlie describes a couple of incidents:

Dr. Cortez was our Colombian FAO-PINA director, the guy with the little used Russian GAZ jeep. I remember he had an office in Tunja, fleshy face, Castillan lisp, and his manicured nails were always impeccable. Did he have a private practice? Was he a public health MD? He did have the three piece wool suits in apparent abundance. He did seem..... well, functional, almost.

Once and once only did Dr. Cortez show up in our town. Nicely three piece suited, he stepped out of his Russian jeep briefly, and may have had coffee. The conversation was limited and brief. Matters of our program were superficially treated if at all and he was down the road.

One rather cool cloudy day we were puttering around the house doing inside chores and pushing papers. There was a pounding at the door and our young Colombian friends said excitedly, "your brothers are here to see you." We went to the portal and looked out and down the grassed street came some gringos in nice suits and good haircuts, three to four, I think. They stepped in briefly to look around and introduced themselves as embassy personnel. They didn't care to linger. They had just heard that we were "out there" and being on a spin around Boyacá, they wanted to satisfy their curiosity. We walked them back to the municipal plaza/square and there sitting just out from the big eucalyptus tree on the grass was a giant Lincoln Town Car type limo with small US flags snapping in the breeze on each corner. Adios.........[15]

---

[14] Charlie Lenkner, personal email, August 18, 2009.
[15] Ibid.

All Volunteers bumped into strange people in strange places. Sometimes the contact was pleasant and once in a while not so pleasant, but these occurrences were always interesting. Charlie describes a couple of such occasions:

One time we were at the extreme edge of our veredas when we passed in front of an old but beautiful, large, traditional hacienda. It appeared a bit let go, but was still in sound condition. We assumed it might be vacant or that a caretaker was not capable of keeping up or just preferred not to. A pleasant man with a grand mustache, brown snap brim hat and sad large deep brown eyes appeared and invited us up onto the fine porch for tinto. There were old deer antlers, native species, attached to the posts of the porch. This was something I had not seen before in Colombia.

The man was a medical doctor of sophistication and social grace. I gathered that he had returned to his ancestral home, but didn't ask him out right. It seemed he was maybe ill, but the illness was not apparent in his posture or actions. Had he come home to die? He appeared alone. We gave him our genuine attention and general concern. He gave us hospitality and tinto. We finally took our leave to ride on, but somehow our parting words felt inadequate.

Once as we were traveling by road to Bogotá I was looking out the window and saw an atypical cyclist peddling south toward Bogotá. This fellow appeared to be of Native American origins. He had a wide tired Schwin-like bike that was packed with his worldly equipment. The bike had coaster brakes and no gears, one speed, however fast he could peddle.

He was dressed in a white T-shirt and khaki slacks with sturdy boots. Most notably he sported a wide brimmed, black, felt hat with crown, crease & brim, reminiscent of Gen, G.A. Custer, and he was wearing a pair of heavy leather gauntlets with fringed cuffs.

By luck we later spotted him in town headed our way on our side of the street pushing his bike. Being amazed and curious I spoke to him. He did not speak Spanish but US English. He said he was a Sioux or Lakota from South Dakota originally. But his father made a living as a tuna boat skipper out of San Diego. This was apparently where he had started his vision quest, peddling to where we saw him. He had pushed and peddled his way to a physique like Arnold Schwartzeneger on steroids, but talked like one who spends most days and nights in his own company. He was headed for Tierra del Fuego after which he would decide to peddle home or catch a different ride. We may have passed him some pesos, I don't remember.[16]

Besides the PINA Volunteers in Boyacá, there were two ETV types from our group in the department. These two were Marge Mohler and Tom Gallaher. Tom was near the Abbotts, actually in Duitama.

Duitama, Boyacá is about 200 kilometers north of Bogotá and several hours by bus [Tom writes]. Duitama was located toward one end of a wide Andian

---

[16] Charlie Lenkner, personal email, Aug, 18, 2009.

plain at an elevation of about 8500 feet. Arriving when I did at the end of the rainy season, everything was remarkably green.

Duitama was a rather large town, with a population of several thousand. The town boasted a large and impressive Cathedral the site of the Diocese of Duitama/Sogamoso. Like many of the towns in the department of Boyacá, it had been founded in the mid to late 1500's. The Spanish colonial architectural heritage was less evident here than it was in several other smaller towns in Boyacá.

I had been assigned to work with three ETV Volunteers who had already been on site for almost a year; in fact, all three were scheduled to leave Colombia within the next several months.

Elaine was a tall, willowy blond from Texas, who after over a year in Colombia, had really begun to dislike, perhaps despise is a better word, Colombian men, because she felt she was being constantly harassed. It was tough being a "blond goddess." When she visited ETV schools I would frequently accompany her, because she wasn't harassed when she was with me.

Judy was a petit, dark eyed señorita from Boca Raton, Florida. With her dark hair, dark eyes and fluent Spanish, Judy was occasionally mistaken for a Colombiana.

Jeannie was from Wisconsin though not as petit as Judy, she was also dark eyed and raven haired. All three women lived in a small house at the edge of town.

Since Duitama was a transportation hub, with numerous busses leaving daily for Tunja, Sogomosa, Valle du Par, Santa Rosa, Bogotá, and parts north, south, east and west, their house became a sort of Peace Corps Hostel for all Volunteers returning to their sites who had missed the last bus. There were guys in search of a home cooked meal, or guys just wanting to spend time with some attractive gringas.

One day I distinctly remember walking to their house and finding the floor covered with sleeping bodies, there must have been about eight or nine guys crashed, asleep on the floor. This was unusual; normally it was only two or three and sometimes the inn had no visitors at all.

I lived in a small two room cabin on a finca about a mile or two outside of town, no electricity, no running water, but I did have a bed and a sleeping bag which I must have been given by Peace Corps in Bogatá, which I'm glad I had because it was cold at night. Each morning, after partaking of a delicious breakfast with the family I stayed with on the finca, I would walk into town and go to the girls' house where it would be decided which sites would be visited that day and who I would accompany. My Spanish was at that time still pretty rudimentary so I would have been pretty useless by myself.

I have never been so exhausted in all my life as I was during those first few weeks in Colombia; I don't remember being that tired during marine corps boot camp, and that was strenuous. But this was much more tiring, it required a constant focus. It required so much effort to understand what was being said to me and so much effort to speak; when I got back home in the evening I was exhausted. All I could think of was going to sleep. Of course that was when the family I was staying with would send over their son, a boy of about 8 or 10, to keep me company and *chalar* (talk, chat) so I wouldn't be lonely.

On most days we would either visit sites where TV's were already installed and work with the teachers to get them comfortable using the programs in the classroom, or we would visit schools to determine possible new ETV sites.

Jeanie had been a teacher in the States and she would often conduct workshops for teachers to help them prepare and incorporate more hands on experimental learning techniques than the rote drilling and, memorization normally used in the classroom by most teachers. I assisted at a few science workshops she conducted.[17]

So Tom received his initiation into Colombian ETV in Boyacá. It was a chance to learn from the gals who had been part of the very first ETV group in Colombia and gave him time to improve his Spanish. All this would stand him in good stead when he changed sites and moved to the coast where it would be his responsibility to commence a program.

The second ETV Volunteer from our group in Boyacá was Margaret Mohler who was located in Tunja. As with Tom and the rest of us, she was learning her trade and struggling to pick up the language.

Like Gerry Volgenau, Tom Gallaher, Lisa Hufnagel, I was a utilization Volunteer [Margaret recalls]. I would visit schools helping teachers get used to having lessons taught via TV. We helped arrange class schedules, held teacher training sessions and twice I worked in day camps for kids during school vacation periods

In the day camps we included art, music and organized physical education classes because those were not part of the usual curriculum. The first day camp was in Duitama and went so well I set one up in Tunja. I believe Bob Bezdek came to Tunja for my day camp and brought bows and arrows. No one was killed or injured, so I consider that day camp a success.

I had two favorite schools I visited. One educated children whose parents were serving time in prison. Those children were toddlers and up in age. Primary education went through the 5th grade. The other school was attached to Tunja's liquor factory and served the children of the workers. I always received a tour of the factory (probably due to being a gringa with blond hair) and ended up bringing home one or two bottles of *creme de cacao* or *creme de cafe*. What I really wanted was a bottle of rum which was pretty tasty.

I never lived with a Colombian family while in Tunja, always with other Volunteers. A lot of our time was spent in buying food and preparing meals as two of the guys ate with us daily.

One weekend I was the only one staying in Tunja, and I awoke in the middle of the night to see some man lighting a match while standing in the doorway of my bedroom. I was so scared I couldn't even scream, but I made enough noise so the robber knew I was awake. He fled without taking anything. My room must

---

[17] Tom Gallaher, personal email, Oct. 21, 2009.

have been the first one he visited as my purse and money were in the dining room untouched. I called Colombian friends who called the police. After a half hour the police came from a distance of four blocks. Nothing could be done. I only saw an outline of the robber. The following day my friends came with a pearl handled gun for me. And no, I didn't take the gun.

I accompanied an ETV Volunteer to the actual prison which is on the highway connecting Tunja and Duitama as she was assigned that school for visits. I remained outside while she visited inside. We walked back to the highway to get a bus back to Tunja. Now, Colombian buses are colorful, noisy, crowded, live animals, people occasionally getting sick, etc. Well, this bus was practically empty and even had cloth headrests. We'd never seen such luxury on a bus! We rolled into Tunja knowing this bus was on its way to Bogotá. After a brief discussion, we decided to stay on the bus and get lunch at the Crem Helado. Since trips across department lines were "illegal", we scrunched down when we saw our Volunteer Leader driving through the Tunja bus "depot" plaza. Doris and I had a delightful ice cream lunch and caught a bus back to Tunja late in the afternoon.

Our only Thanksgiving away from the states was cause for a Volunteer celebration. One of the Volunteers, Larry Peterson I believe, brought six live turkeys to Tunja. We nearly caused a riot when these turkeys were beheaded and plucked. I think 38 Volunteers spent Thanksgiving in Tunja. The whole Boyacá crew came. That was the day our Peace Corps team was defeated by the National Police team.

I remember a couple of parties up at Lago de Tota, going to three movies in one day with Gary Peterson and Bruce Borrud, and entering the Tunja Christmas parade with our rendition of Santa's sleigh with reindeer which no Colombian understood.[18]

As with Tom, Margaret acquired experience in ETV and the language during her stay in Boyacá. Like Tom, she was about to gain a whole new prospective on Colombia. After their initiation in Boyacá, both Volunteers would be going to the coast, Tom to the port city of Barranquilla, and Marge to the old fortress city of Cartagena.

---

[18] Margaret Mohler, personal email, May 19, 2009.

10

NORTE DE SANTANDER AND THE VENEZUELAN FRONTIER

Before my (the author) transfer from Boyacá to the Cauca Valley, Bruce and I decided to go on a little paseo of our own. We wanted to explore the north country, that is, the north of Boyacá on up toward the Venezuelan border. We planned a trip up the spine of the Cordillera Oriental. We would take ground transportation through northern Boyacá, Santander and Norte de Santander clear into Venezuela. This would give us a chance to visit some of the sites the Volunteers from our group had in Norte and see the country in between.

So we caught a *Sevisio Publico*, a Colombian cross-country taxi, in Tunja. One of our group's ETV girls from Tunja, Marge Mohler, a PINA girl from our group, Carol Oakes, who was stationed in Sotaquira (a small town in Boyacá not far from Guateque where Jerry Schaeffer and Brian McMahon are stationed), and Jerry Brelage from our group who had come over from Tolima, went with us.

We traveled most of the day, getting to Bucaramanga about 4:00. Quite a change. We started dropping as soon as we left Tunja, back down into coffee, sugar cane and banana country. First we'd seen since Puerto Rico. We crossed a mountain range, very steep, dry with only cactus and shrubs for vegetation.

Bucaramanga is lower and quite a bit warmer than anything we've been in for a long time. It is the cleanest, most modern city I've seen in Colombia with neon signs, modern architecture and clean, wide streets. After we found rooms and ate, we took in a movie, "Quo Vadis." The theater was very modern with a stand selling <u>cold</u> Coca Colas. We're all trying to figure a way of getting transferred.

Also, the black market is a going thing here. You can get all sorts of radios, electrical appliances, etc. that you can't get elsewhere in Colombia or are terribly expensive.[1]

Bucaramanga was the capital of Santander, the department we had been traveling through most of the day. It straddles the mountains north of Boyacá, but unlike our department which runs east out onto the Llanos, Santander spreads west down into the Magdalena Valley between the Eastern and Central Cordilleras.

From what we saw, the department, at least as represented by its capital, seemed to be much more progressive than Boyacá. Perhaps that is why there is no one from our group stationed in that department. In fact we ran across no Peace Corps Volunteers in the city at all.

Left Bucaramanga at 10:00 and crossed more mountains. But this time the mountains were real lush, almost like a rain forest. Once we got to the top of the mountains, the terrain leveled out into rolling hills, miles and miles of open country. It looked like the northern plains of Montana. Then we dropped back

---

[1] Gary Peterson, *Colombian Diary*, Apr. 10, 1965.

down into the heat, finally arriving at Cúcuta, hot and sticky. And it is dirty, the streets are crowded with people and garbage. There are an awful lot of cars here, all with Venezuelan license plates.

The next day we finally found some PCV's here in town and learned how to get hold of our friends. We called Carol Scharmer and Jim Finkler, two of our group who live outside Cúcuta in a little town called Bochulema and told them we'd be out later. Then we caught a taxi for San Antonio, Venezuela.

In San Antonio we bought syrup, brown sugar and radios. San Antonio is a small town, mostly shops supported by Colombians. The border guards' search was very superficial.

Back to Cúcuta, then out to Bochulema. A very nice little town, clean, green and up in the mountains a little so it's not so hot. Jim lives in a house which has been rented by PCVs ever since Colombia 1 (the first group in Colombia), I understand. So there's a collection of tools from CARE and former Volunteers. They are supplied with everything, typewriters, filing cabinets, wood working tools, anything you could want.

Carol lives across the street, but they cook and have parties, at Jim's place. Jerry, Bruce and I slept at Jim's and the girls stayed over at Carol's.[2]

During visits like this you often learned more about the other members of your group than you ever did during training. Jim, for instance, grew up in a close family in Milwaukee, Wisconsin. His mother had spent two years in a tuberculosis sanitarium when he was 7 through 9 years old. He started working at 12, delivering papers, brewery laborer, cement layer, bank teller, all the way through college, attending Marquette University. Looking back Jim has some thoughts on his time in Bochulema.

James Finkler

I had the benefit of having a great partner during my tour. Carolina Scharmer and I worked very well together and I felt we were a good team.

We were successful in developing better health and nutritional habits in the families in our area. We had a latrine project and were reasonably successful with the "Quarto S" programs in the schools. I also hope that by having organized programs and presentations and meetings where individuals had the opportunity to listen and discuss subjects without constant interruption, they learned things could be accomplished by and for themselves.

The experience was fantastic for me. I learned a great deal about myself and my strengths and weaknesses. I also found it to be beneficial in my work experience and handling encounters and relationships with individuals of different backgrounds.[3]

[2] Gary Peterson, *Colombian Diary*, Apr. 11, 1965.
[3] Jim Finkler, personal email, Aug. 21, 2008.

Carol Scharmer

Jim's partner, Carol Scharmer, was from Baltimore, Maryland, a graduate of Essex Community College where she majored in physical education. She had demonstrated her abilities in this field during our rock climbing excursion in Puerto Rico, scaling cliffs that denied many of the guys. But it was her quick smile and consistent cheerfulness in training and in Colombia that added so much to our group. She met all challenges with courage and an upbeat attitude that lifted those around her. Beyond her contributions in education and nutrition, she was one of those who was truly an ambassador of good will for the United States.

Another Colombia '64 Volunteer, a former resident of Bochalema, we just missed seeing was Freddie Faulkner.

Originally from Canford, New Jersey, Freddie was a graduate of Harvard University and had worked as a hospital attendant and farm laborer during his student years.

Freddie had first been assigned to Bochalema, but stayed for only about three months, then moved on to Ocaña on the other side of the mountain, the west slope of the Cordillera Oriental. Ocaña was a city of almost 60,000 people in 1965, the second largest city in Norte after Cúcuta, the capital. But before Freddie left Bochalema, he had a near death experience which may have provided some impetus to his site change.

Freddie, Jaime (Jim Finkler) and Carol were hiking up into the mountains above Bochalema to reach a vereda in a remote area. They were following a trail in the bottom of a deep gorge with shear vertical walls pressing in on them. The trail was narrowed even further, at one point, where it passed through a great rock that was split so that there was just room for a single person or animal to slide through.

I am about half way through this gap in the boulder [as Freddie tells the story] when suddenly a fifteen hundred pound bull with mean looking horns appears from around the corner of the rock and charges full tilt right at me.

Carol and Jaime, behind me, are scrambling to get out of the confined area of the split rock, but I had no time to escape. With the bull coming right at me, I did my best to avoid those nasty horns by grabbing the bull's head with both hands as he charged at me.

I was sure I was as good as dead. I felt like I was in front of a roaring freight train. But somehow the bull tossed his head at just the right moment and I was thrown up on top of the boulder as he stampeded through the split in the rock and on down the gorge.

Frederic Faulkner

Before I could even climb down off the rock, two men showed up and were very apologetic about the incident. It seems they were trailing the bull down the mountain when it got away from them.[4]

---

[4] Freddie Faulkner, telephone interview, Nov. 23, 2009.

In Ocaña Freddie worked out of the Secretary of Agriculture's office and accompanied the Colombian *agronamos* on much less dangerous trips to the surrounding countryside, small towns, schools and veredas.

When not out in the campo, Freddie's time was spent in the office in Ocaña where he became acquainted with an attractive Colombiana, the secretary. The relationship grew to be much more than just an acquaintance, though courting in Colombia is anything but permissive or easy. There were dances, movies and evening visits at Cecilia's home, always well chaperoned of course. At 10:00 in the evening Cecilia's mother would escort Freddie and the boy friends of Cecilia's sisters out the front door. She was raising eight children by herself, her husband having died a few years earlier, and she tolerated no nonsense.

On one particular night, the electricity seemed especially unstable. The lights would dim and even go out for a few moments from time to time. Freddie smiled knowingly at Cecilia who seemed to pick up on an idea he was forming and she smiled back.

The next time the lights went out, Freddie leaned over to find Cecilia right beside him. Concluding she must have understood his meaning and slid over toward him, he planted a big kiss on her cheek at the same time the lights came back on. But Freddie discovered to his horror it was not Cecilia sitting beside him, but her mother. He decided the old gal was not only quick on her feet, but very perceptive; probably none of his sly messages to Cecilia had escaped her notice.

Besides work and courting, Freddie spent a good deal of time with the Catholic Archbishop located in Ocaña. Though not Catholic himself, Freddie expended many an evening with the reverend exchanging ideas and imbibing a social drink or two, another example of how many Colombia '64 Volunteers built wonderful and productive relationships with the clergy in order to improve the circumstances of the people, objectives both parties were working toward.

At the end of his tour, Freddie was offered a position with the Department of Agriculture in Cúcuta if he would extend a year. Considering the progress he was making in his courtship and his increased effectiveness as a Volunteer, Freddie accepted.

His assignment in Cúcuta was to run a program designed to educate teachers, government officials, farmers and campecinos in modern agricultural practices. The courses consisted of three weeks of class work held at various towns and cities in the department. Often the army was used to transport class members from their homes to the class sites. When available, army barracks were utilized to house attendees. "I believe I accomplished twice as much in that last year as in my previous two years in Colombia," Faulkner summarizes.[5]

One of the courses was held in Tibu, north of Cúcuta, a town in the middle of Colombia's richest oil field. "The town turned out to be a miserable, dilapidated, neglected Indian village."[6] No boisterous boom town with free flowing money and all the vices that go with it here. Apparently, none of the oil money was being left in the town.

Much of his success in this new job must be attributed to the fact that Freddie could get almost anything he wanted from the governor. As was the case with the Archbishop in Ocaña, he became good friends with the chief department executive in Cúcuta, spending many an evening conversing about the country's problems, world events and

---

[5] Freddie Faulkner, telephone interview, Nov. 23, 2009.
[6] Ibid.

the United States. Though he did not abuse his friendship, if he truly needed something Freddie could count on the governor to provide it.

Finally, the move to Cúcuta brought to a head Freddie's courtship of Cecilia. Now literally on the other side of the mountain, it was a case of follow through or sever ties. Freddie and Cecilia were married three months after the move.

Bruce, Margaret, Carol (Oakes) Jerry and I had a delightful stay with Jim and Carol. They had a very nice town and wonderful accommodations.

Read magazines while the girls fixed breakfast and lunch, then we went swimming in a pool here in town. Think of that, a town swimming pool to use whenever you want. Then the girls fixed supper. A real restful day.[7]

But all things eventually come to an end and the next day we were back on the road, taking a roundabout route back to our site. Marge, Carol and Jerry left earlier to catch a flight back.

Wednesday we went back to Cúcuta where Bruce and I caught a plane for Bogotá. The plane was a little two engine job, but it got us there. First time I've seen the El Dorado airport in daylight. It's real fancy. As modern as any in the U.S. Ate and saw movies the rest of the day, finally meeting Marge, Carol and Jerry at the late movie. They came in on a later flight via Medellín. We bedded down at the Pit.

Just before we left Bogotá this morning, Bruce and I ran into the Lenkners, the couple who are moving to Boyacá from Tolima. Well, we rode out to our site with them. They had already rented a car (a publico taxi) to take them to Sogamoso. We spent the rest of the day getting things back in shape around the place.[8]

Donald Lydic

A Volunteer from Colombia '64 in Norte we did not get to see was Don Lydic stationed in Chinácota about 20 miles south of Cúcuta, a town of about 2,600 at the time. Don was the other Nebraskan in the group, a graduate of the University of Nebraska. Originally Don had been assigned to a government agricultural farm on the outskirts of Cúcuta, but the facility had no faculty, no workers, no growing crops, no livestock and no money. There were buildings and fields, but no programs or government support to start any. This was an idea whose time had not yet arrived, or at least the money to carry out the idea had not yet materialized.

After three months of frustration with nothing to show for his efforts to get things started, Don began looking for other opportunities. Fortunately for Don, Chinácota, a town in the department, was losing a Volunteer couple (the

---

[7] Gary Peterson, *Colombian Diary*, Apr. 13, 1965.
[8] Gary Peterson, *Colombian Diary*, Apr. 15, 1965.

Beavers, who were terminating) that had started several ag projects in the town and surrounding veredas. Don received permission from Peace Corps to relocate to the town and take over those projects.

As we separated in Bogotá for our return trips to our sites, Carol Oakes certainly had no inkling that she had just been introduced to the department she would soon be moving to. She was quite content in Sotaquira where she was staying with a family that provided her with a room so she would be safe, or so she thought. In the evening she ate at a hotel with the local judge, his secretary and whatever transients happened to be in town.

"Every night the judge would have me read the newspaper to him and anyone else interested, then he had me explain what I had read," Carol says.[9]

At first this test/quiz was nerve wracking and stressful. But the judge seemed to have infinite patience and Carol began to pick up the language quickly and not just speaking, but reading as well.

Carol Oakes

With her Spanish skills improving so rapidly, Carol was able to make a real contribution; she could carry on actual conversations and even speak to small groups of women about nutrition for families and how to prepare the vegetables and proteins their families needed. She was weeks and months ahead of the rest of us in her language facility. But her stay in Boyacá was cut short.

One night the father of the family she was staying with became intoxicated while playing tejo with his friends, not an unusual event, but this night he had something to prove. Had he lost money gambling at tejo, had a fight with one of his buddies, or was just in an evil mood? Carol never found out what his problem was, but after coming home, he took out his gun, staggered into her room and pulled the trigger.

The shot went wild, but the explosion scared Carol, quite literally, right out of bed. She didn't even wait for her heart rate to slow to something approaching normal, but grabbed some clothes and by morning was on her way to Guiteque and the protection of Brian McMahon and Jerry Schaeffer.

"Ever the heroes, Brian and Jerry let me stay for a couple of days to get my head straight and then we contacted Peace Corps in Bogotá."[10] Carol's clothes and other items were picked up by Peace Corps and brought to her in Bogotá where she was interviewed by Peace Corps staff to determine her fate.

The site at Chináquita, Norte de Santander came up. With the Beaver's departure, Don Lydic had relocated to the town, had taken over and already expanded the ag projects there, but the nutrition end was being neglected. Here was an opportunity for Carol. She would be moved to Chinácota where she would share not just the site, but, as it turned out, Don's house. Don used one half the house and Carol the other. To make the situation respectable, they acquired a maid, Doña Luisa Cardenas, who proved to be a real blessing.

[9] Carol Oaks Ford, telephone interview, Nov. 15, 2009.
[10] Carol Oaks Ford, personal email, Nov. 17, 2009.

"She kept our house," Carol writes, "did the laundry (got it as clean as new), and fed us. I was planning on bringing her to the states some time later, but she became ill with cancer and died before I could make the arrangements."[11]

Now a local could report to the town, through the gossip channels, that the American's were indeed honorable people and could be looked to for help. Carol and Don would become an effective pair of Volunteers in this Colombian border area.

> We each had a mule for our 4-S meetings [Carol says] and for getting around
> to the veredas. A town boy helped with our rabbits and caught the mules for us.
> His name was Jose. Don and I paid for his colegio education.[12]

Eventually, Don developed one of the true rabbit farms in Colombia. Campesinos, farmers and breeders would bring female rabbits to him to mate with his outstanding bucks. Rabbits from Chinácota spread all across Colombia thanks to the network of Volunteers Colombia '64 provided. Gardens, nutrition, 4-S clubs flourished in the area. As the end of their tour drew to a close, Carol would extend to the end of the year (1966) and Don would transfer to the north coast where he took over a program started by Jeff Andrews another member of Colombia '64.

---

[11] Carol Oaks Ford, personal email, Nov. 17, 2009.
[12] Ibid.

11
CONVENTS, GLACIERS AND A WEDDING
ON THE CARIBBEAN COAST

While the Tolima and Huila Volunteers toiled away in the upper reaches of the Magdalena River, two members of Colombia '64 were headed for the other end of that great water way. After their initial introduction to Colombia and the orientation meetings in Bogotá, Eugene Roberts and Jeff Andrews flew north to the Caribbean coast, landing at the old Spanish citadel of Cartagena. From the coast, they traveled south into the hot coastal plain of Colombia away from the cooling breezes of the sea.

Roberts found his site, San Jacinto, "right on the main highway running south from Barranquilla along the Magdalena River."[1] His new surroundings were certainly a far cry from the Maryland family cattle operation he was used to. Eugene was from Glenn Dale, Maryland and was a graduate of Yale University where he had been on the varsity wrestling team. He had also worked for the Dept. of Animal Husbandry at Penn. State, so he had an excellent background for the agricultural work Colombia '64 was being asked to perform. All his training and experience would provide only a starting point, however, in dealing with the new environment Roberts now found himself in a strange culture, language, and crops he had only read about.

Eugene Roberts

Some 30 miles to the north of San Jacinto, closer to Cartagena, Jeff Andrews pulled into his town, Maria la Baja, after traveling 50 miles by bus, passing fields of rice, cotton and tobacco, and crossing the once consequential Canal de Dique (see Append. II). Turning off the highway for a couple of miles, the bus reached Jeff's site, a town of several hundred people. It was not a city of extensive amenities, there were no paved streets or electricity, and running water was intermittent. Many of the thatched roofed houses had only hardened clay floors. There was not even a school for the children of the town. When weather permitted, classes were held beneath the comforting shade of a large "class room tree."

Jeff Andrews was from Morriston, Florida, a small community approximately 20 miles west of Ocala, so he was no stranger to heat and humidity. Nevertheless, the topical climate of Colombia's northern coastal plain would require getting used to, even for this native Floridian.

Jeff found his accommodations primitive at best, consisting of a hammock in a one room thatched roofed edifice that was shared with two Colombian guys. All meals were purchased in the town's only restaurant… compacted clay floor, thatched roof, and fresh meat hanging from a wire stretched from one wall to the other… loaded with flies! The family pig, undoubtedly destined to be a future

---

[1] Eugene Roberts, telephone interview, May 27, 2009.

lunch or dinner, was allowed to roam around and find tasty morsels on the floor under the tables.[2]

In the center of the village stood a very large Catholic church. Andrews would need the cooperation of the padre who officiated at this church to accomplish any community development projects in the area. The padre had in mind some of these projects himself, but may have been a little skeptical of the new arrival when he discovered that this *Norte Americano* was a Protestant, and not just a Protestant, but a Southern Baptist Protestant! Irregardless, Jeff persisted in establishing a working relationship with the padre and after many "interesting" discussions during which the padre "helped" Jeff to understand where he was "wrong," the two reached an accommodation. Agreeing to disagree on religion, Jeff and the padre found they could work together, "hand in hand"[3] for the betterment of the people of Maria la Baja.

Jeff Andrews

Jeff was able to secure a few packets of seeds and two rabbits. It was a beginning, although a meager one. Shortly, the two rabbits succumbed to some mysterious tropical malady, but his garden projects caught on. His venture into tropical horticulture expanded from one demonstration garden to thirty enterprises scattered around town. Though tropical diseases and insects were a constant problem, this was one area that showed potential. "The kids loved growing things and occasionally the adults would enthusiastically join in to help with preparations for planting. Cooking the collards, radishes, tomatoes, corn, etc., was another LARGE project in itself."[4]

Simultaneously, Jeff's living circumstances also began to improve. He went, "from a hammock and a room shared with two other fellows to a cot and a room alone in a nice, new spacious hospital which could not be opened for lack of funding. His eating ritual went from the grit (not grits) of the local restaurant, to the scrumptious meals provided by the German nuns operating a, "colegio on the edge of the village."[5] All male volunteers of Colombia '64 lost weight except R. Jeff Andrews who gained 20 pounds. Life was slowly settling into a more tolerable routine.

Jeff was soon engaged in gardens, 4-S club, a rejuvenated rabbit program and even some English classes. Working with the padre, he began to work on some of the community action projects that they both felt were of prime importance in bettering the town's conditions. Jeff says that,

....once I made peace with the local padre, the villagers were more accepting of my efforts to assist them in raising their standard of living. I went on several trips to Cartagena the provincial capital, with "leaders" from Maria la Baja to meet with government officials concerning funding for schools, roads and medical help.

---

[2] Jeff Andrews, personal email to Gary Peterson, April 14, 2009.
[3] Hocicon, Issue 2, July 1965, page 3.
[4] Jeff Andrews, personal email to Gary Peterson, April 14, 2009.
[5] Hocicon, Issue 2, July 1965, page 3.

The Colombian Agency charged with providing assistance to us and helping us in our efforts to improve the living standards of the people with whom we lived, was PINA. Jose Rojas Pinella was the administrator in charge of the province and tried to assist with gardening equipment, seeds, brochures and other useful items for the 4-S programs. Unfortunately, he was limited in what he could offer and limited in his ability to make unilateral decisions. Victories were hard to come by.

However, Dr. Rojas was instrumental in setting a meeting for me and the village leaders (including *el padre*), to meet with the Governor of the Province in Cartagena. The Governor was, of course, 45 minutes late for the meeting and could only hold out a slim promise of funding for a school for Maria la Baja. The villagers pointed out that those classes were difficult to hold in the rain and lightening under the big "class room tree!" He finally agreed to work hard to get the funding for a new school for Maria la Baja and before I left Colombia, construction had begun![6]

Every volunteer carried away with him or her a few exceptional memories having spent 20 intense months in Colombia. One of those unforgettable, poignant memories for Jeff was the night he, the ole Southern Baptist, spent in a convent. The episode began, as most profound experiences do, without fanfare. "As is my usual procedure, I walked over to eat supper with the nuns at the colegio. Huge black clouds seemed poised, ready to spill their ever-abundant reservoir of water on the ugliness of poverty and hunger of Maria la Baja."[7]

In spite of the threatening rain clouds, Jeff didn't even bring his rain coat, but made a dash for the colegio several blocks away. He made it to the school/convent and sat down for supper with the nuns and three girls who stayed at the colegio. During the meal, however, the menacing dark clouds opened up with a torrent of rain, the kind of instant downpour only experienced in the tropics, rain so intense you can't see across the street.

The cook suggested that I would have to stay the night. It was a joke of course. I laughed. Later while rocking to the beat of the pelting rain this preposterous idea was again submitted, this time by the head *madre,* or more correctly, the *Madre Superior.*

"Thank you very much, but I believe it will soon stop."[8]

But the rain didn't stop or even let up. Jeff waited as the table was cleared and one by one the nuns and girls drifted off to take care of their nightly duties. Left alone with just the pounding of the rain and his own heart beat for company, Jeff began to feel a little deserted. He could hear noises coming from down the hall and finally he decided to investigate. The closer he got to the source of the sounds the more intrigued he became. With just a bit of trepidation, he decided, "guess I better go join them, sounds like they are having fun."[9]

---

[6] Jeff Andrews, personal email to Gary Peterson, April 14, 2009.
[7] Hocicon, August 1965 issue, page 3.
[8] Ibid.
[9] Ibid.

A perfect scene of contentment, just what one would imagine seeing nuns do at night. Two of them were untangling thread they had evidently gotten from the factory in crude form. One was crocheting and the other was cutting pictures of well-dressed kids from what seemed to have been a Sears & Roebuck catalogue. The cook sat at the feet of the two working on the thread, fighting the mosquitoes. A couple of the young girls were sitting behind me mumbling the creed or rosary or whatever one says.[10]

Again one of the nuns suggested he stay the night, but Jeff insisted he had to get home. Another nun asked if Jeff was afraid to spend the night with them. In spite of the invitations and teasing, Jeff held to his conviction that he had to get home. But after another attempt to leave only to find the down pour worse than ever and nearly falling on the slippery, wet rocks of the pathway, he acquiesced and consented to stay the night.

The four nuns and three girls quickly produced a bed, mosquito net and linens, and then arranged Jeff's sleeping quarters on one side of the activity room. When all was in readiness, the nuns retired leaving the three girls to entertain their house guest. A board game was produced and, "the monotonous tones of the praying *madres* coexisted with the gleeful noise of the game, as the three girls and I rolled the dice to see who would begin 'the chase.' When three authoritative knocks on the door sounded, we were in the middle of our game and the gringo was leading. Hardly had the sound from the knocks ceased when the game was boxed and put away. I was left with only a glass of water and a *Kolcana* (the Colombian version of Coca Cola)."[11]

"As the stillness of solitude descended and the dark curtain of night fell around the earthly stronghold of Godliness, the epitome of ironies burst upon my irreverent mind. Tomorrow it will have been exactly 22 years since having been born. My status had fallen or risen, according to one's point of view, from the cradle of Baptistism to the bed of Catholicism. After this night in a convent, what more can life produce?"[12]

For six months Roberts and Andrews were alone, as far as the Colombia '64 group was concerned, in their north coast outpost, but then others began to arrive. These were ETV folks coming from Boyacá and Huila being reassigned to open Colombia's school television program in this part of the country. First on the scene was Tom Gallaher from Boyacá, a shift from the high mountains to the sultry coast.

Before being transferred to Barranquilla [Tom writes], my first six months in Peace Corps, were spent amidst the green hills and valleys of Boyacá in what coastal Colombians referred to as *Tierra Fria*. I'd spend the rest of my time in the Peace Corps in Barranquilla. It was there I would meet, fall in love, and marry the woman who would become my wife. So I have many found memories of *la costa* and its inhabitants, the *costeños*.

Situated midway between the old colonial walled city of Cartagena and another old Spanish colonial town, Santa Marta, Barranquilla was the largest

---

[10] Hocicon, August 1965 issue, page 4.

[11] Ibid.

[12] Ibid.

city on Colombia's north coast. It was the first settlement in Colombia and the final resting place of Simón Bolívar. In comparison to the colonial architecture and historical points of interest within the old walled city of Cartagena and the beautiful white sandy *playas* (beaches) and turquoise waters of Santa Marta, Barranquilla was a gritty, bustling port city, hot, humid, dirty, and crowded, so different from the cool green hills and valleys of Boyacá. Situated on the east bank of the Rio Magdelena on a series of hills, the city rose gradually upwards for several hundred feet from the banks of the river. Barranquilla was, to say the least, a little short on charm.

The oldest part of town, and the center of commerce, was a few hundred meters in from the river. I was puzzled by the configuration of the sidewalks, in this part of town. Frequently they were several feet above street level and stairs were cut into the sidewalks at each corner to allow one to climb up from the street. The further one got from the river and the "*centro commercial,*" the lower the sidewalks became until after a mile or so the sidewalks were just like sidewalks anywhere else in the world. Only when the rainy season arrived did I realize why the sidewalks were elevated so far above street level. The city had no storm system to drain away the rainfall. As the rain fell and the water rushed down hill, the streets gradually turned into raging rivers and if you weren't on an elevated sidewalk, you were in danger of being swept away. The torrential rains caused huge potholes to form during the rainy season; many capable of swallowing a small car. I even witnessed a few cars being swept away during the two years I was there.

During my time in Barranquilla it was impossible for me to walk down the street without hearing the sensuous, driving *cumbia* rhythms pouring out from what seemed like every store front. The infectious beat seemed to permeate the air. When you heard the cumbia, your feet just wanted to start dancing. For almost two years, whenever I heard the cumbia, which was every day, I felt like I was dancing. The music was so *alegre* (joyful), it was next to impossible to keep still. Costeños were born with rhythm in their blood, and dancing with a *costeña* was like holding quick silver in your arms. If such music were as ubiquitous here in the USA, our vaunted worker productivity would no doubt suffer a precipitous decline, but we all might be a little happier and a little healthier.

Barranquilla was a large city. There must have been twenty or thirty Volunteers in the city and another twenty in the surrounding campo. Peace Corps also had a regional office in the city, and in contrast to Boyacá, where I could sometimes go for several days without seeing any Volunteers, other than the women I worked with, it was almost impossible not to meet one or more Volunteers every day. In fact the structure of the ETV program made it virtually impossible not to be involved with PCV's on a daily basis.

A typical day would start with my taking a bus to the *Officina Technica* which was an office within the Dept. of Education that supervised "*Television Educativa.*" The office opened at 7:30 AM. Upon arrival, I'd spend a few hours with our Colombian counterparts "*charlando*" and figuring out, more or less, what we were supposed to do. Then before you knew it, it was noon and time for siesta. The office closed down until 2:30 and everyone went home for a nap. Usually a few of us walked over to the Peace Corps office or went to the Liberia National which was a big book store in downtown Barranquilla where you could get a cold *refresco*, a *jugo natural*, something to eat. Not your typical Volunteer's day.

For the first few months, most of our time was spent deciding which schools would be eligible to receive the television sets which were being donated by the Allianza Para Progresso, and had yet to arrive. We also had to schedule workshops to instruct the teachers in how to integrate the programs they would be viewing into their curriculum. Carolyn, an ETV Volunteer from another group, took on the responsibility of developing materials to instruct teachers on how to utilize the T.V. programs they would shortly be receiving. Carolyn was a graduate of Columbia University Teachers College and had all the proper pedagogic credentials. With some help from her Colombian colleagues, Carolyn wrote a book which was eventually adopted by the Ministry of Education to be used in all the normal schools (the Colombian equivalent of our teachers colleges) to help prepare teachers on how to best use educational television programming.

We spent a few days a week visiting schools throughout the department of Atlantico in order to determine which schools were going to receive the "*televisor.*" Occasionally the Minister of Education would accompany us to a school and proceed to give a long exhortation about what a great country Colombia was and what great benefits would accrue to the nation from being able to utilize the latest advances in educational technology to improve the development of the children who were the "*futuro del pais.*" After hearing "his speeches" a few dozen times I was astonished at, how long they lasted, how similar they were and the bravado of his rhetorical flourishes. After the speech was finished, we were always served tintos and *pastales* and another hour or so would pass exchanging pleasantries.

It was from the minister that I learned the importance of visiting every school, even the most remote; to create the impression that everyone would be given equal consideration lest they think they had been discriminated against and treated unfairly. He made me aware how deeply political the educational system was.

When the TVs finally arrived we had to deliver them to the schools and get them installed. And while it was frequently possible to install two sets a day in the city, we never were able to install more than one out in the *campo* due to the distances between schools and the poor conditions of the roads.

To carry the TVs to the schools we needed a means of transportation and this was provided in the form of a jeep on loan from the *Departamento de Obras Publicas* (Department of Public Works). This was a remarkable vehicle. It was a Russian jeep given to the Colombian Government as part of Russia's foreign aid program.

Apparently in order to build up some good will in Latin America, and to counter our Alliance for Progress, the Russians also started a foreign aid program. One of the first offerings of their program was a gift of 500 "jeeps" to the Colombian government, which the Colombians graciously accepted.

Somehow the government of the Department of Atlantico, got their hands on several of these Russian jeeps, one of which we had the use of from time to time to take our good ole' 'merican TV's out to install in Colombia's schools.

The jeep was incredibly ponderous. It was like driving a tank. It was slow and seemed to be made out of cast iron. There were no shocks, so you felt every pothole and there were a lot of pot holes. The writing on the instruments was in Cyrillic as was a small book that I took to be a driver's manual. Not too surprising, when you consider the jeep was built for the Russian Army.

Growing up in New York City, then being in the military and at sea, I had never driven a car before I joined the Peace Corps. Now here I was, responsible for getting these TVs delivered.

A Colombian friend offered to help me get a drivers license. We went down to the local police station to get the license. The jefe at the police station asked me if I knew how to drive. Before I could answer, my friend spoke up "Of course he knows how to drive, can't you see he's a gringo? All gringos know how to drive." So I paid the fee and walked out with my very first drivers license *HECHO EN COLOMBIA* (made in Colombia). The next day my friend gave me a few hours instruction and I was good to go. And the amazing thing is I never even came close to injuring anyone, and had only one fender bender.

The biggest problem with the Russian jeep was we only had use of it on an intermittent basis and we were never sure when we'd get it, or how long we'd have it. Needless to say this resulted in a lot of down time. Sitting around during one of these periods of inactivity, it dawned on me that our program, as good as it was, had a fatal flaw. The TV's were all donated. We installed 'em, maintained 'em, and trained the teachers how to use the programs in their classrooms. The officials in the Colombian Department of Education who had been assigned to work with us, could just as easily be transferred, when we left. There was no fiscal support for the program within the Department of Education. The gringos were funding everything. I felt that unless a section was established within the Dept. of Education, with its own director, its own staff and its own budget, the program might just fade away when we left. Our Colombian counterparts agreed that would probably be the case. Carolyn and I tried to figure out the best way to institutionalize the program so that it would survive our departure and continue under Colombian leadership.

In order to gain support for the ETV program I wrote a series of articles for the local newspaper about the program. Every time there was an installation of a "*televisor* " at a new site we would try to have the Minister of Education and the Director of the Office of Educational Television present to be photographed presiding over the ceremonies. The minister was a real politician and he loved all the free publicity. Eventually I was able to get the owner of the city's leading newspaper El Heraldo to write an editorial in support of *TELEVISON EDUCATIVO.*

We were able to get a legislator to sponsor a bill that would establish a separate office with its own director and its own budget within the Dept. of

Education. When it came time for the *Assemblea* to vote on the matter, the minister had me speak to the assembled delegates.

Naturally I was a bit nervous but all the speeches I had listened to over the previous months stood me in good stead. I was able to get up and repeat dozens of the empty platitudes I had been listening to for the last several months. I told them what a great honor it was for me to be able to speak to them. I told them of the great warmth and hospitality the Colombian people had shown us. I recalled the greatness of the Colombian people, the friendship between the U.S. and Colombia, the importance of education for "*futuro del pais*," the "*podoroso empleyo*" the legislators of Atlantico would set for the rest of the country, of how education would lift up the children and make for a better and brighter future for the Colombian people, and how, despite its small size, the Department of Atlantico would set an example for the rest of the nation. How the people and children of Atlantico would be the beneficiaries of their vision and foresight, etc., etc., etc.

When I finished I was expecting they would rush the podium, lift me up on their shoulders and carry me off the field in triumph, like college football players do to their coach after winning the" big game." That didn't happen, but they did stand up and gave me a round of applause.

Even better the bill passed and a separate office was established within the Dept. of Education and the director was my Colombian counterpart Santander Crespo. We received a budget of 30,000 pesos per year, and our own Russian jeep.

All this time I had been working closely with Carolyn, the ETV Volunteer from another group. When you work with someone and see them almost every day you soon get to know them really well, and the more I got to know Carolyn, the more in love I fell. No matter what disappointments we had and hardships we faced, she was always cheerful and upbeat, generous and kind.

My living expenses were so minimal that I was able to save some money each month that enabled me to buy an engagement ring. We were in Cartagena for an ETV conference, and Peace Corps had put us up at a hotel on the beach. We were walking along the beach one evening, the moon was almost full. I stopped under a palm tree and got down on one knee, just like in the movies, and proposed. I remember telling her that I wasn't sure where I was going or what I wanted to do, but I knew that I loved her. Her response was that we would figure out our future together and she said, "Yes!" A few months later, April 2, 1966 to be exact, we were married in the Church of Nuestra Señora del Carmen in Barranquilla.

A Colombian friend once said a better name for the Cuerpo de Paz (Peace Corps) would be the Cuerpo de Paseo (Corps of Travel), because Volunteers were always going somewhere.

Shortly before we were married, the school teachers, who hadn't been paid in several months, went on strike. It appeared that the strike would be a long one. We decided to take a trip and visit parts of Colombia we might not get to visit otherwise.

We had been thinking about traveling by boat down the Amazon River when we finished our PC service. So we decided we'd travel to the Chocó and take a boat down the Rio Atrato as a way of preparing ourselves for a trip down the Amazon. At the time we went to the Chocó, it was one of the least developed departments in Colombia. It had less than 20 kilometers of paved road.

We flew to Medellín, then at dawn left by bus for Quibdó, the capital of the Department of Chocó. I believe the paved road ran out shortly after we left Medellín. It was a long and tiring trip. We didn't arrive in Quibdó until mid morning the following day. During the course of the trip the complexion of the passengers became progressively darker the farther we went into the Chocó.

The Chocó was settled by black slaves who escaped from the gold and emerald mines in Antioquia and fled into the jungles of the Chocó. We were told, there were villages in the jungles where they live much like their ancestors lived in Africa centuries ago.

The other major ethnic group is the Amerindians who live in isolated settlements in the jungle. At the time of our visit, the only town was the capital Quibdó and that wasn't much more than an overgrown village with only one paved street that was only about a quarter mile in length.

There were no bridges or motorized ferries in the entire department. The way you crossed rivers was in a canoe or on a raft that was pulled by a rope hand over hand from one side to another.

Sometime in the afternoon I became aware that Carolyn and I were the only white people on the bus, everyone else was black. An hour or so later we came to a wide river. The bus drove onto a rather insubstantial looking raft that had been tied up next to the river bank. We had been on the road for several hours and everyone got out of the bus to stretch their legs, while the ferrymen pulled us across the river.

I was standing next to the rail near the edge of the raft and Carolyn was standing near the bus. A man came up to me and began a conversation. After we had been talking for a few moments, he reached out his hand and began stroking my arm. Oh no, I thought to myself, this guy is gay and he's making a pass at me. What am I going to have to do, whack him in the head? As these thoughts were running through my mind, out of the corner of my eye I see a woman talking to Carolyn. Suddenly this woman reached out and stroke Carolyn's arm. Then I realized what was going on. This guy had never been this close to a white man before and he was curious to find out if my skin felt any different, and once his curiosity had been satisfied, he withdrew his hand as did the woman who had been stroking Carolyn's arm. Our journey continued uneventfully, until we arrived at Quibdó.

Quibdó had to be one of the ugliest towns in Colombia. The little village sat on the banks of the mud colored Rio Atrato. The town actually occupied only one bank of the river, the other side was mostly scraggily second growth tropical forest. There was only one road into Quibdó. The sight that greeted you when you first entered town after being ferried over the river was the back walls of a series of ramshackle buildings. The buildings perched like herons, were set on spindly poles raised fifteen or twenty feet above the muddy banks of the turgid

Rio Atrato. They huddled close together as if for mutual support and stretched out alongside the chocolate colored river for about a mile or so. On three sides Quibdó was bordered by jungle and on the fourth side by the river.

Except for a stretch that was paved and ran for about a quarter of a mile or so in front of the buildings that lined the rivers banks, all the roads were unpaved and muddy. Gradually they petered out to footpaths into the forest as you neared the edge of town.

The one stretch of paved road seemed to exist solely for the purpose of providing the towns fleet of taxis (I counted two) an opportunity to drive their passengers up and down the main street. The only passengers I ever saw in the cars were Amerindians, who had come into town to trade. After selling their produce, some of them would take a ride. As the cars drove slowly back and forth, up and down the town's only paved street, you would see them sitting in the back seat smiling contentedly dressed only in loin cloths, with a bright feather or two of some tropical bird in their hair.

As I recollect we stayed in Quibdó for about two or three days waiting for a boat to take us down the Rio Atrato.

The best thing I can say about our trip down river was it only lasted a week. It was incredibly boring and monotonous, the scenery never changed, dense tropical jungle crowding down to the banks of the river. Every other day or so we would come to a small clearing in the jungle and there would be a few forlorn looking buildings and thatched huts. The color scheme was several shades of green and the muddy brown of the river. We got enough of a taste of what a trip down the Amazon might be like, that we decided to forgo that experience.

Barranquilla sits at the mouth of the Rio Magdalena, about a hundred kilometers from the Sierra Nevada de Santa Marta, a mountain range that has the steepest vertical ascent of any mountain range in the world, rising from sea level to almost 19,000 feet in about 50 miles. In the early morning coolness, just before dawn, one could occasionally catch a glimpse of the snow capped peaks of the Sierra looming up across the folded plain of the Rio Magdalena Valley. It was a magnificent sight, quickly obscured by the heat and haze rising from the swampy lowlands of the Magdalena river valley. During the day, one would never imagine that a mighty range of mountains lay just barely one hundred kilometers away totally obscured by haze and mist. I was determined to hike the heights of these mountains the first time I had a chance.

One day a Volunteer from Valledupar wandered into the Peace Corps office in Barranquilla and told us about a group from the University of Pennsylvania that was planning an expedition into the Sierra.

He was planning to join them, so I thought I'd go along as well. Our thinking was they might be able to use some people with language skills to help out with local guides, and that would be us.

We left for Valledupar the next morning and joined up with the team from the University. It was quite a large group over twenty people as I recall and several fields of study were represented, ornithologists, geologists, botanists etc.

We were helpful in finding a few guides for them and some mules to carry their equipment.

The expedition set off with Dave and me bringing up the rear driving a few mules ahead of us. We made camp the first night at about 6,000 feet in preparation for the next leg which would bring us up to about 12,000 feet where we would be positioned near the foot of a glacier which began at about 16,000 ft. My dream of scaling this renowned mountain to the summit seemed about to come true.

Next morning the expedition set off early. Dave and I had to round up a few mules and pack up some equipment, so by the time we got started it was mid morning.

Growing up in the Bronx I didn't have much experience in "mule driving" so progress was slow. Sometime around mid afternoon we came upon two women, who were part of the expedition, sitting patiently beside the trail waiting for us to appear. One of them had slipped and sprained her ankle. Her friend stayed behind for company. The rest decided to press on and left them behind, knowing that we would soon be along. Even with our assistance the woman had difficulty walking, so we were slowed down even further.

Besides leaving the two alongside the trail for us to pick up, the group had neglected to leave them any food or extra water; perhaps they thought we were a walking commissary, but that was not the case. We had no supplies, neither food or water, or shelter. All that was with the main expedition somewhere up ahead. Our mules carried only books and scientific equipment which was a considerable amount as they planned to be in the Sierra for a month.

I realized it was imperative we catch up with the main expedition before night fall. By now we were above the tree line. The only articles of clothing we had were jeans and t-shirts, adequate during the heat of the day, but hardly suitable for the night when temperatures would get down to freezing. We were very hungry, having had nothing to eat since early morning. By now the ladies canteens were empty and we were all thirsty.

As soon as the sun set it became noticeably colder, and the expedition was still nowhere in sight. Right about then I began to wish I had done a little advanced planning and was regretting my spontaneity.

Fortunately, within a short time we came upon a small Indian village, actually nothing more than a few stone walled huts with thatched roofs. There was a fire burning inside one of the huts so the village seemed to be inhabited. I don't recall them having any food, but they did have water which they shared with us and for which we were very thankful.

Noticing how inadequately we were clothed the Indian women quickly bundled Dave and I into one of their huts and lay down beside us to keep us warm. That night I slept nestled between two Indian women, along with Dave, the two gringas, and a few small pigs in a little hut. I can honestly say it wasn't the best night's sleep I've ever had, but at least I survived.

We finally caught up with the rest of the group the following day; they had made camp beside a beautiful mountain lake adjacent to and several hundred feet below the foot of the glacier which covered the highest peak in the Sierra Nevada, Pico Colon.

Seeing the snow capped peak at such a relatively "short distance" away, renewed my determination to get to the top. I had often dreamed about climbing a snow capped peak and now I'd have a chance. I was not going to allow my lack of experience and equipment to deter me. After all, the peak was only a mere 3,000 or so feet higher and only about sixty percent of that was over snow and ice, perhaps seven or eight miles round trip; I'd be back well before dark.

After a hearty breakfast, I began my trek early the next morning. My equipment consisted of the clothes on my back, hiking boots, a sweatshirt, a small backpack lent to me by a member of the group, and a hiking staff that had also been given to me by a member of the group. The backpack contained, bread, cheese, nuts and raisins, and a flask of water.

It was a sunny day, not a cloud in the sky. It probably didn't take me much more than an hour or so to get to the foot of the glacier. There was a slight breeze that made it cool and even a little chilly in the shade, but in the sunshine it was very pleasant. I felt great, strong, well rested, and excited to move ahead.

I had been walking on the glacier, for only a short period of time when I experienced my first mishap. My foot broke through a soft spot in the crust and I sunk down to my knee in the snow. Aside from getting some snow down my boot, it wasn't too bad, although it did give me pause to consider what I should do if this were to reoccur.

About a half hour or so later, I hit another soft patch and broke through the crust once again. I pushed on, but now I was breaking through the crust frequently, often as far down as my knees, with almost every other step. It was hard work, lifting my legs up out of the snow. My pants and boots were soaked; my breathing had become heavy and labored.

Finally, I had to admit that I was not going to be able to get to the top, of the mountain, and that what I was doing was stupid, foolish, and dangerous. So I turned around and started back down.

On the way back down, I slipped, fell, and broke through the crust, falling into a small ice chasm. The chasm wasn't very deep, probably not more than eight or nine feet. I was shaken up by the fall, but not seriously hurt, no broken bones etc. But I was unable to grasp the ledge to pull myself up. When I realized that I couldn't get out quickly, panic set in. I tried to climbing up the walls, but they were icy, there was nothing to hold on to and I kept slipping back.

Pretty soon my t-shirt and jeans were wet and clammy from the ice. I had to face the prospect that I might never be able to get out of this crevasse and that I'd die there. It was all my fault for being so stupid and foolish and not taking any precautions.

To make a long story short, I never was able to get out of the ice chasm, and perished on the slopes of Pico Colon.

Actually, the hiking staff I had been given was like a ski pole and having it no doubt saved my life. The pole was steel tipped and had a little round cup about six inches up the shaft to prevent it from sinking too far into the snow.

Using the steel tip, I began chipping away at the icy wall. After an hour or two I didn't have much to show for my efforts, the progress I made was agonizingly slow. I was beginning to think maybe I'd never get out of there alive.

Then I had the idea to chip away at the lip of the hole above me in the hope that the ice might be thinner there. A shower of snow and small chunks of ice rained down on me as I worked away. Eventually I had chipped away enough material so that I was able to climb out.

By the time I finally pulled myself out it was beginning to get dark. My clothes and boots were wet from the snow and ice. I began my descent trying to carefully retracing the way I'd come up, so as to avoid another accident. Fortunately, there was a full moon and I don't recall having any difficulty finding the base camp. It being beside the lake was a big help.

When I got back to camp I stripped off all my wet clothes and dried myself off. Someone gave me a cup of hot water laced with rum. The next thing I remember was awakening the following morning feeling hungry enough to eat a cow. I left the following day and was back in Barranquilla within a few days.

I did make a second trip into the Sierra Nevada, this time on a humanitarian mission. Peace Corps had a doctor in Barranquilla. Some how or other he got wind of the fact there were isolated groups of Indians, living up in the Sierra, and from time to time some of them would come down from the mountains looking for medical help. Two of these Indians had recently been seen in Santa Marta. The doctor didn't speak any Spanish, so he asked me if I would help him locate the Indians in Santa Marta and if we were successful, accompany him into the sierra.

The doctor had a backpack full of meds and we drove over to Santa Marta. It didn't take long to locate the two Indians. They were members of the Kogi tribe, the same tribe I had spent the night with on my previous trip two or three months prior. Only one of them spoke Spanish, but from what he was able to tell me, I knew they were looking for a *medico*.

We agreed to leave for the village the next morning. We left at dawn and following their directions I drove into the Sierra. After about two hours driving we came to the end of the road. It was still early in the day so we left the Jeep by the side of the road and plunged into the forest. I remember asking Juan, which was the name the Spanish speaker went by, how long it would take to reach his village and being comforted by his reply that it was not very far.

From the moment we left the Jeep, our guide's pace never slackened. We took no rest breaks, nor did we stop for lunch. Our guides seemed impervious to hunger and fatigue. Finally, late in the afternoon, we came to a clearing in the forest. Someone had carved a small *finca* (farm) out of the dense foliage. There were several rows of scrawny looking corn stalks, a few banana trees and some chickens pecking away at the dirt in front of a thatched roofed hut that stood at the opposite side of the clearing.

A small, raged looking, bare foot compesino came out to greet us. He was the first new person I had seen all day, and his finca was the only sign of habitation we had seen since entering the forest several hours earlier. For the first time since we had left the Jeep early in the morning, we stopped.

Inside the darkness of the hut, I could see a small child peering shyly out at us. The father ordered the child to bring us same water. While we were waiting the doctor had me ask the compesino, how far it was to the Indian village. Not very far was his reassuring response. The doctor, however, was not satisfied with his response. Noticing the lengthening shadows and the impending arrival of night, he pointed to his watch and asked me to ask him how long it will take us to get there? Will we be there in an hour or so? Gesturing toward the doctor pointing to his watch, I asked the compesino if we would arrive at the village within the next hour or so. He assured me most definitely that we would. When I informed the doctor of his response, I could see him relax.

Wanting to arrive in the village before dark we were soon on our way. We needn't have hurried, we spent the night sleeping in the forest and arrived mid morning in the village. It wasn't until the next day that I came to realize how absurd my questions had been. Here I was asking a man who had probably never seen a watch in his whole life, a man who measured time the same way our ancestors had centuries ago: sunrise, mid day, sunset. To parse an hour, a period of time that had no meaning for him was ridiculous.

We spent two very busy days in the village or "*major dicho*" (better said) the doctor spent two busy days examining folks giving out meds, and cleaning up wounds, etc. He was fascinated by the experience. I remember him remarking that he had seen things in that village, that he'd never experienced in the States - conditions that no longer existed in the U.S.[13]

Just as the American doctor discovered conditions in the mountains of Colombia so different than anything he would see in the United States, Tom came to understand how different even day to day situations were in Colombia, differences Volunteers experienced, but may not have even recognized.

I never realized how great it was to be a dog in America until an experience I had in Colombia. Carolyn, my wife, got very sick, and the doctor suggested we move out of the place where we were living into a healthier environment, where she could get adequate rest and better food.

As luck would have it, an AID director in Barranquilla was taking his family back to the U.S. for a month vacation and was looking for someone to house sit for him for the next thirty days.

It was the perfect solution for us, so we moved in. Before leaving, the director told us that we would only have one chore to do while they were out of the country. We'd have to feed the dog, and walk him once a day. The dog was a German Shepard, who answered to the name Yankee. I no longer recall the owner's name, let's just call him Mike.

Mike takes me to a big freezer and opens it to show me the dog's food. He informs me that Yankee gets a pound of ground steak each day and that I will

---

[13] Tom Gallaher, personal email, April 21, 2009.

need to take it out of the freezer to defrost in the morning. Each day's ration was prepackaged in its own plastic bag to make it easy for me.

Looking at 30, one pound packages of frozen ground steak, I realized that Yankee was eating far better than either my wife or me. So I decided that we would share our food with the dog and he could share a little of his food with us. For the next thirty days, Yankee received the typical *"comedia Colombiana,"* yuca, rice, platano, and a pound of meat per week which I purchased at the local market. And we ate the dog's food. It's startling to realize that dogs eat better in the U.S. than half the world's population and Yankee had been eating better than we had been eating for the last two years.

When Mike and the family return he was surprised to see how thin Yankee appeared.

"What happened?" he wanted to know. "Why was the dog so thin? Had I forgotten to feed him?"

I showed him the empty freezer and told him I couldn't explain it either. Perhaps the dog has worms. "Maybe he should take him to a vet and have him checked out," I suggested.

I must confess, I had no guilt feelings whatsoever and Carolyn, with the help of her new diet, had recovered completely.[14]

Colombian jails were notorious for their bad conditions. Actually, all South American prisons and holding tanks had that reputation, with Peru and Ecuador being the worst. Still, a night in a Colombian jail would not be considered a picnic. From experience Tom can say,

.....I hope not many of our group ever had the occasion to spend a night in a Colombian *cárcel*, especially over something as stupid as a typewriter.

Dan Dobin was a PCV working in co-ops in Barranquilla and for a short time we had rented a house together. One day he came to me and asked for my help in retrieving a typewriter that someone had taken from the co-op where he worked. Of course I agreed to help.

We went to an office building and walked up to the third floor. Dan led the way into the office and pointed to the typewriter, "that's the one, take it." So I took it over the protests of several people that gathered around in the office. We went to the office of Dan's co-op where I dropped off the typewriter.

A short time later we were walking down the street when someone pointed us out to the police and shouted out, "There they are!"

The police ordered us to stop. Dan started running and urged me to run as well. I wasn't going to run; I had nothing to fear from the police. I had merely taken the typewriter and returned it to its rightful owners. Besides it was undignified for me to run, and it would be difficult for me to escape anyway, as there probably weren't to many 6' 2" red heads in Barranquilla. I continued walking until the police accompanied by the irate individual from whose office I had taken the typewriter, caught up with me.

"Tell us where the typewriter is," he demanded.

---

[14] Tom Gallaher, personal email, April 21, 2009.

I told him the typewriter had been returned to its proper owners. He instructed the police to have me show my certificate of ownership, and when I couldn't produce any proof, the police hauled me off to the local *cárcel*. I thought I'd be there only momentarily and that Dan would show up soon and everything would be resolved. Never in my wildest imagination did I think I'd spend the night behind bars.

The cell was hot and stinking and crowded. There wasn't enough room to lie down and I wouldn't have even if I could have. Dawn didn't come early enough for me. I got out early next morning thanks to Carolyn. She had heard what happened. She got hold of Dan and had him return the typewriter so I could be released from jail. The whole experience sort of soured me on Colombian jails.[15]

A few months after Tom Gallaher's move from Boyacá to Barranquilla, more ETV folks from Colombia '64 began to arrive on the coast, this time it was in Cartagena. Like Tom, Marge Mohler was being shifted from the mountains of Boyacá to the tropics of Colombia's coastal plain.

I transferred to Cartagena after spending the first year in Tunja because Cartagena became a new site for ETV. Gerry Volgenau was to be our ETV Volunteer leader. Jeanne (Ellefson) Meier and I taught and trained the teachers on Saturday mornings and worked with them in the schools during the week.

When we first arrived, we lived with a Colombian family. But after a few weeks it became apparent that having two more people in this house was really a hardship for the family. Jeanne and I found an apartment in old Cartagena.

The family convinced us to come to their barrio every Wednesday for dinner and bring our laundry. That family eventually immigrated to Ohio as the father found work in the construction industry there. They're now in Texas where the weather is more to their liking.

Our Cartagena apartment had three rooms plus a bath and was located over a tienda with the owners living in an apartment behind the store. We entertained our neighbors with our gringo antics like lowering a basket with pesos to buy Pepsi from the tienda down stairs.

The neighbors actually brought chairs out to watch our project to rid our place of mice. Our entrance on the street side had about a 6 inch gap between the door and the sill. We figured we could nail a board making the door flush with the sill. We modified the door, but the mice problem continued. Our neighbors just laughed at us because, as they later told us, the mice weren't entering at the door, but in the hole in the wall created by the water pipes. We kept very little food in the apartment after that.

Cartagena has a rich history and the buildings in the old walled city where we lived were really neat. You could go up on the walls and walk the ramparts.

One story I heard is that prison cells were part of this wall that faced the water. When high tide came--well you can imagine what happened to those prisoners.[16]

---

[15] Tom Gallaher, personal email, April 21, 2009.
[16] Margaret Mohler, personal email, May 22, 2009.

By January 1966, Colombia '64 had increased its presence on the Caribbean Coast from just two, Roberts and Andrews, to five, adding Gallaher, Mohler and Gerald Voganeu who would serve as the ETV leader coordinating the effort to establish a functioning system in the Bolívar Department. Along with the Volunteers stationed on the coast, would come visitors. Colombia's north coast, so different from the mountainous interior, would become one of the group's favorite vacation destinations.

Meanwhile, Jeff Andrews had done some expanding of his own. During the last few months of his tenure, Jeff had branched out, working with schools all over the department of Bolívar including the city of Cartagena. Utilizing UNICEF seeds and tools, and PINA for animals, his goal was to establish gardens and livestock programs in as many of the department schools as possible. The program proved so successful that when he ended his tour, PINA and the Peace Corps looked around for someone with experience to carry on the work.

Don Lydic of Boyacá rabbit ranch fame was offered the job if he would be willing to move to Cartagena and extend for a year. Since his draft board had turned him down for a deferment to go to graduate school, Don decided, why not?

Jeff had been working with about 40 elementary schools in Bolívar, 12 of these had active programs going when I arrived. I worked out of Cartagena and was successful in expanding the program and extending it to families associated with the schools. We sold the seeds and animals to individuals, at a low price, but it was enough to be sure they were serious about starting a project. Most of the teachers in these schools were great and were the real backbone of the program.

One school even tried importing ducks especially bred for laying eggs. The theory was that they would be less susceptible to the tropical diseases. The school ordered the ducks, but I never learned how they worked out. I left before the project really got under way.[17]

Jeff, ready for another hard day in the campo or maybe feria.

---

[17] Don Lydic, telephone interview, Nov. 19, 2009.

12

COLOMBIA'S NORTH COAST
SMUGGLERS, BUCCANEERS AND A DESERT IN THE SEA

As Margaret Mohler indicated in the last chapter, Gerald Volgenau was also moved to Cartagena, though he came from the hot country of Tolima at the other end of the Magdalena Valley instead of the mountains. Gerald would be the ETV leader coordinating the effort to establish a functioning system in the Cartagena area. But Volgenau's story of the coast begins, conversely, many years later and in a different Latin American country – actually in Panama City, Panama on December 23, 1989.

Twenty-four years had passed since I ended my tour as a Volunteer in Colombia. Now as a national correspondent for the Detroit Free Press and Knight-Ridder Newspapers, I was called in the dark hours before breakfast to grab a suitcase and head for Panama.

We, that is, the United States, were invading. The goal was to oust Manuel Noreiga, the *de facto* president. He was a classic South American strongman who had fallen from U.S. grace. For decades, the CIA had loved Noriega. He was their darling as an "intelligence asset." But now President George H.W. Bush viewed *Cara Pina* (Pineapple Face) as a "narco terrorist," the man who had foiled all attempts to democratize Panama. So we went to war against him and his military backers. And if a thousand Panamanians died in the process, well such was the price of democracy.

Like any war, it proved to be dangerous for journalists. By the time I left Detroit, a couple of photographers had already been killed.

On the morning two days before Christmas, another reporter and I were traveling in a van with some Marines. We'd seen some action the day before and now were headed toward the U.S. military headquarters.

Sometime before noon, our van was crawling up a switchback road to the offices of the U.S. Military's Southern Command. The Command was located on a hilltop in Balboa, a rather luxurious part of what had been the U.S. Canal Zone until 1979. The Command had been set up in the former U.S. Officers Club. That would be home base for me for several days, a place to return to after chasing around on combat missions. Officers gave press conferences there. You could wash in a sink (no showers) and, in my case, I ended up sleeping on two tables pulled together in a patio.

As we drove toward the Command, I looked out the van's window just in time to catch sight of something that jerked my thoughts far from Panama's microcosm of fire fights, Humvees and Blackhawk helicopters. I nudged the Marine corporal sitting next to me.

"See that church?" I said. We were passing the Balboa Union Church.
"I got married in that church."

He looked at me as though I had stepped off a space ship. But it was true.
Pat Hill and I decided to get married in the spring of 1965 while we were still in Espinal. The date would be in November. And we thought it would be in Cartagena.

Cartagena and the department of Bolívar were going to be new sites for Educational Television. I was being sent there as the ETV coordinator and Pat, who extended her tour by a year, would be working in the schools as a teacher trainer. We were soon to be joined by a technician and two more Volunteers for the schools, Marge Mohler and Jeannie Elephson. This arrangement worked out fine. Better than I might have imagined.

Pat, Jeannie and Marge were experienced in this classroom work. Actually the word "experienced" does not say it all. They were pros. They understood that the Peace Corps' most important contribution to Colombian education was not TV sets, not even the programming with expert, on-camera Colombian teachers. That electronic wizardry was just a foot in Colombia's educational door. The important job was to bring modern teaching methods to teachers who for literally centuries had never moved beyond basic rote learning.

These Volunteers could not know how prescient they were. ETV soon proved to be short lived -- an educational fad. But what would remain, at least for some teachers, was a better, more sophisticated view of teaching and learning. Jeanne, Marge and Pat knew their pedagogy. I, on the other hand, was not so great at it. So the Peace Corps did what so many organizations do with incompetents. They promoted me.

And despite that awkward experience with the Girardot city archives back in Tolima, I was far better at negotiating with local and even national officials than I ever was when trying to explain the benefits of the Socratic method.

In order for the Peace Corps to bring ETV to Cartagena, the government was required to supply certain things: office space, telephone, a jeep, two Colombian teachers to work as my counterparts and eventually take over the program, and finally, someone to learn the technical aspects of TV, like hooking up antennas and such. Somehow, I managed to get it all done with the help of the officials' secretaries (who really ran the place) and a liberal distribution of contraband Marlboro cigarettes.

For me, Cartagena proved to be a steamy place with a history of buccaneers and remarkable moments with one-legged street people, a Salvador Dali-esque film festival and a bullfight that might have been imagined only by the love child of Gloria Steinem and the Colombian artist Fernando Botero.

When fall arrived, Pat joined me on the coast, and our marriage plans began to jell. The date would be November 27th. My mother could fly down from Colorado Springs. Pat's parents would make the trip from Orlando, Florida. All fine and good. In fact, pretty darned romantic. I was already imagining a wedding in the shadow of Cartagena's 300-year-old El Castillo de San Filipe de Barajas. This was a centuries-old walled city with cobbled streets, whispering palms and the quiet lap-lap of the Caribbean Sea against the shore. But as the big day approached, circumstances changed. And I must say that they changed in *un estilo Latino* (Latin style). It was yet one more demonstration that, like Dorothy, we were no longer in Kansas. All the judges in Colombia went on strike.

Now in the United States, autoworkers go on strike. So do hotel waiters, airline pilots, truck drivers, steel workers, school teachers, fire fighters and even police officers. But for the life of me, I cannot remember even a single instance when judges hit the picket line.

But this was Colombia and here the judges went on strike. I can't recall why they struck. Probably for more money. But it may have been for air conditioned court rooms or fancier robes or a chance for a bigger slice of the graft. Who knows? Whatever the reason, they were serious. And being judges, whose words quite literally are law, they were unlikely to cave in very quickly.

Now understand the nature of this strike. Everything that required any sort of legal imprimatur demanded a judge. It needed his agreement, his signature, the stamp of his official seal. Marriages, which of course were our concern, were halted well before any I dos could be spoken. Grooms, brides, priests may all have been ready. But without a judge to sign off on it, why bother?

And not just marriages hit a judicial road block. Trials slammed to a halt in mid course. Civil suits went unsettled. And guys who had been sent to jail on charges of being drunk and disorderly -- typically an overnight penalty -- simply stayed in jail for weeks... and weeks.

October came and waned with no strike settlement in sight. We needed a Plan B. We could not go back to the states to get married. That would have been a simple solution. But the Peace Corps did not allow such early returns.

Then Pat came up with a brilliant idea. She had friends who were Volunteers in Panama. With a little help from them to find a church and such, we could get married there -- in the Canal Zone.

At that point and as it had been from the beginning, the Canal Zone was officially America. It was as American as, say, Arizona or Connecticut.

Volunteers in Panama were allowed to go into the Zone. So this was a loophole. By shifting the wedding to the Zone, we could get married in America without actually going to America. And so we did.

It was a small wedding in what seemed like a very big church -- just a handful of people gathered at the altar. The onlookers were mostly Volunteers, most of whose names I never learned. As I look back, I really only knew two people -- my mom and, of course, Pat.

Pat looked more than fetching in a pure white gown. I, on the other hand, looked like a Bataan Death March survivor. My weight had dropped dramatically while living in Colombia's tropics. At five-foot-11, I weighed only 140 pounds. In my new dark suit, the one I'd bought the day before, I looked like a kid in his dad's clothes.

But no matter. After all I was _only_ the groom. As any guy who ever has stood at the altar can tell you, the groom's presence is required but not particularly important.

The ceremony came off as planned. Words were said. Rings exchanged. Papers were signed. No judge was needed.

And later we went for dinner. Pat's dad, a former Navy officer, chose the place. And wouldn't you know, it was the place I'd end up almost two and a half decades later -- the officers club in Balboa.

To walk the streets and high parapets of Cartagena is almost to hear the swash and buckle of this storied Caribbean gold port. In fact, Cartagena has more history -- especially of the sword flashing bloody kind -- than almost any other city in the Americas. And it certainly is one of the oldest European-founded cities in the western hemisphere. Cartagena got its start in 1533. That's very early -- just 41 years after Columbus stumbled onto the Americas and a full 32 years before the Spanish founded the oldest existing city in the United States -- St. Augustine, Florida.

The founder was a Spanish nobleman, Don Pedro de Heredia. He recognized that Cartagena's wonderful, deep water harbor would be a great place to load ships with gold stolen from the locals.

It should be noted that Heredia was not a born adventurer. *Nueva Granada* (as Colombia was known) was not really high on his list of places to go. For him, a hot night in old Spain was lots of booze, women and an occasional barroom brawl. Unfortunately the local authorities soon wearied of this bad behavior and issued an ultimatum. Go west young noble or go to jail.

So in true conquistador style, Heredia showed up on the coast of South America with 150 men with swords and muskets and then proceeded to steal as much gold as the Spanish ships could carry. If any native objected, Heredia simply had him killed. After all they were only Indians and not even Catholics, so who cared?

In short order, Cartagena grew to become one of Spain's most important gold ports and was attracting the eyes of privateers from England. That meant what in today's vernacular might be called "the letting of defense contracts."

Over time, the Spanish erected some seven miles of ramparts to protect the port city as well as *El Castillo de San Felipe de Barajas,* a huge fort to fend off attackers from the land side.

Building these fortifications was not cheap. In 1756 when the final bill came in for all that construction, Spain's King Carlos III took one look at the totals and picked up a telescope. Peering out to the west from his window, his majesty said: "For this price, those castles should be seen from here."

Historically Cartagena is as famous for the people who attacked it as for the people who lived there. Looking for quick plunder, France and England sent some of their most famous privateers to Cartagena. They included John Hawkins and his nephew Sir Francis Drake.

Drake, who was called El Draque, managed on one foray to capture the city, destroy almost a quarter of its buildings, including a recently completed cathedral, and the government palace. And then to further thumb his nose at the Spanish, Drake made them buy it back for about $200 million in today's dollars.

Needless to say, Spain's King Philip II was miffed. He offered an $8 million reward for Drake's head. But as it turned out, King Philip had about as much luck at capturing Drake, as President George W. Bush did in nabbing Osama bin Laden.

Attacks on Cartagena went on for almost 200 years. But the attackers were not always successful. One of the last attacks came in 1741, just 35 years before the American Revolution. British Admiral Edward Vernon, along with colonial troops, staged a massive attack on the city with 186 ships and 23,600 men. It was a bloody siege. But to Spain's credit, the defenders held off the Brits with just six ships and 3,600 men. Imagine the Alamo with the Texans winning. King Carlos' may have griped about the cost, but he got his money's worth with the San Felipe fort. No enemy ever captured it.

But even when the city was not under siege, Cartagena was a harsh place. It was a slave port. The Spanish and Portuguese crammed their ships with thousands of Africans and brought them to the Americas. Heredia, the city's founder, led the way. He brought in Africans to cut cane so roads could be opened. It did not take long for the Spanish to discover that the local Indians made lousy slaves. Once in chains, they tended to die quickly. Soon Cartagena gained notoriety as one of Spain's two officially sanctioned trading centers for black slaves. The other was Veracruz in what is now Mexico.

Also the Spanish Inquisition set up its unique shop of horrors in Cartagena. Thousands of accused heretics were tortured to death in the Palacio de La Inquisicion from 1770 to 1811. The building, now a museum, still stands.

If Cartagena is known for its violent past, it also has gained fame as a home for artists and writers. Unarguably, Colombia's and Cartagena's most famous author is Gabriel Garcia Marquez, who wrote one of the 20th century's greatest novels, "One Hundred Years of Solitude." As a young man Garcia worked as a journalist in Cartagena and later used the city as the setting for his novel, "Love in the Time of Cholera."

Less well known but close to my heart and the hearts of Cartageneros is the poet Luis Carlos Lopez. An odd statue stands in one of the city's less prominent plazas. Displayed are two rather battered shoes; one lying on its side, the other standing. It is a tribute to Lopez and to the city. After a long absence, the poet returned to Cartagena and described the city as comfortable as putting on a pair of old shoes. The city loved that image. So the statue was erected which Cartageneros variously call *"Las Botas Viejas"* or *"Los Zapatos Viejos."*

To say that Cartagena was different in this time than other places in the Colombian nation is not a particularly brilliant observation. Colombia is filled with unique places, entirely distinct from the others. For the most part, this variation is isolation due to geography. The country has lots of mountains. Big mountains. And for centuries it was pretty darned hard to get around. So Colombia became a place of enclaves, each with its own personality.

Cartagena, like much of the Caribbean, has tall people (as compared to the shorter Indian stock of the interior). This is due to the strong African influence. *Costenos'* walk (stroll is probably more accurate) is unhurried, the only sensible way to move in such a hot and humid place. Their gait is languid, loose-limbed and always in the coolness of the shady side of the street. As a result, Cartageneros don't sweat. You could always spot the *Cachacos*, those people from the interior. Speed counts with them. They quick step along, migrate to the vacant sidewalks in the sun to build up more speed and, in minutes, their clothes are soaked.

Heat, in many ways defined the city in the 1960s. One of the two movie theaters had no roof. You sat under the stars which were often better entertainment than the film. To eat in the city's single restaurant with air conditioning was to emerge with your glasses fogged. It was a city that smelled of fish and the sea, of stagnant water, of perfume and body stink, of dust and flowers.

Cartagena -- unlike the grey, stone cities in the mountainous south -- is brightly lit, dressed in yellows and whites. It is a place of music. Even if no music is playing, the coastal people move like dancers who are listening to their own internal guitars and *tambores*.

The city is romantic. The clip-clop of moonlight carriage rides of the parapets, dinners of grilled lobster, Costeña beer and *chipi-chipi* on the porch of the restaurant *Capilla del Mar,* soft breezes, and evening of *guayabera* shirts and the caress of white cotton dresses on brown legs.

Like the rest of the country, Cartagena was a city of extreme wealth and extreme poverty. The rich tended to hang out in Boca Grande where tourists stayed at the Hotel Caribe. The poor, like the poor everywhere, were relegated to sour neighborhoods with stagnant water in the streets and sometimes inside the houses, bare light bulbs at night, corrugated tin walls and bare-bottomed children with distended stomachs.

And Cartagena was -- and is -- a magnet. It was a port city that drew people from all lands. Even a few cruise ships came. (Chaperon to a 14-year-old girl, "Get away from that Colombian guy. Don't talk to him." "But, but ... he's an American. In the Peace Corps.")

For Colombians, Cartagena is a favorite vacation spot. And happily for Pat, the other Cartagena Volunteers and me, it was one of the spots not to be missed by Peace Corps Volunteers. Most of them ended up at our apartment. Each arrival signaled a chance for a gathering, a party. Rum would be drunk, guitars played, people sang folk songs for heaven's sake and Mexican rancheros. No ear buds, no Walkmen, no commercial television. Not much of interest on the radio, except an occasional hours-long broadcast of a speech by Fidel Castro from across the waves. We made our own entertainment.

Perhaps my favorite example of Cartagena as the world's agora is Christmas. It was truly an international event right in our apartment. Out on our deck, you could see the Caribbean's blue-green waters, a five-year-old Colombian girl with a blindfold tried to swat a *piñata*. Food flowed in like a cholesterol tide. Pat cooked the traditional American dinner -- turkey, dressing, mashed potatoes, the whole shebang.

Irene LoRe, a Volunteer whose Italian grandmother taught her a thing or two, showed up with enough ravioli to feed the Vatican guard. Ester Jimenez, the elderly lady who lived downstairs, produced coastal-style fish tamales steaming inside their traditional wrap of *bijao* leaves.

Two local Volunteers created a Christmas tree after finding some pine boughs which were tied together and made to stand up in an inverted stool. We had no fake snow, tinsel or colored glass balls. So we decorated the tree with Christmas cards and children's drawings.

Peace Corps Volunteers started showing up in late morning. Ready to party, they stopped for a quick snack, drank a beer or two, pulled on swim suits and headed for the beach which was three minutes down the road. When they got back, they still found plenty to eat and drink. It was an inland sea of comestibles.

More people came. And more. They showed up from all over the Colombian coast and from deep in the interior. Peace Corps staff members from Bogotá made a surprise visit, along with a dignitary from Washington. CARE Rep. Don Cronin drove his Jeep over from Barranquilla.

A borrowed phonograph was thumping out cumbias and sambas. The windows were open. Of course, it was hot. So the music was an open invitation for anyone within ear shot. The neighbors came by and ate and drank and danced -- and stayed. And so did people who were just passing by on the street. People no one knew.

It was all fine and festive. The food was endless. Patton's army could not have eaten it all. Everyone drank rum as though Prohibition would start on the 26th.

And they danced. Only stopping occasionally to rest for a few minutes to drink another beer and then dance again. They danced in the midday swelter and in the early evening when the air refused to cool and then well on past midnight when even the hardiest started to stagger a bit.

And we laughed. We laughed as though laughter had just been invented and everyone had to try it out and, once having tried it, needed to do it again and again.

Almost nothing about this Christmas might be described as North American traditional. No snow. No Santa. No roasted chestnuts. No Frosty the Snowman. No paper satchels from Macy's, Gimbals' and Sac's. It was simply my favorite Christmas of all time.

The omnipresent lottery ticket sellers were as much a part of the Cartagena scene as the city walls. But here on the coast, these hawkers had a distinct subgroup -- a one-legged variety. These were former fishermen done in by their former trade.

These fishermen used no nets or long lines with hooks. Theirs was a more explosive style. They used to pair up and go out in dugout canoes with several sticks of dynamite. The guy at the back would paddle; the one in front would stand with one bare foot on the prow, light the fuse and when it had burned down just enough, he would throw.

Boom!!

Dead fish rose to the surface by the score, white bellies to the sun. Much easier than trying to use hooks and lines. In seconds, the job was done. All they had to do was scoop up the corpses.

But at times, the dynamite pitcher got a little too casual. He'd light a long fuse and then, while it was burning down a bit, he would stick it in his back pocket -- maybe so he could light a cigarette. Sometimes he waited just a bit too long.

Boom! His anatomy was changed forever.

If he lived -- and many did not -- the fisherman suddenly found himself making a career change – lottery tickets anyone.

Cartagena did not have a full-blown bull fight season like Bogotá. But it did have one fight while I was there. And if nothing else, that single event showed that bullfight fans are among the most vicious in the world.

The *corrida* (bull fight) was held in the city's bull ring. It was not a big, fancy cement structure like in the capital, but a rickety old collection of grandstands.

The *matador* (killer), in this case, was not a man and not really a matador. She was a woman who fought Portuguese style, that is, on horseback. In Portugal she would be called a *caballería* (horsewoman). The other notable thing about the Portuguese style is that the bull is not killed, at least not in the arena.

So the bull came out. Black and vicious, his horns hooking first left and then right with the speed of a cheetah. The *picadors* (mounted bullfighters) did their job, jabbing him with their lances. They rode horses that were heavily padded to avoid goring.

Then out she rode, the caballería. She was glorious in black with a traditional flat-brimmed hat. Her job was to set the *banderillas* (small darts with streamers attached).

If you are unfamiliar with bullfighting, the banderillas are colorful, sharp sticks which the bullfighter stabs into the shoulder of the bull. The idea is to weaken the neck so the head droops down. With a hanging head, the bull then opens up his shoulders which allows the bullfighter to jab a sword straight into his heart.

She was a beautiful rider on a stunning black horse which she guided with just her knees. Her art was to ride up next to the bull, leaning far out from the saddle and, using both hands, artfully stab in the banderillas. Simply, hers was a brilliant display of horsemanship and courage.

But as wonderful as that spectacle was, it was not enough for the crowd. Taunting and yelling, they demanded that the slight woman get down off her horse and, like a traditional Spanish matador, cape the bull from the ground and then kill it with a sword thrust.

It was dreadful.

She was brave to be sure. But she simply was not big enough for the job. On the first pass, she caped the bull, reached high with the sword and tried to stab this moving mountain of fury. The blade only sunk in a few inches and then immediately flipped out, blood running down the bull's flank.

It was ugly. The bull was not getting an honorable death, he was being tormented. The crowd broke out in hisses and boos.

She tried again. And again. Each time she failed. Finally, the bull staggered to its knees from sheer exhaustion and loss of blood. At that point, a man – another bullfighter – came up with a short-bladed sword and killed the bull with one powerful stroke to the forehead.

The ballet of the bull fight had ended in an execution.

To my memory, film festivals in the 1960s were held in Cannes and maybe a few other places. They certainly did not appear in such out-of-the-way venues as Banff, Park City and Telluride. And more, it was hard to even imagine one in Cartagena.

But the city fathers were nothing if not ambitious. A festival was scheduled. I think it was the city's first. Famous guests were invited.

Cartagena had just the two movie theaters. The one with no roof and the one with air conditioning. To make up for the lack of venues, the city also opened up the bullring for movies. Folding chairs were arranged in rows in the arena, right on the sand. A screen and a small stage were set up at one end.

We got tickets for the arena to see "Billy Liar," a British comedy with Tom Courtenay. I did not mind that it was two years old. I had not seen it. And what's more it featured Julie Christie. It's the film where she first caught the world's eye.

Now understand, even in this go-along-get-along coastal town, this festival was a big deal. All the fancy folks showed up. Men wore their best *guayabera* shirts; women sucked in their tummies and squeezed into their fanciest party dresses. Everyone was doing his best impression of sophistication.

I went with Pat, Jeanne and Marge. We dressed nicely too. But instead of an evening of coastal sophistication, the festival that night was more of a Mack Sennett comedy Latino style. Only minutes after we sat down, two carefully coifed women got into a screaming match over seating.

"This one's mine!"

"No, it isn't! My cousin was saving it for me!" And so it went until one slapped the other. They finally were pulled apart. What a show.

And then someone lighted firecrackers in the old wooden grandstands behind us. These hijinks led to an actual fire. Not a big one, but with plenty of smoke. Just enough to be entertaining.

Once the blaze was snuffed, the emcee called the honored show biz guests to the stage. That night apparently was Mexican movie night in terms of celebrities. One by one they trotted down the sandy aisle and climbed steps to the stage. But instead of being dressed in tuxes and eye-popping gowns, they looked like tourists in Acapulco. They were wearing shorts, t-shirts and running shoes. And they all looked, well, rather sweaty.

Their explanation: "Sorry, but we flew in on Avianca." The country's national airline. The Volunteers, who well knew that airline, began to laugh. "And not only was the plane late, but they lost our luggage."

This was an Avianca classic. We tried hard to stifle our laughter. It was only polite. The rest of the audience was in fact cowering in embarrassment.

More Mexican movie people came to the stage. A producer, a director, some actors including Lola Beltran.

Now Lola Beltran was not only a movie star, but hugely famous and beloved as a singer of *rancheras,* the emotional Mexican love songs. In spike heels wearing a long colorful scarf, she carefully walked up the steps to the stage, was introduced to cheers and then she politely stepped back to join a line of luminaries.

At just the moment of that backward step, she disappeared. Vanished. One second she was there; the next she was gone. All the remained was her long, long scarf which briefly floated in the air before tumbling in a heap on the stage. Lola Beltran, the beloved Lola Beltran, had fallen off the back of the stage.

The audience was struck dumb. They were horrified. People rushed to her aid. They helped her to her feet. She was still unsteady, but she bravely waved to the crowd. Soon only the groans of embarrassment lingered in the crowd. Fortunately the movie was on tap.

Minutes later, "Billy Liar" glowed onto the screen. As a fan of British comedies and especially of Julie Christie, I liked it. But to tell you the truth, the film was something of an anticlimax.[18]

Gerry, Tom, Marge, Jeff and Eugene experienced the Colombian coast in an up close and personal way for an extended period of time, at least several months. But to gain a different perspective, or maybe not so different, on this area of the country, we have the recollections of the Lenkners who traveled along this sea coast on a vacation and visited not only the major cities already mentioned, but even ventured out to the Guajira Peninsula, a strange land, a desert jutting out into the sea.

One of our most pleasant times [writes Charlie Lenkner], was spent visiting and touring the bay fortifications of Cartagena with Gene Roberts. It was a wonderful introduction to the Colombian north coast and its people.

The coasteña life style was as open and auditorally animated as the cold country was *cerado* (closed) and wasn't edgy like Tolima. Windows and doors were open, radios and some TVs were on, folks yelled and glided (their slow effortless walk), sticking their heads in doorways or coming out to chat.

There was evidence of a little money as some houses were large and more in our style of individual house on a lot, not built wall to wall as in the older parts of town and most other cities. They did remain 3rd world sensible in that tethered in the yard around the house were goats. They mowed the "lawn," didn't see any Toros or Lawn Boys. These houses were usually two story and like mini forts, four walls, few windows on the exterior, with the court yards and openings inside.

We were there during part of the political campaigning, leading up to the voting under the rules that the parties alternated power, but not necessarily the candidates (see Appendix III). On the coast, politics appeared to be an in-the-streets kind of thing. There were crowds, banners, posters, noise. There was a

---

[18] Gerald Volgenau, personal email, Jun. 10, 2009.

fairly strong conservative sentiment which we never knew enough about to link to other things historically. There were Rojas Pinella posters and supporters. Kind of like the running of the bulls, such entertainment was best enjoyed from the window of one's hotel, high up and overlooking the crowds in the streets, at least by the not so fleet afoot and the obvious gringo.

We took the bus to Santa Marta. From the bus, Barranquilla seemed to have even less charm than say Bakersfield (California).

We crossed El Rio Magdalena and it was not a pretty sight; it had less tropical allure than in Tolima certainly. I envisioned crowds of sharks and caimans lurking expectantly, grabbing assorted chunks of protein washed down from the interior.

Ciénaga, a coastal town along the way, was not exactly like San Diego either. Starting about here I began to marvel that there were any caimans left, as vast hordes of them had apparently been captured as infants, gutted, preserved, and were being offered as coin purses, handbags, door stops, paper weights, hairbrushes, tooth brush holders and neckties at every tourist stop. Preserved sharks' jaws were big also, as well as shark teeth. I hoped there were a few predators and scavengers left alive and functioning to clean up the big river.[19]

Santa Marta wasn't San Diego either, it was better. It now seems that time spent off the beach or not dancing and drinking rum & Coca Cola was time wasted. By some conjunction, now a mystery, we met the Fenimores here and enjoyed the white sands and clear blue waters of a quiet cove together.

Unlike any other city we visited, Santa Marta seemed to have a host of young bucks interested in and training for *boxeo* (boxing). They were running, punching, shadow boxing, rope skipping on the streets and in the parks. I attributed it to recent Cuban and Caribbean basin successes in that sports endeavor.

The fight I did see was unexpected and it left me feeling sick to my stomach. It was between two women in a park on the crowded central walk. It was silent, serious and sad. Hanks of hair were removed and garments suffered. I don't know what precipitated it or how exactly it was ended. Little was solved, and two who had little, now had even less

We, of course, saw the Quinta de Bolívar, pretty and nicely kept. I can't remember if it was Bolívar's summer or winter get-away. My guess is, it was his, whenever-it-was-better-there-than-in-Bogotá retreat - I'd say any of about 365 days a year.

Santa Marta was the location of one of the major banana plantations of the UNITED FRUIT CO. of Boston who wielded considerable power for decades in Central America and the Caribbean.

We took a self-guided tour. It was impressive with the company town, the administrative building, no doubt the infirmary or clinic, dormitories, intra plantation railroad and such. I'd say the architecture was patterned on the bungalow style from British East India and other tropical installations. There was not much going on there. We did see some Colombian men across the way

[19] Charlie Lenkner, personal email, Aug. 11, 2009.

mainly trying to down a quantity of cane rum of local manufacture and swimming in an irrigation ditch of water from the mountains. If they had other assignments they had been set aside.

Ships coming into Santa Marta often had an open house, ship board tours when they docked. We went on board a British war ship, complete with British Marines whose uniforms were reminiscent of the U.S. equivalent. A German freighter unloading cars and taking on bananas also put down the gangplank. Later we met some of that crew on the beach. They were by and large big dudes, piano mover, pro-football big, except for the very outgoing and fairly conversant in English, Herman.

He was stout, but certainly short and hailed from Hamburg. He was, in any case, happy to have a break, off ship and on the beach. We were learning about life and work on a freighter and Melody asked him about his work, his particular role. He answered, "wok, wok, wok; wok in the fu'gin hold, wok." She had her answer. It seemed because of his size, he was sent down the tubes or pipes and passageways to clean and inspect.

I had come to Colombia carrying a reprint from a mountaineering journal with details on the Sierra Nevada de Santa Marta peak and like Rojo (Tom Gallaher) harbored some considerations of climbing it. The material was provided by my old Scout Master who was a WWII Marine in the South Pacific and had climbed mountains on several continents. He had provided me with, in addition to the handout, some pointers from his climbing experience. So 18,000 feet meant something to me. But I couldn't imagine how I was going to find time to mount an assault on the high peak and complete my assignment while making the world safe for democracy. I did enjoy seeing the mountain as we flew by on the way to Riohacha.[20]

The Lenkners moved on from Santa Marta to the east passing by the Sierra Nevada de Santa Marta with its 19,029 foot Pico Cristóbal Colón which, unlike Tom Gallaher, Charlie did not attempt to climb. Melody and Charlie's destination, Riohacha, Guajira, on the Guajira Peninsula, was further east along the coast than anyone else from our group traveled, as far as I know. This peninsula lies in the rain shadow of the Santa Marta Mountains and is one of those queer anomalies found in South America. Like the deserts on the coasts of Peru and northern Chile, this is an arid wasteland on the shores of the sea. Just another incongruity typical of Colombia - the country's only desert is surrounded on three sides by water.

The first thing I remember as we headed into town [says Charlie of their visit to Riohacha], was the sight of a very long wooden quay or pier that extended out into the water, the Caribbean. It was above the water some 10-20 feet and there were buildings along the part closest to shore. It was wide enough and strong enough to hold cars. I know that because parked on the pier were more Mercedes Benzes than I had personally ever seen in one place in my life. I'm guessing 6 to 8. And these belonged to.........yes of course, Customs, the *Aduana, el Aduaneros*. We never witnessed anything coming into or going out

---

[20] Charlie Lenkner, personal email, Aug. 11, 2009.

from the pier in our short stay. When they had traffic it must have paid handsomely, though apparently not often.

I had been interested to see the *Departomento de la Guajira* because on the map it seemed so lightly settled and appeared to be fairly flat. That was in fact the case. The soil seemed capable of growing something other than brush, but that was about all there was for vegetation. What one might use for irrigation water was another question. There were in fact places where bulldozers were clearing and leveling, for what purpose I never determined.

The population seemed to be made up of at least equal numbers of indigenous people, those of mixed blood and pure European. The Indians were usually on the move across the flats, on foot. They were not small or puny people. The men favored felt Stetson type hats with wide brims, rayon or nylon long-sleeved shirts and thongs of a native design. The women wore sandals of similar origins. Some men sported watches and transistor radios that they held up to their ears as they walked. The ladies carried loads on their backs assisted by trump lines or bands across their foreheads. They had their heads covered with some cloth and wore mumu type dresses, plenty loose enough to afford lots of ventilation.

We had learned of Volunteers in the area and as was the custom were given shelter and conversation for a brief stay. Supper was made up of small mussels from the beach just out a ways from their house. The little clams had most of the sand washed out of them and the mussels went into a spaghetti sauce. We slept in their living room in hammocks with the anti-rat disks on the suspending ropes.

The next morning the Volunteers took us for a walk down the beach. There, not far up from some trees along the shore, probably mangrove, were several vehicles and out of the trees there emerged modern pirates, judging by their appearance and attitude, and their porters. Being transported were wholesale lots of American cigarettes, Scotch whiskey, Scandinavian wooden matches, Japanese electronics and shirts made of synthetics. We had observed the ready availability of U.S. smokes and the fact that they were lit with good matches, but we hadn't, up till then, had the complete picture. Now we understood the source.

Our Peace Corps hosts showed us through the trees down to the beach and we saw the smuggler's fleet. They were large dugouts, that must have been made from huge trees. They were so big that they were powered by inboards, Ford V-8s. These sailors, we were told, made fast, night runs out to the Dutch Antilles, the ABC islands (Aruba, Bonaire & Curacao). Score one for free enterprise.

Back in Riohacha we had time or took time to look at the not unattractive but plain faced city that architecturally could have fit anywhere in Mexico or our southwest (in an appropriate time period.) To say it was quiet would be an understatement. The only things pretending excitement were Rojas Pinella posters and they were mute.

It was probably siesta time. The sun was bright, the air still as we came to an interior plaza whose walls were all uniformly solid. It was nice, tile roofs, paved surface, maybe three or four entrance/exits at the corners and there was a small tidy refreshment kiosk with thatched roof and an attendant. We walked in and ordered a welcome gaseosus. Barely had we taken our first swigs when a U.S. made Jeep with a mounted 50 caliber machine gun and several riflemen pulled through each entrance. The men were all equipped and neatly uniformed and looked like they knew what they were doing. None looked right at us and we elected not to look back, not to look at anything but our sodas, in fact we did not move. As quickly as they had come, they backed out and disappeared.

The next day we got on the plane for Cartegena and a return to the altoplano. That was the beauty of living in someone else's country, every day was different, no two alike.[21]

Colombia's north coast has been the gateway to its heartland. On this stage, the scenery changes, canoes to sailing ships, to steam propelled paddle-wheelers, to diesel screw driven all steel hulls. And the population has been modified by invaders, Caribs, Conquistadors and African-Colombians (the last came not of their own accord). Yet throughout the millenniums, this land-sea frontier has never ceased to throb with activity. It has remained vibrant and essential, Colombia's connection to the outside world.

---

[21] Charlie Lenkner, personal email, Aug. 11, 2009.

13

GAMBIANOS, PAEZ, RESCUING MISSIONARIES
AND A PEACE CORPS BABY

Milton Scott drank in the scenery as he rode along with the Peace Corps leader from Popayán who was maneuvering the roadway cut into the side of the mountain. They were traveling through the high mountains and deep valleys of the Cordillera Central just east of the wide Cauca Valley from which they had come.

Scott wondered just what he had gotten himself into, requesting a solo site. Most Volunteers were stationed in pairs and even those that were not, were usually placed in close proximity to a veteran Volunteer who could show them the ropes.

In Scott's case, however, he would be quite alone in terms of any Norte Americano closer than two or three hours by bus, and the buses were infrequent visitors to his village, the leader explained.

"There are only two busses a week to Paniquitá," the leader went on, "both leave in the pre-dawn hours. The Tuesday bus goes to the Popayán market and comes back late at night. The Thursday bus goes to the market in Silvia still further up the mountain. Either way you're out for a day or if you stay over, it's a week."[1]

Undaunted, Scott could think of this only as an adventure and an opportunity to do some good. The vegetation was interesting and even the climate was comfortably cool as the Jeep climbed to nearly the 7,000 foot level. These were temperatures much to his liking.

Milton was from Owosso, Michigan and had graduated from Houghton College in Houghton, New York with a B.A. in business administration. Like most of the Colombia '64 group, he had some farm experience, but his knowledge and skills would soon be tested in this exotic environment.

As Scott and the leader pulled into town, Milton could see why this had been designated a one Volunteer site. Paniquitá had at best, maybe 500 residents. The population of the town and surrounding area was Paez Indian with a sprinkling of mestizos in Paniquitá itself.

Milton Scott

No one in the village owned a car. There were no motor vehicles in town at all. The only way in or out was on foot, horseback or the twice weekly buses. There was no electricity or telephones. If an emergency occurred – well, there would just have to be no emergencies.

The town was dominated by a Catholic church where Father Carlos Aritaga officiated assisted by four nuns. The nuns also taught in one of the two schools in town. They ran the girl's school while two male teachers brought in from the outside taught at the boy's school across the street. All this Milton learned from the leader and from the padre who greeted them as they arrived in town.

Father Aritaga was older, at least he seemed to be to the 22 year old Milton, but quite spry, and as it turned out, very progressive, working hard for the betterment of his flock.

---

[1] Milton Scott, telephone interview, May 28, 2009.

It was Father Aritaga who had been the prime mover in getting a Peace Corps Volunteer assigned to his town. He had already arranged for a small house for Milton and had a family who would provide his meals. So, finding some of the amenities that taxed many Volunteers upon their arrival on site were already taken care of for Scott. On the other hand, the true isolation and primitiveness of the town was impressed upon the new arrival as he became familiar with the area.

A few days of exploring revealed there was no weekly market in Paniquitá, an absence not unusual in small villages in Colombia. The local population depended almost entirely on what they could grow themselves and obtain from the markets in Popayán down in the valley and from Silvia further up in the mountains.

About the only cash crop grown in the area was a fiber producing plant the locals called *cabulla*. Known as *fique*, and by several other names in various parts of Colombia, the plant (Furcraea andina) is native to the Colombian Andes and was used by the Indians long before Europeans arrived. The Spanish found the fibers so useful; they exported the crop to Venezuela and to several Caribbean Islands.

The plant grows close to the ground, similar in appearance to a pineapple plant, but with much larger leaves. The long, green, leathery skinned leaves contain fibers not unlike hemp. They are used for making rope, garments, hammocks, packaging, sacks, handy crafts, even tapestry.

The people of Paniquitá and the surrounding area grew the cabulla and stripped the fibers from the leaves. Bails of the raw fiber were often stacked in town awaiting shipment to markets. Father Aritaga had been the driving force in organizing a cooperative to market the bails to the outside world, securing better prices and lowering transportation costs.

The cooperative also operated a tienda in town which imported a beef animal once a week, did the butchering, and sold the meat on Sunday morning so people could make a purchase after Mass as they departed the town for home. Every part of the animal was used, down to the tripe and kidneys. Other than the Sunday meat sale, the store carried only the bare essentials, matches, soap, needles, thread, items a household might need in an emergency and could not wait for the trip to the markets of Popayán or Silvia.

The cooperative's tienda was not open every day, nor was the only other store in the town, a privately owned tienda. For the most part, the population was very self reliant. The diet was primarily corn, much of which was raised locally though some of the grain was imported as it took twelve months for corn to mature at this high altitude. Families grew potatoes to supplement the corn diet and raised, or rather kept around, a few chickens which were used as fighting cocks and to eat. They were good foragers, small, feisty and about as palatable as shoe leather unless the carcass was boiled for an interminable length of time.

As was the case in much of Colombia, good nutrition in the diet was sadly neglected. About the only vegetables Milton could find were in a small garden grown by the nuns at the girl's school to augment purchased food for a very limited hot lunch program the nuns supplied the two schools. It seemed there was plenty of work to be done here.

Once acquainted with his new surroundings, Milton set out to find a source for improved seed varieties and small live stock. In Popayán he discovered a *granja* (agricultural experiment station) run by the Cafeteros. Here he obtained good seed from plants bred for the area. He used these to increase the production of the nun's school garden and with this as an example, induced others in town to start gardens.

From the Cafetero granja, Milton next picked up some White New Zealand rabbits and began a rabbit project with the nuns. Rabbits worked well at the school where Milton could keep an eye on their care, but did not catch on with the general population. A more acceptable protein source was needed and chickens seemed to be the obvious solution. The people were already accustomed to eating chicken and were somewhat familiar with their care. Before Milton could act on this new approach, however, he was overcome by illness.

At first Scott just didn't feel well and then some of his glands became swollen. A trip to the doctor in Popayán confirmed he had mumps. Though he never became incapacitated or even felt all that bad, Peace Corps insisted he spend a week in the hospital in Popayán because of the complications that can occur when an adult male gets the disease.

While in the hospital, Milton was alone in terms of visitors. Of course he had no family in country to attend to him, which the Colombians found strange and lamentable. Often during his stay, Colombians, perfect strangers, there to visit relatives, would stop by Scott's room so he wouldn't be lonely. Milton was sometimes annoyed by these interruptions, but mostly he was touched by these people's compassion for another human being they saw as suffering alone.

When Milton's friends in Paniquitá learned he was in the hospital, they became very concerned. Their experience with hospitals was that this was where people went to die. People went to the hospital in Popayán and disappeared - forever. When Milton showed up back in Paniquitá a couple of weeks later, the town's people were much relieved to see him in the flesh, and not a little surprised.

While in the hospital, Milton ran across two Peace Crops nurses who were there training the staff in special areas. "One of the nurses was instructing in surgical procedures," Scott remembers.[2]

Like most male Volunteers in rural Colombia, Milton lost some weight during his tour in South America. "It was rumored that I lost a lot of weight while I was sick. But I only lost, maybe, ten pounds while I had the mumps. Most of my weight loss was just due to the campo diet and occurred over the months I was in Paniquitá."[3]

Not long after Scott returned to his site after his bout with the mumps, the town celebrated a momentous occasion, the arrival of electricity. Since no one in Paniquitá had electrical appliances, the new energy source was used almost exclusively for light, a relatively easy and inexpensive installation especially the way the villagers did it. In one or two, sometimes three, of the main rooms of each home, a simple pull-chain ceramic light fixture was mounted on the ceiling and connected to the town's electricity. The bulb was left naked, no shade or covering, so as not to impede the distribution of all the available light. No subtle, defused back lighting here, just bold, stark brilliance.

Milton, on the other hand, being conversant in all the potential applications of the new type of energy, installed not just lights, but in one room he connected the wiring to a wall outlet. Next he hustled back to Popayán to purchase materials to build a chicken

---

[2] Milton Scott, telephone interview, May 28, 2009.
[3] Ibid.

brooder. Finally, he ordered one hundred unsexed Road Island Red chicks from the granja in Popayán.

It took some convincing, but gradually Milton sold the pullets off and made enough money to buy more chicks so he could repeat the process. His main problem was teaching the people that though these big, fat, red chickens required a little more care than the native truculent breed, they would lay more eggs and produce much more meat. The roosters could even be used to improve the native breed. With a little experience, the new chickens caught on and became a major factor in improving the local diet and economies of many families.

Much of Scott's success he attributes to Father Aritaga. Though a Protestant, Milton attended Mass on Sunday and very often the padre would encourage his congregation to visit with the Peace Corps Volunteer and try his ideas. Because of Father Aritaga's promotion, Milton was able to reach not just the people in town, but many of those from the surrounding area.

Another avenue to reach people in the outlaying veredas was through the schools. There were four small, mixed sex schools outside Paniquitá. Each school had one teacher who welcomed Milton and were only too willing to help out with demonstration gardens and chicken projects. In this way Scott was able to affect not only the nutrition of the families in and around Paniquitá, but even the economy of these people.

For diversion there were books, especially after the coming of electricity, and there were the long evening talks with Father Aritaga who proved to be a fount of knowledge and something of an intellectual, curious about anything Milton could enlighten him on. In Popayán there were movies, restaurants and usually a few Volunteers in for a visit. But the most frequent outing was a ride even further up into the mountains to Silvia for a visit with the Fenamores.

"Paniquitá was in the same direction from Popayán as Silvia and probably 2/3 of the way to Silvia as the crow flies," Milton recalls.[4] Mary Ann would put on a good feed, usually even dessert and Bob was often ready with some adventure, or misadventure, he needed help with. The high mountain town became a regular stopover for Milton, during his months in Colombia.

On the front cover of the fourth edition of the *Peace Corps Handbook,* published July 1966, is a picture taken high in the Andes of South America. In the foreground are three figures with their backs turned toward the camera. They are swathed in ruanas up to their chins so that they become three dark silhouettes with no distinguishable features. Perched on the three heads are three hats that do catch the light, hats that might be described as Bowlers or Fedoras except the top is pushed down so it is flat like a Trilby hat. The hats are unadorned except for one which has a leather thong laced around the brim.

Facing the three figures, and the camera, are a young blond woman wearing a dress and sweater, and a young man in a Levi jacket and straw hat. Both are holding small rabbits. Behind them are parts of a rock wall, a section of rough hewn split rail fence, part of a building with a corrugated steel roof, and in the distance tower desolate mountains devoid of trees or other discernable vegetation. The scene is a poster perfect picture of the Peace Corps in action, two American youths in some remote and forgotten land working

---

[4] Milton Scott, personal email to Gary Peterson, Feb. 18, 2009.

with an exotic people eager to learn what these interlopers might be able to teach. And such an evaluation would, in this case, not be far off the mark.

The three silhouettes are, in fact, Guambiano children in front of their school located nearly 10,000 feet above sea level in the Cordillera Central of Colombia. The young man and woman are Bob and Mary Ann Fenimore from Tacoma, Washington, members of the Colombia '64 group.

Both were products of rural backgrounds themselves, Mary Ann from a family owned farm and ranch, and Bob who had spent his summers on his uncle's dairy farm. At six years old, Mary Ann was driving a farm tractor. Bob graduated from tending dairy cows to farm laborer at ten and construction worker at twelve. Both their families maintained large gardens, bottling some 1,000 quarts of produce to feed their families through the winter.

Mary Ann and Bob met at Pacific Lutheran University where Mary Ann majored in physical education, graduating in 1964. She put herself through school working in a drug store while Bob played football and worked at a service station where he learned something about auto mechanics.

Mary Ann Fenimore

After Mary Ann's graduation, the Fenimores married and then filled out an application for the Peace Corps. This couple possessed exactly the kind of experience the Peace Corps was looking for in a South American Volunteer. That fall Bob and Mary Ann boarded a 727 for Denver and then an old DC-3 to Lincoln. It was the first time either of them had ever flown.

After Nebraska and Puerto Rico, Bob would say, "In short, we thrived on training. Some of the best education I have ever received in my life and I still use those skills today. They helped set me on a new course in life and we never looked back except to keep saying, 'this is a way better ride than I ever thought I would get out of life when I was growing up. I never would have believed it if you had told me.'"[5] Next stop – Bogotá Colombia for orientation.

From Bogotá, the Fenimores flew to Popayán, the old Spanish capital of the Cauca Valley. Bob described the modern city as, "steamy hot Popayán which by the way was a very beautiful colonial town with churches having interiors to die for."[6]

But the Fenimore's stay in Popayán was short. Very quickly they were on their way to the mountain fastness that would be their home for the next two years. Their outpost was Silvia, a town of about 1,500 people, "located at 8500 feet in a beautiful narrow valley alongside the Piendamo River. At that time there were two streets of cobblestone, a central plaza with a lovely church. The streets ran east and west along a bench about 75 feet above the river. Pristine. The hills on both sides were covered with a carpet of green Kikuyu grass cropped short by horses and cattle. Surrounding the town were large fincas of thousands of hectares owned by absentee landowners. The town itself had people of

---

[5] Bob Fenimore, personal email, March 24, 2009.
[6] Ibid.

mestizo extraction."[7] "The town even had a tourist hotel for the tourists from Cali, who came for a rest,"[8] in the cool, refreshing climate of the high mountains.

Upon their arrival, the Fenimors learned about the Volunteers who had preceded them at the site.

There had been two male Volunteers in Silvia for the two previous years-- community development guys [Bob recalls]. I believe their names were Robert Salafia (a Julliard school of music grad I was told, who wrote lots of music with no piano). He had managed to get a school built in a small, high up vereda and befriended a lot of people. Sadly, he died of brain cancer within a year of returning to the USA we were told. The other was Paul Mundschenk who had worked with the Guambianos up one creek valley and helped organize cooperatives. There had been a married couple for a while but their marriage blew apart and they terminated early before we arrived. One other Volunteer had been sent in just before we arrived from another group that had come one year previously--Jack Ward from Western Montana. Wow, did that guy know his agriculture!!!

Bob and Paul left almost right away, but Jack stayed on. We had our own place and Jack had his. Mary Ann did the cooking as was the custom. We had our horses out of town at a finca owned by the Christian Missionary Alliance as that is where the previous Volunteers kept them and we inherited their horses-3 head. One was a complete knot head and we sold him. A missionary bought him and pastured him high in the mountains on unbelievably steep terrain. One time he gave the horse *purgante rapido* (rapid purge) for intestinal parasites. The horse threw himself down in pain as it started to work and fell out of the field and rolled about 300 feet to the bottom of the side hill!! Fortunately, there were no broken bones. That was how steep almost all the fields were the people we worked with owned!!

Robert Fenimore

We rented a lovely old home with three rooms on the street, a court yard in the middle and three rustic rooms in the back. The back door opened up onto about a 1/2 acre of land that ran down to the river and was fenced all the way around. We now had a basic framework to begin with. We had electricity off and on, one running water tap that had water most of the time, and an inside toilet. Cool. We turned over and worked up the courtyard and put in a demonstration garden.

Tuesdays were market day in Silvia and the day the people from all around came to buy and sell. The activity started at 3-4 a.m. with buses arriving with produce, hogs being butchered, horse loads of goods coming out of the mountains and then arrived the "Indians" carrying massive loads of potatoes weighing 50 pounds or more traveling with no shoes, walking for 2 hours or

---

[7] Bob Fenimore, personal email, March 24, 2009.
[8] "Billy Goats and Vitamin Pills," *El Hocicon*, August 1965 Issue, p.4.

more down the mountain – Guambiano, indigenous people. We were told there were about 7,000 spread out all thru the mountains but we never knew for sure.

They all wore the same clothes. Very colorful. The men wore woven wool ruanas made by the women who hand spun the wool working constantly while sitting or walking. They then used a crude loom to weave the ruanas for the men and skirts for the women. Both men and women usually wore two to three of each for warmth. The men wore bright blue wool wrap around skirts, black bowler hats (with flattened crowns), and very colorful scarves with all the colors of the rainbow. The women wore the same except their skirts were of a woven material and the ruanas were of blue wool. The blue wool was purchased and highly valued. Also, as a show of wealth, the women wore strings of white trade beads around their necks. Some having a number of pounds of them, so many they could not turn their heads, but had to turn their bodies. And, all with no shoes. Huge feet, cracked from walking in mud, over rocks, down steep trails while carrying massive loads as almost no one had horses. To poor![9]

The other indigenous people that lived in the region were the Paez who dressed in clothes common among the mestizo population, that is, dark pants, suite type jacket, light colored shirt, ruana and hat. Amongst all these populations dietary deficiency was a severe problem.

There were high levels of malnutrition, kwashiorkor (protein deficiency), and in some areas 80% child mortality before the age of 5 [Bob laments]. So, so sad. This seemed to be worst with the mestizo people for some reason. They had huge families with many deaths. The primary food in the area was potatoes, onions, some wheat in places, corn and a small twisted little tuber they called oca (Oxalis tuberose). It was a very starchy little fella-about ½ inch in diameter and 2 inches long and bright pink. And, of course, there was yuca where it could be grown. All this went into the soup pot.

Starvation was everywhere. Almost no protein at all because of the cost. They did have some scrawny chickens but could not afford to eat the eggs or the chickens. Eggs were worth one peso and 10 hours of very hard labor netted 5 pesos. Chickens would sell for 35 pesos. So you can see--they would sell the eggs or chickens in town to buy flower, sugar, salt etc.

They grew their crops on very steep mountain sides and ran the rows up and down the mountain because that is how they had always done it. That led to huge erosion problems and loss of what precious little soil they did have.[10]

Nutrition was the obvious immediate problem. Methods of enhancing the diet in rural settings was what the Fenimores had trained for and market day provided the opportunity to engage the people from all over the region.

On Tuesdays the town grew to many thousands. The streets were packed with people. The mountains disgorged an unbelievable number of people. We worked

---

[9] Bob Fenimore, personal email, March 24, 2009.
[10] Bob Fenimore, personal email, March 25, 2009.

with Paez and Guambiano Indigenous people and the town filled with them. We set up a custom of opening our home to the people on market day and served coffee and "*pancitos*" (small breads) to people that stopped by for a visit. We had visited the schools where the previous Volunteers had worked and told the children to have their parents come to see us when they came in on Tuesday. Well, that word spread quickly and very soon we were getting visitors.

Our demonstration garden in the courtyard was a hit right off. We showed people lots of vegetables they did not know about and said that if they would work up a garden plot we would come out and give them the seeds, fertilizer and show them how to plant the vegetables. Their part was the garden plot prep. This way we initiated visiting homes with families as well as schools. So gardens were our in and we showed them how to grow, harvest and prepare the vegetables. Actually, mostly they ate soup so it was a snap teaching them how to use the vegetable.

We were surprised at the response! Soon we were making appointments on Tuesdays as to where we would be going the following week and quickly we had big "trap lines." We would go to someone's home and plant and explain as best we could with our limited Spanish and they always seemed to really appreciate the visit, information, education, etc.

We would use the opportunity, as the weeks and months passed, to introduce other ideas and notions. IE--no one had an outhouse!! Intestinal parasites, amoebic dysentery and diarrhea were rampant. So, to initiate this idea of outhouses we started with the schools.

Whenever we went out to plant a garden in an area we would stop and visit some of the other houses and introduce ourselves and then make our way to the local school. Well, that was grand - Mary Ann having her certificate as a teacher was so delighted to be with the children. The teachers so loved having the time with Mary Ann because they stayed in the school alone as part of the teaching assignment. We introduced school gardens and slowly befriended the children's parents who would then come to visit on Tuesdays. In time we had the local men help us dig a latrine hole and then help build the outhouses. The children were delighted as well as the teachers. You can imagine the mess, contamination, etc., before the outhouses.

I remember, we talked to the foreman of the ranch owned by the missionaries and explained outhouses and sanitation and suggested that maybe he would like to build one for his family plus the others that worked on the land. A few weeks later when we went to get our horses he proudly announced he had built one and did we want to see it? - "you bet." We walked over to his home and there was a beautiful new outhouse - well constructed, nice door and everything. But it was placed on two large beams right over a small stream that ran by his place! Oh well. He got it partly right but---.

Why would he not think this was alright since the town of Silvia had sewer lines from indoor toilets that were all collected into one line that flowed into a flume that dropped 50 feet directly into the Piendamo River! Then just downstream from there was a pristine arched stone bridge that, we were told, was built by Simón Bolívar as he was coming thru this area and off that bridge they dumped all the town's garbage right into the river. No wonder there was such a high death rate among the people and especially the babies and young children!!!!

The schools varied in size from 25 to 75 students. One huge school up the valley must have had a couple hundred Guambiano pupils. Jack worked with that one as well as Mary Ann and I. A number of schools had nuns for teachers but these were the larger schools so there could be a mother superior to look after her flock. The school gardens went over great and the children took to them quickly and brought their parents to see them as well.

From there we worked on initiating a school lunch program for the children where a huge pot of soup was cooked and served at noon. For this program we contacted CARE and got them involved. They were grand and soon we were receiving shipments of powdered milk, soy powder for a protein source, bulgur, flour, cracked wheat, etc. and the parents would come in on Tuesday and haul the supplies out to the schools. Thus, each day the students received a hot meal. Often this was the only meal they ate at times when the families were in between crop harvests.[11]

Gardens, latrines, and school lunches were programs that would improve the lives of the people in and around Silvia immensely, but to combat some of the worst of the malnutrition problems, a means of supplementing diets with a dependable protein source was needed.

As soon as we had the garden program initiated, Jack, Mary Ann and I set out looking for rabbits. We spent two days traveling by bus, stopping anywhere we could get a lead as to where we could find rabbits. One here, another there and finally we found a place where we could purchase a number of "Californias", white rabbits with black ears and tails, that had been bred specifically for meat. So, with rabbits in hand we headed home.

Next was to build cages. The local priest who we had befriended suggested a 14 years old boy named Alfredo Guerrero. What a gem. He took charge - multi talented and a hard worker. The big benefit was that he also helped us with our Spanish.

Most of the people we worked with were Indigenous and Spanish was their second language with many of the women not speaking Spanish at all!! The men's Spanish was of mixed quality so they would often copy our incorrect Spanish thinking we knew best. This was very funny until we were evaluated for our Spanish proficiency. When we terminated, the government gave us a proficiency test in Spanish and told us we talked like "Indians." We explained it could not be any other way since they were the ones who taught us.

The biggest fights Mary Ann and I had in the first 6 months, were over who would answer the door when someone knocked!! Our trick on the street was to initiate the conversation so we knew what the topic was. At the door, the other person initiated and often we did not have a clue as to what the hell they were talking about!!

---

[11] Bob Fenimore, personal email, March 25, 2009.

One day a lovely couple came to the door with a little baby and we talked to them not knowing what they were saying. This was about 3 months after arrival and we were very green. They were Guambianos and Alfredo came to the door with us but stood back in the hallway and listened. The people told their story. We listened carefully saying *"muy bien, muy bien"* (very good, very good) not understanding anything except a few words.

Finally they left and as we turned Alfredo's very dark face was white as a sheet! He said, "why did you say *muy bien*? They were telling you that they had had twins and one of them had died."

Oh my god. We felt terrible. All we could do was to keep learning and moving forward and Alfredo proved to be a good and patient teacher plus interpreter.

We would eat breakfast at his mother's smoke filled (from the fire) cubby hole restaurant at the market on Tuesday and he would help us haul our baskets full of produce, which was a weeks supply, back to our house and then help out as 50 to 100 people would come by for coffee. We now had the rabbit hutches built, nest boxes made and babies happening. And, believe me with rabbits it can happen fast - at one point a year later, we had 200 rabbits and supplied other sites all over Colombia with their starter rabbits.

We explained protein, nutrition, and rabbits as a protein source and told them that if they would build a hutch we would supply a pair free with the stipulation they had to give two back to us in the future or give two as a starter pair to a neighbor, providing they swapped the new male with us to prevent inbreeding. We would then go out and show them how to kill, skin, dress and prepare the animal. We also tattooed all our rabbits for positive identification with birth dated as well as blood lines.

Mistake number one, do not just let the blood run on the ground!! Catch it and fry it up!! Well, makes sense when you think about it - free protein. And, get over your notion that intestines are to toss. That idea comes from the land of plenty. You eat all the rabbit including the head. Believe me, when you are hungry you eat it all!! We were also able to get the schools going with rabbits. It was pretty easy with the rabbits because they and all their parts just went into the soup. The big problem though was they did not want to kill them (they would become pets) and they always thought the rabbits were lonely being separated so they kept the males with the females all the time which led to all sorts of problems (the males will kill the newborns). So, we saw we needed to look for another protein source.[12]

As in other sites, the next source for protein, usually tried after rabbits, was chickens. People already knew something about keeping the birds and how to prepare them, but the pitiful specimens raised in the area provided neither meat nor eggs in any quantity.

So, we ordered 100 Rhode Island Red unsexed day old chicks, built a brooder and we were in the chicken business. We kept good records and found that the people were extremely interested in the project. Then we had the idea of selling

---

[12] Bob Fenimore, personal email, March 25, 2009.

the one month old cockerels to improve the inbred chickens they had at home. Well, that was a hit. We sold them at cost and away they would go with one chick tucked in their shirt to keep it warm. Since many of them lived so high up in the mountains that it often froze at night, they would take the bird to bed with them to keep it warm.

By the way, to say "to bed" is probably not correct in that most had no beds or blankets but slept on an old cow hide on the floor in their clothes with all the family huddled together to try and stay warm. We could not believe it when we first saw it.

Anyway, the roosters worked great! It took a few months but soon there were half breed chickens running around and weighing twice as much as the native chickens and laying way more eggs.

We also wanted to try and speed up the process so we kept the 50 laying hens and some roosters, and folks could buy fertile eggs from us at cost! This way, when they had a 'clucky or broody' hen they would come and buy or trade for a dozen eggs to put under the hen. This really sped things up. I do believe this was one of our best projects.

We also sold eggs in town and with what we made from egg sales we were able to pay all of our expenses for purchasing, raising the entire flock. We showed our visitors all the figures. Actually we explained the paper to them because virtually all were illiterate. They did value education though so it was never difficult to get parental help on school projects.

We also tried white meat birds for fryers but the people did not like them. The national dish is *Sancocho de Gallina* and that takes an old bird well boiled that has lots of flavor. Our 8 week old birds were tasteless in comparison. So, that project was a flop but we broke even and gained experience.[13]

With chicken projects going, the Fenimores decided to try something with a little more size. Pigs looked like a good bet, as they didn't require the feed that cattle would need and yet would produce more meat then a chicken. Unfortunately, the arrival of a sow to the Fenimore household happened to coincide with a town waste disposal system problem. The sewer lines running through the nunnery in town plugged up and backed up the sewer that went through an adobe wall to the theater next door. "The nuns knew it was their fault, but were not 'fessing up.' So the swine (got the blame and) had to go. We looked pretty silly taking our big sow out of town in a wheel barrow."[14]

Goats were also tried as a potential source of meat and milk. This seemed to be a natural solution to the protein problem. Goats can live on almost anything and don't require a lot of attention or care, at least according to their reputation. After some scouting around, the Fenimores were able to secure four nannies and a billy goat. This looked like a sure thing, but goats, like all livestock, are susceptible to problems.

The billy got sick [Bob remembers] and we did not know what to do. I took the early 4 a.m. market bus to Popayán to the vet who said he did not have any idea what the problem was, but sold me some penicillin. The billy died anyway.

---

[13] Bob Fenimore, personal email, March 25, 2009.
[14] Ibid.

I was sick. We had worked so hard to find, transport, care for these animals and now we had 4 nannies and no billy. That one really was painful.

Then a few days later one of the fellows we worked with came to see us. He had borrowed money equal to one year's labor for a milk cow for his family. A short time later the cow up and died. Again, I was sick. I could see there were doctors for the people but no veterinarians. The guy in Popayán never left his office and actually just sold antibiotics, feed and vaccines.

There was a huge need!! People are always going to eat and they need vets to help keep their animals alive. That was the turning point for me and I decided to go back to school and start over again after Peace Corps. I started corresponding with Washington State University Dept. of Agriculture. They were a huge help with our projects and furnished invaluable advice plus I 'knew' professors already before I arrived back in the states. Strange how a goat dying can change a person's life.[15]

So after trying rabbits, pigs and goats, it was the chickens that turned out to be the real winner. They survived in the high altitudes, could maintain themselves with only limited assistance in feed and, with the new stock, produced sufficient meat and eggs to make a difference in the nutrition of the mountain people. And it was the chickens that helped give Jack and the Fenimores access to people even outside the seven veredas and six schools they were working with directly. This was particularly true of the Paez Indigenous peoples. The Guambianos had been the first "Indians" they had worked with, but gradually they were able to reach the more distant Paez.

The Paez people were much more reserved and harder to make contact with, but once the word got out about the little cockerels and fertile eggs they started to arrive on market day. We were very pleased because some had come 2-3 days from back in the central *cordillera - Tierra Dentro* they called it and it was. Some lived at over 14,000 feet!! They later reported back that the roosters and eggs performed well and they were pleased and grateful. This allowed us to reach many, many people that we could never visit because of time, distance and remoteness.

We had a brooder that held up to 150 chicks and wound up having a new batch of chicks every 5-6 weeks or more frequently. We made a pen that stood up off the ground to keep the 4 week old chicks in that were ready to sell and then we started a new batch.

Problem!! The floor of the pen for the chicks was wire and one night we woke up to a hell of a racket with chicks squawking. We ran out and found a damn possum (*duchamp*) was hanging upside down and chewing off the feet of the chicks as they protruded down thru the wire!! We were sick. All the chicks recovered and we changed our way of housing. The possum did not fare so well.

One man got enough money together to buy 50 unsexed chicks and raised them up before we left. He sold the 6 month old roosters and made enough to pay for all his investment (wire, housing, chicks, feed) and had 25 laying hens free. He was the living example that would carry on after we left for home.

---

[15] Bob Fenimore, personal email, March 25, 2009.

The local village people also caught on as well as the missionary fellow and they both started big poultry operations. The missionary asked us "how do you get so many people to come and visit you?" We said that from what we had seen - when people are starving and you help them learn how to feed themselves and if you can alleviate disease they will follow you anywhere - nothing magical. And, I guess it was a way of saying that maybe a combination of physical and spiritual could work.

I think one thing that really helped Mary Ann and me was that we loved the people. And, we cared about them and not for them. We held them as able and never engaged in any give-away programs. They had to participate fully and then we all worked together for the common good.

And customs in the area really aided us as well. The Guambianos were a unique, distinct, proud group of people. Some of the last remaining Indigenous people in Colombia we were told. They were wonderfully gentle, handsome, and some were very tall.

All around them in the mountains to the east, north and south, were the Paez people. They were ferocious in the sense that they did not like the government authority and even the army did not mess with them. Folks said that this was historical, that they had resisted the Conquistadors. There were untold thousands and no one could give us any real number. Slowly they warmed to us and we overcame their suspicious. So, we were watched carefully and finally accepted.

Since they lived so far out, they came to us, and market day was perfect. They bought seeds, fertilizer, chicks, fertile eggs and gathered lots of educational materials. They had adapted the western style of clothes so were not easy to distinguish from the mestizos except by their uniformly darker skin color. They seemed to have mastered Spanish quite well. They were extremely proud, but curious once they started to trust us.

The Guambianos, on the other hand, were more welcoming and inclusive, maybe because they were closer to town. Also, they were fierce about maintaining their distinctive dress. It was amazing. Almost to a person they did not accept the "western" dress. The women were constantly spinning wool and they wove the ruanas for the men and skirts for the women. The men knitted the small hats out of wool that all the babies and children wore. Then once the children started school they would adopt the adult style of dress right down to the bowler hat for the boys. So, they always stood out.

The way they were treated, spoken to and regarded by "Colombians" was appalling. Huge discrimination and I do not believe I am understating the situation. The Paez and particularly the Guambianos, because of their dress, were treated as second class citizens or not citizens at all.

The men always walked in front and the women behind. Often the men were tall and well built. Extremely good looking people who would give a smile quite readily if they were shown kindness and attention. This made our work so much more pleasant because they lacked that "macho" edge so common in Latin society.

And laugh, they loved to joke and with the Guambianos it was to tell a story on themselves and what fools they were. Oh, for the howling. And with that we were off and running, sharing stories of life. We saw it as "sweet reprieve" from the suffering they endured all their lives. Born into, lived in, and died in grinding poverty. Sometimes we would weep at what we saw. And, we could not "fix" it. But, we could laugh with them.

The Guambianos had a tradition of "*mingas.*" That is where a group of up to 25-30 people would get together as a work party and work on one persons field, build fences, harvest, build a house from scratch etc. So, we used that for community development projects-especially at the schools because they valued education so much.[16]

Nutrition and sanitation were two deficiencies the Fenimores had found appalling upon their arrival in Silvia. Poor nutrition they were combating with gardens and livestock, and outhouses were a means to improve sanitation. Still, the use of surface water from rivers and streams for drinking and cooking, the same water used for disposing of everything from garbage to human waste, was horrifying to the Volunteers. The practice had been to dig small ditches running from the river or streams to the schools or homes often through fields and by other houses where refuse would be deposited in the running water.

They searched for a means of mitigating this sanitation disaster. Finally, they discovered that UNICEF had pumps that could be used to pull water from wells. They applied for and eventually received a shipment of these pumps from the United Nations agency. These were not high powered electric pumps - none of the schools outside town had electricity. They were hand pumps of the type used in rural areas in the United States at the turn of the century, but they were just what the Fenimores needed. The pumps were for wells for the schools; that would be the place to start.

But first the wells had to be dug. As the wells got deeper and deeper, Bob was having some serious doubts. "No way was I going down in that hole. Oh my god!!! But, they did. So, wells were dug for the schools and pumps installed--fresh clean water. Yahoo."[17]

We also received a Zinvoram machine for making mud bricks and again we had huge mingas, stomping mud, straw and cow manure together to make bricks and then to building additions onto the school, out houses, etc.

As a bonus, the folks borrowed the machine and carved into the side of a hill and used the dirt to make bricks and from that they built a house!! Cool. Whenever we got together it was a great opportunity to talk agriculture, nutrition, sanitation, parasites, disease control etc. And, we had fun.

While we were there we experienced a big crop failure in some areas and they had only the little pink ocas. Some areas ate only these things boiled, for almost six months!! That is all. It was grim.

One market day one fellow came to our house for coffee and as he was leaving took a little bag out from under his ruana and said, "I know it is difficult

---

[16] Bob Fenimore, personal email, March 26, 2009.
[17] Ibid.

for all of us in this time of famine so I want to share some of what I have with you." It was a little bag of ocas. And he left. Mary Ann and I looked at each other in disbelief. May I someday be able to achieve that level of kindness and caring. It humbled us to tears. I still shake my head in remembering that moment.

The Guambianos were poor and disenfranchised. All their good land had been taken from them and they had been pushed to the steep marginal land. You would have to see it to believe what they had to farm. Their main cash crop was potatoes - delicious little yellow potatoes with deep eyes. Yum!!

Problem was that once harvested they sprouted in 15 days. You guessed it, everyone harvested at the same time. The only place to sell was in town on Tuesday and often they would only get a five to one return on their planting. IE-Plant one pound and harvest five. Lots of work with little return. Another problem, the bottom fell out of the market and they would get money equal to the price of 15 eggs for a 50# sack of spuds. The potatoes were bought by middle men who then sold them the next day for 5-10 times as much in Popayán or Cali. So sad.

As luck would have it we were at a conference in Bogotá and went to the Rockefeller Institute and toured their research facility. They were doing work with over 200 varieties of potatoes and we told them where we lived and our situation, etc. They asked us if we were interested in taking some potatoes to try with the stipulation we had to let them know how it worked out in our area. We thought they would send us a couple of pounds sometime later.

About a month after that, the market bus from Popayán honks in front of our house and we go to the door and they say they have some potatoes for us. "Where do you want them?" We are looking for the little bag, but they unload 1000 pounds of potatoes!!!!!! Damn, that is a lot of French fries.

Now we had our work cut out for us. We put the word out that we had potatoes and put forward this scheme. We give you 5-20#s of potatoes. You plant and fertilize them. When you harvest them you must give the same amount we gave you to someone else. And, they must do the same when they harvest.

"Promise?"

"Yes, we promise."

Well, come harvest time they get 40 to 1 instead of 5-1 and the bonus was that they could store them in their houses for 6 months. This meant that now they could bypass the dealers in Silvia, go to Popayán or even Cali and market directly eliminating the middle men. The small coops were already in place and we were told that it worked well.

We also convinced them to contour farm around the mountain to stop erosion. When we went back 10 years later it was the contour farming, potatoes and chickens that had persisted and really changed lives.

We have been told that the mayor of Silvia and the governor of Cauca are both Guambianos - we have not verified this. The Guambianos now have their own market buses and roads to the villages so they can do their own deliveries and not be captives of the town market.[18]

---

[18] Bob Fenimore, personal email, March 26, 2009.

Jack and the Fenimores worked in seven veredas and six schools outside Silvia where there were no roads, only trails. Mary Ann remembers doing,

.......all our work on horseback. We kept them at the missionary's finca and would tell them the day before when we needed them. It was about a 1/2 hour walk to get there. By the way, their names were Bob and Marge Searing and he was a second generation missionary for the Christian Missionary Alliance. They were extremely kind to us and helped with the transportation of things we needed from Popayán in their little 1948 Ford pickup. We also had many meals and evenings with them. But, we were careful to not be associated with them religiously as we walked that same fine line with the Catholic Church.

A Swiss priest lived across the street from us and we became great friends. He was in his 70's and kept bees. He had been a prisoner in China for many years - oh for the stories. He would actually ride way out with us at times when we had gardens, outhouses, school lunch programs etc. we wanted to initiate and he would give Mass. The people were astonished that he would come out because it was the first time in their memories that a priest had visited in their area. He would ride along in the rain with his pipe in his mouth upside down so the tobacco would not get wet! Incredible. He spoke Spanish with a heavy Swiss/German accent. We loved him and he us as well as the people - Padre Julio.

Well, people flocked to the schools and often we had to do Mass outside. A fiesta. He would do his service and then say, "I came today to talk to you about your spiritual life and care for it. Now, Bob and Mary Ann are going to talk to you about the care of your bodies. Please listen carefully. They are very interested in helping with your health and that of your children."

We were shocked the first time he did that. It was like having the blessings of God. And, in no time a program was started and work spread. I guess if Padre Julio says this is a good thing it is a good thing. We were so appreciative.

As I said, we did all our traveling on horseback and we rode for hours every day. Tuesday we set up visitations and then went into the mountains 3-4 days a week. We got up at 6:00 a.m. every day to care for all our animals and usually out the door at 8 to get our horses. We were saddled up and on the trail by 9. Up, up, up we would ride often up to 11-12,000 feet and then ride the ridges to get to where we were going. Our horses were incredible 8-900 pound Paso Fino steeds and tough as nails.

Very well broke. Often we had to go through lots of gates and they were trained to walk up to the gate and turn sideways so we could open the gate without getting off. They would back up and let us go through and then maneuvered around so we could close it again--all without dismounting!

We would visit homes and work on the gardens, with the rabbits, chickens, notions of compost piles, use of manure to fertilize the gardens (the soil was so poor and worn out) and then we would be served coffee in huge bowls and sweetened with a crude sugar (panela).

They would seat us and often only had one or two chairs for the entire house or we would stand in the kitchen by the wood burning stove if it was cold or they had no chairs at all. The stove was built up off the floor about 3 feet and wood was fed into it and there was no chimney. The smoke just went out the roof and over time it collected dust, grease, debris and this all hung down from the ceiling in long strings many feet long over the stove. We are sure that occasionally one would fall into the soup and maybe that is what gave it such good flavor.

Once a school teacher at a school about 5 hours ride out decided to honor us by feeding us chicken soup. Now, this is above and beyond what a normal visitor would receive The chicken represented 7 days hard labor for a working man!!! Imagine serving guests a meal equivalent to 7 days work.

Bob got the special piece of bird and as I am eating, up floats the head with that eye looking at me! It still had the comb and wattles attached and the beak along with some pin feathers still in the skin of the neck.

We took very good care of our horses and they served us so well. Grunt and sweat up those mountains and in all sorts of weather. If we promised to come, we came even if it was raining hard. We had big ponchos that would spread out in front of and half way down the side of the horse and back almost to the tail. We held the reins under the poncho and the heat of the horse kept us warm. We put plastic on our hats and it was tolerable. But, the trails were red clay soil that turned to greasy mud up to 2 feet deep and all this on steep trails.

Often we would visit 5-6 houses and it would get late and we would lose daylight and have to ride home in the dark. The trails were so steep we had to lean back in the saddle and hold a tight rein in case the horse fell forward. We could not see the trail and had to let the horses see for us.

I remember one time my horse was walking on a very steep muddy side hill and his feet slipping out from under him. We went down. I wound up straddling him as he lay on his side not knowing what to do. Suddenly he just stood up again and I was back in the saddle.

We depended on those horses and we got to be good friends. I see how people talk about how a deep relationship develops between horse and rider. And, they had to depend on us and trust us as well. Often we had 8-10 hours riding in one day. When we had far out places to go, we would have Alfredo go and get the horses so we could leave a 7 AM. Since we were essentially at the equator it got light suddenly at 6 AM and then the curtain fell at 6 PM.[19]

Bob and Mary Ann had been in Silvia for a few months when a new family arrived from the States. This was Tom and Judy Banks, Wycliffe Bible translators, who had come to the mountains to translate the Bible into Guambiano, a monumental task.

They chose to live high in the mountains with their three small pre-school children, staying in a small, cold house at about 11,000 feet [Bob writes]. We became friends, especially as Judy needed a female friend that could speak English. They spoke almost no Spanish. Again we were careful to not get stirred

---

[19] Mary Ann Fenimore, personal email, March 27, 2009

into their program in any way, keeping the balance. When people asked, we just said that we were friends only.

After they had been there for a number of months, word came down the mountain that Tom and Judy were sick. Evidently they had been ill, had gone to town and had received a diagnosis of hepatitis. But then chose to go back up the mountain and wait it out-- to this day we do not know why. Anyway, the word we were given was they were really ill and not able to care for the children.

So, we grabbed some supplies, groceries, what medicines we had and mounted up. We rode the 2 1/2 hours up to their place.

Oh my, were they ever sick. Both parents were so weak, they could barely get out of bed. But they would have to, to get to the back door so they could throw up. Then back to bed until the next bout a few minutes later. They were so, so weak from the vomiting and dehydration, they could not take care of themselves let alone the children. We really worried they would die - and with 3 little kiddies.

We cleaned the place up. Then we tried to find something Tom and Judy could keep down. Everything we tried just came back up and they were getting weaker and weaker. Without a doctor or hospital, or intravenous feeding, we just had to experiment with what we had or could get locally. There was every possibility one or both parents might die if we could not find a solution. Finally, we found they could suck on hard candy to give them a little energy and they could keep some water and hot tea down if they just sipped it. Eventually the vomiting slowed down and they were able to sleep.

With the Banks beginning to revive some, we turned our attention to the children. They had two children in diapers that had to be changed frequently; cloth diapers that needed to be washed out which Mary Ann did heroically, while we were trying to stabilize the parents. With both parents down, but beginning to come around, the next thing we discovered was huge round worms - some up to almost a foot long - coming out of those children!! We had our challenges, making do with the meager supplies we brought and what we could find at their place or buy from the Guambianos.

We stayed there for a week and slowly the parents started to regain their strength and were able to take care of the children. For the first few days, caring for five people and trying to nurse the parents back to health was a grim task. It was the rainy season; everything soaked down with drizzle, clouds to the ground, cold (no heat at all in the house and temperatures close to freezing every night). But, we were young, tough and intrepid. Foolish maybe? Oh well, we all recovered.[20]

After several months as part of the Silvia team, Jack Ward's time was up. He would be heading "states side." The Fenimores were sorry to see him go. "We will be forever indebted to him for all he taught us about agriculture. He was from a family of 12 children and he was a survivor. Boy did he teach us a lot. Skinny as a bean pole, he could eat. Being from a huge family, he knew that when the food was passed his way you better get what you wanted because the plate might not be coming back with anything on it. I

---

[20] Bob Fenimore, personal email, March 26, 2009.

am sure he has forgotten more about raising animals than we will ever know."[21] The only good thing about his leaving was that he took his two kinkajous with him. "Good riddance of those biting buggers that ate 100 bananas a week (well, we ate a few of them as well so that is a bit of an exaggeration)."[22]

With the departure of Jack Ward, the Peace Corps looked around for a suitable replacement and finally settled on Eugene Roberts. Eugene was plucked from his coastal site of San Jacinto near Cartagena and transferred to the mountains of the Cordillera Central.

> Silvia was a complete change from the heat of the north coast [Eugene explains]. It was a beautiful area. The Gambiano Indians we worked with were said to be similar to the Indians of Peru and there was a story that the Spanish had used the Gambianos to build the Camino Royal (royal highway) from Peru through Quito, Ecuador to Popayán. The tale relates that the Gambianos were captured in Peru, used as slaves. Upon completion of the road, they were released in the mountains above Popayán where they live today. There is some evidence to back up this story because of the similarity in language between the Gambianos and Peruvian Indians and the fact that they live in a sort of enclave surrounded by the Paez indigenous people.[23]

The Fenimores were pleased to have a member of their group join them and were not slow in dividing up the work in Silvia and the surrounding area.

> Eugene was kind, gracious and easy to get on with [Bob recalls]. We supplied him the horse Jack had left and he took over the area to the north up the valley.
>
> I think it is only in retrospect that I can fully grasp our ignorance at the gap between this "gentleman" and us. Even as he revealed stories about himself it has taken decades to appreciate our differences in upbringing. I believe his great- great-grandfather on the Roberts side was the first governor of Maryland. What a history.
>
> He arrived with a cassette player (we had never seen one) with tapes of Joan Baez and would even let us play it when he was away. We did not know Joan Baez at that time. We were truly country bumpkins - naive country kids from rural Washington. I recall some trainees at Nebraska from the East would ask us if we still had "Indian problems" and if we had indoor plumbing yet? Maybe they were joshing us but I'm not too sure.
>
> Anyway, Eugene also had this tiny espionage camera he loved. We loved it too, but the pictures were so small! Like a postage stamp. Like we should talk. We had splurged and had a Kodak instamatic.
>
> So, Eugene got his own residence but ate with us. We had a deal. We had a can for food that we all put equal shares into and Mary Ann would cook dinner while I did chores. Eugene would eat with us and tell us stories of girl friends

---

[21] Bob Fenimore, personal email, March 26, 2009.

[22] Bob Fenimore, personal email, March 26, 2009.

[23] Eugene Roberts, telephone interview, May 27, 2009.

from Smith. It seemed like a strange name for a school. Anyway, he was great. Telling us tales of his registered Black Angus cattle - he loved the Baralermere line as I recall - travels, airplanes etc. The void between us, how we were raised, astounds me to this day.

So, he took up his work and was great to be around, very amiable and a hard worker. Enthusiastic I think was a phrase used a lot in our group. Eugene was with us for several months and then went to Bogotá for the last few months of his tour.[24]

Eugene Roberts and Jack Ward worked with the Fenimores in Silvia reaching into the surrounding country generating new ideas and promoting changes that made life better for the mountain people. They were an effective team furthering progress in nutrition, sanitation, agriculture and education.

With Eugene in Silvia, Milton Scott's visits meant there were four Volunteers from Colombia '64 in town at the same time, a good gathering for stories and an exchange of information.

We grew quite fond of ole uncle Milti [Bob relates]. He softened over the two years and we did too, I believe. We all found we needed each other and were not here to do it all alone. Face it; we were just kids for goodness sakes, pitched into a foreign country, language, low levels of awareness of the world and highly indoctrinated in the ways of "the best country on earth." So, we welcomed Milton's visits, stories, history, and his laugh.[25]

On one of these social calls, Bob Fenimore confided to Milton about a problem they were having with a chicken thief.

Someone was breaking into our chicken house - actually a room at the back of the house where there was a window that looked out on our pasture that ran down to the river. We had an outside run for the birds and the thief was coming in thru the window. He would steal two to three birds at a time out of our laying flock of 50. Remember, these were not just laying hens, they were our source of fertile eggs for distribution to the mountain people and represented over one year of work and tender care. They were family--get the picture?

So, after repeated visits and the loss of about 15 hens we were fit to be tied. Not to mention that each bird was worth 35 pesos which was 7 days hard labor of 10 hours per day for the people we worked with!!! Damn man, we are talking serious coin here. After the last visit we had put in bars in the window, but this thief was not to be deterred. The wall was torn open. We had tried everything. We even had Alfredo sleep out there and when he did--you guessed it --no thief. I have to admit that even our faithful employee's name appeared on our radar screen. For shame.

Anyway, Milt was over for a visit and all three of us put our heads together and we came up with a scheme. Send Alfredo home. Tie a string to a brick in the

[24] Bob Fenimore, personal email, March 27, 2009.
[25] Ibid.

unrepaired wall. Run the string under the chicken house door, across the garden, over the patio, under the kitchen door, across the kitchen, and tie it to a frying pan precariously balanced on the edge of the counter ready to fall at the slightest tug.

After some trial runs we honed our skills and placed a rug on the floor so that when the frying pan hit the tile floor it would not make too much noise. We were set. Snickering all the way, we went to bed thinking "that this was a real brain storm."

We had not been in bed half an hour and "bang" the frying pan hits the floor. We had carried our idea even further because we actually had a plan! We had procured a two foot long piece of fire wood that was two inches in diameter with a triangle shaped cross-section and if the pan goes down we were to dress quietly and I was to sneak out the front door, run to the corner, down the steep alley to the river, jump over the fence and sneak up the pasture to the chicken run. Milt in the mean time was to wait till my estimated arrival in the back and then enter the hen house.

So, shaking with anticipation and honestly dreading what we might encounter, not to mention the quart of undiluted adrenalin running in our veins, we leapt into action.

As I tore up the pasture I discovered something we had overlooked. I had a sprinkler running to water the grass in the chicken run and this had rendered the whole backyard a soggy mix of mud and chicken manure.

Milt yells to me that the thief is in the hen house and is coming out the window. I enter the chicken yard while Milton is in hot pursuit right behind the thief. We caught him in the yard and I shined my flashlight in his face afraid it would be Alfredo! But I had never seen the guy before. We both grabbed him at the same time. He resisted and I whacked him over the head with the fire wood. Down we all went into the mud and manure, but we were totally oblivious to all that. The guy thought we were going to kill him which probably gave him extra strength. Somehow he managed to get to his feet and escape. Down the hill he ran.

Now remember, I had played football since grade 7 plus two years on scholarship at the University level and I had been the top tackler for both of those years. It was a beautiful open field tackle from behind. Now this guy must have really thought he was going to die.

Milt caught up with us and I am yelling at the thief to lay still or we would bash his brains in. All the time he was kicking and fighting back. Finally I said to Milton,"lights out move Milt" (referring to a move taught to us by 'Deadly Duddly' the self defense guy back in Nebraska). So one of us lifted one of his legs and the other gave him repeated karate chops to the old "family jewels."

He was still struggling when Mary Ann shows up in her night gown with the biggest damn butcher knife I have ever seen in my life. In her loudest berserk Norwegian voice, she yells at him that it may be in his best interest to do as he was told! That did it. The guy was convinced and he gave up.

So, we hauled his sorry ass up and into the house and sat him on a rug in the front room. Needless to say, half the villagers and all the dogs in town were awake by now. The whole town was in an uproar. The front door was opened and people poured in from the street.

What a picture. The bad guy sitting on the rug with a gash in the top of his head, hair, face and clothes covered in blood. Milt and I covered with blood, all three of us caked in mud and chicken manure, and soaking wet. Mary Ann in her nightgown was standing over us all holding this huge menacing butcher knife!

"What are all these folks going to think about this?" I thought in a moment of panic. "They will all think we have gone completely crazy."

The police showed up. It was revealed this guy was a local slime bag that would go down to the river where the women were washing clothes - they hung the clothes on the fence to dry - and he would steal their clothes. He was well known, but had never been caught so the town's people were cheering. He was the brother to one of Alfredos best friends so he knew every time Alfredo stayed over. By the way, the piece of firewood was one that Alfredo kept to defend himself when he slept in the chicken house.

Well, the guy spent a few months in the local jail. His parents were mad at us because we caught him. And in Colombia prisoners are not fed by the government. It is up to relatives to feed the inmate. This guy's mother was not happy having to bring food three times a day for her 25-30 year old criminal.

We were stopped on the street until we left and were thanked for catching the guy. He was a thug and had intimidated the village for years. Good riddance they would say.

What an experience we shared with Milt.[26]

One of the hard and fast rules in the Peace Corps was that if a girl got pregnant, she was automatically sent home. If the young woman was married, the couple's tenure in the country was terminated. The Colombia '64 group understood this. We were told this repeatedly in training and at every conference. No Peace Corps Volunteer had ever had a baby and remained in country. It just was not allowed. But then the Fenimores were not just any Volunteers.

About a year into our stay [Bob relates] Chuck Brady, our local "boss" for Peace Corps from Cali, paid us a visit. He asked if we would like to take over the Peace Corp rep job in Popayán, have a Jeep, travel around and visit sites, oversee projects, etc.

We thought about it for about one minute and said, "We came to Colombia to be with and work with the people. And, we love Silvia and the folks here. We are flattered. Thanks, but, no thanks. And, oh by the way Chuckie boy, since we seem to be doing such a nice job, how about looking into getting permission from Peace Corps for us to have a baby?

Well, guess what? He got back to us a couple of weeks later and said, "Yes - I received permission from Washington - the only stipulation is that it not

---

[26] Bob Fenimore, personal email, March 27, 2009.

interfere with your work and that you come to Cali periodically for checkups." Cool.

Well, Mary Ann being of full blood Norwegian breeding stock got pregnant almost right away. So, off to Cali.

The Peace Corps doctor said, "Here are the rules, checkups every 3 months, keep doing what you are doing, lots of exercise, eat well, you are to gain no more than 15 lbs or I will hospitalize you to get your weight down and Bob, here are your midwife instructions! But we actually prefer that you come to Cali two weeks before due date."

So, away we went. Mary Ann went on as normal. Well, why not? Her role models were Gambian women who went in the house and had a baby and at times were back in the field working the same day. She flew to deliver rabbits to the coast, traveled on buses, walked a million miles in routine matters and continued to ride horses. We met a Colombian doctor who would do the delivery and set that all up. So far so good.

About the 7th month she could not get up on the horse without help because her tummy would not clear the side of the horse so she could swing up in the stirrup even holding onto the horn. I had to help her up. She would get a foot into the stirrup, grab the horn and I would wolf boost her butt for balance so she could get her belly and Chad (we had a name for him by this time) up and into position so she could sit down in the saddle. Cute.

Then well into her 8th month her horse stumbled on the road and almost went down. She pulled back hard on the reins to keep his head up, to keep him from doing a summersault. We decided that that was the end of her riding, just could not take any more chances. I would ride out on my own and people knew she was home so they took to stopping by during the week for supplies, seeds, chickens, etc. So we kept everything running.

The native women loved seeing Mary Ann pregnant and came to teach her how to spin. "Well, if you are going to be a good wife you have to learn to hand spin, don't you?"

Two weeks before due date we went to Cali and walked miles every day from boredom. Met lots of nice people. The people at the local hatchery where we had purchased chicks offered us a job! Go to the states and train for 3 months and then come back to Cali to run the hatchery and breed stock farm. Thanks, but, no thanks. I had decided on vet school.

So, the due date arrives, but no Chad. In the mean time we wrote up our termination report plus a training booklet Peace Corps had asked us to write. Not sure what ever happened to them. Chuck and Melody Lenkner, and Dennis Burkholder had come to Silvia to cover for us. We had spent a week crafting a beautiful composite of all we had learned, resources, government agencies, private agencies etc. and we worked on typing it all up while waiting.

Now we are one week over – still no Chad. Time is becoming critical. We had been asked to terminate one month early and return to New Mexico to help train our group's replacement Volunteers and to do that we wanted to go to our termination conference in Bogatá in about 10 days. So, they tried to induce the delivery. Not pleasant and did not work.

Finally, two weeks late, off to the hospital. Labor for a few hours, but not hard and the doctor went home for lunch. Well, wouldn't you know, into full blown labor a few minutes later. The doctor rushes back, hustls into his gown saying in his limited English, "Mary, don't puush. Don't puuuh."

Now in place-"Mary, puush". One push and out pops Chad's head. Push number two and Chad flies out and hits the doctor in the chest and the guy has to catch Chad like a football bobbling him and trying to not drop him.

I guess these Norwegian women are bred to have children easy! Ha. And the condition Mary Ann was in was unbelievable. Well, maybe Mary Ann would not feel that way, but afterwards we all had a good laugh. That was about 1 p.m.

We stayed the next day to get all the paperwork straight--Chad is a dual citizen and the Colombian officials said he will always be a "Colombian".

Mary Ann wanted to go to the termination conference so we flew the next morning, maybe not the best idea. But in Mary Ann's mind,"why not? The Gambianos would do it!"

The rest is history. Lots of trials those first few weeks but he survived, is now fluent in Spanish and a handsome First Peace Corps Baby.

We returned to Silvia and, oh my, was he a hit with the people. The people we had worked with came with their blessings and admiration and of course we were so glad to be able to share him with them.

Now it was time to wind down projects, tie up loose ends and off to the next adventure in New Mexico. Peace Corps asked us to consider training for and working towards being local and/or country directors and again we declined. I guess the pull of learning to care for animals was too great.[27]

It had been a great adventure, the mountains, the Indigenous people, gardens, horses, chickens, pigs, goats, missionaries and a baby. Taking measure of things from the perspective of an older and, perhaps, wiser person, Bob considers his attitude at the time.

In reflecting back I think there certainly was an element of arrogance, elitism and exclusion on our part towards the town's people of Silvia relative to the indigenous and country people or campesinos we worked with. It stemmed from our work and love of the people and the condescension of the towns people towards "our" people. "Indios" were at the lowest rung on the social ladder. This was very painful to us and it certainly gave us pause to look closer at our own racism which we have had to do battle with all our lives having been indoctrinated with it from birth.

We loved the indigenous people we worked with and as such, when we heard people talk so disparagingly and act in such horrid ways towards the Guambianos and Paez, we really disliked it. I guess I give this as a sort of mild justification of our feelings about the "town people" in general. The truth is that I believe mountain people (the Guambianos and Paez) were seen as barely human. Their pain and suffering seemed to be separated from the towns people and even though they purchased supplies, contributed immensely to the local economy thru the tourism they engendered (people came specifically for market

---

[27] Bob Fenimore, personal email, March 27, 2009.

day in Silvia to see the Guambiano people), sold goods and produce in the market, they were held in disdain and contempt.

I do generalize here, but the pain I felt and continue to feel is deep. It is hard to understand deep racism. It is irrational at times and particularly in Silvia where if people bothered to look in the faces of one another, they would see their aboriginal ancestry staring back at them - mestizo. It is sort of like hating yourself which I think they did at some level, but unconsciously. The women would grow hair on their legs and point it out. We would ask why and they would say, "Indians can't grow hair on their legs." I guess this was offered as proof of their closer ties with their Spanish ancestry.

Then the Cali tourist would arrive and condescend to the folks from Silvia! And god forbid, a real Spaniard shows up - *Creme de la Creme.* I sure did learn a lot about them and myself thru it all.[28]

Finally, the Volunteers of Colombia '64 departed from the mountains of the Cordillera Central high above Popayán. Eugene Roberts had already left to go to Bogotá for his last few months in Colombia. The Fenimores were headed back to the states where they were to train the next Colombian group and then on to veterinary school at Washington State University. Milton Scott left Paniquitá for graduate school at Harvard Business School. All would agree their experience in the mountains of Colombia had left an indelible imprint on their lives. Certainly, their hope was that they had made some difference in the lives they touched in this high mountain fastness.

---

[28] Bob Fenimore, personal email, March 27, 2009.

14

A WORD ON COLOMBIAN TRADITIONS AND CUSTOMS

One of the first challenges faced by Volunteers arriving in country was the food in Colombia. In the big cities, like Bogotá and Cali, there was an almost infinite variety of fares. In the smaller cities, Tunja or Popayán, the cuisine was Colombian, but protein was still plentiful. In the campo, however, the menu tended to run to starch, potatoes in the high country, yuca and plantains in the valleys and coastal areas. Rice was served everywhere. But meat was rare. If you were served a piece of chicken or an egg, you were being honored.

So it was customary for Volunteers in the campo, who had been eating almost exclusively starches, to order a large steak whenever they were in the city. Forget the side dishes, potatoes, rice, carrots, etcetera, they're bodies craved meat and they would generally load up.

Now when your system is used to starches and all of a sudden your stomach is filled with protein, it reacts somewhat violently. Diarrhea would set in and you quickly found yourself confined to your room where facilities are close at hand. Eventually, your system becomes accustomed to the protein rich menu and you can enjoy your stay in the city.

Upon returning to the campo and the starchy cuisine, your system again rebels and constipation becomes a problem.

However, Volunteers quickly learned there were several pills in the medicine kit supplied to each site that counteracted the effects of diet change. A few pills upon reaching the city and presto, you could fill up on meat and still attend the theater without discomfort. Back in your site, a few other pills and the body still functioned as it was supposed to. The balance of dosage was critical, but most Volunteers soon learned how to deal with the gastric problems of diet changes.

Colombian food was one thing and then there were Colombian beverages, drinks Volunteers were quite unaccustomed to.

> Aguardiente and tinto were the two drinks of choice in Colombia unless beer was on the menu. Aguardiente, made from fermented sugar cane juice, had a licorice flavor and was highly alcoholic, 100 proof plus. It was the national drink of Colombia and was offered everywhere a Volunteer went, straight of course, in shot glasses, and it was impolite to refuse. I never developed a taste for the stuff.
>
> As far as tinto went, having never heard of espresso, I didn't really understand what it was, but everyone drank it from small demitasse cups with lots of sugar. I guess it gave you a big shot of caffeine, but I did not relish it...as I would say a Starbucks cappuccino.[1]

Coffee was also served as *café con leche* (coffee with milk). This was regular coffee diluted with a healthy amount of milk served in an ordinary sized coffee cup. Some sugar was added to make a rather pleasant drink.

---

[1] Richard Bennett, personal email, May 6, 2009.

The beer drinking was endless and I remember well the men at small tables completely covered with empty beer bottles. The best drinking time I remember was during each town's patron saint's birthday, when traveling bands would come to town and play cumbias all night in big tents. Everyone danced, the men drank, and the bars had to put a bar across their door about 6' high to prevent drunken partiers from riding their horses in to get more alcohol.[2]

There was a good reason for the bottle covered tables. "While drinking beer in a cantina, the waitress does not keep a tab. She simply leaves the bottles on the table (at times so many bottles that they threatened to tumbled onto the floor) and when everyone gets up to leave, she counts the bottles to determine the amount owed. Simple and efficient. Not to mention that it foregoes arguments about how much was drunk, paper checks and perhaps complicated arithmetic problems for waitresses who probably never finished grade school."[3]

Speaking of cantinas, most of us quickly learned the Colombian etiquette of asking for service in a restaurant or bar. In the United States, it's not unusual to wave your hand at a passing waiter to get his attention. In my experience, this hand waving allows the waiter to ignore you by simply looking or feigning to look in another direction. On several occasions I had waiters simply wave back at me.

In Colombia – and in other Latin countries as well – the style is to hiss at a waitress.

"Ssssssst."

As an American, this hissing seemed rude, at least at first. But the thing is: Everyone did it. The waiters did not seem offended. And what's more, it was really effective. For a waiter to look in another direction simply did not work as an excuse for not coming to your table.

Other forms of commanding waiter attention also emerged. For those men who wore big rings – especially ones with college emblems – they simply banged them on the table to get a waitress to come by. Usually three sharp bangs on a table top did the trick.

The waiter-come-hither form that I never adjusted to was hand clapping - usually by men of substantial means. Leaning back in their chairs like Latino pashas, they would slap their hands together. Clap, clap, clap. To me, it seemed arrogantly imperial.[4]

Another custom of Latin America that the Volunteers were well aware of, but still took some getting used to when they encountered it face to face was the double standard in morals. This ranged from the annoying - "Something else that became more of a nuisance rather than a compliment as time went on were the flirtatious remarks called out

---

[2] Richard Bennett, personal email, May 6, 2009.
[3] Gerald Volgenau, personal email to Gary Peterson, April 4, 2009.
[4] Ibid.

by men as we gringas and local women strolled along on the sidewalk. This was more common in Bogotá and the larger cities."[5] - to the dangerous.

In a somewhat unnerving way, Bogotá's men and Colombian men in general all seemed excessively attracted to fair-haired women – blondes, *rubias.* One story circulated about a Peace Corps woman who was not only blond, but who was considered something of a babe. It was said, one sex crazed Bogotáno literally tackled her as she walked along the sidewalk on the Septima.

So women Volunteers were cautioned: be careful how you dress. Wear nothing at all revealing or tight fitting. This sort of dress just added to the notion seen in Hollywood films that all gringas were genetically prone to be sluts. Best advice: when out in Bogotá, wear a raincoat even if the sun is shining. No one suggested an Arabic *chador,* but that might have worked too.[6]

This dichotomy in the morals of the Latin culture was personified in the custom of keeping a mistress.

Professionals like doctors and lawyers and certainly a number of businessmen rarely brought their wives to restaurant gatherings with other men. Instead, they displayed their machismo by bringing their mistresses. In fact, seeing men with mistresses in restaurants was as common as rice with dinner in a country where *arroz con pollo* is the national dish. As a result, mistresses were generally accepted and even delighted in – at least by other men.

The doctor arrives at a table of men in a local cantina.

"Hey guys, I want to meet Maria Consuela." Everyone nods, smiles and admires. Maria and her kith invariably were curvy, wore the tightest fitting dresses that only years later would be matched by Spandex. They often were amusing and usually seemed smart enough to make me wonder how they ended up in such untenable positions.

However, one mistress told me that life as a kept woman was far superior to that of a wife – at least as long as it lasted. She said, you get to go out to parties, bars, dance clubs, eat in fancy restaurants, be plied with nice clothes and jewelry and sometimes lived in fancy apartments subsidized by their lovers. Meanwhile the wives stayed home to yell, try to keep the kids corralled and weep over the unfairness of it all.[7]

Another practice that took some getting used to was the proliferation of beggars in the cities and along the roads.

After living there for several months, seeing the crippled and infirm (some with fake bandages) along the market routes became commonplace to me. At

---

[5] Carolyn Hawkins Denton, "Memories of Caloto, Valle de Cauca and Ventaquemada, Boyaca," July 13, 2009.
[6] Gerald Volgenau, personal email to Gary Peterson, April 4, 2009.
[7] Ibid.

226

first sight though, it was very alarming to see so many soliciting for a *"limosna."* [8]

Particularly disturbing to the newly arrived Volunteers were the children begging in the streets of Bogotá. Those of us who only ventured into the capital on occasion were always distressed by this show of poverty and neglect.

Though not as wrenching, there were other habits of Colombians that initially irritated the newly arrived Volunteer.

A characteristic that seemed to particularly irk women Volunteers was that Bogotános – in fact, men all over Colombia – seemed to think of their country as one giant urinal. They saw no reason to give special respect to historic cathedrals, museums or historic forts on the coast. If Colombia's national monuments had one thing in common, they all smelled like piss. [9]

This habit was not confined to just men, however. In the vicinity of a good party where there was lots of beer being consumed, women would also relieve themselves in an adjacent field or roadside. This was facilitated by the use of the full skirts which they wore. This annoying habit was more prevalent in the mountain areas then in the low country.

Another interesting oddity which seemed to be peculiar to the hot country, if not to just the Cauca Valley, was the institution of the town clown.

There is a newspaper story in El Paes about a town clown in Palmira. Most of the small to medium size towns have one of these types hanging around. I'll tell you about Santander's clown. He's a tall (about 5' 10") Afrcan-Colombian, husky, walks stooped shouldered with a slow shuffling walk. He runs errands and does the town's odd jobs like announcing town council meetings and dances. He acts the part of an idiot, but his costume tips him off. His clothes are simple and bright, dark pants with a red shirt.

I saw this guy one day with his hair arranged into points. All the hair on his head was combed out into cone shapes that stuck out from his head some three inches. And on his head he had a smooth, hard shell with little figures of cows and horses stuck on it. And taped to the end of his nose he had an egg. In this getup he was wandering around the market place. People would look him over and then would pay no more attention to him. They just seemed interested to see what kind of costume he had on that day, but made no fuss over him. [10]

On the more positive side, I found Colombians to often be very inquisitive about world events and particularly happenings in the United States. The U.S. space program was followed closely by a great many people. Colombians would ask me questions about the program as if I were an expert on the subject. I tried to stay informed by listening to

---

[8] Carolyn Hawkins Denton, "Memories of Caloto, Valle de Cauca and Ventaquemada, Boyaca," July 13, 2009.

[9] Gerry Volgenau, personal email to Gary Peterson, April 4, 2009.

[10] Gary Peterson, *Colombian Diary*, Apr. 25, 1966.

news reports and reading Time magazine as that was the only English publication available in small towns.

This was in the middle of the Gemini program, part of the overall effort to put a man on the moon. But at the time, no one knew what to expect when we reached the moon. I remember there was still concern over what the surface of the moon might be like. Would it support a space craft? Was it covered by a deep blanket of dust, several feet or even miles deep? Colombians would argue over these questions as if they personally were going to experience whatever was there.

All these questions were answered by the Surveyor landing which the Colombians were quite excited about. At the time it was hard for me to stay up on events with limited access to new media especially anything from the States.

> The U.S. really came through with the Surveyor moon shot [I wrote at the time]. Now I have to get a paper this morning for that, and a radio to listen to for the Gemini shot.[11]
>
> I listened to the astronauts come down yesterday. I think that was the first time I have ever listened to a landing.[12]

This was a subject I could talk about with the town's people and often came up as a topic of conversation. Many times, after a successful landing of a Gemini crew, a Colombian would say to me, "you must be proud of your country's achievement." This was said without jealousy or animosity. It was just a heartfelt congratulations on a job well done and a desire by the Colombians to share in this achievement of mankind.

Finally, there were Colombian politics. Let me review a few words I wrote on the Colombian election that occurred in late January 1966.

> As you know, there exists in this country what is called the National Front. That is, both traditional parties support the same candidate for the presidency trading off the position every 4 years – one term Conservative, the next Liberal. And this year is the election. Carlos Lleras R. is the Liberal candidate and therefore the candidate of both parties. The papers are full of the campaigning for him and of the head of the other party, Mariano Opina P.
>
> But today in the paper at the bottom of the front page, there is an article about Gustavo Rojas Pinilla, one time dictator of Colombia, and his disastrous attempt at a campaign speech in Popayán, at least that is the way the paper put it. There are posters around promoting everyone and his brother for President, but that doesn't seem to mean much. Actually, there are three major candidates besides Lleras the National Front candidate, Rojas the former dictator, a Communist, and another candidate who I never heard of. Anyway it will be interesting to see if Rojas's flop in Popayán was really all that big a flop.
>
> Camilo Tores, a defrocked priest who has become quite famous for his controversial speeches, in fact that was why he was defrocked, has changed his name to Helio, so says the paper. Camilo has been running around ever since I arrived making speeches about returning some of the power of the government

---

[11] Gary Peterson, *Colombian Diary,* Jun. 2, 1966.
[12] Gary Peterson, *Colombian Diary,* Jun 7, 1966.

back to the people. He has gained something of a following in Colombia. He gave a speech in Santander in which he said, that the people must rise up and demand more power, but not by violent means, as that might cause U.S. intervention as it did in Santo Domingo. Well, last month Camilo announced that he had joined a band of bandits that call themselves the National Liberation Army.

Early this month he got married and just the other day he changed his name. Kind of interesting to see what happens to him.[13]

While on my trip to Peru and Ecuador, I heard what happened to this reformer.

News flash – remember the de-frocked priest I mentioned a while back who had joined the bandits in Colombia? The papers down here in Peru say he was killed by the army in a raid on a bandit camp.[14]

The last few months I was in Colombia, national elections were held. This election was carried out on two separate days. First were the elections for the congress.

Today is election day and the town is overflowing with people from the rural areas. The army is here also and has the voting area marked off. Whenever anyone enters the area he is searched. They're really making sure that no one causes any trouble. All the voting places have guards and when the boxes were taken to a central place for counting, they had an army escorts. I don't think there will be any tampering with the ballots in this election.[15]

The election is over and it looks like the Frente Naciónal did all right with some from the other two parties getting in. That is, the extreme conservatives and the communist party. The complete results should be in the paper today. Now we wait for the presidential election.[16]

Following the elections for congress, the election for the president was held.

Elections are over. Heard some of the reports on the radio last night while I was eating. Sounds like Lleras, the National Front candidate, won fairly easily.[17]

The National Front would stay in power which meant the two parties would coexist peacefully, putting a final end to the Violencia. While the civil war between the two Colombian political parties did come to an end, it bequeathed to the country a certain lawlessness featuring the old roving guerrilla war groups now turned into bandits. Gradually, these were being hunted down and exterminated. The country seemed to be on the path to political and social stability with every opportunity for economic prosperity. The growth of the communist movement had stagnated. And the invasion of the illicit

---

[13] Gary Peterson, *Colombian Diary,* Jan. 29, 1966.

[14] Gary Peterson, *Colombian Diary,* Feb. 18, 1966.

[15] Gary Peterson, *Colombian Diary,* Mar. 20, 1966.

[16] Gary Peterson, *Colombian Diary,* Mar. 22, 1966.

[17] Gary Peterson, *Colombian Diary,* May 2, 1966.

drug industry had not yet hit South America. Criminal gangs and the associated violence appeared to be on the wane (see Append. III).

Much is made these days about Colombia's drug cartels and violence. Guerrillas in the hills, death squads, rampant killing and kidnapping of politicians, soldiers, wealthy business people and even gringos. Back in the 60s, it was a bit different. I do not think drugs played that big a role in 1965. The guerillas were, for the most part, Maoists. Their gripe was political, left over from the 1950s which suffered a near endless war between the countries political liberals and conservatives.

While time and drugs changed Colombia's guerilla activities, some things never changed. One was a rebel leader in my era known as Tiro Fijo (Sure Shot). His real name was Pedro Antonio Marin, who later took on the *nom de guerre* Manuel Marulanda Velez. As a backlands *gueriero* leader, he survived for more than five decades, starting in the mid-1950s. Never captured, he thrived during my years in Colombia, later became a founder of the infamous FARC (Revolutionary Armed Forces of Colombia). He died on March 26, 2008. Not from army bullets or in a police raid, but prosaically of a heart attack at the age of 75. He was not only a legend, but a rarity of endurance.

Being a guerrilla in Colombia typically was a young man's game. Young men in their teens often joined a bandit group for a few years. They saw it as a short-term gig. They went off to the hills to live a life of adventure, to shoot guns, and go on a few raids. Then after a year or two, they went back home to become garage mechanics or store clerks. For them, time in the jungles was a youthful, if sometimes lethal lark. That's not to say they did not do bad things.[18]

As has been mentioned by several Volunteers, the festivals and carnivals were one of the highlights of life in Colombia. Even the small towns had their town saints day and at least one or two other fiestas during the year, when work came to a halt and the town gave itself over to parades, dancing and celebration. During these festivals, Colombians were bent on having a good time. But even more importantly, they wanted us as guests in their country to enjoy the events.

Certainly one of the charming attributes of Colombians, and perhaps Latins in general, is empathy for others. This was shown in the visits Colombians, perfect strangers, made to Milton Scott when he was in the hospital in Popayán so he wouldn't be alone (Chap. 13). And there were hundreds of other cases where Volunteers were shown this side of the Colombian character. The intent of the Peace Corps in Colombia was to improve the lives of the people in that country, but looking back from the vantage point of all these years, the process worked both ways. Colombians had much to teach these young Americans and the astute Volunteer came away with an education and a new prospective on life.

---

[18] Gerald Volgenau, personal email to Gary Peterson, April 4, 2009.

15

THE CAUCA VALLEY
COMMUNISTS, BANDITS, BEES, AND GOLD

Assembling the chapters of this book, has given me an appreciation for the temperament and outlook of the Volunteers of our group. Bruce Borrud and I had worked together in the high country for almost five months. Bruce was easy going, had a wonderful sense of humor and, it seemed to me, infinite patience. He was kind to the people we worked with, without being condescending. With his self-assured manner, Bruce gained the respect and confidence of the naturally reserved and cautious highlanders. I believe they understood his genuine concern for their welfare.

I learned a great deal from Bruce and the people of Boyacá which helped equip me for the rest of my tour in Colombia. After five months in the mountains, I was moving to the low elevations of the Cauca Valley. The differences could hardly have been more striking. As if to prepare me for the transition, a surprise awaited me in Bogotá.

Upon arriving in the capital, I checked in at the Peace Corps offices to let the staff know I was on my way to Cauca. It was in Bogotá, "I heard that the university students were setting up road blocks and demonstrations. The staff advised me to keep moving rather than stay overnight in Bogotá. I immediately caught a cab and headed for the airport. The cab driver tried four different routes before he found one that wasn't blockaded. Startled and a little uneasy, I caught a plane for Cali."[1]

I was leaving the Cordillera Oriental behind, and beginning an acquaintance with Colombia's more violent character. Boyacá was, for the most part, isolated from the ugly hangover of the Violencia and the emerging Communist movements, but Bogotá and the Cauca Valley were not. I was on my way to work in a nucleo and was only vaguely aware of what that implied.

In Cali, I boarded a bus for Santander, one of the open air, colorful models, not the school bus type I was used to. Then it was on to Popayán, the capital of the Cauca Department, where I met Jeannette Reeser (my new partner) and Carolyn Hawkins (my replacement in Boyacá). I also met most of the Cauca PCVs as they were all in town for a termination party for the Volunteers of Colombia #8 and #12 who were heading home to the U.S. None of these veterans seemed too concerned about the potential for violence in the department, but it was unsettling

My colorful new mode of transportation.

[1] Gary Peterson, *Colombian Diary,* May 20, 1965.

for me to learn at the party that,

> ......there was a large Communist population at the university in Popayán which would, on occasion, attack anything representing the United States. It's here in Cauca that the Peace Corps leader's Jeep was blown up during Easter week. The head of the U.S.-Colombian Educational Center in Popayán (an American) had a gas bomb thrown into his home a couple of months earlier. Now both his house and the Peace Corps Leader's house have police stationed in front of them and there are police detailed to stand outside at this party.[2]

The nucleo I would be working with was established, I was informed, because of the bandit activity in the area. Though not as intense in 1965 as in Tolima or Huila, Caloto did lay claim to its own bandit leader up in the mountains above the town. There was even a detachment of Carabineros stationed in town whose purpose was to track down and eliminate these same guerillas. Yes, this was certainly going to be different than Boyacá.

The bandit leader who lived in the mountains above Caloto was Telmo Abilio Fernandez, alias Tijeras (Scissors). I wondered what this guy was like; would he stand out in a crowd? Was he a tall man or short? Did he have an entourage following him

Caloto Market

[2] Gary Peterson, *Colombian Diary,* May 22, 1965.

everywhere or would he blend in? Some of these questions were answered though in an indirect way.

I may have actually met Tijeras, though I didn't know it at the time. This was at one of the town's festivals which lasted a couple of days. Cleaning up the following morning with some of the town's people, I was informed that the bandit from the mountains had actually been at the fiesta. I said I would certainly have liked to meet him and asked why someone had not introduced me. My friends told me that I was a good guy, but I was still an *Estadounidense* (United Statesian) and they just didn't trust me that much. The only way these bandits survived was because the locals protected them.

Distinctions between Cauca and Boyacá extended to more than just the aftermath of the Violencia of course. In Boyacá, you could walk a mile or two from our hacienda and climb or descend a thousand feet. Here, the Cauca valley floor was flat as far as the eye could see, although the town was located on the perimeter of the valley with mountains rising just behind the nucleo at the edge of Caloto. The several veredas and schools the nucleo worked with were all out in the valley except one that was in the mountains. But this vereda of mostly Amerindians received less attention than the others.

Another difference from Boyacá was that I would not be starting from scratch, as Bruce and I had had to do in Ventaquemada. Carolyn and Jeanette had already paved the way. Carolyn tells about those first few months she and Jeanette struggled to get started in the hot Cauca Valley.

Jeannette Reeser and I were placed in Caloto, a tropical area where pineapple, yuca, bamboo and fique grow. We were the most fair-skinned people in that area, but soon became good friends with Nolva, the cook's daughter. She loved to play basketball and volleyball and was a good athlete. Her mother, Celia, had the only restaurant in the village. Celia had several regular customers besides the two of us. Some of those were city officials and the "carabineros," (mounted police) who patrolled the area and were particularly alert at that time because of a recent kidnapping of a sugar refinery owner.

Mr. Knudson and a *directora* from a neighboring nucleo at my house.

We began our work by getting acquainted with the principal of the local school and other teachers. The school (a nucleo) was built with Alliance for Progress funds, a program begun under former President, John F. Kennedy's administration. The "margola", the school's van, was driven by Antonio and used to transport the campo team to the satellite schools. There was also a Catholic school for girls in Caloto.

Many young children in the rural areas suffered from malnutrition for lack of enough protein in the diet. Instead of formula or breast milk, babies were often given "panela

233

water" which was comparable to brown sugar water. We began by trying to introduce them to Incaparina and get them to incorporate it in the foods they prepared.[3]

So after her initiation to Colombia and Peace Corps work in Caloto, Carolyn was moving to the high country of Boyacá and I descended, in a physical sense, to the Cauca Valley where I would have to become accustomed to the heat and, in the wet season, the humidity. "I was drinking seven or eight sodas a day when I first arrived, usually two at a time."[4] It took a couple of months for me to acclimate.

Racially there had been much more uniformity in Boyacá. Nearly all were Amerindians with metizos and some pure caucasians in the towns and cities especially in government positions and business owners. In Caloto, on the other hand, you could find all possible variation.

Take the nucleo for instance. The director, Mr. Knudson (pronounced Nudson) was of Norwegian extraction. Part of the time I was in Cauca there was an agronomo at the nucleo that was Italian. Gallego, the *majordomo* (foreman/grounds manager), who I worked with on the nucleo ag projects, was Amerindian or mestizo. One of the male teachers looked to be a mix of several races including black and oriental. Antonio, the nucleo van driver and Obidio, the nucleo carpenter, were African-Colombian.

The population of Caloto and surrounding area was a mixture of black, Amerindian and Caucasian with a sprinkling of Asian, and there was every possible combination in between.

In colonial times Caloto had been one of Spain's prosperous gold producing sites. In fact it was the Spanish that imported the Africans to work in the gold mines and later the rice plantations of the area. That was after intense forced labor had decimated the indigenous population (see Appendices II and III).

The era of commercial gold production had long since passed, but there were still flakes to be found if one was willing to put in the time and effort. Many of the women in the area sported gold earrings or necklaces made from gold they had panned themselves. I was always impressed with how brilliant these pieces were. Essentially pure gold, they had a much brighter yellow-metallic luster than commercial jewelry in the United States.

Caloto had two paved main streets that ran on either side of the central plaza with a third shorter parallel street further north. A number of cross streets intersected these avenues and there were additional dirt streets further out. In the center of town was a plaza, clean and well kept except during coffee harvest when coffee beans would be spread out to dry in the streets and plaza.

The town's main industry was a regional hospital which employed three doctors and a platoon of nurses and other support personnel. The area was agricultural, with coffee beans, chocolate and sugar cane (converted to panela) being the chief cash crops. The hospital, nucleo, several stores and small businesses were enough to keep the town's one or two thousand inhabitance reasonably well employed. The town was generally clean and well maintained.

---

[3] Carolyn Hawkins Denton, 'Memories of Caloto, Valle de Cauca and Ventaquemada, Boyaca," Jul. 13, 2009

[4] Gary Peterson, *Colombian Diary*, Aug. 28, 1965.

To get to Caloto, you usually boarded a bus in Santander about thirteen kilometers away on the main highway between Cali and Popayán. Santander was a town of about 4,500 people and had its own Volunteer, Bill Higgins, a community development PCV. Many a time I would get to Santander, miss the bus to Caloto and have to stay at Bill's place where I was always welcomed.

So I arrived at my new site and found a place to stay in the town's only hotel. My room was concrete with a high ceiling and no windows. It was cool and damp which I didn't mind as I was going to need some time to acclimate to the heat.

Jeannette immediately took me under her wing and introduced me around town. There were the doctors, the town's business people, the mayor and her secretary and Celia, the black lady that ran the best (and only) eatery in town - "a sort of boarding house. Breakfast: 2 eggs or meat, rice, café con leche and a couple of rolls. Dinner: soup, rice, couple of slices of tomato, *platino*, a banana and yuca. All this for 5 pesos a day, that's about 25 cents."[5]

As Jeannette, or Juanita as she was called by the Colombians, took me from place to place, it became clear my new site mate was more than just well thought of by these people. Jeannette was pretty with light brown hair, blue eyes, freckles and a perpetual cheerfulness. She spoke Spanish like a native – town's people would tell me she had almost no accent – and the Colombians adored her. During our meanderings that day, I watched her speak to the mayor, the doctors at the hospital, the shop owners and the guy sweeping the street with the same deference and respect. It made no difference if a person's station in life was elevated or humble, Jeannette would talk to them and take an interest in their lives. She would make jokes, which her command of the language allowed, and cheer them up. If one of our missions in Colombia was to be an ambassador of good will,

Jeannette Reeser

I would have to say Juanita had already achieved that purpose in spades.

Jeannette was from Pine Meadow, Connecticut and had attended Seton Hill College in Greensburg, Pennsylvania. Her interest in the Peace Corps was sparked by an event that had occurred a couple of years earlier. While attending a presidential speaking engagement, Jeannette had actually shaken hands with President Kennedy. The incident served to channel her desire to be of service in the direction of the Peace Corps. She applied and after the preliminary tests, found herself on the way to Lincoln, Nebraska. That handshake with John F. Kennedy would lead to Jeannette's two years of living and working in the Cauca Valley of Colombia.

Whereas Bruce and I had been on our own in getting established in Boyacá, here I had plenty of help. Bill and particularly Jeannette had seen that I was properly introduced. Mr. Knudson made sure I was integrated into the nucleo staff.

Celia became much more than just the lady running the boarding house where I ate. Her family saw to it I was taught the social graces. Celia had two daughters, Nolva and Lilia, in their late teens or early twenties and a son of ten or twelve, Gerardo. Celia found two or three houses in town for me to choose from and guided me on how much to pay for rent. I picked a four room duplex. The building was concrete with two rooms and a

---

[5] Gary Peterson, *Colombian Diary,* July 8, 1965.

kitchen open to a patio in the center. Across this patio was a wall that divided the whole house in two, my side and another for the family occupying the other half of the house. It was strong, simple, and airy with running cold water and a toilet.

Nolva and Lilia spent several evenings teaching me the Colombian dances so I would not be a total social dunce and Gerardo introduced me to the town's soccer field where there was always a pickup game. Besides soccer and basketball, other popular games were pool – there were three or four establishments in town with pool tables – and Chinese checkers. I could hold my own in basketball, improved at soccer, but never achieved parity in checkers or pool.

So I settled in, obtained a bed from some PCVs that were leaving for the States and made my own desk, table and book shelves. There were already garden projects, chickens and rabbits at the nucleo, at the five satellite schools and in the associated veredas. They even had a couple of experimental fish ponds out in the communities. My job would be to carry on these projects at the schools and veredas, and teach agricultural classes at the nucleo. I also became involved peripherally in Jeannette and Bill's Vilachi project.

> Jeannette and I went to Santander. Then with Bill, we went up to a vereda, Vilachi, to a fiesta to raise money for another grand fiesta in June. It's this vereda that Bill and Jeannette are proudest of. Bill has been working with the junta there in building the school and Jeannette has been working with the women in nutrition, etc. Now she is about to help with the school lunch program and Bill is helping them build a kitchen for the school.[6]

Gallego in his nucleo garden domain.

I advised in the planning and layout of a garden and suggested a chicken project as a possible meat source for the lunch program.

However, most of my work was centered in the nucleo in Caloto. I worked closely with the nucleo majordomo, Gallego, on the nucleo's projects. We improved the chicken flock by introducing breeding stock from the experimental farm in Popayán.

I instituted the tattooing of the rabbits (in the ear) so they could be tracked and a record kept of their breeding program. The chickens and rabbits were then used to upgrade the rural school's animals and the farm stock of local breeders.

---

[6] Gary Peterson, *Colombian Diary*, May 23, 1965.

During those first few months in Cauca, insects came to be the bane of my existence. First I was introduced to the army ant which could decimate a garden in a single night. More than once I was called to a rural school or family garden that was being invaded. Usually I was too late, but I did become familiar with this South American pest.

"Most of these ants were from half to three-quarters of an inch long, but there were a few that were at least one inch in length. These had great big heads, out of proportion to the rest of their large bodies. The oversized ants with monster heads seemed to be soldier ants that attacked anything threatening the column. These ants apparently just work at night, forming a living highway, up trees, across the tops of walls, though cracks, transporting edibles back to their nest."[7] I have seen a column of these ants be just an inch or two wide or at other times it might be a couple of feet wide, a mass of swarming ants consuming everything in its path.

There were all kinds of stories about these insects, how they would kill small animals and even babies, then consume them in a matter of an hour or two leaving only a pile of clean white bones. I thought these were just wild stories until I was bitten by one of the big headed creatures and found out just how nasty a sting they have. Through experimentation we eventually found a couple of insecticides that would kill the ants and we saved our gardens from these ferocious predators.

Having checked the ant problem, next it was bees. Bees were one of the items the nucleo did not have when I arrived though honey was a prized local commodity. I searched for someone who could help us start a bee hive. Finally, I located Paul Anderson, a Cauca Volunteer who specialized in bees. He brought a box-like hive and some bees to the nucleo and gave us instructions on bee keeping – keep the hive clean, remove any dead bees and let the honey makers do the rest.

This seemed to be an easy win. Get some bees, establish a hive, harvest the honey, how hard can it be? - I should have known better.

Gallego and I worked on establishing the hive in the garden at the nucleo inserting the frames for the bees to deposit the honey on. We tended the hive carefully and watched the bees multiply. Gradually, Gallego took over the project and the bees became so used to him, he could get right into the hive to work without smoke or protective clothing. All went well for about a month then disaster struck. Suddenly the bees started dying – in large numbers. Gallego and I cleaned out the hive, but the next day there were more dead bees.

After careful observation we discovered what the problem was with the bees. When Paul brought the bees he didn't have enough Italians, the real good honey bees, so he brought an Italian queen, but the workers were the native black bees. Now there are enough Italian workers so they are trying to throw the blacks out. As one of the teachers said, "Even the bees have racial discrimination." I figure before the fight is over the colony will be cut in half, but I don't know what we can do about it. So we just wait and see.[8]

The inter-racial battle went on for weeks. It looked like the native blacks were even recruiting help from local bees outside the hive; a major insect war was on. Since the

---

[7] Gary Peterson, *Colombian Diary*, Aug. 4, 1965.
[8] Gary Peterson, *Colombian Diary,* July 31, 1965.

queen was Italian, all the workers being produced were also Italian. Eventually the Italians won and were able to take over the hive and defend it from the indigenous bees in the area. We divided the colony into several hives, each with their own queen. These, we were able to distribute to the satellite schools and campecinos. Several locals who had little or no land became bee keepers commercially and were able to supplement their family's meager incomes in this way.

Having learned something about bees, Gallego and I became aware of another potential problem, African bees or "killer bees" as they were labeled in the newspapers. These were bees imported from Africa as part of a breeding program in southeastern Brazil. Though slightly smaller than European honey bees, the African variety is a much more prolific honey producer. They do have a drawback, however; they are very aggressive and tend to swarm around a perceived threat stinging the interloper to death.

Of course, the bees escaped from the experiment station in 1957 and began interbreeding with native bees in the jungles of Brazil, killing a few people in the process. They spread south into Argentina and northwest into western Brazil. Officials and beekeepers were on the lookout for these little savages in Colombia at that time. Gallego and I, likewise, kept an eye out for these little beasts.

Interesting to note that after I left Colombia, the African bees did invade the country, then spread into Central America. By 1990 they had crossed the Rio Grande into Texas and by 2003 had moved into southern California and central Nevada. The good news is they are adversely affected by cold weather and may have about reached their northern territorial limit.

Boy proudly displays his rabbit hutch.

In August school dismissed for summer vacation. All the students and many of the teachers at the nucleo left for their homes, some went on vacation trips. The satellite schools closed and the teachers left to visit parents and friends. Work slowed to a crawl so it seemed a good time to take vacation myself.

Our group had arranged a one year reunion at the resort in Melgar for the end of August. Steve Burgess and I planned to leave from there and play tourist for another week, Bogotá, then on to the Amazon. It would be a trip I had dreamed about for a long time. Growing up on a ranch in Montana before the days of television, I had read a great deal. One of the subjects I found fascinating was the great South American river. I had read Friar Gaspar de Carvajal's account of Francisco de Orellana's discovery and voyage down the length of the river in 1542. I had read about the man-eating cayman and pink dolphins in National Geographic. There were books describing giant catfish, a myriad of monkeys and brightly colored birds all inhabitance of the jungles and waters of the Amazon basin. I had read stories of natives hunting with tall bows and long arrows or with deadly poison tipped blow-gun darts. And always there was the great river, so large it was almost an inland sea. Now I might have the opportunity to see all this for myself.

Jeannette, Nolva and I caught a bus for Cali, then at 11:00 AM we left by bus for Melgar. We rode all night arriving at the resort at 8:00 in the morning. After two days of reunion, Steve Burgess and I left for Bogotá – next stop, the Amazon

We flew up and over the mountains, then straight and level across the great expansive Llanos and then over the jungle. Below us was the green canopy of the tree tops with an occasional blue ribbon of a river parting the trees. Finally we reached the Amazon and the Colombian town of Leticia.

> Very nice little town of about 2,000 people. The guy who runs the place, Mike Tsalickis, is an American of Greek extraction, speaks Greek, English, Spanish and Portuguese. The buildings in town are generally new or at least well maintained. It is a clean town without the usual beggars. The people say they have no problem with stealing, even leave stores open at night. It really seems like a frontier town due in large part, I suppose, to its isolation. An airplane comes in about once every two days and a regular boat once a month. There are no roads connecting Leticia with the rest of Colombia.[9]

Most of Colombia is well to the north of the Amazon. There is only an arm of the country that stretches down to the river. So Colombian territory only runs for a few miles along the north side of the river. To the east is Brazil. The west is Peru and across the river is Brazil again. Leticia is Colombia's only port on the river, but moored at a dock were two Colombian Navy gun-boats, the sum of the countries Amazon fleet.

The Amazon is hugely expansive even here, 1,700 miles from its mouth. It is amazing that ocean-going ships can cross three-quarters of the South American continent on this river arriving at Leticia and sail another 300 miles further upstream to Iquitos in Peru. The river is two miles wide here and the southern river bank can only be seen on a clear day from Leticia. The Amazon has multiple channels with some large islands out in the river. The river banks are high in most places and composed of river mud. Flooding must keep foliage from covering these banks as the jungle is quite dense just a few yards off the river. It is all together an impressive body of water.

> Monday morning Steve and I took a ride to an Indian village, down stream. An American couple with 2 children went with us. They're here in Leticia waiting to catch a ship down river. They plan to go by boat all the way to the Atlantic.

> In the Indian village Steve and I bought a set of fishing bows and arrows (oversized, just like I had expected). We visited a Brazilian town called Benjamin on the south side of the river. The village looked like a frontier town out of the old west, mostly constructed of wood with wood walkways and dirt streets. It is nothing like the comparatively modern Leticia.[10]

When we first arrived in Leticia and visited Mike's establishment we were mesmerized by the quantity and variety of animals he had in cages in a couple of open air sheds. There were huge anacondas and smaller snakes, birds of every size and color as

---

[9] Gary Peterson, *Colombian Diary,* Sep. 6, 1965.
[10] Gary Peterson, *Colombian Diary,* Sep. 8, 1965.

well as tapirs, ant-eaters and hundreds of chattering monkeys of various sizes, shapes and colors. Only a young river otter was allowed to wander freely about Mike's facilities. This little guy was the office pet and had the run of the place.

The disposition of all these animals we discovered Wednesday morning. Actually, Tuesday night Mike told us about the cargo plane lined up for a trip to the north coast and then on to the U.S. So Wednesday morning we helped load boxes, crates and cages onto trucks bound for the airport and a trip north. Apparently this is done every few months. I was surprised to learn that most of the monkeys do not go to zoos, but to university and pharmaceutical labs to be used for test work. The snakes do go to zoos because exotic snakes do not survive in captivity for long and have to be replaced regularly.

As we completed the loading, Mike was telling us of his ideas on methods to ship Amazon pink dolphins to the U.S. and Europe. So far his attempts had been unsuccessful, but he was not deterred and would keep trying. He figured if he could deliver a healthy specimen it would be well worth the effort.

He also told us about a National Geographic film crew that had been there a week earlier. Mike explained how he hauled out one of his big boas and wrestled with it in a pond beside the river.

"We put on a real good show," he said.

A tapir – one of Mike's captures.

Years later, back in the U.S., I saw his National Geographic special on TV. And there was Mike down in the water and mud grappling with this huge snake. He had coils around his legs and a loop across his chest. He appeared to be struggling mightily to free himself from this great monster. It looked, for all the world, like he would surely be crushed or drowned. It was indeed, "a real good show."

At about the same time, I ran across an article in a National Geographic magazine that explained Mike's background. He only told us he had been down there for about twelve years and had learned to hunt animals in the Everglades.

"My father used to dive for sponges, like most of the Florida Greeks.....I've collected animals ever since I was a kid in Tarpon Springs," the article quoted Mike. "I worked south from the Everglades, and 17 years ago I hit Leticia. But it was nowhere till I got air travel going."[11]

The story also described Mike's animal collection.

___

[11] "Colombia from Amazon to Spanish Main," *National Geographic,* August 1970, p.272.

Buying monkeys and birds on the Amazon.

"At Mike's home and zoo I saw more animals in five minutes than I've ever saw in the bush. Several hundred native trappers bring him anacondas, pumas, rare birds, porpoises, manatees, monkeys, marmosets, and other animals."[12]

Steve and I went on one of Mike's buying trips down the Amazon. We left at 6:00 in the morning with two of Mike's workers and returned at 3:00 the next morning. On the buying trip we would stop every few miles along the river and hike back several yards to a thatched roof hut. Often these huts had no sides, just a roof. Lounging under the roof, in hammocks, or outside on the ground would be a man and his family or sometime just a woman and kids. The man or woman would stand up and greet the boatman. The guy (or woman) might have a couple of monkeys, some birds or a snake to sell. Some animals were purchased from people just paddling up the river. We came back with 24 monkeys, 30 parakeets, a large cayman skin, a fresh small cayman skin, bananas, platino, and a rooster. Quite a trip.[13]

At one stop, during a thunderstorm, we pulled into shore to gain shelter. Before we left, the boatman tied a cord around the neck of a two foot cayman and tossed him overboard. We dashed for the hut just off the creek bank. After the storm had passed, we went back to the boat to find the craft had moved up against the creek bank trapping the cayman underwater. The animal was dead, apparently drowned. The only knife we had was a jackknife my brother, Bob, had given me the previous Christmas. So while we

A typical "house" on the Amazon

[12] "Colombia from Amazon to Spanish Main," *National Geographic,* August 1970, p.272.
[13] Gary Peterson, *Colombian Diary,* Sep. 9, 1965.

motored on down the Amazon, the boatman's brother used Bob's jackknife to skin the cayman.

That afternoon an ocean-going passenger ship arrived and docked. "The boat everyone has been waiting for all week finally arrived this afternoon. It came up river from Brazil and will be going on to Iquitos in Peru. It will stop on its way back down river in a week or two. The whole town turned out for the event and boarded the ship."[14] Most of the locals settled on the rear open deck and ordered cocktails. I wondered around and talked to some of the crew. These men were from all over the world, an Indian, Portuguese, British, Canadian and a couple of Germans. It was certainly an international crew.

The ocean liner was not the only vessel to put in at Leticia that day. "Two PCVs and 4 tourists arrived before sunset. They had come down river in a small boat from Iquitos by themselves, some 300 miles. It must have been quite a trip. They were sunburned, exhausted from paddling and out of food, but they had made it. If they had had another few hours on the river, they would have been in real trouble."[15]

The last night we were there, one of Mike's workers took us out on the river on a cayman hunt. These hunts are conducted at night so you can use a bright searchlight to spot and blind the reptiles. When the beam of light hits a cayman, all you see are the two yellow eyes shining in the dark. You aim your shot gun right between the eyes and pull the trigger. It's crude, but effective. It was a short hunt and we only killed a couple of 'gaters, but we did get a feel for how it was done.

> This morning we said good-bye to everyone, picked up our tickets and boarded the airplane. We are now somewhere between Villavicencia and Leticia, Steve, me, the 2 other PCVs and 2 young tourists. This is a Satena (Colombian military air transport) plane, seats are cloth hanging along the sides of the plane. There's no heat or pressurizing system. It's starting to get cold. It will really get frigid when we climb to get over the mountains into Bogotá.[16]

Before we left Leticia, Mike invited us to go along on a monkey hunting trip he was preparing for in a few days. Steve was really tempted; he had to think long and hard before he finally decided to go back with me to civilization. It would have been quite an expedition.

The vacation in Melgar, Bogotá and especially Leticia had been refreshing and stimulating. Now I was ready to get back to Caloto and the challenges at the nucleo. But what I found upon my return was chaos.

School started on the 4th of October, but the director, Mr. Knudson, was on leave going to school in Venezuela and no one had the authority to sign checks. There was no money for the nucleo to purchase food, gas, or other supplies. At the same time, the department teachers (those in the satellite schools) were out on strike. So, no school in the campo and the nucleo was trying to get by running half days to conserve supplies. Also, there was a gas shortage because a tanker of gasoline had sunk at the port of Buenaventura depriving our area of fuel for vehicles.

---

[14] Gary Peterson, *Colombian Diary*, Sep. 9, 1965.

[15] Ibid.

[16] Gary Peterson, *Colombian Diary*, Sep. 10, 1965.

And to top it all off, I had a run in with a local cur. "On the way back from the nucleo this mangy dog ran out and bit me. Now I'll have to keep track of the dog to see that it doesn't die in the next 10 days. There is the possibility that it has rabies and I will have to have the vaccination shots."[17]

There were, however, some bright spots during this almost consistent run of bad luck. For one thing, the dog didn't die and I avoided the thirteen rabies shots in my stomach. Also, because of the disruption at the nucleo, substitute director, teachers on strike, half day school and no gas, Jeannette and I gained some freedom to explore new areas, especially the mountain veredas, which the nucleo seemed to neglect. Often we worked with the hospital personnel who were more interested in the veredas in the mountains than the nucleo. And to facilitate these expeditions, Jeannette had purchased a horse.

Yesterday, Jeannette and I decided to ride horses up to Todevio. Peace Corps was considering putting a Volunteer up there. We were only planning to be gone for the morning, but we didn't get back until three in the afternoon. The town is way back in the hills. We rode up this trail that wound through the mountains and some beautiful scenery. Half the town's population looked like they were police or army. This is one of the places where there is supposed to be high bandit activity. The people themselves are Indian.[18]

Saturday Jeanette, Dr. Yacub (one of the doctors at the hospital) and I rode horses up to a vereda in the mountains behind Caloto to see about putting a hot lunch program in the school. There are no roads, only a trail that wound higher and higher up into the mountains. Doesn't look too promising, just too isolated. But the med team wants to see what can be done to improve the conditions for the school children and the people in this remote area.[19]

A Carabinero leaving Caloto for a patrol in the mountains.

Today Jeanette and I went up to Huella another vereda in the mountains behind Caloto. We talked the driver of the hospital comuneta into going up to the end of the road and then we hiked another half hour to the school. We spent the rest of the morning up there and part of the afternoon, coming back on foot. I showed the kids how to build *aras* (raised mounds) to drain their gardens and we planted

---

[17] Gary Peterson, *Colombian Diary*, Jan 6, 1965.

[18] Gary Peterson, *Colombian Diary*, Sep. 28, 1965.

[19] Gary Peterson, *Colombian Diary*, Nov. 29, 1965.

several varieties of vegetables that should do well at this altitude. Jeannette worked with the school cook on the lunch program, suggesting ways to vary the menu and how to make better use of the food that they get from CARE.[20]

The people in these mountains are Pais (Paez) Indians. Spanish is their second language. In fact most of the women and children do not speak Spanish so communication is a problem much of the time. They have little, but seem to be willing to work to better their lives. They are so appreciative of any help, instruction or attention you give them.

With bus schedules now so erratic, I was forced to rely more on my bicycle and Jeanette's horse for transportation. During trips into the campo, I would sometimes smell a terrible stench. When I investigated the source, it often turned out to be some animal that had died and was rotting in the heat and humidity. But sometimes I would fine a small plot of land, a house and a rack of chocolate beans drying in the sun.

Chocolate beans on rack to dry.
Note the outhouse in the background.

Chocolate was a good cash crop for the small land owner. It was labor intensive, but brought a high price. The large, almond-shaped beans were stripped from the melon-like pods and placed in a pile, then covered with banana leaves and allowed to ferment. After fermentation, the beans were laid out on racks to dry. The smell of the drying beans would carry for half a mile or better. It was almost overpowering up close, but it was a means for the campesino to make some good money if he was willing to put forth the effort and take the risks which included diseases, insects and adverse weather, the usual plagues inflicted upon farmers everywhere.

It was at this time that I developed a garden kit to give to people, particularly kids, who were starting gardens. "These kits consisted of a variety of seeds, and some insecticide powder. I gave kits to teachers at the nucleo and in the satellite schools. Now if I'm not around and one of the students gets his fence built and the ground turned over, the teacher can give him the kit and he can plant his garden, no fuss, no bother for the teacher. This is also in case it starts to rain early this year. There are several kids that have gardens ready, but have no water."[21] These kits also worked well with 4-S clubs and proved a boon to expanding garden projects in the veredas.

Aside from work, I did some gold mining, on a very limited basis. After all, this was one of the great gold mining areas of colonial Spain.

[20] Gary Peterson, *Colombian Diary*, Jan. 25, 1966.
[21] Gary Peterson, *Colombian Diary*, Feb. 11, 1966.

Planting a garden at a school in the campo.

Celia, the woman who cooks for us, took Jeannette and me down to the creek yesterday and showed us how it is done. Her father brought her a gold panning pan from their country. They are from a town on the other side of the valley up in the mountains. She says where she comes from everyone has a pan and everyone goes out and pans a little. The pan is a big round wooden bowl, shaped like a Chinese hat, with the point in the middle. We dug around in several spots, spent about half an hour and came up with some real gold. I think if you really worked at it you could make better wages than the common laborer does around here. Celia said that this was a bad day and there was a better spot further up the stream.[22]

We went panning for gold again yesterday morning. Celia took Jeannette and me further up the creek to a spot that has a reputation as a rich gold area. She had also found a little pick in addition to the panning bowl. We panned for about an hour and a half and did get a small amount of gold. Jeannette and I split the haul. I'll have to go out and really spend some time at this, one of these days.[23]

But of course I never did. Always so much going on and so many things to do, that spending hours panning for gold, somehow, lost its allure.

And finally, right after Christmas, there was the Cali *feria*, an event rivaling any *carnival* in Colombia, a celebration not to be missed. I met Ron Halter and Steve Burgess there and we took in the bull fights of course. Many of the matadors were first rate, coming from Spain on the off season. But one of the unique features of these ferias is the dances that go on all night in the *casetas*.

---

[22] Gary Peterson, *Colombian Diary,* Nov. 12, 1965.
[23] Gary Peterson, *Colombian Diary*, Mar. 25, 1966.

These casetas are really something, great big buildings or tents with a dance floor in the middle and tables all around. And this is the first place I have seen in Colombia where you could dance and talk to a girl without being introduced and without the mother sitting between the two of you. I have a taste of what Rio de Janeiro's carnival must be like.[24]

Bill Higgins, our horse and a couple of turkeys.

Reflecting back on the fall's events, I think Bill Higgins's departure was one of the most trying occurrences. Bill, a member of an earlier group, had completed his tour and headed back to the states. He was a good friend and had put up with my bad Spanish and cultural gaffs with grace and humor. His leaving made me think of how different things were going to be for him.

There had been a number of going away parties for Bill which will give you some idea of how popular and well thought of he was. He could walk into the mayor's office and be treated with more than just respect, able to walk into any of the Cauca Department offices in Popayán and get an audience at a moment's notice. All this would change upon his return to the States.[25]

Besides the Amazon, my other great interest in South America was Peru and the ancient Indian civilizations that had flourished there. Again, since boyhood – all that time to read at the home on the ranch – I had been fascinated by the Incas and earlier cultures that have left archeological ruins, pottery and gold objects behind. I was somewhat familiar with statue-like pottery of the Mochica, the gold work of the Chimú, the stone carvings of the Chavin, the textiles of the Paracas, the gigantic figures and geometric designs laid out in the desert recognizable only from the air, made by the Nazcas and the architecture of the Incas. Now was a chance to see these artifacts for myself.

I had made arrangements with Chuck Brome, my old fraternity brother from Montana State, to meet at his site, Guayaquil, Ecuador. We would travel to Peru and then on to Bolivia to visit Don Durga, the third fraternity brother in the Peace Corps in South America.

[24] Gary Peterson, *Colombian Diary*, Mar. 25, 1966.
[25] Gary Peterson, *Colombian Diary*, Nov. 29, 1965.

I had decided to go by the land route to Peru in order to see the country. Great idea on paper, but as it turned out, difficult to execute. The highway from Santander to Popayán was closed for construction and I had to catch a ride with a departmental engineer I knew just to get to Popayán. From Popayán to Pasto, the capital of Nariño was an overnight bus trip. The bus was so crowded that I didn't even get a seat and so I sat on my suitcase in the aisle until the guy next to me started to vomit and I decided to move. I stood up the rest of the way to Pasto. We arrived about 9 in the morning. The worst bus ride I have ever had."[26] I spent the rest of the day exploring Quito, the Ecuadorian capital.

You can ski or breathe, but not both.

The next morning I was up at 4:00 and caught the *autoferro* (train) that runs from Quito to Guayaquil. It dropped from Quito at over 9,000 feet to Guayaquil at sea level in less than 200 miles. We passed some of the highest mountain peaks in South America, Cotopaxi (19,347 feet) and Chimborazo (20, 561 feet). Several of the mountain tops are perpetually covered with snow. Being right on the equator, these peaks are dazzling to look at. It is easy to see why the Incas called this northern section of their empire, "The land of the shining mountains."

An Ecuadorian on the train told me that there was a ski resort on one of the mountains, for a few years. He said it finally closed in spite of the fact that it operated year round. The problem was, he said, that you could ski or you could breathe, but you couldn't do both. Good story and the people in the train car all had a good laugh and I laughed along with them though I suspect I was, at least partially, the subject of the gayety. But the passengers were jovial and congenial and it was a pleasant trip.[27]

Guayaquil is a city unlike anything I had seen in Colombia; it is definitely a tropical port.

The city, nearly 700,000 people, is the largest in Ecuador. It is built next to a river, a couple of miles from the sea. Some of the ships are unloaded right in the river, but most are docked in inlets along the coast, then the cargos are hauled overland a few miles to the city.

The down town area is not too bad, fairly clean and the buildings look nice, but the urban housing areas are jungles. People live in straw mat houses or shacks. With the heat and humidity, there is a variety of insects hard to believe.

[26] Gary Peterson, *Colombian Diary,* Feb. 18, 1966.
[27] Gary Peterson, *Colombian Diary,* Feb. 25, 1966.

Insects up to six inches in length and so many that on some sidewalks where they have died from the sun and heat, they cover the pavement and cause a terrible stench.[28]

Chuck and I left Guayaquil and traveled by boat, taxi and bus to the border. Here the road literally ends. Peru and Ecuador were technically in a state of war, though this condition has remained for decades. It all stems from a war between the two countries in 1941. Both countries had claimed the area east of the mountains down into the Amazon basin. During this short war, Peru occupied this area reducing the size of Ecuador about in half. A conference of South American countries met in Rio de Janeiro to settle the dispute. Ecuador received some of the territory on the east side of the Andes, but Peru was given the Amazon area. This is the same territory that runs up to Colombia at Leticia. Ecuador, to this day, claims this area and maps in Ecuador still show this region as part of the country, their "Amazonas." Thus, the semi state of war between the two countries.

We had to exit the bus at the end of the road and walk across the border where our passports were checked. Then we boarded a greyhound type bus for the 22 hour ride to Lima.

The museums in Lima, some of them private, were terrific. I remember one that featured Moche pottery. The Moche civilization flourished along the Peruvian coast north of Lima from about 0 to 1000 A.D. The pottery, mostly of the stirrup-spout type, was wonderful in quality and variety. Many were in the shape of individual's heads like portraits were done in European societies. Some were of people in various kinds of clothing, soldiers, groups of people, even whole scenes.

Other museums had the black-ware of the Chimú, bright colors of the Tiahuanaco pottery and the pots and bowls with distinctive art work of the Nazca. There were silver and gold objects of the Chimú and Inca.

Inca stone work in Cuzco.

One of the most amazing items was the embroidered mantle from the Paracas culture. This was a green, orange and black cape of the finest cloth. Though ancient, about 4,000 years old, its preservation was made possible because of the dry climate of the southern Peruvian coast.

From Lima we flew to Cuzco, the old Inca capital. High in the mountains, the city is a mix of colonial Spanish, Inca and modern structures. Along the streets of Cuzco are many fine examples of Inca stone masonry work. A number of the walls bordering the streets were parts

---

[28] Gary Peterson, *Colombian Diary*, Mar. 25, 1966.

of ancient Inca buildings and were used by the Spanish as foundations for their buildings and walls. No mortar was ever used by the Incas, yet the stones are cut and fitted so exactly that you can't get a knife blade between them. This stone work is most remarkable.

The next day we took a train to Machu Pichu. "On the trip, there were nothing but tourists with us, three Mormon missionaries going home from Argentina, three stewardesses from Pan Am and lots of older people."[29]

Machu Pichu

The ruins are breathtaking. The site was never located by the Spanish and when Hyrum Bingham discovered it in 1911, he thought he had found the lost Inca stronghold from which the Incas had fought the Spanish for years. Eventually, this proved to not be the case, but it was true this site survived as an Inca village, probably a religious site, long after the rest of Peru had been conquered by the Spanish.

The buildings, partially restored at the time, sit in a saddle between two peaks. Yet, this small plateau is several hundred feet above the river and guarded by steep mountain sides difficult to climb, but easily defended. The whole impression is one of isolation and remoteness. It is beautiful with towering mountains, deep gorges, jungle and rushing rivers on all sides.

Sacsahuamán – the Inca fortress above Cuzco.

---

[29] Gary Peterson, *Colombian Diary*, Feb. 26, 1966.

Back in Cusco, we took a taxi to see the old Inca fortress that guarded the Inca imperial capital city. Sacsahuamán was stunningly massive. Huge boulders, taller than a man have been fitted together to make a series of walls, one above the other forming an impressive fortification. The walls are not straight, but zig-zag so that defenders would have a clear shot at attackers attempting to scale the fort walls. The whole structure is overpowering in its immensity.

In Peru we ran into several interesting people from all over the world. In Cuzco we met a girl from Jamaica who is teaching in a British school in Lima. She was charming, partly I suppose because of her manner of speech. We rode back from Cuzco to Lima with the two Australian boys, brothers from a ranch in Victoria. They were on a two year world tour. And in Lima, amazingly, we ran into Doug Dunn and Steve Burgess on their way to catch a cruise ship back to Cartagena, Colombia.

Chuck Brome and the teacher from Jamaica, high in the Inca ruins.

Saturday morning we flew from Lima to Guayaquil, faster and much easier than the land route. There, Brome and another Volunteer gave me a tour of the poor barrios. What a mess. The flimsy houses are built on stilts over a swamp. The morass is divided by roads of piled up dirt which are raised above the water level of the swamp. There are no sewage or water facilities. The disease rate must be astronomical in this place.[30]

A disappointment for Chuck and me was not getting all the way to Bolivia and seeing the other Montana State Phi Sig working as a Peace Corps Volunteer in South America. Our plan had been to take the train from Cuzco along Lake Titicaca to La Paz. However, once back in Cuzco we learned the tracks had been washed out and the train would not be running for days, maybe weeks. With the way blocked and time running out, we took a few extra days in Lima and Guayaquil and called it good. I flew back to Colombia from Ecuador, a much easier trip.

By the time I returned from my Peruvian adventure, winter was a hard reality in the Cauca Valley. There would be some rain two out of three days and it was cool, much to

---

[30] Gary Peterson, *Colombian Diary,* Feb. 28, 1966.

my liking, though the natives complained of the freezing weather. To the average resident of Caloto, anything below 60° was frigid.

The nucleo, I discovered, had some additions. Señior Knudson had obtained title to a finka to be added to the nucleo, a project he had been working on since I arrived. I had thought he was dreaming, but he had indeed pulled it off. And with the land he had obtained an extra position, an agranamo to supervise work on the finka. To fill this position Knudson had talked an older gentleman, Don Angel, into coming out of retirement to run the finka.

Don Angel was an interesting guy. Italian by birth, he had come to Colombia as an adult. He would tell us about the Mafia, the drug trade which at that time came through the Mediterranean from Turkey – this was before the illicit drug industry in South America had blossomed. He had many stories about his youth in Italy and World War II. He had nothing but praise for the United States and particularly for the Martial Plan that put Europe back on its feet after WWII. We had many long discussions about why U.S. aid had been so effective in Europe, but seemed to be so ineffective in South America.

Work settled into a routine. I taught ag classes to the boys in the nucleo and worked with the campo team in the veredas and schools in the valley. Garden projects were now proliferating almost spontaneously. I worked with families directly and with kids through the schools, but there were also families starting gardens on their own initiative. I was often approached for seeds which I could obtain from CARE or the ganja in Popayán. I would provide seeds, but insisted the garden spot be prepared, fences built and insecticide on hand before I gave anyone seeds.

Rabbits, bees and chickens projects were also becoming more numerous. These were usually worked through the nucleo, although I would advise parents and children on the construction of hutches, beehives and chicken coups individually.

Winter was also the season for basketball, which didn't make a lot of sense to me as all the courts were outside and subject to the rains. I played many a game splashing down the "floor" which was concrete or dirt. I played on a couple of different teams, none of which did very well. I had

Lunch time at the nucleo.

better luck as a coach than a player. I coached two boys teams, a Caloto first team and second team.

Last night my team (Caloto's second team) played again. We almost didn't find a ride to Santander because the bus wasn't running. Finally, the kids got 10 pesos together and offered to buy the gas if someone would take a car. Dr. Usubioga, the head of Medico, finally said that he would drive.

We arrived so late the boys had no time to warm up and went into the game cold. The team we were playing was considered to be the best team in the tournament in the second category. I thought we were going to get killed, but the boys really came through. At half time we were 2 points behind, but the other team was so sure of themselves that they hadn't put in their real hot shots.

The second half, they jumped ahead at first, then my team started to gain and with 3 minutes left we were 3 points ahead. One minute and we were only 1 point ahead, but the boys were able to stall for the last minute.

They have really improved over the last 3 games. Mostly it has been in confidence. The first game they were sluggish and acted like they were just going through the motions. Last night they played like they really wanted to win. I have taught them the zone defense which is not commonly used by teams at this level. On offense, I have tried to get them to look around and pass the ball. Last night was the first time the zone worked very well and it fell apart some times. They still dribble too much, but they are passing more and more, especially to the guys under the basket and that really paid off last night. The kids really felt good and I enjoyed winning more than if I had been playing."[31]

Caloto officials attending Easter celebration.

My second Easter in Colombia was to be very different from my first.

In Colombia, *Semana Santa* (Easter) starts the weekend before Easter and goes strong all week. After celebrating with the people in Caloto, I headed for Popayán. There were parades in the capital every night of the week with concerts in the afternoons and church services in the morning.

In the processions were one or two bands and many floats, each carried by eight men. These are maintained by the affluent families in Popayán and are carried by the men of those families. The floats are actually platforms with figures on them depicting scene from the Bible. The figures are all life sized with a canopy over the whole scene.

---

[31] Gary Peterson, *Colombian Diary,* Jun. 19, 1966.

Of course, the town was just packed with people, most from Cali, but there were people from all over Colombia with a sprinkling of Volunteers and other gringos. I even ran into two students from England.[32]

A program that became increasingly important in 1966 was the institution of school lunch programs in the nucleo satellite schools. This required some kind of stove since schools were not equipped with any type of heating devise. Due to the hot climate, fireplaces and heating stoves were a rarity in the area.

The story of school lunch stoves goes all the way back to Boyacá where Bruce and I started to build one for that vereda school. When I arrived in Cauca, one of the first things I encountered was a project to promote a stove for school and home use at the Cauca department fair.

This was a brick stove that was designed by the Volunteers in Pispomba for the campesinos. It costs about 150 pesos for the materials and will burn wood or coal.

Tuesday we decided to draw up a set of plans for the stove. So while Herb and Earl finished the stove construction, I drew up the plans. I worked in the PINA office. PINA has a larger staff here than in Boyacá, the director, a nutritionist, a secretary, two clerks and three UNICF Jeeps.

Wednesday we were ready to start on the booklet and who shows up, but an arts and crafts transfer from another department who was in Puerto Rico at the same time we were. So we enlisted his help with the drawings, while Herb wrote the instructions and a civil engineer and I put the plans and illustrations on stencils.

Thursday we worked on the booklet all day until 2:00 in the morning.

Friday we finally finished the booklet about 4:30 in the afternoon, just in time to take it over to the fair.

Saturday we spent touring the fair grounds and helping with the demonstrations. It was similar to a fair you would find in the western and midwestern states with permanent buildings to house the livestock and exhibits. As for livestock, there are more horses than anything else. Most of these are fancy riding horses of the rich. I found both dairy cows and beef animals on display, Normandia, Charolais, Brahma, Red Polls and native Criollo. The machinery exhibit (farm equipment) was much smaller than you would find in the states. Booths were everywhere, including garden demonstrations, chicken brooders, rabbits and a rabbit cooking demonstrations by the PINA girls. Our stove was featured in one booth along with the instructions we had worked on. And the nucleo at Caloto had a booth of furniture they had manufactured.[33]

I used variations of the design presented at this fair on several stoves constructed in the Santander area and in the Caloto nucleo satellite schools. Some of these school lunch programs were in operation before I left Colombia and others would come on line later

---

[32] Gary Peterson, *Colombian Diary,* Apr. 12, 1966.
[33] Gary Peterson, *Colombian Diary,* Jul. 1, 1966.

Obidio and me at the nucleo.

with the support of the community development Volunteers and nucleo personnel. Obedio, the nucleo carpenter worked with me on the stoves around Caloto.

Sunday Obidio and I went to La Quebrada and finished that stove. There are still two cement pipes to put up as chimneys, but Don Gorge can do that himself. I'll come back out and show him how it works later.[34]

Obidio was one of the finest people I knew in Colombia. He was quiet and unassuming, intelligent, cheerful, conscientious and a self-starter. He is one of the people I wish I had kept in contact with. Ah, things we regret now that we are old and those opportunities have slipped away.

And finally there was the stove for the school lunch program in Vilachi that Bill Higgins and Jeanette had worked so hard to build. Since Bill's departure, a replacement Volunteer had taken over.

Monday John and I went to Vilachi and finished the construction of the stove at the school. It is supposed to be ready for a big fiesta on Sunday.[35]

The stoves proved to be one of the successes in this hot climate. Though designed for cooking, I suspect they were also used for heat on some of those "cold" rainy days.

Besides the Amazon, the other area of Colombia I wanted to see was the Llanos and at one point it looked like a visit to a remote part of this vast plain was possible. Jeannette, with her inimitable talent for meeting and getting to know people had chanced across a couple from the far reaches the Llanos. I jumped at Jeannette's suggestion we pay them a visit.

Jeannette and I are planning on a trip to the eastern end of Colombia to the territory of Vaupes to visit a young couple who are studying and documenting the language of the local Indians. They live near the capital, Mitú, I understand. We plan to leave about the 23rd of May and I will be taking 5 days vacation.[36]

---

[34] Gary Peterson, *Colombian Diary,* Jun. 29, 1966.
[35] Gary Peterson, *Colombian Diary,* Jun. 24, 1966.
[36] Gary Peterson, *Colombian Diary,* Apr. 27, 1966.

Now, Mitú, on the far side of the Colombian Llanos very close to the Brazilian border, is among the headwaters of the Rio Negro. To reach their site, we were going to fly to Mitú, then take a bus and finally paddle the rest of the way in a canoe. It would have been one great adventure, but alas, it was not to be. "Oh, yes, got word we're having a PINA conference on May 28th and 29th, so Jeannette and I won't be going to Vaupes, not now anyway."[37]

Jeannette and I never made that expedition to the eastern wilderness. One of the reasons for not being able to take advantage of this opportunity was that time was running out. With only a little over two months of service time left, there was much to do.

Caloto Plaza

Back in Caloto I had many loose ends to clean up before leaving. I had tests to prepare for my classes at the nucleo. I also had a site survey of a town up in the mountains above Popayán to finish up. The padre in Cajibio had been pressing for a Volunteer for his town and Peace Corps agreed to take a look.

I made the trip to Cajibio for a two day stay. One evening I had dinner with the priest in his rectory. It was like a scene from the Middle Ages. We ate at a long table. A four course meal served with two varieties of wine by a servant girl, efficiently and silently. At this large table were the padre, myself and his nephew.

---

[37] Gary Peterson, *Colombian Diary,* May 23, 1966.

The priest was from Switzerland originally, but he had been in South America for some time. He told me he had been assigned to Cajibio "to straighten it out." He said when he arrived the town was a mess, but that he had gotten the streets paved, a new school built and was working on a sewer system for the town.

The padre's nephew was from Spain and spoke with a lisp. Later I was told that the native Castilian Spanish of the upper classes will have this lisp. Its use goes back to a Castilian king who had a lisp and his court adopted a lisp in their speech so as not to embarrass him. Another story for the gringo? – I don't know.

Just before I left, Jeanette, Nolva, Lilia and I took a trip to Cali and went to a football (soccer) game. I don't remember who was playing, presumably Cali and another city team. What I do remember was the delightful time we spent together. Celia, her two daughters and young son were like family. Many evenings we spent playing cards or board games. Celia looked out for me, to be sure I wasn't taken advantage of. The girls taught me to dance and instructed me on Colombian edict. Nolva and Jeannette became good friends. While in Colombia, I met many fine and generous people, but to me, Celia and her family will always represent the very best of the Colombian people.

Monday, Tuesday and Wednesday we had our termination conference in Bogotá with people from Washington. And last night there was a cocktail party at the director's house. Two of the guests were the linguist and his wife who have been in Vaupés where Jeannette and I were going for vacation, but didn't make it. After talking to them I regret even more not making the trip. They are in some of the wildest parts of Colombia, basically virgin territory.[38]

The meetings were productive, but not without a special twist characteristic of Colombia '64. Our group just had a knack for pushing the envelope to the outrageous. We had two special guests at our conference who were investigating the Peace Corps in Colombia, but were novices as far as our work went and ripe for a little skullduggery.

The two guys, who were from Washington, were not familiar with Colombia or agriculture. We found this out the first day. Well, the second day we decided to play a trick on them aided and abetted by their ignorance. We made up a story about a feed that we said was hot stuff as a livestock feed for rabbits, chickens, goats, etc. But, we said, this feed, "FINA," was just not available most places and hard to get almost everywhere in Colombia. Everyone contributed some of their special knowledge off the cuff. It worked out to be a really great con.[39]

Jim Finkler remembers the incident and reports some of the details:

The purported product was FINA, *Fomenta Integrada Nutricion Augmentada* and was only available in Venezuala and because the Norte Volunteers, Carolina, Carol, Don, Freddy and me, were closest to the border we supposedly smuggled the feed across the border. It was excellent feed, we said, and produced very rapid growth in rabbits and other animals. Volunteers would

[38] Gary Peterson, *Colombian Diary,* Jul. 28, 1966.
[39] Gary Peterson, *Colombian Diary,* Jul 31, 1966.

come from all over Colombia to our sites to pick up the feed. We were the distribution center in Colombia.[40]

Our con was finally interrupted because the two gentlemen had to leave to catch their plane. Our director left with the Washingtonites and we toasted our success in pulling this sham off.

> The director came back to our conference, after driving the two guys to the airport, and said that all they talked about was how they were going to dig into this and find out what the problem was, why this animal feed could not be made available in Colombia. The director said he had a hard time keeping from laughing out loud, but was able to contain himself at least until he deposited his two guests onto the plane.[41]
>
> I understand Peace Corps and maybe the Department of Agriculture were still trying to find this FINA a year later [Burkholder adds].[42]

Main Street Caloto

Returning to Caloto to clear up a final few items, I had a couple of experiences that I have often thought of in relation to the town. The first occurred one clear quiet morning when I was up early and the rest of the inhabitance were still snoozing. The sun was not yet up and I had wondered over to the main street just enjoying the quiet solitude of the morning. The only living thing in sight was a big dog striding down the street as if he owned the town. The Colombians called these animals "*lobos*" (wolves), but they were obviously dogs, not wild K-9s. They looked like German Shepherds, but were bigger than a large Shepherd.

The magnificent animal completely ignored me as he passed my position on the sidewalk, trotting down the middle of the street.

Suddenly, a small fuzz ball of a dog, a little yapper, came scooting out of a doorway along the street. This obnoxious little mutt had the habit of sneaking up on people from behind and nipping at their heals, then emitting its piercing bark, all of which was extremely annoying. Yet, no one in town dared punish this nuisance for fear of looking like a brute picking on this pipsqueak of a dog.

---

[40] Jim Finkler, personal email to Dennis Burkholder, Jul. 26, 2009.
[41] Gary Peterson, *Colombian Diary,* Jul 31, 1966.
[42] Dennis Burkholder, email to Jaime Finkler and the group, Jun. 29, 1966.

As was its habit the little cur circled around behind the "wolf" barking and nipping at the big dog's hind legs. The majestic K-9 ignored this irritation, so the little yapper was emboldened and moved up from the hind legs to the front legs, a bad mistake in judgment.

The big dog didn't even break stride, but merely turned his head, reached down and grabbed his antagonist in his mouth and tossed it across the street so that it bounced off the wall of one of the buildings lining the avenue.

The little mutt howled like he'd been butchered, more from surprise than from actual injury I suspect. The wolf continued down the street totally unconcerned while I laughed until tears rolled down my cheek. Like most everyone in town, I had wanted to kick that little dog many times. It did my heart good.

Another experience that has stuck with me happened a few weeks later after a particularly long hot spell. The weather had been stifling, but that morning the heavens had opened up and expelled a brief though significant down pour. The smell of the damp earth was wonderful I thought, as I left my front door and headed for the Carabinero's office to collect some information.

Before I even reached the street that ran in front of my house, I heard the clatter of horse's hooves coming toward me. Down the street galloped a horse at full speed with a kid of about twelve riding bareback. Passed me they flew, enthralled in the exuberance of the freedom and sheer joy of life it seemed to me.

About half a block passed me, the boy turned the corner entering the town plaza at a full gallop. That's when disaster struck. The horse's hooves slipped out from under him on the wet pavement and the animal crashed to the cement pinning the boy's leg under him.

As the horse struggled to his feet, I could see the boy was injured and I rushed up the street to see if I could help.

At the corner where the accident had occurred was one of the town's old timers sitting in a chair that was rocked back on two legs so that the top of the chair rested against the wall of the town office building. He was smoking his pipe and staring off into space as he did for many hours every day. At the sound of the horse crashing to the ground, he merely turned his head in the direction of the incident and drew another puff on his pipe.

By the time I reached the boy, the horse was on its feet and the lad was sitting up holding one leg and sobbing. He was scraped up pretty badly, but then I noticed what was apparently the source of his real pain. The big toe of his left foot was out of joint. Instead of being in front of the ball of the foot, it was on top of it forming a "Z" with the line of the foot.

By this time, the old man had raised himself from his chair and ambled the few steps over to where the boy and I were in the middle of the street.

Still puffing on his pipe, he reached down and took hold of the boy's foot with one hand. With the other, he grabbed the boy's dislocated big toe, then he gave a sudden but strong pull.

Amazingly, at least to me, the toe popped back into place. The boy let out a yell, or scream, that must have been heard clear across town. Without even saying a word, the old man stood up and ambled back to his seat against the wall facing the plaza.

I helped the boy to his feet and back onto the horse. The bravado and gaiety were gone as the kid guided his horse across the plaza and off toward the north side of town.

I eyed the old man, but he was once again, lost in his thoughts or dreams, and I wondered what stories he might have to tell if only I could break through his self-imposed isolation.

So, as I packed to leave, I played my last games of soccer and basketball with the youth of Caloto and actually won a couple of rounds of Chinese checkers and pool. Or did the towns people just want me to leave thinking I had at last achieved something approaching their level of play. I suspect it was the latter. The Latin concern for other people's feelings was nearly always evident among these generous people.

Jeannette stayed on a little longer than I did. She was in the process of finding a home for her dog. Both of us had acquired dogs some time during our last year in Caloto. The two animals were from the same litter, Jeanette has reminded me. I named my hound Thor and Jeannette named hers Tiki. One of my last tasks before leaving was to turn over Thor to one of the Carabineros who had taken a real shine to him. Jeanette gave hers to a nurse who lived across the street from her.

Jeannette and friends at my house.

I have also learned about an experience Jeannette had with the doctors from Popayán at about this time. On a visit to the department capital, Jeannette was asked by a couple of the doctors if she wanted a ride back to Caloto since they were coming up to the town for a conference. Jeannette readily accepted, trading the hot and dusty bus ride for a relatively comfortable ride in the doctor's Jeep.

However, in Caloto the good doctors ended their conference with a party of their own. By the time this was over, they were in no shape to drive back to Popayán themselves. So they implored Jeannette to take them back. Though Jeannette protested that she had never driven a Jeep, the doctors would not take no for an answer. Finally, Jeannette agreed to drive them back over the highway (dirt road). With more grit than good sense, she piled into the driver's seat and headed for the main road, "with the two doctors giving her all kinds of instructions and advice."[43] She learned to drive the vehicle as she went along and in spite of the construction and sheer cliffs that terrified her, especially in the dark, she managed to get the now sleeping medicos to Popayán.

---

[43] Jeannette Reeser Cannon, telephone interview, Dec. 16, 2009.

Through the years, Jeannette has stayed in contact with Nolva and through her with the rest of Celia's family. Jeannette would return to the U.S. leaving behind a town that loved her and a resident doctor who had asked her to marry him, completing a journey that had begun when she shook hands with President John F. Kennedy at a university assembly some four years earlier.

16
THE UNFORGIVING LLANOS

The Llanos, that flat grassland sweeping from the foot of the Andes through northeastern Colombia into Venezuela, conjures up visions of a lone horseman driving a herd of cattle, of dust and suffocating heat in the dry season, and clouds of insects and stifling humidity in the wet months. This great plains of northern South America, almost totally devoid of population, has all the mystery and foreboding of the Amazon jungles to the south. Here there are millions of acres of waist high grass, slow moving streams and rivers populated with mosquitoes, venomous snakes, man eating piranha and fifteen foot caymen where only the rawhide tough llaneros, Cebu cattle and occasional leather skinned Indian dare venture.

It took Niclolás Federman, the first European to cross the Llanos, two years to accomplish the feat. He left Coro, Venezuela on Lake Maracobo in 1536 with 300 soldiers, 130 horses and a large number of native bearers. When he finally reached the area where Villavicencio is today, 60 miles southeast of Bogotá, he had only 200 men and less than 100 horses left (see Append II).

Other explorers crossed and recrossed the Llanos, most looking for El Dorado. Philip von Hutton claimed to have found Meta (the city of El Dorado) in 1542, but was beheaded by rebels upon his return to Venezuela before he could mount another expedition and conquer the city. Jiménez de Quesada, governor of New Granada, led a campaign from Bogotá in 1569 into the plains to find the fabled riches, but had no luck. Others searched, the last being Antonio de Berrio in 1584 who left from Tunja with one hundred men and searched near the head waters of the Oronoco, but again found nothing. Perhaps El Dorado's riches are still there waiting to be discovered.

About the only Spanish who actually lived in the Llanos were the Jesuit fathers who established missions with associated cattle ranches to support them. When the Jesuits were told to leave South America in 1767 by the Pope, many of these cattle operations were sold to private firms and thus the Llanos cattle industry began along with the llaneros, the cowboys of the Llanos, and their legendary endurance.

The Llanos is also where Simón Bolivár recuperated and reorganized for his final push to Bogotá and the defeat of the Spanish at Pointe de Boyacá. A sizable part of his army was made up of the tough, mounted plainsmen.

So the Llanos has always fascinated me and I became even more intrigued as I met people from that great enigmatic expanse.

In the Bogotá airport, on one occasion, I ran into two families from the Llanos. They were Americans who were there to see off some of their teenagers being sent to the U.S. to school.

The parents had come to Colombia in the 1940s and had built ranches out on the plains. Their stories were reminiscent of the early cattlemen of the U.S. northern plains, circa the 1880s. It seemed to me they were living a wild and adventurous life.

Another time I happened to encounter the governor of one of the territories of the Llanos. He tried to convince me to go back with him and set up my own ranch in his territory. He said I could have all the land I wanted. When I asked him about restrictions on the land one could legally obtain – I did know there were such laws in Colombia – he informed me he would take care of any potential government interference, for a cut of course.

His idea was to create a quarantined herd of cattle that could be kept isolated from other cattle and thus be kept free of hoof-and-mouth disease, a debilitating infection common in South American cloved hoofed live stock.

"But that would require a lot of expensive fencing," I protested.

"Nonsense," was his comeback, "you just find a fork in a river and run a fence from one branch to the other, thereby eliminating the need to fence the other two sides."

"How about piranha?" I inquired, having heard all the stories about these ferocious carnivores.

"No problem," he assured me, "they are only dangerous when you have to cross a river during the dry season. Then you run an old cow into the water up stream and let all the piranha attack it while you drive the herd across down stream."

The good governor seemed to have an answer for every objection, though I took all this with a grain of salt. He was still in salesman mode as he left to board his plane back to his eastern governance. Sadly, I never made it to his territory or even to the Llanos except for a short stop over on the way back from the Amazon, but others of Colombia '64 did spend some time there.

Tom Gallaher paid a visit to Villavicancio, enticed by, what else, feminine wiles. Tom was stationed in Duitama and was visiting Sogamoso, 20 kilometers down the road, when the circumstances that brought about this trip to the Llanos began to coalesce.

There was another ETV Volunteer stationed in Sogamoso, I met her one day after I had been in country about 2 months. She had a sultry, browsy way about her that I found irresistible. When she asked me if I would like to accompany her to the Llanos to scout out potential new sites for ETV, I immediately agreed. To be honest about it, the thought crossed my mind that she may have had other things in mind besides scouting out new sites.

A few days later we were on a bus to Villavicensio "the gateway to the Llanos" which lay at the foot hills of the Andes. The bus trip over the *páramo* (high, desolate, cold plain) was quite an ordeal. After leaving Sogamoso, we climbed a gravel road a few thousand feet up to the bleak heights of the páramo. The land was flat almost devoid of vegetation, except for a few spindly shrubs. A chilly, moist wind blew across the páramo. The sky was a dull gray, clouds scudded overhead so close it almost seemed you could reach up and touch them. Fog and mist curled around the large stony outcroppings which from time to time rose up to punctuate the bleakness of the páramo. As far as I could tell the road petered out soon after we started across the high plains. For a while we drove beside a shallow stream which meandered until it finally disappeared. We had been on the road for several hours, without seeing any sign of life, when suddenly as if a curtain had been drawn, I could see shafts of sunlight breaking through the clouds and patches of blue sky and there right in front of us spread the Llanos, thousands of feet far below, glistening in the sunlight, stretching to the horizon.

From the edge of the cliff we were perched on, we slid and skidded down the mountainside through a series of switch backs, dropping thousands of feet until in an hour or so we arrived at our destination Villavicensio.

Aside from our bus, and few Jeeps, I could see no other wheeled vehicles in town. I felt as if I had stepped back a hundred years in time, to Dodge City in the 1870's. Most of the traffic on the muddy, unpaved main street consisted of men on horseback and a few horse drawn wagons. My feeling of being back in the American frontier was further reinforced by the large number of hombres with side arms.

I don't remember where we stayed that night but it was in separate rooms.

Next morning we paid a visit to the *Alcalderia* (mayor's office), my companion did most of the talking as her Spanish was much better than mine. Somehow I wound up with the Alcalde at an Army base. Immediately upon our arrival the Capitan (the post commander) broke out a bottle of Aguadiente, it wasn't even 10 AM. Good Colombian hospitality required a host to offer you a "*trigito*" and to keep offering until you finally accepted. Well that's what happened. After saying no for perhaps a dozen times, because I didn't want a drink especially not at 10 AM - I agreed. But I had totally lost my patience by then, so instead of sipping my drink I tossed it down and immediately signaled for another. I knew any good macho Colombian host would not allow his *cajones* to be called into question and would follow suit. My intention was to get them all stinking drunk, so next time when I said no thanks they'd take me at my word. The Capitan and all his comrades drank up. As soon as my glass was refilled I tossed down the drink, the Capitan and all his buddies did the same. After several more rounds of drinks no one was feeling any pain. Then the Capitan invited everyone to take a trip down river.

We all piled into some dugout canoes which were lying on the river bank. It was then that I notice the Captain and several soldiers were carrying rifles. The Captain saw me eying the rifles.

"For to kill the *caimánes*," he told me.

We began to drifting down river with the current. There was plenty of beer in the canoes in case we get thirsty and some folks were thirsty already even though we had just started. After we had been on the river for a half hour or so someone spotted some caimánes (cayman).

"Let's shoot the caimánes," someone shouts.

I'm in the canoe with the Captain the Alcalde and two other soldiers. The Captain hands me the rifle he had been holding. I must have looked a little dubious so he urges me to go ahead and take a shot. I was a little unsteady on my feet as I stood up in the canoe, but what the hell. I heard a fusillade of shots going off all around me.

I fire at the caimánes, the recoil of the rifle knocked me backward and in falling I manage to tip over the canoe and we all wound up in the river. When I surfaced I noticed two other canoes also tipped over as well, from a combination of too much aguadiente and overzealous marksmanship, I suppose. With so many bodies in the water the caimánes had an abundance of prey. Obviously I made it safely to shore. I regret to say I cannot say the same for everybody else.

Not that the caimánes ate anyone, all the shooting and noise must have scared them off, but a couple of the soldiers almost drowned trying to get to shore.

That evening there was a *baile* (dance) to which my companion and I were both invited. My date, or so I thought of her at the time, looked ravishing or at least like she wanted to be ravished. Well that's what I imagined as I escorted her to the baile. After we had been dancing for a few hours I suggested that we call it a night and go back to where we were staying. She wasn't ready to leave just yet, she said, she wanted to dance some more. We danced a few more times and I again suggested we leave. She still wasn't ready to leave and said I could leave without her.

This upset me. It was beginning to look like I was going to spend another night in my room alone – not exactly how I had this planned. I stomped off the dance floor, but before I reached the front door my anger got the better of me and I turned around and went back. There she was dancing with some other guy. Now I was really hot under the collar. I went up to her and told her since she had come with me, she was damn well going back with me and I reached out to take her by the arm.

The guy she had been dancing with pulled out a big gun. "No Señor I think the lady wants to stay."

I took one look at his gun and immediately agreed. "You're absolutely right, she must stay!!!"

My father taught me never to disagree with a man who has a gun, particularly if you don't. For a second the thought crossed my mind that Deadly Dudley and my Marine Corps Sergeant might disapprove of my action, but I quickly put that aside and left. I guess I was lucky I wasn't a Colombian. Had that been the case, he may have pulled the trigger.[1]

Having gotten over my illusions about Nicole, I spent a few days exploring the town and surrounding area. I met a Colombian who spoke English and had been to school in the states. He invited me on a visit to his ranch. I accepted. Turned out his ranch was a few hundred miles outside town. We flew out there in a small twin engine plane. After we landed he told me his ranch encompassed all the land from the foot hills of the Andes east to where we were standing. He was one of the *latifundistas* (large land owners) we had been told about in training. It was a great experience to see a part of Colombia I had only imagined.[2]

A few days later, I returned to Villavicencio and went on to Sogamoso. I did not see Nicole again, nor did I care to.[3]

A few miles north of Villavicencio, where Galleher had his encounter with the Llanos, another Colombia '64 Volunteer was trying to adapt to the plain's harsh conditions and the even more intransigent population. Guacavia, a village in the department of Meta, of which Villavicencio was the capital, was as forlorn as any site in

[1] Tom Gallaher, personal email to Gary Peterson, October 21, 2008.
[2] Tom Gallaher, personal email to Gary Peterson, Octorber 22, 2008.
[3] Tom Gallaher, personal email to Gary Peterson, October 21, 2008.

Colombia. Dennis Burkholder from the northern plains of the United States (North Dakota to be exact) found himself in a,

......remote outpost on the western edge of Colombia's vast eastern plains. Gaucavia could barely be called a village, with two dusty streets intersecting in a "T" in the center of town. A cluster of houses constructed of miscellaneous boards, cane, and bamboo coated with a plaster composed of a mixture of mud and manure lined the two streets. These white-washed, structures, had thatched-roofs and dirt floors. A few run-down tiendas supplied the town's essentials with one store doubling as the once weekly meat market. The population of the village was a couple of hundred not counting the students at the boarding school where the Peace Corps Volunteer was scheduled to teach English, agriculture and nutrition.

There were two other significant structures in this tiny village and both were of vital importance to the inhabitants: an impressive cathedral stood out from the surrounding squalor and served the 99.5% Catholic population - Dennis comprised the other 0.5%, but he pretended to be Catholic because it was either that or be considered a communist. More importantly, there was a Policia Headquarters manned by the military officers who were inordinately proud of the fact that they had carbines and live ammo. Some of these soldiers appeared to be too young to be soldiers – a bit disconcerting.

Richard Falxa of Buffalo, Wyoming was a veteran Volunteer finishing up his term with the Peace Corps who accepted Dennis into his house and site located about ¾ mile from town. Guacavia had been one of the original sites to host Volunteers and was fortunate to have been staffed by some of the early legends of Peace Corps Colombia. Don Ricardo was truly a super Volunteer with a shopping list of accomplished community action projects. He tolerated this new Volunteer and shuddered at his poor command of the language privately. Truth be told, he did not think this new addition to his site measured up. But Richard was too much the gentleman to ever say that out loud.

A few months later, Richard ended his service leaving Dennis alone in this desolate village. Really alone. There was no Volunteer within a hundred miles of Guacavia. There was no one who spoke English to be found. Rodney Spokely was to have been Dennis' partner, but he had been delayed in coming to the country for medical reasons and when he did arrive he was sent to a different site (see Chapter 6 on Tolima).[4]

Dennis settled in as best he could. With no one to talk to but Spanish speakers, his language skills improved rapidly and he developed a routine work schedule. He did have occasional visitors, though sometimes these were not welcome or even human.

A boa constrictor slithered its way into my kitchen where I was eating lunch. In total fear and outright panic I grabbed my machete and winged it at him with such force that the tip of the blade stuck in the cement floor causing the machete to break. The clatter must have annoyed the boa constrictor, for it made its exit

---

[4] Dennis Burkholder, personal email to Gary Peterson, May 11, 2009.

to the yard where it lingered. Finally, some neighbor kids came over and hauled the monster down to the river and depositing it in the water.[5]

Other than these interludes of rare excitement, Dennis worked on the program he had been trained to carry out. As with the other members of Colombia '64, these began with simple projects in agriculture and nutrition.

Alone, El Gringo, as the villagers called him, began working on garden projects, rabbit projects, latrine construction projects and he also taught classes at the school. The rabbits hated Dennis and scratched him and bit him -- damn them anyway. Dennis hated the rabbits back. It was not a happy relationship.

The gardens were another matter. The soil was extremely fertile and any plant that bore its fruit above the ground thrived. The Volunteer grew a tomato that weighed 3 lbs, nurtured a pole bean plant that went up, then down, then up and half way down again on a 10' pole. The instructions for planting green beans were simple. Put the seed in the ground and get the hell out of the way.

Villagers took notice and asked for help in planting and maintaining their own gardens. These garden projects produced an abundance of vegetables and several villagers eventually turned their enterprises into a profitable cash crop.

The children in the area were not healthy, a perennial problem in Colombia it seemed. 1 in 5 died before age five. There were very few bathroom facilities or toilets. The preferred place for villagers to relieve themselves was in the fields or gardens or rivers. Education was crucial to the understanding that latrine usage was necessary. It was an uphill battle.

Purina Corporation provided a high-protein mixture (Incaparina) to one of the organizations Dennis worked with that was free of charge to families who would mix this supplement into the diet of their young children. It was similar to oatmeal in consistency and had to be disguised pretty well to be palatable. Even though it was free, it was not used by the families. Incaparina was to become one of the three elements that turned around the public opinion of El Gringo.

Dennis won a raffle at the school with the prize being a freshly weaned pig from a neighbor's litter. "Pig" as he was named took up residence in the pasture corral in back of Dennis's house. Pig (not to be confused with Dennis's dog named "dog") subsisted on a diet of field corn and scraps. One day Dennis mixed some Incaparina into Pig's feed. Pig loved it. Pig thrived and grew quickly. The villagers knew that Pig had brothers and sisters just down the trail. Within two months Pig was twice the size of his siblings. The villagers were impressed. They had to admit, El Gringo could sure grow vegetables and pigs. Dennis was becoming known for his expertise in agriculture, but gaining real acceptance was another matter.

Unfortunately, it was a different event that gained their respect. Don Jaime had been a thorn in Dennis' side ever since his arrival. Jaime was reputedly backed by someone of influence, perhaps linked to the Violencia, but nonetheless one not to be messed with. Don Jaime liked to make fun of El

---

[5] Dennis Burkholder, personal email to Gary Peterson, May 11, 2009.

Gringo by saying things about him in Castellano that he didn't think Dennis understood.

One night after several bouts of Aguardiente and several *cervezas* (beers), Don Jaime challenged El Gringo to a game of billiards. Dennis was not a novice at this game and was on the verge of winning when Jaime called him a dirty word.

Well, the village youth had been happy to teach Dennis all the dirty Spanish words, so he understood clearly what Jaime had called him. Buoyed with liquid courage he suddenly grabbed Don Jaime with both hands. Holding his shirt, Dennis lifted the trouble maker up and slammed him onto the billiard table. El Gringo then grasped each side of Jaime's reddening face and called him every dirty name he could think of, pretty much every dirty word in the Spanish language, culminated with the granddaddy of them all, *"hijo de puta!"* Dennis accompanied this parting shot by slamming Jaime's head on the table one more time. There was dead silence in the room. Dennis wished the onlookers a *"Buenos Noches, Que duerme con La Virgin"* and walked home convinced that he had just written his airplane ticket back to North Dakota.

The next day El Gringo walked to the school with a foreboding knowledge that he was in deep trouble. Would the townspeople just stay away from him now and give him the silent treatment or would they be openly hostile to him? Surely someone would get in touch with Peace Corps headquarters in Bogotá soon if they had not already done so, and he would be gone.

Dennis approached the first person he had seen since the previous night and waited to see if he would even be acknowledged. Nodding slightly, the villager said, "Buenos Dias, Don Daniel." Daniel was the town's translation of Dennis (Dennis the Menace of the comics was translated into *Daniel el Tavioso*). Surprised, Dennis walked on toward the school. Villager after villager approached him all with the same greeting. "Buenos Dias, Don Daniel!" The name "El Gringo" was forgotten. Don Daniel had dared to challenge Don Jaime. Word of the events of the previous evening had spread quickly through the pueblo. Before the night was even out Don Daniel was known in the town as someone of consequence. It was a new day dawning.

If this seems to sound like something out of a western movie it should not be surprising. The Llanos was the Wild West of Colombia (Ok, technically the Wild East). The men fancied themselves great horsemen, fighters and lovers. Machismo was their defining character value. The men boasted about their possessions: (in order of importance) my horse, my gun, and my wife.

The men did not work very hard. They drank; they raced their horses, and spent the rest of their time working on their reputation as a great lover and romantic. The women worked, took care of the children, prepared the meals, washed the clothes, and took care of the house. The women of Colombia could be exquisitely beautiful until age 18 or marriage whichever came first, at which time the ravages of their workload and perpetual pregnancies took their toll.

Because he was in a remote site and alone, Peace Corps designated the Guacavia as a hardship site which allowed Dennis unlimited rest days away from the site without having to use vacation days. It also provided him with 250 extra pesos a month bringing his total paycheck to 1,600 pesos a month ($75 dollars more or less). His lifestyle was Spartan. The rent on his shack cost 60 pesos a month, laundry ran about the same, and the meals brought three times daily to his home by the neighbors cost 300 pesos. The menu was unchanging. Breakfast was a fried egg on rice with water-based hot chocolate to drink, lunch was fried platano with rice and beans, the evening meal was a vegetable soup, yuca, an occasional slice of meat and a hunk of bread. The monthly budget left Dennis with 1,200 pesos a month to spend on whatever. "Whatever," however, was limited. A game of billiards cost 1 peso, a warm beer cost 1 peso, a warm pop cost about 40 centavos. A bowl of chicken noodle soup and a hunk of beef cooked on a vertical wood stake next to a blazing fire was available on market day once a week for 4 pesos. There was nothing else on which to spend money.

That's where unlimited rest days came in. Bogotá was a hair-raising ½ day bus ride through the mountains. In Bogotá Dennis could find Peace Corps friends and spend his money. Peace Corps money was communal. If you had money, you spent it. If another Volunteer was out of money, you gave him some of yours. It was similar to playing a two year long game of Monopoly and not caring who won.

Every two weeks Dennis would take a one hour trip on a small open-sided bus (*chiva*) to Villavicencio where he could pick up his mail and eat some good Chinese food and have COLD beer. There would be a few letters from a faithful girlfriend and several from his parents. For twenty months there was no communication with his parents other than through these letters. That seems stranger now these forty-some years later than it did then.

On one of these trips to "Villavo", Dennis was in a bar where he met the crew of a U.S. Air Force C-47 that was transporting a load of gasoline 55 gallon drums to a group of Wycliffe Bible Translators who were living out on the Amazon. After a dozen rounds of cerveza it became the consensus of the group that, "you might as well fly with us if you want to see the Amazon. Just be at the hotel at 6 a.m."

Promptly at 6 a.m., a slightly hungover Dennis met the part of the crew that managed to show up for breakfast at the hotel. The six man crew was down to 3. The group traveled by cab to the Colombian Air Force facility where the C-47 was parked off to the side of the graveled runway. After a careful pre-flight check of the engines (the pilot did a pull-up on the motor mounts of the two engines and gave each a precursory glance and pronounced them good to go.) The plane took off and quickly rose above the clouds which made getting a view of the Llanos impossible. The 3rd crew member lay down on the barrels of gasoline and fell into a drunken slumber. A queasy Dennis sat in the uncomfortable drop down webbed seat and jolted along for several hours of bumpy travel. Eventually, the co-pilot left the cabin and came back to have a smoke and offered Dennis the opportunity to go up front with the pilot. Dennis didn't think lighting up a cigar in the presence of a cargo of gasoline was a good idea, but said nothing and went up to join the pilot.

"The weather is too bad, we are going to have to go back to Panama." The pilot seemed to think nothing was unusual about Dennis going to Panama.

"Um, I don't have my passport." Dennis said. "I have to go back to Villavicencio."

"I was just kidding. We have to go pick up the rest of the crew anyway. We might as well give you a look at the Llanos. I'll drop us down under the cloud cover."

With that he took the plane into a screaming nose dive emerging below the clouds about 300' above the ground.

"Take a look!. Flat grassland. It's like this for thousands of miles and the only thing you see besides grass is an occasional river. Well, look at that, would you. A herd of cows."

The next ten minutes made an indelible impression on the young man from North Dakota. The pilot put the plane in a dive right at the cows sending them splay-legged running in abject terror. The terror was shared by the newly installed co-pilot. After six passes with the genuine U.S. Air Force Government Issue aircraft at a height of maybe 8 to 10 feet off the ground the pilot grew bored with the exercise and pulled up to 150 feet. Taking hands off the wheel he asks, "Ever fly one of these before?"

Without hesitation Dennis replied, "Nope, don't want to either."

"Well, at this rate we are going to hit the ground soon, so maybe you should learn how to fly."

The pilot was enjoying his passenger's distress. "To go up you pull it back, like this!" The plane climbed into a near stall. "To go down, just push it forward like this." The plane plummeted toward the ground.

With no choice the frightened passenger came up with the perfect solution, "I think I am going to be sick!"

Not wanting his passenger to get sick in his plane the pilot pulled the airplane up above the clouds and headed the craft back toward Villavicencio. The remainder of the flight was uneventful until arriving back at the city. To give notice to the rest of the crew to get to the airbase, the crusty old veteran pilot buzzed the hotel twice and headed to the air field, landed and parked the airplane at the far end of the runway on the grass. Ten minutes later the truant crewmembers walked out and rejoined the crew who had busied themselves with the task of rolling the barrels of gasoline out of the door of the airplane and letting them bump onto the ground. The bewildered Volunteer asked what they were going to do with the gasoline and was told that the crew would be back in a couple of weeks to try it again.

"Well, what about me? What should I do?" Dennis asked.

"Well, I guess if I were you, I'd jump that cyclone fence and hike back to town before the soldiers show up. We're heading for Panama."

With that they started up the aircraft and took off without bothering to get clearance. With no other alternative, Dennis climbed over the fence aware of the drone of the departing aircraft. It was a long walk back to town.

Back in Guacavia, the days had become routine for the Volunteer. Long dark boring nights alone separated from any close neighbors. Reminders of the Violencia were everywhere, but Dennis did not share the fears of the villagers who refused to walk alone at night, nor did he join in the custom of walking with other men while holding hands as a source of security.

One day without warning, the Peace Corps sent out an official to Guacavia who told Dennis to pack up his belongings and accompany him back to Bogotá where he would be given a new assignment. The official said that the Peace Corps had been contacted by someone from Guacavia who told them that it would be a good idea for Don Daniel to leave. It had something to do with stories of a man, a Jaime somebody, who had been heard making threats against the American's life. [6]

So the town bully, who wouldn't challenge Dennis openly, again, had been making threats behind his back. Did the menacing promises really represent truly dangerous intentions or were they merely the meaningless utterances of a slightly deranged and humiliated individual? Dennis wasn't particularly worried, but the Peace Corps was not about to take any chances. Dennis was hustled back to Bogotá.

The Llanos was left devoid of Colombia '64 Volunteers except for occasional visitors. The great grassland of Colombia was left to the llaneros, the cattle, the Indians and the mosquitoes. Only occasionally would a PINA/ETV Volunteer pass this way, usually making just a short stop on his/her way to somewhere else. The Llanos would remain an enigmatic frontier to the Volunteers, not unlike the perception most Colombians had of their eastern domain.

---

[6] Dennis Burkholder, personal email to Gary Peterson, May 11, 2009.

17

GOLD MINES, FREE ENTERPRISE AND OLD PEACE CORPS SITES

So Denise Burkholder originally from the Great Plains of North America (North Dakota) moved from the great plains of South America, the Llanos, to the mountains of the Cordillera Central. This middle mountain range of Colombia begins in the department of Huila as we've seen, close to the site of another Colombia '64 Volunteer Richard Bennett. It runs north touching Cauca, Tolima, Valle Del Cauca, then through the heart of Caldas, terminating in central Antioquia.[1] Along the spine of this range are located some of Colombia's major cities, Armenia, in the south, to Perfira, Manizales, and Medellín in the north. Dennis would be deposited about half way between the last two.

At first they didn't know what to do with me having arrived in Bogotá on such short notice. After a few days, they decided to send me to Marmato, Caldas, a gold mining town perched way up on the side of a mountain. (Marmato was established in 1520).

Quite a few Europeans and some American companies would eventually established mining operations there, but at the time I arrived it was strictly a struggling Colombian enterprise. The question was what was I supposed to do there.....the answer was......you'll think of something. And, of course I was again alone in a hardship site. Beautiful place. Bizarre.

They had me do a series of site surveys in my last few months. Towards the end I was asked to stay on as a Volunteer Leader, but my draft board was becoming impatient with my stay in the Peace Corps so I headed back to the states with Jarussi and his dumb macaws. Also an interesting story (see Chap. 18).[2]

From the heat of the Llanos to the cool slopes of the Cordillera Central, Dennis had lived in two of the extremes of Colombia. Now he was headed home to an anxious draft board and an unknown future.

To the north of Dennis was the department of Antioquia where one of the ETV Volunteers was assigned, in Medellín. Here, perhaps more than in any other part of the country, the people are noted for being industrious, motivated and inventive, especially when it comes to business. Antioquenians have a reputation for being entrepreneurs and sharp businesspeople.

The departmental capital, Medellín, reflects this character of the people in one of the most modern, clean and well run cities in the country. It is no accident that when the illicit drug trade exploded in South America, the first center of the cartels was Medellín. If there is a business opportunity, the Antioquenians will discover and develop it faster than anyone in the country. Colombia's involvement in the drug trade would blossom and expand here until the Medellín drug lords were superseded and wiped out by the Cali

---

[1] Another department, Quindio, has been carved out in these mountains since then.
[2] Dennis Bukholder, personal email, May 11, 2009.

cartel. Anioquenos might be the most inventive and entrepreneurial, but they were apparently not the most militant and ferocious.

However, Colombia's involvement in the illegal drug trade was in the distant future in 1965 when Elizabeth Hufnegal disembarked from the flight from Bogotá and surveyed her new home. Liza, as she was known by the Colombians, was a graduate of Syracuse University in mathematics. She was another member of our group more at home with academics than with agriculture and nutrition, and therefore a good choice for the ETV program. Here in Medellín she would be situated far from anyone else in our group. Still, it was a comparatively modern city, with amenities not available in most of the country.

Medellín was the "City of Eternal Springtime" and it breaks my heart to know how it has become overrun with the drug industry. It was well-named as the temperatures were always moderate, the landscape mountainous and green, the city well-nurtured by the sun every day. It was my first experience with Paradise and I loved being there; only Hawaii comes close.

Elizabeth Hufnagel

I went to Medellín after meeting with John Neff, the Peace Corps Colombia Director. He said he had been looking over my transcript and asked me if I would be interested in joining a small group at the University that was organizing an effort to introduce the "New Math", SMSG (School Math Study Group), into the curriculum. I was ambivalent because I had trained in Educational TV Production and was eager to experience it, so I agreed to try to do both. Big mistake! No way was I going to be able to get on a local bus out to the rural areas with all its scheduling uncertainty and get back to the university in time to meet with my new group or to teach an evening class. I am talking busses with the chickens and goats, and running on South American time using Colombian equipment. I wrestled with it for a time, but ultimately decided to work with the university group.

But in October of 1965, just about the time I was feeling adjusted and fully functional, I got word that I had been granted emergency leave to see my mother who had gone through major surgery and subsequently had come down with pneumonia and was asking for me. I was given a month at home to decide my next step. I decided I was needed more at home.[3]

Elizabeth would be the first of our group to head home, but she would be followed by others leaving for school or to work in Peace Corps training programs. The bulk of Colombia '64 would leave at the scheduled termination date of August 1966, but a few would stay for a few months, up to a full additional year.

Liza was at the north end of the Cordillera Central in Medellín. Dennis was to the south at Marmato, the gold mining town, and still further south near Pereira, Caldas Betsy Long was stationed. Betsy thought she would not make it through training because of her North Carolinian accent, but would come to master Spanish completely making it

---

[3] Elizabeth Hufnagel, personal email, Feb. 1, 2010.

part of her life ever after. She would also become enamored of her part of the Colombian mountains and sent an invitation for all to come and enjoy.

Caldas is a must to see before leaving Colombia. Its three major cities (Manizales, the breath-taking mountain-top capital; Pereira, the city with the perfect climate and friendly people; Armenia, in the heart of Quindío where the best coffee grows) are each competing for supremacy, thus dividing Caldas into the "three fincas" of Risaralda, Quindío, and Caldas. Who knows whether this division will increase the co-operation or invite strife between the regions of the *cafetal*.

Betsy Long

An hour from Pereira by campo bus in the heart of Risaralda is Altagracia, where my *acción comunal* partner and I are working. Although it is a tiny pueblo overlooking the Cauca Valley, this populated area with its six veredas is filled with compesinos for and against the Padre—*como siempre*, the struggle for power continues.

When's the perfect time to visit Caldas? Why, during the ferias of Manizales—January 25-30, 1966. You'll be entertained with fiestas, fiestas and more fiestas, *corridas*, flasks of wine, dancing at the casetas, a paseo to the *nieve* (snow) de El Ruiz (18,000 ft.), and the fantastically barren land which might be equal to that found on the moon. This week of *verano* (only week of the year when it doesn't rain every day) is famed for its beautiful weather which shows all of the scenery of Manizales to its best advantage.

Hasta Cartegena y las ferias de Manizales.

Also, we are looking for more rabbits for Altagracia. (We had a slight epidemic of coccidiosis.)[4]

Betsy found a site that had a Peace Corps history so initial openings had been made. Here was a situation different than that presented to most Colombia '64 Volunteers. Betsy's site had already had agricultural Volunteers for some time and substantial progress had been made in terms of agriculture, but not in nutrition. Betsy's particular expertise was just what this area needed at this time. Her introduction to Caldas was, however, anything but auspicious.

I arrived in Pereira on Avianca airlines after our brief orientation in Bogotá. I had difficulty with Spanish due to my heavy Southern accent. I was not able to roll my "Rs." After 6 months in Colombia, South America, I was capable of two-way communication. No longer did I have to wonder what *como amanecio* (how did you greet the dawn) meant?

I was initially met by Tom, the Peace Corps Leader, in Pereira. He wanted me to meet the local Volunteers at the Swiss ice cream parlor in town. We left all my bags in the Jeep in front of the parlor and, of course, everything was stolen. Fortunately, I had Lloyds of London insurance so I was able to replace

[4] Betsy Long, "Caldas—The Department with the Mostest", El Hocicon, Jan. 1965 (?), p. 7.

some of the things. The biggest challenge was replacing shoes that were gringo size. Later, my parents were able to find someone from North Carolina who was traveling to Bogotá on business. They sent a "care" package to the Peace Corps office, which eventually I received.

We traveled in an open green Peace Corps Jeep, on a dusty unpaved road that led to my site, Altagracia. The town turned out to be a small village of about 50 to 75 families with an additional 6 outlying veredas. At my site, I was assigned to replace three Volunteers who would soon be completing their service (Tony, Pablo, and Carlos). These Volunteers were working in conjunction with a nucleo that had been built to draw the community together to combat the violence left over from the Violencia. Fortunately, the area experienced little of this terrorism while I was there. The old Volunteers had taught many of the campesinos how to raise vegetables, bees and rabbits. Unfortunately, they had no time, or the knowledge, to teach the families how to cook them. That's where I came in, working with mothers and families concerning nutrition and sanitation.

It was a one hour ride in an open air bus (chiva) over an unpaved road from Pereira to the village of Altagracia. I usually rode the chiva with a live chicken or pig next to me or a burlap bag of oranges, a stalk of bananas, a caged tropical bird, or a bag of coffee beans. The top of the chiva often carried produce that was secured with a rope. A helper hung onto the back of the chiva, and he gracefully and skillfully jumped on and off of the back as he delivered and plucked up items along the way.

This was considered a "developed" part of the Colombia, thanks to the Federation of Cafeteros. Homes had electricity and running cold water. The houses were built of guadua (bamboo), then covered with a mixture of mud and manure; when the walls dried they were white washed with *cal* (lime). The walls of the mud homes became completely odorless when dry and were great for hanging decorative posters.

Pablo and Tony offered to show me the nearby veredas. We mounted the Peace Corps horse and two others borrowed from neighbors. All through the valleys, we rode to homes where we visited the gardens and became acquainted with the families.

Soon after this initial visit with most of the families the Volunteers had been working with, I was walking behind a police horse that was trained to kick, a trick I was completely unaware of. I was kicked in the mouth and laid out semi conscious with three loose front teeth. I was lifted into the back of a pick-up truck carrying coffee beans. We rode over an hour to a hospital in Pereira where Tony had already made friends with the nuns. It was recommended that I stay in the city for the weekend to be certain of a positive recovery. Recuperating at the PCV's apartment, I started passing out again. A second trip to the doctor was in order and I was diagnosed with having worms. I was treated with de-worming pills and was soon able to return to Altagracia.

I inherited many projects such as rabbit hutches and a lush school garden, bee hives, and family gardens. Because the families had not yet learned how to use the produce, my work was cut out for me. I had a teenage assistant, Nelly, who accompanied me on many visits, especially when we were assisting with the garden projects and harvesting.

For a family to give up a piece of land that could be growing coffee took much convincing. It worked in many cases, although the people were only used to eating onions, tomatoes, platinos (cooking bananas), and yuca in their *sancho* (campesino soup). Chicken was rare. As a guest, you knew that you were honored if the soup had protein in it. Once, I was served sancho with a chicken foot submersed in the liquid. Of course, I ate while the family watched. This was the Colombian campesino custom. Guests or the father were always served first. Machismo was alive and well.

Hospitality was always present even in the humblest home. Upon arrival, I was served "tinto", delicious Colombian coffee, sweetened with panela. Needless to say, dental problems were widespread and there was no dentist available.

The priest had invited Peace Corps Volunteers to the site, but he later ran the Peace Corps out. I saw the church remain half built, while the Padre's house was completed with brick, tiled floor and a television set (the only one in town).

I'll never forget the delicious taste and smell of *empanadas* (chicken, rice in a corn meal *masa* - dough) fried on Sunday a.m. outside of the church. It only cost a couple of pesos. It was a delicious Sunday treat.

I worked with the school nucleo team that included an agronomist, a teacher, a shop teacher, and an extension person. We tried to make weekly visits to five surrounding veradas. My Colombian counterpart was the community nurse, Dona Rosalba, who already had the confidence of the community. Together, we organized classes at the health center on the day when the doctor came, which was once or twice a month. We taught basic nutrition and health classes, one on one and in groups. I borrowed the Peace Corps projector and U.S. AID films for many of our presentations.

I taught the mothers how to make an oven from a 5 gallon oil can, using metal pieces from shipping crates for the racks. Since eye diseases were prevalent due to cooking directly over an open wood fire with heavy smoke, I was able to communicate in Spanish various eye care options. Also, I taught the mothers how to effectively use Incaparina. The mothers were taught how to make formula by adding a small amount of Incaprina. If too much was added to boiled water, the infant would get diarrhea. Incaprina could also be added to the *arepas* (grilled corn tortillas) or *sancocho* (soup) to add nutrition.

Initially, I lived at the nucleo and ate with the staff for 6 months. After eating mostly starches and gaining 10 kilos, I decided that I must move and cook for myself. Later, I lived in a mud house by myself up the hill from the nucleo.

I remember experiencing my first earthquake in this house. I awoke in the middle of the night in a house where I lived alone. I heard noises and a few things falling. I prayed that I would be safe. The next morning, my neighbors told me that it was a *terramoto* (earthquake). There were more small earthquakes during my stay. There were also rock and mud slides that often blocked the road for hours.

Finally, I lived where the previous Volunteers had lived. I had an indoor flush toilet and an outdoor cold shower. I inherited a two burner electric stove and a tiny oven. I often bought a kilo of beef and prepared corned beef and cooked half of it in the pressure cooker. The backyard also had a rooster hut on stilts and a banana tree and coffee trees. I always had a huge pot of boiled water covered to provide potable drinking water. I remember buying bananas by the stalk. I usually consumed and shared lime sautéed bananas and banana fritters with the neighbors and visitors.

I hired my neighbor, Inez, to wash clothes, make arepas and to look after the house when I was visiting homes. Of course, there was no refrigerator at any of the places that I lived. All beds were made of guadua slats and the mattress was just a cover filled with straw. For a few months, I had a dog named Muneca (doll) and a horse for transportation. The pastures were not sufficient to feed the horse; thus Peace Corps said that the horse must be sold.

Biweekly, the town butcher rendered a cow and hung it over a concrete slab near the entrance of the tiny movie theater.

One of my best friends was Dona Mary, wife of the police chief. We spent time together with her two young children. We discussed Colombia and the way of life for women. In the 60's, women were considered aggressive if they tried to push officials to do something before they were ready. Patience was extremely important and everything needed to be done with respect for the Latin way of life. Work inside and around Altagracia had to proceed slowly.

I remember parades to honor a saint or the candles lighting the homes on Christmas Eve. The lights shone across the hills.

In order to increase the campesino's confidence in the military, there was a special day when soldiers from the base in Pereira came to the nucleo to cut hair, pull teeth and play basketball and soccer with the youth.

I went to Pereira weekly for shopping, mail and visiting with other Volunteers. At the same time, I was able to network with staff at the Children's Hospital. This is where malnourished children stayed for 3-6 months recovering their health through proper nutrition. The mothers were mandated to attend daily nutrition classes in order for the child to participate in the program. I saw children with bloated stomachs from parasites and severely bleached hair with mottled skin turn into handsome, dark haired, smiling child. Always, the first course of treatment was the "pulgante" or de-worming medicine, then the implementation of proper nutrition and sanitation. Families were encouraged to use the latrines which they had dug and installed with the help of the first Volunteers. The seeds of change continued to be planted, but it all took so much time and patience.

At my site, I saw a family of seven children lose the 5 youngest children to malnutrition and dehydration. The mother washed clothes in the stream for her tiny income. The father was disabled from having tuberculosis and stayed at home in the barrio where they lived on donated land. It was a terrible role reversal for the macho Colombian male to stay at home. I continued to talk to the family about participating in the children's hospital program in Pereira. It was always a question of time and money for transportation, and the fatalistic attitude, "it's God's will" always pervaded. Only the strongest children lived past the age of two.

The last big project I worked on was a community family planning seminar at the school. It took months to line up a doctor, a more liberal priest, and an educator to conduct the training. I spent days talking to families, especially the mothers who were in the homes. The fathers were in the hills picking coffee. Of course, they all seemed interested and promised to attend. Little did I, a gringa and a single lady, know that only the men would attend? Women were not allowed this information, especially in a mixed group. At least the seed was planted, but it may take generations to succeed with family planning in Colombia.

As my time to complete service arrived, everyone was asking for a *recuerdo* (remembrance gift). To Colombians, if you admired something that someone was wearing, they gave it to you. Some of the things that I gave away were articles of clothing, posters, and some kitchen items. *Asi es la vida Colombiana!* (That is the Colombian way of life.)[5]

And so closed out Colombia '64's role in the lives of the people of the Cordillera Central. Elizabeth, Dennis and Betsy, a small contingent of our group had been spread out in isolated outposts in this mountain range in the very heart of Colombia. Hopefully, some of the things they taught remained to better the lives of these people they worked with. As Betsy says, "at least the seeds were planted."

---

[5] Betsy (Rosita) Long Bucks, A Southern Gringa Goes to Colombia, Jul. 2009.

18
BOGOTÁ AGAIN

While the Volunteers of Colombia '64 were scattered across the country like chaff in a strong wind, three members of the group stayed in Bogotá. Their assignment was to work in educational television in the capital city and here they would remain, more or less, for the duration of their time in South America. As Marge Mohler points out, "Gerry Volganeu, Tom Gallaher, Lisa Hufnagel and I were ETV utilization volunteers,"[1] and were shipped out to the far reaches of Colombia along with the ag/nutrition people. However, Robert Bezdek, Louie Jarussi and Ken Waissman would have Bogotá as their base of operation for the next twenty months.

At six feet, two inches and 200 pounds, Jarussi was, "not as tall as old Gigante, but tall enough to really stick out in a crowd walking the streets of Bogotá or any other place down there."[2] He describes some of the benefits and problems of living in this big city along with various aspects of their program.

I will say that the ETV program in the Peace Corps was a challenge and fun as I remember it as a 20 year old. Two parts of it were centered in Bogotá, programming and technical installation. Ken Waissman worked in the production of most of the programming that was televised over the country and I worked in the technical section that fixed and installed the televisions all over the northern area of Bogotá and many miles into the interior. We had other sections of technical support, one being in Cartagena, another in Cali and others spread out over the nation.

Our base site was in Bogotá. All of the lessons were printed there and then sent out to the surrounding schools in the country that had televisions installed. The lessons were then broadcasted and the teachers had the guide book to preview with the kids before the live broadcast was sent over the air waves. Ken Waissman worked hard in the production of the programming and its transmission.

All of us worked with counter parts whom we helped train and they, in turn, were helping us with the language barrier. Some of my days were spent in the Bogotá office repairing televisions and watching our counter parts do the same. Other days we would be scheduled to go out into the surrounding areas both in and out of Bogotá to install or repair televisions that were already in use.

I never was very comfortable with heights and some of those roofs were really high and not very strong. I weighed over 200 pounds and a couple of times I fell through those clay tiles and scared the crap out of the teachers and kids underneath.

I remember going to what I thought was the end of the world in a 4x4 Jeep shifted into four wheel drive and low range, then strapping the TV and antennae on the back of a burro. I followed the animal up this mountain trail to one of the many remote villages we served. Then we had everybody looking at us while we

[1] Margaret Mohler, personal email, May 19, 2009.
[2] Louis Jarussi, personal email, Sep. 3, 2008.

put in the first television they'd ever seen, attaching it to a generator for power. Man it was powerful to feel that we had that kind of impact on human beings. The town's people thought we were some sort of gods. It was a very humbling experience and it was this type of exposure to the people in Colombia that has changed my life and how I view things in the world.

After I had been in country for six months, I was promoted to being in charge of technicians country-wide. Not that I was the best to do this job, but I was next in line when another group terminated. In my new position, I flew to each department to see how their supplies were doing and offer any technical assistance I could. I did spend lots of time in Cartagena and Santa Marta for obvious reasons.

I lived in the second story of the Balalaika restaurant there in Bogotá. The owner was a Russian by the name of Victor who spoke at least six languages. His wife was Hungarian. They had immigrated to Colombia many years previously to escape the oppression in their own countries.

I ate really good meals of authentic Russian and Hungarian food and was amazed at the variety of ethnic groups from all over the world that would come to the restaurant to eat and listen to the music. I think it was because old Victor could speak their languages. Hell, I had my hands full with just Spanish and it was humbling to listen to Victor and his wife speak in Russian, Chinese, Spanish, French, and other languages I didn't even recognize. So I was introduced to a whole new world of international travel and influence just by being in Bogotá and living in that restaurant.

I recall one evening I was sleeping and two robbers with machine guns had entered and robbed the restaurant at gun point. Nobody was shot, but it sure scared the heck out of everyone. After that Victor hired two thugs to watch the door at all times.

Living in Bogotá had its advantages and disadvantages, but I think what I enjoyed most was seeing other Volunteers come through and many times they would stay with me as they were getting ready to terminate or were getting medical attention.

One time a Volunteer had come to town because he had lots of worms in his bowels. He was taking medication to kill them and was staying with me for a few days.

We went to a movie one night and, of course, it was packed. The movie started and all of a sudden this putrid smell hit me in the face and the locals were saying not so nice things about the aroma. I didn't know what it was. However it passed and things were okay for about 10 minutes. Then again it hit me, a smell like rotten fish. Well, my friend was belching up the gas created by the dying worms in his gut. So we got up and left before they threw us out.

At least two of the downsides of living in the big city were that poverty and death were right under your window and you saw it and smelled it every day as you walk the narrow streets or drove through particular areas of the city. There were the groups of small kids who were sleeping in the doorways as you walked home at night after a movie, or you might hit some bar and see bodies lying on the curb.[3]

Not all of Louie's time was spent on ETV work. Sometimes he was given tasks that took him to out of the way places. One such adventure was a trip to Buenaventura, Colombia's west coast port, gateway to the Pacific. At one time, before trains and airplanes, this port city was the life line of western Colombia, Cali, Popayán, the Cauca Valley, their window to the outside world. Though still important as a means of getting bulk goods to the valley, particularly fuel, Buenaventura's significance had declined with the advent of modern air and ground transportation.

Our director asked me to fly to a dingy place on the pacific coast called Buenaventura [Jarussi writes]. I left Bogotá in a jet, landed in Cali, got on a twin engine plane flew to some remote location and then got on the smallest passenger plane I have ever seen and flew low over the jungle landing in the hot dusty coastal town of Buenaventura.

My mission was to find and drive back a brand new Jeep equipped with a winch and all the other whistles for our director. Heck, I didn't even know how to get out of the town. But with my Spanish improving after a year and half, I was given directions to drive on this muddy, dirt road carved out of the jungle for about 15 hours till I hit Cali. Can't get lost, there aren't any other roads out there, I was told.

That west coast was certainly like you would envision, the kind of dense jungle and high humidity portrayed in the movie the "African Queen" with Bogart....only without the hippos. After driving day and night I made it to Cali, and it was like arriving in an oasis of civilization in the middle of an uninhabited desert.

I think I remember seeing only 2 trucks on that jungle road in all that time. All I could think of was, what would I do if this new Jeep stopped and I couldn't get it to go any further? I was never so glad to get to any place in my life.

Cali was very nice, pretty, good climate, clean, and good looking ladies. It was the only place I found in Colombia where I could buy real apple pie. Some gringos had a little cafe where they did prepare some American dishes including that pie. I think all the Volunteers in that area would go there when they could.

I spent a nice night in Cali and after visiting with some fellow Volunteers and drinking a little aguardiente, I felt much better. I made it to Bogotá the next evening and the director was really happy to receive his new toy.[4]

Though Colombians were usually thoughtful and careful in their dealings with each other and outsiders, there were occasions when they seemed to abandon caution and good sense altogether. Such was the case on one of Tom Gallaher's visits to Bogotá when he stayed with Jarussi. The six foot two, 200 pound former Marine was invariably congenial and easy going which may have led to the Bogotáno's deficiency in judgment.

---

[3] Louis Jarussi, personal email, Jun. 27, 2008.

[4] Louis Jarussi, personal email, Jun. 28, 2008.

One morning I put Tom in a cab to go to the airport [says Jarussi]. He was flying back to Barranquilla on an early morning flight, before dawn. But an hour later he was back at my place looking a little the worse for wear.

He said the cabby took him to a seedy part of town and pulled into an ally. As the car slowed down, he said he knew something was up. The next thing he remembers a guy pulled open the back door and tried to crawl into the car and grab him. Tom punched this would-be robber in the face as hard as he could and the man fell back out of the car. Then Tom put an arm around the driver's neck and squeezed hard yelling at him to get the hell out of there as fast as he could. A short distance away, Tom jumped out of the cab and then found another taxi to take him back to my place.

Bogotá was full of crime at that time and you had to be really careful where you want and with whom. But any thug bent on rolling an American should not be picking on a 6 foot 2, ex-Marine who was raised in the Bronx or he's liable to get the shit kicked out of him.[5]

Jarussi also had opportunities for experiences with the sea, some dangerous, but all educational for a kid from the prairies and mountains of Montana. And Louie was always game for an adventure.

We had one of our ETV meetings in Cartagena. I ran into a few of the guys that were already in Cartagena from the group before us. They had borrowed a boat, so on the weekend we loaded up that poor old boat and headed out into the ocean.

There was a very small island, mostly rock and sand, that was about an hours ride from the beach. We were going to snorkel and look at the fish. We dropped anchor about 20 feet from shore. The water was about 6 feet deep there with a sharp drop-off.

The first guy to jump off the boat landed on a sea urchin. The spines went clean through his foot. I remember this loud shriek and lots of swearing. We didn't know what had happened. He had us drag him back into the boat and we saw the spines that had run through his foot. We pulled them out with pliers and poured good old aguardiente on his foot.

We swam for a couple of hours before we went back; the injured guy had been drinking anyway and didn't want to rush back to shore. So he drank more while we looked at the huge fish that swam around that island.

However, it was a learning experience for those of us from the middle of the United States where we didn't have to worry about creatures of the deep like sea urchins. On my other ventures in the ocean, I was very careful and I always looked for things that might bite, sting and or stab me.

One of the girls at a meeting I attended was swimming by the hotel in Cartagena, and was stung quite badly by many jelly-fish. I think she had to see the doctor. It scared the crap out of all of us.[6]

---

[5] Louis Jarussi, personal email, Jul. 15, 2008.
[6] Ibid.

While Jarussi was roaming around Colombia from his base, the Balalaika in Bogotá, directing the maintenance of the ETV equipment, Robert Bezdek, the former student for the priesthood, was being introduced to, not just TV repair, but studio type equipment in the main ETV studio in the capital.

I was selected to work with the high-tech PCV (a real electronic genius) who would literally fix something super-technical at the television station when it would not send out a signal or in today's computer jargon, 'when it crashed.' This was the station that would telecast the program material to the schools during weekdays. Within a very short period of time, I realized that I was in way over my head, and thus the Peace Corps staff moved me out to work with Bogotá teachers and superintendents in educational television.

The last six months of our tour, some officials from the American embassy asked me to work with them to get movie projectors out to Peace Corps Volunteers with the agreement that the projectors would be returned periodically for repairs to keep them from ruining the film. In other words, the projectors would have been junked unless they were routinely repaired."[7]

The years Bob spent in seminary studying for the priesthood gave him a different prospective on Colombian ecclesiastic affairs, certainly different than those in our group that were Protestants, but his background provides special insight unlike even the other Catholics of the group.

On the outskirts of Bogotá, I worked with a Spanish missionary priest, and he was one of the holiest men I ever encountered. In fact, he invited me to stay with him for two to three days during Holy Week (Semana Santa); schools had no classes during the week before Easter. He told me, in general terms, about the confessions of the men, who were finally coming back to the Catholic Church after years of operating as bandits. He told me their shocking confessions about how many men they had killed during "La Violencia." There would be estimates of 30, 40, 50 or many more, which is still very difficult for me to comprehend.

When there was a teachers' strike in Bogotá, I joined Ron Halter for a couple of weeks in El Salado. I was flabbergasted with the priest, who woke up everyone probably around 6:00 A.M. with his scratch record of AVE MARIA on the loudspeaker.

He would say that it was time to wake up and for the wives to fix their husbands breakfast. Then, 30-45 minutes later, he would use the loudspeaker again to tell the men to go out to the fields and for the women to come to mass at the church. Around 9:00 when the newspaper would arrive, he would interpret the articles and even the comics (sometimes laughing) to the people. At noon and again at 6:00 p.m. he would play the Angelus. If there had been a death that day (frequently the case in the two weeks or so that I was there), then there was no evening music. When there was not a death, the teenagers would dance in the

[7] Robert Bezdek, personal email, Oct. 13, 2008.

plaza to the music the priest played. Afterwards, he would tell everyone to go to bed.

As someone with a high level of Catholic training, I could not believe the control this priest had over the community. Of course, Ron put his unpopularity in perspective with the priest's extracurricular activities.

I think it would be quite difficult for a priest in another Latin American country to have this type of control over people. In Mexico, for example, this simply would not have happened, and I certainly did not hear of anything like this during the number of years I lived and did research there.[8]

Robert was in and around Bogotá for his twenty months in country. During this time, he experienced some of the seamier and more turbulent side of the city.

We had to live with Bogotános picking our pockets. I had three or four encounters, and I had to admire how good these people were at their "trade."

There was the time I had to cross a line between soldiers on large riot-trained horses and students who were protesting the U.S. invasion of the Dominican Republic a few months after we arrived. I have never been so scared in my life when a soldier with his sword out headed for me on his galloping horse. I thought I was dead for sure. But the soldier pulled up right in front of me and I made it to my house alive.

I have kept the newspapers with the pictures of Father Camilo Torres, who joined a guerrilla group to protest the injustices he saw in Colombia and then was killed by the soldiers.

Another time I went to a Bogotá school in my Peace Corps Jeep. The trip to the school was uneventful. But the return was difficult because soldiers made me detour around an area where they had surrounded Sangre Negro, one of the notorious bandits who supposedly had killed an enormous number of people. The soldiers eventually killed him, and the incident made the front page of the newspapers the next morning.[9]

The article in El Tiempo spread the news of the killing across the country. I read about it out in Caloto, Cauca. Sangre Negro (Black Blood) alias Jacinto Cruz Usma had been operating in northern Tolima for years. He apparently went to Bogotá to see a girl friend.

This was often the downfall of many of these bandit leaders. As long as they stayed in their own territory, they were safe, protected by family and the people who either loved them or feared them. But trips outside of that safe zone quite often lead to disaster.

In the case of Jacinto, I remember reading that he had been trapped in a building and the army and/or police had evacuated all civilians from the area, but were afraid to enter the establishment and flush out this bad guy. Finally, the army brought in an artillery piece and leveled the structure killing the bandit.

[8] Robert Bezdek, personal email, Mar. 8, 2009.
[9] Robert Bezdek, personal email, Mar. 9, 2009.

The third member of this Bogotá contingent of our group was Ken Waissman, who worked in Colombian ETV. He had been recruited specifically for this program. His background, education and talent were put to good use. Ken was not just a talented program director, but was an artist, pianist and play director. Besides the strictly academic side of the operation, Ken developed an entertainment/educational program that was broadcast to the Colombian school children.

I produced and directed a twice weekly program called *"La Casa de Musica."* A kind of forerunner of "Sesame Street." Through songs and instruments, the children practiced math (half-notes, whole-notes, quarter-notes) and were helped with their reading by singing lyrics that were projected on the TV screen. We also taught them to make instruments so they could play along in an early version of interactive TV.

La Señorita Amalia

The hostess was a member of the Colombian aristocracy, Amalia Samper, a musicologist who had trained in Europe and in the United States with the famous composer Carl Orff. She had a pretty, cherubic 'Shirley Temple' face, surrounded by a head full of blond curls and wore a 'fairy tale' like pinafore. On each program, she was visited at the window by a large puppet burrow named Pasqual and a puppet cow named Rosa.

The Peace Corps had engaged Stanford University to do a study of what effect these Peace Corps produced educational TV programs were having. (A kind of Colombian Nielson rating.) To promote our show and stack the cards in favor of our getting high ratings, I sold the Peace Corps office and the National Network on sending us out into the field to do 'live' performances of the show. We performed in theaters, assembly halls and church recreation centers.

I realized from the very first 'live' presentation that the 'fan' and 'star' syndrome hadn't been invented by Hollywood. It was natural and came from within. I walked out onto the stage, faced the standing room only crowd and in Spanish asked them who we were about to see? In one voice the kids shouted back, "La Señorita Amalia!" And then from off-stage, Amalia Samper began playing the show's theme song on her *tiple*, a Colombian instrument that was the size of a guitar but strung like a ukulele.

As she walked out onstage, a shocked silence fell upon the startled faces of the children. I suddenly realized that their shock was due to the fact that they hadn't conceived that the black and white image they watched on their television screens was a real "live" full-color human being! Within an instant, a large number of kids were screaming and running toward the stage. Fortunately, there had been security down front and they jumped in front of the stampeding youngsters and eventually got them back to their seats. From then on we always made sure we had plenty of security guarding the stage and the isles.

The price of admission for the kids was to bring one of the instruments we had shown them how to make - a drum, a triangle, rhythm sticks . . .

On one such occasion, after the show I was checking the Jeep to make sure all the props (and the puppets) were secure when I noticed a little boy about six years-old peering into the back of the Jeep. I asked him what he was looking for and he said, "Pasqual" (the burrow.)

"Oh, Pasqual already left," I said. "He took the train back to Bogotá."

The little boy started to cry. I asked what was the matter. He held out a hat he had been holding behind him. It was a hat we had shown the kids how to make on the show. "I stayed up real late last night making Pasqual this hat, but I couldn't get close enough to give it to him." He had added his own special touches: two holes at the top for Pasqual's ears. In crayon on the front he had written: "To Pasqual from . . ." and had then written his name, his school, his town and his department. When we began these ETV programs, these kids barely knew the names of their villages let alone their departments.

"I'm going to see Pasqual when I get back to Bogotá," I said. "So if you give me the hat, I'll give it to Pasqual. Now, keep watching the show because Pasqual is going to show up wearing your hat." Smiling, the boy handed it to me.

The shows were taped ahead so it took about a week for Pasqual to arrive at the window wearing the new hat. "Pasqual, where did you get that hat?" asked 'La Señorita Amalia.' "It's from my good friend..." the burrow announced and proceeded to give the boy's name, his school, his town and department.

Ken and Amalia reviewing the day's script.

A couple of weeks later, I was at the U.S. Embassy for a Peace Corps event and a couple of Volunteers from the boy's area came over to me. "You have no idea what you did," they said. "They carried the boy through town on their shoulders because his name had been mentioned on national television."

By the time I left, our twice weekly show was now seen four times a week (so I guess we passed muster with the Stanford University 'Nielson' group.) I had trained a talented young Colombian, Hector Escallon, who had been working in the videotape room, to take over as director. Hector went on to become a major commercial producer and director at the national network.

In 1999, I was invited to dinner at the Colombian Ambassador's home in Washington, D. C. When I arrived the Ambassador and his wife greeted me; they were both diminutive and looked like a couple of kids! I wanted to ask if their parents were home. Actually their ages were forty-two and forty-one respectively. With child-like delight, they told me that as children they had been fans of "La Casa de Musica."[10]

Augmenting his talents, the experience Ken gained in Colombia no doubt helped him in his career when he returned to the United States.

It was Ken's talent and audacity that lent much of the character and special moments of entertainment to our group. From his productions of skits and plays during training to his arranging an introduction to Harry Bellefonte back stage in Lincoln, Nebraska. From the con job of the Washington visitors to our final departure bash with a special guest, Ken was always coming up with the unexpected and entertaining.

For some months Jarussi, Bezdek and Waissman were the lone representatives of Colombia '64 in the capital city. But gradually other Volunteers from our group began to drift in from various parts of the country and took up residence and positions in Bogotá. The first of these was Arlene Ratliff, who, was originally stationed at the Nucleo Escolar de San Jose near Dolores, Tolima with Jerry Brelage. After the Army Jeep bombing, the pair was moved to another nucleo which didn't work out. Both Volunteers eventually asked to be relocated. Jerry, of course, asked to be moved back to San Jose, a dangerous step even for a male Volunteer, but totally unacceptable, to Peace Corps, for one of our women. Arlene accepted a position in Bogotá working in the PINA office, planning and writing nutrition classes. Here she became acquainted with Martin Rorapaugh.

I met Arlene after she was brought in from the Nucleo Escolar due to the Violencia as mentioned [Martin writes]. I was with the Educational Television project (Colombia 65-01-02).

We were married at Juzgado Quinto Civil in Bogotá on October 28, 1965. Our church wedding was held October 28, 1966 at the Union Church of Bogotá. We honeymooned in Cartagena.

We had a second floor apartment in the apartment house of Raquel Gomez de Garcia. Raquel was a particularly feisty lady. Two incidents that I won't forget:

First, one day a person started loitering around the outside steel door to the apartment building. Raquel opened her window (on the fifth floor) and told him to move along. He told her that the sidewalk wasn't hers and he'd stay as long as he wanted. At this point Doña Raquel stuck her pistol out the window and started firing down at him from above. It didn't take long for him to decide that he'd stayed as long as he wanted to.

Second, one afternoon Raquel came home from the open market with her groceries which included a truly bedraggled looking loaf of French style bread. We asked her what had happened to the bread. She said that a man had

---

[10] Email from Ken Waissman, Aug. 8, 2010.

attempted to swipe her purse so she had beaten him about the head with the French bread until he fled.

She was a great landlady, and our apartment was never broken into. A rarity in Bogotá.

During the remainder of our stay in Bogotá, Arlene worked with the National Ministry of Nutrition. I believe she was writing national standards.

I worked at the HJRN educational television studio. I was responsible for four grades of Natural Science programming as well as two series of programs for the rural Mothers Groups. These were 15 programs each. One was on Public Health and the other was on Nutrition. I was also charged with training Colombian Producer-Directors. This all went well and I was able to turn the programming for which I was responsible over to a Colombian counterpart when I left.

One of Arlene's good friends was a young woman named Betsy (Long). Arlene often spoke fondly of many of the Volunteers in your group.[11]

Eventually, not long before termination time, Eugene Roberts would show up and finally, Brian McMahon would arrive, though Brian's stay did have its difficulties. "Towards the end of his tour Brian's apartment was robbed of every single item in the place including the light bulbs."[12] Brian didn't have the protection of a feisty landlady like Raquel and so he became one of the many victims of house burglary. In his case the thieves left nothing of importance. He was wiped out of all the things he had collected and saved from the various trips around Colombia.

Finally, most of the remaining Volunteers of Colombia '64 showed up in the nation's capital for termination. There were the final closing of accounts, turning in of last minute reports and that last physical. And of course there was that last party.

"I seriously doubt that any Peace Corps group ever hosted a more spectacular going away party then our event."[13] Our group was not about to leave Colombia with a whimper, no, we would go out with a resounding cannon-like boom. The party was planned by the Volunteers in Bogotá led by Ken Waissman and Eugene Roberts. Louie Jarussi talked the owners of the Balalaika into using the restaurant for the party. Arrangements were in the final stages and it looked to be a fine party. But Ken Waissman and Eugene Roberts decided it needed an added touch, something special, something out of the ordinary. And there on the Tequendama Hotel marquee was the answer, Jayne Mansfield, the blonde sex symbol, was the headliner at the hotel's night club. Ken and Eugene decided that the Broadway and Hollywood star was just what the party needed.

First, "Ken had the ETV art department make an Honorary Peace Corps Plaque for the star."[14] The plaque would be presented to Miss Mansfield at the party. But how to get an invitation to the performer was the question. Jerry Schaffer relates the story told to him by Eugene Roberts as to how he and Ken went about inviting this special guest to the party.

---

[11] Martin Rorapauph, personal email, May 21, 2009.

[12] Dennis Burkholder, personal email, Jun. 29, 2009.

[13] Dennis Burkholder, email to the group, Jun 30, 2009.

[14] Ken Waissman, personal email, Aug. 7, 2010.

Eugene and Ken were in the U.S. Embassy [Jerry writes]. Ken saw some Embassy stationary that was unattended and stuffed a couple of sheets into his coat pocket. They returned to the hotel and typed a letter to Jayne Mansfield encouraging her to attend the Peace Corps party and signed it using the U.S. Ambassador's name. They tried to deliver the letter to her at her hotel, but the clerk would not give out the room number. So they went from floor to floor. They found a room with a Colombian soldier standing guard. They pushed him aside and gained access to the room. They delivered the letter to Miss Mansfield's manager.[15]

The pair waited for a reply, but heard nothing. Time was running out. Well, Eugene and Ken decided that desperate situations call for desperate measures.

Waissman and Roberts 'crash' a rehearsal for Jayne's act that was about to open at the Tequendama Hotel. As the rehearsal breaks, Waissman and Roberts approach Ms. Mansfield, show her the plaque and invite her (personally) to the Balalaika party where they plan to make her an Honorary Peace Corps Volunteer.[16]

Receiving a tacit acceptance, the two Volunteers leave not fully satisfied, but with hope their special guest would make it to the party. So with preparations made, the final party for Colombia '64 began.

I think the band was the #1 band in Colombia, "Los Flipperes" [Dennis Burkolder recalls]. We all were assessed a sum for the party and meal, but those who had more gave more. Etched in my memory was throwing in 1 and ½ months pay because I never could spend all my pay in my site and surely had no use for it since we were leaving.... Something like 2,300 pesos, I think. I remember the 1 and ½ months pay thing as I never again in my lifetime spent that much on one night's party.

It was truly a great party and the group enjoyed their last hurrah with the gusto typical of Colombia '64. Then just as the party is beginning to wind down,

......Jayne Mansfield showed up with her entourage [Dennis writes]. I had pretty much made up my mind that I didn't like her because she had indicated earlier that she wasn't coming. But she danced and talked to anyone who wanted to meet her, was intelligent (!!!!), fun and witty.

Jayne drank imported American whiskey to the tune of 800 pesos. She wore a white vinyl jacket with huge black polka dots on the front and small ones on the back, black and white vinyl skirt and high boots.[17]

[Ken remembers] a member of another ETV group, wearing a 'forties' Zoot suit he bought especially for the party, ended up in the men's room with Jayne

[15] Jerold Schaffer, personal email, Nov. 15, 2009.
[16] Ken Waissman, personal email, Aug. 7, 2010.
[17] Dennis Burkholder, email to the group, Jun. 29, 2009.

switching clothing. She emerges wearing his Zoot suit and he makes an entrance wearing her vinyl jacket and mini-skirt. The crowd roared their approval.[18]

By now Miss Mansfield and her entourage had run up quite a food and beverage bill. Also, the contracted time for the band and use of the Balalaika were just about up. If there is one thing the group learned in Colombia it was that you don't end a party before the participants are ready. Waissman extended the party until dawn. In the finest Colombian tradition, he and Roberts decide they would figure out how to pay for it *mañana*. Miss Mansfield danced with all the guys who wanted to dance with her and talked to everyone.

Miss Mansfield accepting the Peace Corps Plaque with the band members in the background.

Jayne Mansfield may have had a very successful night club tour in South America - I don't know. But I suspect she received more applause and collected more good will that night than she ever did at her night club acts.

During all this revelry there just had to be more than one side show.

[Burkholder] remembers some drunk Colombian tough guy who was annoying as hell and eventually someone from the group called his bluff and offered to step outside and settle it. The Colombian kicked off his shoes claiming he was a black belt and Rodney Spokely, the littlest guy in our group, picked up his shoes and threw them over one of those high fences with broken bottles stuck into the cement on the top to keep out intruders. The tough guy slunk off like a beaten dog with his tail between his legs.[19]

Finally, there was the ride back to the hotel. Some dozen of the most hardy who had toughed it out until dawn hailed a cab. "I remember the ride in/on the cab [James Finkler

---

[18] Ken Waissman, personal email, Aug. 7, 2010.
[19] Dennis Burkholder, email to Gary Peterson and group, Jul 5, 1966.

writes]. It was already daylight and I think it was Schaefer, and a few others, probably Freddy because he was always part of our craziness."[20]

Ken and Louie present Miss Mansfield the Peace Corps Plaque at an official ceremony a couple of days after the termination party. Louie was drafted for the task, "because I was the only guy hanging around the Peace Corps office at the time. So I dug out my old wrinkled Montana sports coat and drove over to the studio."

And so the last party in Colombia ended for this group of Volunteers who had first assembled in Lincoln at the University of Nebraska two years earlier. It had been an interesting and eventful twenty-four months. But now each of us was looking forward to moving on with our lives. There would be those staying behind and putting in a few more months, even another year in Colombia. One, Brian McMahon, planned to stay in country and go into business with a couple of Colombians in an artificial insemination breeding company. Others would be returning to the U.S. to help train replacements. And then there were those planning on a tour of South America or motorcycling all the way home.

Little did any of us realize or even give a thought to where we would be in forty years. We were young and restless, and the Peace Corps experience just seemed to confirm our conviction that all things were possible.

---

[20] Jaime Finkler, personal email the group, Jun 28, 2009.

19
TRIPS THROUGH LATIN AMERICA AND HOME

Following the final bash in Bogotá, members of Colombia '64 began to trickle out to the airport and say their good-byes to the country that had been their home for twenty months. Some had already left; Elizabeth Hufnegal had gone home a few months earlier to tend to her mother who had become ill. Margaret Mohler had also left Colombia before the group's final party.

I was only in Cartagena for 6 months [Margaret recalls] and left a couple of months early to take advantage of a program Cleveland had for returning Volunteers. They'd pay for a master's degree in education if we taught in the inner city schools. I had to take some education classes before the school year began and left Colombia for that reason.[1]

Next to head home was Ron Halter.

I had to leave a couple of days before anyone else in order to start my freshman year of college on time. The President of my new school, Park College (currently Park University), sent me a letter while I was still in Colombia. He stated that he had been notified by the Peace Corps that I was looking for a college in the mid-west. He explained that he thought that my experiences would add to the "total school experience" of a liberal arts school like Park, and he asked me to apply for admission. How could I turn down such an invitation?

I flew home on a TWA Tri Star Constellation; the airplane with 3 tails. I was seated next to a German who spoke English with a thick German accent. When we were just past the half way point on our flight home, he turned to me and said "...during ze var, I flew vit de Luftwaffe. Ve are loozing altitude, ve are having problems vit de number 2 engine on ze starboard side." He no sooner got the words out of his mouth, when the Captain addressed the passengers and said almost the same thing. While he made his announcement, the crew "feathered" (shut down) one of the starboard engines. The Captain was confident that the other 3 engines were sufficient to complete our trip to Miami. Needless-to-say, it is hard to forget something like that.

I started college about 2 days after returning home. Because I was 22, my draft board would not give me a school deferment. In the Fall of '67 I passed my draft physical. In February, '68 I started USMC boot camp in San Diego.[2]

The Fenimores returned to Arizona to help train Colombia replacement Volunteers. Others were going back to school, jobs and several had 1-A notices from their draft boards waiting for them - Vietnam was a full blown war by this time.

Adding to the stories I have collected about the Volunteers of Colombia '64, I joined Denny Burkholder and Loui Jarussi who had obtained half a dozen macaws in Colombia

---

[1] Margaret Mohler, personal email, May 22, 2009
[2] Ron Halter, personal email, Jan. 8, 2010.

which we could sell in the United States. He had arranged the sale with a pet store in Chicago, so we were taking a roundabout route home through the windy city. Having disposed of the birds for some much needed cash, we climbed back on an airplane at O'Hara International for the rest of the journey home, Louie and I to Montana, Dennis back to North Dakota.

In Chicago we had many interesting conversations with people about the riots that had dominated so much of the news from the United States the last few months we were in Colombia. These were the riots that began in Los Angeles and spread across the country. Shop owners told us they were in real fear for their establishments and even for their lives at times. The mobs had been one of the things that Volunteers in Colombia were questioned about while we were there, especially the riots in Los Angeles and Chicago which made headlines for weeks at a time. But by the time we arrived in Chicago all was quiet.

Several Volunteers included a bit of a vacation on the way home. One of these was Ronnie Cress who had more problems with getting her dog into the States then we had with our birds.

I had mixed feelings about returning to the United States. I had such a great experience in Colombia, but I also looked forward to getting back to the States. I loved the gathering with my colleagues in Bogotá. I decided to stay a week in Mexico City before going home.

I went through the proper process to prepare my little 10 lb black dog (Tinto) to go back to the U.S. with me. When I went to check in, no one asked about papers for her. She flew with me under the seat or in front of me in a woven basket. No one asked me about my dog.....so I did not say anything.

We stopped in Mexico City and stayed at the Hotel Majestic overlooking the Plaza for a week. What a wonderful time. They put me in a suite for $15 a night and swore I was French, not American, because I could speak Spanish. This was a beautiful hotel where the Mexicans stayed.

From there, I flew to Denver. As I got off the plane in Denver, Tinto stuck her head out of the basket. The flight attendant gave me a long lecture on the rules for carrying a dog on board.

I took her berating for a while, but finally I had had enough. I just told her, "this dog came with me all the way from Colombia, S.A. and she is going with me. Now get out of my way."

My brother was getting married that day and the late plane had already put me behind schedule. I had no intention of missing the wedding. I walked into the wedding late, but what a joy to see all my family.[3]

Some had planned even more extensive and exciting vacations on the way home. Bruce Borrud had concocted a plan to motorcycle home.

My younger brother Bob came down to Colombia when we terminated our P.C. service and our plan was to fly to Panama City, buy motorcycles (we had heard there were no taxes there), and ride back to California on the Pan-Am

---

[3] Ronnie Lou Cress-Kordick, "Retuning From the PeaceCorps," February 2010.

highway. We did fly to Panama from Cartagena (after some sight-seeing in the Colombian city), but found the motorcycles to still be $500 each. With that in mind and the thought of cattle, and other animals on the highways, we decided to take public busses back, one capital city at a time. We would hop on an inter-city bus and travel to the next capital to the north, spend a day or two there sightseeing, and move on.

Our most memorable stop was in Managua, Nicaragua. We had taken a bus from the last capital city to the south and for some reason got in real late (about 3:00 AM) and when we arrived, everyone on the bus hopped off and went home. We were in the middle of town and no one was there. We could go to a hotel, but being PC fiscally conservative and knowing that we were catching an 8:00 AM bus to the next city, we decided to sit/sleep in the central plaza until the morning. In retrospect, probably not a good idea, but at the time it worked.

We went to a park bench, suitcases alongside, laid down, and proceeded to doze/sleep until sunrise. No one bothered us or came along that we know of. This was during the Samoza era in Nicaragua so I believe things were pretty quiet there with his police state in power. After a couple of days in Mexico City, we finished with a 48 hour bus ride that ended in Tijuana, Mexico, where we crossed the border and met our folks who had driven to the border to pick us up. Altogether it took us about three weeks to get back home from Bogotá.[4]

Two other stalwarts did make the trip on two wheels. Jerry Schaefer and Rodney Spokely flew to Panama City and purchased two motorcycles, then set out for home. "Great 5,500 mile trip," Jerry says, "first and last time on a motorcycle."[5] Crossing the U.S. border, they stopped at Bob Bezdek's place.

They had traveled by motorcycle through Central America, Mexico, and then into the U.S. They stayed with me for a day or two in Alice, Texas. [6]

Betsy Long and Carolyn Hawkins had seen Colombia, now they planned to visit the rest of the Continent.

Betsy Long was looking for a travel partner to make the trip around South America after our completion with Peace Corps, and I consented [Carolyn says]. Betsy writes about our travels.[7]

I joined my friend, Carolyn, on a 3-month *huelta* (trip) around South America. We started in Leticia, the Colombian foot on the Amazon. I became ill with a high fever as we stayed in a cheap pension awaiting transportation to Manaus. Carolyn talked to the American Consulate, who helped me get into the tiny hospital, outfitted by the U.S. Navy. It was the only time in two years that I slept in a bed long enough for me. Within 5 days, I was well. I had para typhoid

---

[4] Bruce Borrud, personal email, Jun. 19, 2008.
[5] Jerold Schaefer, personal mail, Jul. 25, 2009.
[6] Robert Bezdek, personal email, Oct 14, 2008.
[7] Carolyn Hawkins Denton, "Memories of Caloto, Valle de Cauca and Ventaquemada, Boyaca," July 13, 2009.

because I had missed a booster shot at one of our Peace Corps Conferences. We were able to hunt for alligators and piranhas by canoe at night before leaving. We also saw a native holding a boa constrictor which he was offering for sale.

Finally, we booked a flight to Manaus where we visited a Brazil nut farm and packing house. We were each given a large bag of nuts that became our snack as we traveled around South America. We also saw cashew nuts growing, one nut attached to a cashew fruit. (The

Man selling a snake along the Amazon.

juice of the cashew fruit was also tasty and very popular.) We visited the ornate Opera house built in the 1920's when rubber was king on the Amazon.

We next took a flight to Belén, at the mouth of the Amazon and then to Fortaleza where the roads began. We rode the bus for two days between each city, Recife and Salvador-Bahia (a two level city with outdoor elevators connecting commerce and homes) where we rested in an inexpensive pension and enjoyed the pristine beaches. In Salvador-Bahia we observed a séance on the beach. Many Africans danced the macumba to the sound of the drums at night on the beach around a large bonfire. This ritual was done to ward off the evil spirits and for healing.

We visited Brasilia, the new capital with many stark white buildings and few inhabitants. We were able to find the U.S. Consulate, a state of the art building.

We then went through Belo Horizonte (the center of gem mining) where we bought a tiny sack of semi precious rocks from a boy selling his "gems" at the bus station late at night.

In Rio de Janeiro, we stayed at a pension where we met some other gringos who were also traveling. We always shared tips with fellow travelers about inexpensive places to stay. We loved the beaches of Ipanema and climbing to the statue of Christ guarding the harbor in Rio de Janeiro. On the beach, I remember hearing people speaking Spanish with an Argentine accent. Comprehension in Portuguese was difficult, but we survived using our Spanish.

After several days in Rio and after seeing the *favalas* (huts on the mountain side), Carolyn and I decided it was time to continue south. Our original plan was to get to the Tierra del Fuego at the southern tip of South America; however, we didn't get that far.

In Montevideo, Uruguay, we took the air boat to Buenos Aires, Argentina. This was the closest that I came to having motion sickness. In Buenos Aries, we remember having tender steak, puffy fried potatoes, a salad, wine and a hard roll for about $2.00 U.S. Ah, what delicious food! The huge trees, flowers, and plazas in the center of the city were enjoyed. This was a very European city. We bought hard rolls, cheese, and fruit for the trip to Patagonia.

As we boarded the train, a tall Argentine man offered to help us get to our seats. He then asked if I wanted to get coffee. I said yes and left my possessions with Carolyn. After going through a couple of cars, we did not get to the dining car, but to a sleeper car. He pushed me into a room. I panicked, got out of the room and ran out of the car on to the platform with him pursing me. Fortunately, the train had not left the station and I was able to get back to my car. But before I could get inside, the train started to move and I fell against the steel stairs cutting my leg. It didn't bleed much, although my pants were slightly torn. I was lucky to be safe and back with Carolyn.

We went through the bleak Patagonia in southern Argentina, which seemed to support only the raising of sheep and goats. We saw young children near the train hoping to get a hand out.

After many hours, we arrived in San Carlos de Bariloche, Argentina. Spring was just beginning. Being in this town was like being in little Switzerland. We climbed the hills and relished the verdant slopes with wild flowers just popping out. We would have liked to stay there but we knew that our $500 each, from the Peace Corps for our resettlement allowance was dwindling fast.

We took a bus to Santiago. In one stop, I ate my first artichoke. Of course, the waitress had to show me how to fix it. Now, it is a favorite.

After seeing Santiago, we went to Valparaíso, on the coast of Chile, where we met a friend from Minnesota who worked there. We then took the train to Portillo, the summit of the Andes, where the World Ski Championships had just ended. What a beautiful site!

From Santiago we flew to Santa Cruz, Bolivia, because there was no viable bus transportation. Santa Cruz was a town with no paved streets. We met missionaries, who invited us to stay and rest.

After a couple of days of the heat, we journeyed to La Paz and felt the altitude immediately, but we enjoyed seeing the Bolivians and their colorful dress. We took a train to Lake Titicaca, the highest navigable lake in the world. We arrived in time for the night boat across the lake, but we were too late to rent a hammock. So once again our sleeping bags were our beds. At dawn, we saw the reed boats and platforms

Machu Pichu

where the Indians lived on the lake. It was bleak and cold at 12,000 feet altitude.

We arrived in Cusco to find there was no place to stay. As it turned out there was a total eclipse of the sun about to take place and this was the best place in the world to observe it. After seeing the wonders of Cusco, we took the train to Machu Pichu. We met scientists from all over the world and the total eclipse happened while we were on the train. What an experience to be in total darkness in the middle of the day! We checked our packs at the hotel and started climbing the ruins. That civilization was awe inspiring.

We returned to Cusco and bought a bus ticket to Lima. An hour from Cusco, our huge bus broke down. The driver had to back down the steep road. He had an 8 year old boy get out at each hair pin curve to let him know how far to back up for the turn. We were going nowhere. Finally, we were able to catch a ride in the back of a large pick-up truck that was carrying Indians and goats. At each stop, we exited to find a toilet. What we found was a hole in the floor. Now we knew why the women wore these full skirts. Of course, we were wearing jeans.

We did eventually make it to Lima and were more than tired. We did visit the Cathedral which housed the glass coffin with the remains of Pizarro, the conqueror of the Inca Empire. (I have been told recently that his coffin has been moved away from the plaza because he was a conqueror.) We were shown around the city by Ernie, a student

Lima Plaza

from my home town of Roxboro, North Carolina. We saw the changing of the guard at the palace and visited the Peace Corps office where a Peace Corps physician examined my leg. He said that it was healing.

We traveled to Guayaquil, Ecuador, and then on to Quito, but after three months of mostly travel by land, we were too exhausted to visit another museum. We returned to Bogotá via air, where I went to the Peace Corps office to see a second doctor about my leg. He said that it was healing, but he did not notice the red ring surrounding the wound.

I contacted my parents and asked them to wire money to me so that I could come home. They met me in Miami. My Mother, a nurse, took one look at my leg and was very alarmed. She had my Dad, a dentist, write a prescription for an antibiotic immediately. She put hot compresses on the leg and elevated it as we drove to North Carolina. The infection was at the stage just prior to osteomylitis, inflammation of the bone. It took six weeks to heal.[8]

Our travels were accomplished by most every means of transportation [Carolyn adds]: bus, plane, train, boat, trucks and afoot - until someone picked us up. What amazed me about the whole trip was the number of contacts Betsy had along the way. That was really great to be able to know someone when you arrived at a place. Also, when we were in Bolivia, she attracted quite the attraction being tall and blonde. There would be a string of kids following behind her, like the pied piper.[9]

One of the mundane things I remember was the night we stayed in Guayaquil. The next morning when we got up, we noticed our rubber flip flops had been chewed on...rats!!! Of course, the space under the door was about 2".

My wallet got stolen in Quito and I had to borrow from Betsy to get back to Bogotá. I, too, had to have money wired so I could fly back to the good ole' USA and buy a couple of emerald rings for my aunt. Landing at the airport in Miami was a strange feeling...cultural shock. Hearing those people announce over the speakers in English with what sounded like a southern accent was truly weird.[10]

And there were those who extended and stayed in Colombia for a few months, some up to an additional year, the Lenkners, Freddy Falkner and his wife, Doug Dunn, Mike Weber (who moved to Bogotá for his third year) and others. Tom Gallaher and his wife not only extended, but, like Betsy and Carolyn, decided to see South America on the way home.

After our group terminated [Tom writes], I extended my service another six months so Carolyn could finish up with her project and would not have to terminate early. When we finally left Colombia in 1967 we traveled all around South America for almost six months by every conceivable method of transportation, bus, burro, train, foot, steam ship, dugout canoe, etc.

Some of our more memorable moments were sleeping out under the stars in Machu Pichu and two days of meeting no one excepting llamas in the high Andes. We sailing across Lake Titicaca on a old steam ship, built in Glasgow, Scotland in 1900, hauled up to the lake and assembled in Puno, Peru.

When I arrived home I had a letter from the U.S. Marine Corps informing me that unless I reported for duty within the next 30 days, I would be considered AWOL and would be immediately re-inducted to finish out my remaining 2 years of service. I had received a two year leave of absence from the Marine Corps Reserve to join the Peace Corps. And I had over stayed by almost a year. By the time I got back, I had less than a week left to report to my unit. Had I not

---

[8] Betsy (Rosita) Long Bucks, A Southern Gringa Goes to Colombia, Jul. 2009.
[9] Carolyn Hawkins Denton, "Memories of Caloto, Valle de Cauca and Ventaquemada, Boyaca," July 13, 2009.
[10] Carolyn Hawkins Denton, personal email, Jan. 6, 2010.

returned in time, I have no doubt my butt would have been on its way to Vietnam.[11]

Finally, there was Brian McMahon who would take up residence in Colombia intending to stay permanently. He had become involved with some Colombians and Germans who were organizing a breeding association to import livestock semen. They're plans were to build an insemination business for cattle, a service common in the U.S., Canada and Europe, but new to Colombia.

So the Volunteers of Colombia '64 split up and went they're separate ways, most returning to the United States. Years later, some of these RPCVs would begin to make contact with each other and organize reunions. Gradually, more and more members of the group were located, but several could not be found. Now, after two years of searching, all the Volunteers of Colombia '64 have been accounted for.

---

[11] Tom Gallaher, personal email, Feb. 2, 2010.

20
THE COLOMBIA '64 RPCVS

By the end of 1967 all the Volunteers of Colombia '64 had departed South America except Brian McMahon. They had returned to the United States to pursue educations, careers, and personal interests. A few were obliged to fulfill military obligations. Over the next forty years, the members of Colombia '64 would spread out across, not just the U.S., but much of the world. Many would become involved in humanitarian enterprises. More than a few would return to Colombia on vacations or service projects.

But how much of an effect did the experience have on the Volunteer? Was the impact for better or worse? It is, perhaps, impossible to know. We can track what became of the members of Colombia '64, but there is no way to determine how their biographies might read had they not spent the time in Colombia. Keeping this deficiency in mind, a brief review of the direction each Volunteer took upon his or her return may give us an indication of the effect. And, perhaps most importantly, there is the Volunteer's own assessment of the impact.

Geoffrey and Janice Abbott

Originally from Connecticut, the Abbotts stayed in the New England area upon their return. They divorced in 1991. Their Peace Corps experience does not seem to have had a great influence on their lives. Geoffrey admits, "I haven't thought about Boyacá for the last 35 years."[1] And contacts with other Volunteers have been minimal. "I think the only RPCVs I have seen in the past 25 years are the Lenkners in 1987, and I have lost contact with them."[2]

> In the years since returning, I have encountered many Colombians [Geoffrey adds], but only one whose sister was living in Duitama within the last few years. It seems most of the Colombians I have met are from Medellín, Cali, or Bogotá, etc. Maybe Boyacá is a good place to stay.[3]

Jeff Andrews

Jeff returned to his native state, Florida, where he picked up a master's degree in international affairs. After a stint in Vietnam with the State Department, Jeff settled in Ocala, Florida building a commercial developing company - convenience stores, small strip centers, fast food units and rental units.

Jeff made a trip back to Colombia in 2007 and found many changes. "I was astonished how much Cartagena has grown. It is quite the city now."[4]

---

[1] Geoffrey Abbott, personal email, Aug. 15, 2009.
[2] Geoffrey Abbott, personal email, Jun. 26, 2009.
[3] Geoffrey Abbott, personal email, Aug. 18, 2009.
[4] Jeff Andrews, personal email, Dec. 8, 2008.

Deon Axthelm

Mr. Axthelm, as he was called by the trainees of Colombia '64, was Peace Corps Training Program Director at the University of Nebraska for several groups besides Colombia '64 including the Bolivian group mentioned in this book. During his career, Deon operated a large irrigated farm, worked for an irrigation equipment company and did research work for the University of Nebraska Agricultural Engineering Department. Eventually, he became known as, "Mr. Water Resource Specialist for the State of Nebraska," working with a state legislator to develop the state's ground water laws and building the organization to develop them.[5] Deon is now retired and living in Springfield, Missouri where he celebrated his 90th birthday in 2010.

Richard Bennett

Richard returned to the United States and married. But he still carried the memories of his Peace Corps days. "I did return once, in 1968 with my new wife on our honeymoon no less, but it certainly hadn't changed at that point since our departure in 1966."[6]

Richard settled down in California where he was raised. "Time passes, and now we are all getting to be old duffers full of memories and stories. I am still involved in agriculture, in the Napa Valley, as proprietor of a 30 acre vineyard, which according to the testimony of several winemakers, produces stellar Cabernet. It must be good because most of the wine made from our grapes sells for over $100 a bottle. I don't drink much of it, needless to say."[7]

Ronnilou Cress Kordeck did run into Richard recently, "I had a delightful visit with Richard Bennett and his wife when we were in Lake Tahoe. He has a beautiful wife and home. We chatted at lunch reliving great memories. He seems to be doing great. I hope they can come to the next one (P.C. reunion).[8]

I have been able to keep up my Spanish language [Richard says]. Living in California in an agricultural community and employing some Hispanics, I find that I speak a little Spanish every day and am always grateful to my Peace Corps experience for that ability.[9]

---

[5] Deon Axthelm, personal email, Dec. 7, 2010.
[6] Richard Bennett, personal email, May, 8, 2009.
[7] Richard Bennett, personal email, May 7, 2009.
[8] Ronnilou Kordeck, personal email, Jul. 9, 2009.
[9] Richard Bennett, personal email, Jun. 25, 2009.

Robert Bezdek

After leaving the Peace Corps, I needed to get a handle on what I had observed in Third World countries. Thus, I went to Ohio State University (OSU) to pursue a masters and a Ph.D. in political science. I took the foreign language exam for a Ph.D. candidate the first quarter at OSU and passed.

For my M.A. thesis, I dealt with a comparison of "interest groups in Mexico and Colombia." In graduate school I developed an extensive file of books and scientific articles on Colombia, but Mexico was next door to my home in Texas and much easier to research. Consequently, I did considerable research on Mexican politics, and my dissertation on Mexican Electoral Opposition was cited by one author as the best general study on that country's opposition up to that time. At OSU, professors recruited me to deal with projects on Latin America, especially Mexico. THE BOTTOM LINE IS THAT NONE OF THIS WOULD HAVE HAPPENED WITHOUT THE PEACE CORPS EXPERIENCE IN COLOMBIA.

I became a Latin American Teaching Fellow under the auspices of the Fletcher School of Diplomacy at Tufts University and I taught for almost two years at the Instituto Tecnológico Autónomo de México in Mexico City. Meanwhile, I did research on three electoral opposition movements during the 1950s and 1960s for my dissertation and traveled to different parts of the country to give lectures at universities as well as to other groups. As to be expected my Spanish continued to improve. The American Embassy worked out a Fulbright for me to teach in San Luis Potosi after I finished my dissertation.

While I was teaching in San Luis Potosí, a new university opened up in my hometown of Corpus Christi, Texas, and the administrators contacted me for an interview. Because of my knowledge of Latin America (especially Mexico) and my Spanish skills, the administrators made the TRAGIC mistake of hiring me to help start this university. Thus, I terminated the Fulbright lectureship earlier than I had expected. I became the Latin American expert in Corpus Christi.

Due to this recognition, Robert traveled, lectured and wrote extensively on Mexican politics in both English and Spanish. At the same time he has been teaching at what is now Texas A&M-Corpus Christi.

The Peace Corps stint was the central experience in my life and that, to a great extent, gave me the framework for my professional career. In fact, my 22 year old daughter will graduate from college in May and plans to join the Peace Corps!!!

Unfortunately, I have no evidence to indicate what type of impact I, or the Peace Corps in general, had on Colombians.[10]

---

[10] Robert Bezdek, personal email, Jan. 11, 2010.

Bruce Borrud

After my return to the USA I immediately started teaching (three weeks into the school year), I was the 7th, 8th, and 9th grade history teacher plus English at our church middle school. They had saved the position for me until I returned from Colombia.

In capsule form, I taught for the next 38 years mostly 6th grade retiring in 2004. I married my wonderful wife Kathy in 1969 and we have three children.

After working in the Los Angeles area for 11 years we headed for the country and moved to Visalia, California. This was a smaller town of 30,000 between Bakersfield and Fresno in the central valley of California.

After 27 years in Visalia we retired to Palm Desert, California (12 miles east of Palm Springs) where we enjoy golf, sun, community, and family. We live in a condo on a golf course and our 3 children bought a condo four houses away. We see our children and six grandchildren often (one of the benefits of living in a resort area).

What was the Peace Corp experience affect on my life? I would have to say that I really didn't reflect on it much to begin with. I just started working and tried to get back to a regular life. I guess I didn't really think about it much until my later years. Frankly, the Las Vegas reunion of 2007 where we shared the Peace Corps impact on our lives was really the first I gave it much thought.

It did have an impact, but I suspect a hidden one. What is it that drives us to be concerned about others, to be eager to help our country, to volunteer for church, community, country club positions? It has to be our desire to make things better. And that certainly comes from our Peace Corps experiences.[11]

Bruce has stayed in contact with some of the Colombians he worked with in Boyacá. He and his wife did make the one return trip to Boyacá and visited his old site and some of the people still there (see Chapter 8).

"Speaking of adventure, Kathy and I are off to Australia this August for three weeks. One of our sons and his family has moved to Sydney for a two year job assignment. He works for Facebook (the social networking site) and will run the Sydney office. So we have a place to stay as a home base while visiting the country for the first time. Should be fun."[12]

Bruce was able to report, "Australia is quite pleasant. Off to Tasmania this weekend with the family for a side trip."[13]

---

[11] Bruce Borrud, personal email, Feb. 1, 2010.

[12] Bruce Borrud, personal email, Mar. 22, 2009.

[13] Bruce Borrud, personal email, Aug. 19, 2009.

Gerald Brelage

Returning to Batesville, Indiana, Jerry also took advantage of his Peace Corps experience in entering the teaching profession. "I think the most interesting part of Peace Corps for me has been to see how most of us have used our experience. For me, it was teaching Spanish, working with Hispanics in our area, being an advocate for Latin America and working in Mexico, Azerbaijan and Nicaragua. I am currently looking at a possible beekeeping project in Colombia. Many of our group used their experiences in a similar manner."[14] Jerry sums up his life and how it was affected by the time in Colombia.

> I taught Spanish for 12 years, school counselor 20 years, school administrator 6 years and private consultant with industries hiring non-English speakers for 5 years.

> Probably the activity I feel most positive about is working as a volunteer the past 15 years with the Hispanics who have moved into our community. This involved working with legal, medical, law enforcement, jobs, housing etc. Due to my efforts along with two other individuals, our community did not experience the negative reaction that most other communities did. I definitely know this would not have happened without the Peace Corps experience.

> Peace Corps was and is still the defining time in my life. I would never have done nor been involved in the programs without that influence. It gave me the opportunity to broaden my horizons. I would never have been able to see the "big picture" without having been exposed to the people and culture during my Peace Corps experience.

> I may have had an effect on the nucleo where I worked in a general way, but I don't think I changed many individuals. For anyone working in an educational setting it is difficult to see short term accomplishments.

> We could possibly attribute Peace Corps influence as an aid in Colombia's recovery from the anarchy of the 80's and 90's. Obviously many Colombians felt there was an impact because President Uribe has requested that Peace Corps return.[15]

Jerry and his wife took six groups of students to Mexico on educational trips and have made four trips to Nicaragua on educational ministries.

Tragically, Jerry lost his wife in a bazaar hay riding accident in October of 2008. Doris, who many of us became aquainted with at the reunions and through correspondence, was an accomplished health care provider with Head Surgical Nurse, Director of Nursing and Director of Infection Control among her offices. Doris will be missed, not just by Jerry, but by all of us.

---

[14] Jerry Brelage, personal email, March 13, 2009.
[15] Jerry Brelage, personal email, Jan. 8, 2010.

Steve Burgess

After returning from Colombia, I went into farming with my dad, but after my experience in the Peace Corps I was not happy living on the farm. So I moved to Garden City, Kansas and went to work for the Layne Western Company, drilling water supply wells and later becoming their district manager. In 1982 the bosses flew out in their corporate jet, closed my office and gave me two choices of transfers, but I refused both of them.

Left without a viable means of support, I started buying rental property. We presently have 250 rental houses and apartments.

I was married in 1970 and we have two daughters. The oldest is doing the bookkeeping and accounting for the business. I think she will blend into the business when her three children get a little older.

In February of 1977 Rodney Spokely and I, with our wives, went back to Colombia to visit our sites. Rodney introduced me to some of the really great Paso Fino farms and hooked me on this marvelous breed of horses.[16]

I did not appreciate the Paso Fino Horse while living in Colombia. All I could think was, what this country needs is a good Quarter Horse. It wasn't until that trip when Rodney showed me some of the good farms and I got to ride some of the really fine horses that I came to appreciate this wonderful breed.

In 1981 I bought my first Paso Fino. Rodney has bought and owned several Paso Fino's.[17] I presently have 15 Paso Fino Horses on an 80 acre farm with a 28 stall barn and an indoor riding arena. It is all Rodney's fault.

I think about my experience in Colombia almost every day. I do not know how it has changed me other than the Spanish has been very helpful with a lot of my clients. We have a number of Somalian and Burmese refugees now living in my community and I can relate to them living in another culture and having a huge language problem. They seem to prefer renting from me rather than other landlords maybe because I understand their difficulties. We have around 100 rental units rented to refugees.[18]

Three years ago the packing plant here in Garden City hired a bunch of Somalia people. I rented 30 apartments to them. One of the Somalis was given the job of interpreter because he could speak English. He gets a company car to transport workers to the doctors and the hospital. He finds and gets people whatever they may need. I asked him where he learned to speak English. He said he learned from a Peace Corps worker who was in his village in Somalia teaching English.[19]

---

[16] Steve Burgess, personal email, Jan. 9, 2010.

[17] Steve Burgess, personal email, Mar. 1, 2009.

[18] Steve Burgess, personal email, Jan. 9, 2010.

[19] Steve Burgess, personal email, Mar. 1, 2009.

Ross Burkhardt

Ross returned home to settle in Hartford, Connecticut where he became, "president and chief executive officer of New Neighbors, Inc., a Stamford based nonprofit community development corporation that develops affordable housing."

"NNI is a community-based not-for-profit organization. For 36 years, it has championed quality housing in Stamford for those least able to afford it. It has built over 300 units of affordably priced rental and ownership housing that have been catalysts for betterment for families and neighborhoods."[20]

"Ross is a former member of the Westport Planning and Zoning Commission and the Westport Housing Authority."[21]

Dennis Burkholder

I returned to the USA (with Jarussi, Peterson and the birds – see Chap. 18) eventually ending up back in North Dakota where I graduated from Minot State, married Beverly and we have two children Heidi and Reed.

Beverly and I taught school for many years in North Dakota. At one juncture we traveled to Colombia and spent several months touring the country with the intent of finding work, but eventually decided against that and returned to the states.

Twenty years later we migrated to Iowa where I was employed by Winnebago Industries as General Manager of the Winnebago Itasca Travelers Club, a position that provided us with the opportunity for extensive travel throughout America for eight years. One of the perks was a company car to travel in!

There is no question that I received more than I was able to give back during my Peace Corps experience. The training, the two years living in Colombia, and the profound influence of my PC friends had a tremendous impact on me. My eyes were opened wide; my horizons were expanded -- and my life was changed forever.[22]

Ronnie Cress (Kordick)

Upon returning to the United States, I remember my mother kept trying to have me hurry up. I told myself that I would not lose some parts of the Colombian culture.

I was nervous when I began driving again. It seemed like I was learning all over. I would have been more comfortable on a horse. There were adjustments we had to make returning to our culture.

---

[20] Ross Burkhardt, personal email, Mar. 31, 2008.
[21] Ibid.
[22] Dennis Burkholder, personal email, Feb. 15, 2010.

The Peace Corps gave me experience that allowed me to land a great job. Colorado Public Health was looking for a nutritionist to work with the local health department around the state and with the migrant farmers. I was not a nutritionist, but a home economist and I spoke Spanish. When I met with the Director of the Health Department, I convinced him he would get more for his buck if he hired a home economist because I was not only educated in nutrition, but also in child development, consumer education and family relations. He hired me as the State Home Economist Consultant. I am grateful for my Peace Corps experience which helped me get the position.

I became an avid mountain climber, skier, and bicyclists. Our experience in Puerto Rico belaying at the dam and the rock climbing gave me the interest in mountain climbing. A major accomplishment was climbing 32 of the 14,000 foot peaks in the Grand Tetons (Owen Technical route). I regret that I am unable to do this now because my asthma and a broken heel that has never returned to its original performance.

I married and traveled a lot for the next four years with my job. I decided to go into teaching home economics in high school since it would involve less traveling because I wanted to start a family. I began in Jefferson County Schools, Littleton Colorado at Alameda High School. An honor at this time was being selected as one of Colorado's Ten Top Teachers of the Year.

After having a son, Joshua, I stayed at home for three years. I returned to teach at Columbine High School, Littleton, Colorado and began studying for my Masters of Educational Administration at Northern Colorado University.

Several years after a divorce, I remarried - a Chicagoan. We moved to just outside Chicago. In 1989, I became an Administrator of Career and Technical Education in one of the High Schools in District U-46 (the largest District outside of Chicago).

My husband and I now live in Sun City Summerlin. I am a joyful granny with my grandson Nicholas. My son, and daughter-in-law live in Las Vegas. After I retired, I have studied for certification in Pilates.

I still feel that Peace Corps is one of my best experiences. My Peace Corps friends mean a lot to me. I have had a wonderful journey on my chosen path and plan to continue on "the road less traveled."[23]

In 2001 Ronnilou Kordick and her husband and two other couples flew to Equitos, Peru and took a trip up the Amazon for 10 days.

Ronnilou has been one of the key people in keeping the reunions going, organizing the Nevada reunion in 2007. She has kept in contact with many of the Colombia '64 group.

About age ....When I went to the Peace Corps 40th celebration in Washington DC, I walked into the convention hall and had to rethink where I was because everyone looked so old. It dawned on me that I was one of them....what a change a few years can make.[24]

---

[23] Ronnie Lou Cress-Kordick, "Returning From Peace Corps," February 2010.

[24] Ronnilou Cress Kordeck, personal email, Jul. 9, 2009.

Douglas Dunn

After serving two years in the Peace Corps, I decided to extend for a third year. It was during this third year that my work program really came together and I had finally developed enough language skills to function effectively. This third year was certainly the most rewarding and fun period of my Peace Corps service.

I returned to the United States in the fall of 1968 to pursue a master's degree in economics at Cornell University. I was then given the opportunity to return a year later in the summer of 1969 for three months to gather research for my master's thesis on the impact of the small-scale poultry program I was instrumental in initiating while a Peace Corps Volunteer. This was a particularly enjoyable experience.

In the fall of 1970 I was hired by the University of Arizona Cooperative Extension, officed in Willcox, Arizona in southeastern Arizona. I was eventually named County Director, with administrative responsibilities for a large county extension office. I also served as Area Extension Agent, Community Development. I worked with rural communities on land use planning, economic development, leadership development, and natural resource conservation. I worked in that capacity for 29 years until I retired in the fall of 1999.

I then moved to Bisbee, a very picturesque former mining town, where my wife and I had purchased and restored a beautiful craftsman bungalow. Our house overlooks the Mexican border. For 13 years now I've been a main street merchant. Acacia Art & Antiques has become the largest business in the Bisbee historic district. While in Willcox and now in Bisbee I have served on various city and county boards and community service organizations. My wife, Donna, recently retired; she was director of the county library district.

Impact: I was fortunate to have had a productive Peace Corps experience with very visible, photographable accomplishments. As my thesis project I was able to document the economic and nutritional impact of the small-scale poultry program I had helped initiate (as reported earlier in this book – Chap. 7). I have done no follow-up as to long-term impact. Unfortunately, the Peace Corps was not established to do long-term development. Rather it was primarily a program in international relations.

The person who most benefited from the Peace Corps was me. Peace Corps was the single most transforming experience of my life. It gave this small town Nebraska farm boy an international perspective and broadened cultural insights. It dramatically changed how I viewed the world and the great diversity of people in it. It influenced my life career and involvement in civic affairs.[25]

Frederic Faulkner

Fred was another Colombia '64 Volunteer that extended for a full year, after which, he and his wife, Cecilia, left for the United States.

---

[25] Doug Dunn, personal email, Jan. 20, 2010.

Mary Ann and Robert Fenimore

The Fenimores left the country for New Mexico to assist in training another group for Colombia. From there it was off to Washington State for more education.

I do believe it was my drive to return to the university and start all over again in Veterinary Medicine that took us out of there and back to school [Bob writes]. Believe me, I had no idea what I was in for. By the way, Charlie and Melody later moved from California to Washington State University. He and I both went thru vet school together for 4 years!![26]

From Washington it was on to Canada. "From 1973-75 (because of our experience in Silvia) Mary Ann was offered a job in a remote native village in Northern British Columbia where we were the only pale faces. Isolated, 75 people, 8 over 80 with 8 deaths in 2 years. Sound familiar? Again, it touched us to our very cores."[27]

Finally, Bob and Mary Ann moved to southern Canada and civilization where they became duel citizens, Canadian and U.S.

Now retired the Fenimores reside in Canada, but are hardly anchored to one spot. "We live for 5 months in the winter in Victoria, BC-Canada then for 7 months in the Rocky Mountains of eastern BC off the grid - no electricity, running water, outhouse, built our own little cabin, etc."[28]

And there is more travel to visit grandchildren, to the states and even Mexico.

James Finkler

Jaime – his Peace Corps name that has stuck with him at least as far as our group goes – is trying to improve his golf game. "Our weather has been horrible and my golf game is in the same category!!"[29]

Since retirement James has been working as an election judge for primary and general elections, volunteers at the local hospital, works at a health club and works with individuals in transition, a church ministery. Jim is also a volunteer worker at in inner city Calthotic grade school and a high school in northern Illinois.

And Jaime is, "trying to get less dumb on his Apple MacBook.[30]

---

[26] Robert Fenimore, personal email, Feb. 16, 2009.

[27] Robert Fenimore, personal email, Mar. 27, 2009.

[28] Robert Fenimore, personal email, Feb. 16, 2009.

[29] James Finkler, personal email, Jul. 8. 2009.

[30] James Finkler, personal email, Jan 24, 2011.

Thomas Gallaher

Unlike most of the rest of the members of Colombia '64, Tom had already seen much of the world when he went into the Peace Corps. He returned to the United States with his wife, Carolyn, also a former Volunteer (see Chap. 11).

After my return I went to Grad school and earned a degree in psychology, a subject which had always fascinated me. I was toying with the idea of becoming a "shrink." In March 1970 our first child was born, to be followed 18 months later by our second, and that put an end to that.

In the summer of 1971, I accepted a position with Peace Corps as the "resident shrink" for a project in Western Samoa.

Our second child was born in Western Samoa and has a name to remind him of his brief sojourn in the islands, Sloan Tagaloa Gallaher. I assisted in the birth of our first child who was delivered using natural child birth. When I took my wife to the hospital in Apia I was prepared to once again assist in the process, only to be told upon arrival that that was not the custom in Samoa. I would not be permitted in the delivery room.

I was led to an empty room and told to wait. It was early morning, still dark. I sat waiting. The sky is just beginning to lighten, when a nurse came out holding a little baby and presented it to me. It's a boy she said......I looked at the child. He had a full head of black hair just like our first child. Then it was time for me to leave; I couldn't do anything more and I needed to get back before my son awoke.

Later that afternoon, I returned to the hospital to find my wife nursing a little baby. When I saw the baby I realized it was not our child. The baby I had seen earlier that morning had a full head of black hair, this baby was as bald as a cue ball.

How could I tell Carolyn she had the wrong baby? How was I going to be able to find out what happened? My Samoan language skills barely extended beyond *Talofa*! You can't imagine my consternation. I didn't know what to do. After visiting Carolyn, I went to the hospital office to try to find out what happened to our son (I hadn't said anything to Carolyn for fear of upsetting her).

Fortunately almost everyone in the office spoke English. I found out that the baby I had been shown earlier that day was in fact the child of a Samoan woman who was already in the delivery room when Carolyn arrived. She delivered her baby before Carolyn, and when the nurse came out with the baby, seeing no one but me in the room, she showed me the baby assuming I must be the father.

Eventually, I wound up on Wall Street first at Smith Barney, then Lehman Bros. and finally Morgan Stanley. I can honestly say that a career on Wall St. was the furthest thing from my mind when I was in Colombia.

Peace Corps didn't carry much weight on Wall Street. I found some outlet for my Peace Corps idealism by working with ex-convicts through an organization in NYC and became involved with Native American causes. I was also active in the Socially Responsible Investing movement. Most of my clients were Charitable Organizations. As a teacher Carolyn was much more involved in organizing hands on "Peace Corps type" projects including a year's teaching assignment in Russia.

Currently I reside in Tiburon, Ca. just across the bay from San Francisco and have 4 grandchildren. After 30 years working for the Morgan Stanley and Lehman Bros representing investment advisors of all types including Hedge Funds, and alternative investments, I decided to go out on my own in 2008 and see how well I could do. So far so good, had a great year in 2009 my clients accounts were up on average 60%.[31]

Ronald Halter

Like many of those returning from Colombia, Ron faced a rather unfriendly draft board. "While there (Colombia), I read *The Night They Burned The Mountain,* by Dr. Tom Dooly. From that moment on, I was focused on becoming a doctor and returning to Colombia to help mitigate the suffering."[32]

Returning to the USA, I immediately enrolled in Park College (KC MO). After my first year, my draft board stated that because I had turned 22, I should have graduated from college; consequently, I was reclassified 1-A. Rather than go into the Army, I enlisted in the USMC. In February, 1968 they sent me to the Marine Corps Recruiting Depot (boot camp) in San Diego, CA. After 10 weeks of hell, I graduated.

A few days before graduation, we were permitted to call home and have family come to the graduation. I knew that it was useless to call anyone in my family back in Ohio. Somehow I found Bruce's (Borrud) telephone number and called him. At the time, I thought I was headed for a rice paddy in less than two months, and I was in real dire need to see a friendly face. Without hesitation, Bruce drove from LA to San Diego for the graduation. We spent the day talking and did a little bowling. I have never forgotten that sign of friendship.[33]

Ron spent three years as a Marine Corps Officer, including a tour in Vietnam. After the Marine Corps stint, Ron "enlisted" in the FBI where he would spend the next 21 years as a special agent.

Retiring in 1999, my wife, Nancy and I purchased a 19th century 40 acre farm in Vermont. The home was built in 1840 and the five story barn was built in the 1870s. Once refurbished, we opened it as a B&B, raised sheep (after lambing

---

[31] Tom Gallaher, personal email, Feb. 2, 2010.

[32] Ron Halter, personal email, Mar. 31, 2009.

[33] Ron Halter, personal email, Oct. 9, 2008.

season I had 80 head), made maple syrup, planted a huge garden, coached high school and middle school basketball, was a substitute teacher and ran for the office of Justice of the Peace in our 600 resident village of Rochester, VT.

I traveled to La Paz, Bolivia, in 1997. While there I learned that although there were Peace Corps Volunteers that were working in the country, they never went to the US Embassy and would not be seen with other Americans. They were fearful of being "tagged" as US agents/spies!!!!....how the world has changed.[34]

Like most of us, Ron would occasionally run across a news report from Colombia. So often it was not good news, but it did bring back memories of places and events.

Just north of El Salado is/was the town of Armedo [Ron writes]. There were 3 or 4 PCVs stationed there. On occasions I would catch the bus that headed north and stop over there. I played chess with one of those Volunteers, Sam Bass, who later became a college professor in Alabama.

Armedo was a relatively large town. It had a movie theater. On one visit, all of the PCVs stationed there and I went to see *Mary Poppins*. When we exited the theater, I was surrounded by at least 50 or so young Colombian children. Initially I was puzzled by the attention, but then I realized that I was tall, slender and spoke English...a Dick Van Dyke look-alike. I did my best impersonation by singing and dancing, until the kid's parents spirited them away. It was a wonderful town where I enjoyed many good times.

Years later, now back in the states, I was devastated by the following report: *"On November the 13th of 1985, the City of Armedo (Colombia) was destroyed by debris flows generated by a reactivation of the Nevado del Ruiz Volcano... a complex sequence of pyroclastic flows and surges erupted by Nevado del Ruiz Volcano in the Cordillera Central of Colombia interacted with snow and ice on the summit ice cap to trigger catastrophic lahars (volcanic debris flows), which killed more than 23,000 people living beyond the base of the volcano."[35]*

Retiring from retirement, Ron sold the farm in Vermont and went back to work as a special investigator for Wal-Mart Stores in Bentonville, AR and then Clarence M Kelley in Lenexa, KS.

My wife and I are currently staying just outside of Fort Campbell, KY. waiting for Bonnie (our third granddaughter) to arrive. There have been some indications of some movement (contractions), but still no Bonnie. Our son returned home from Iraq just before we arrived. He was on his third tour "down range" and had been there for the past 15 months. He was deployed as part of the last of the "surge" troops. Because his unit came home two weeks early, he has to go to work every day (7 days a week) until the 15th...his original return

---

[34] Ron Halter, personal email, Oct. 9, 2008.
[35] Ron Halter, personal email, Mar. 10, 2009.

date. If Bonnie arrives before that, we will baby sit the other two granddaughters while she is at the hospital.[36]

If I hadn't had the opportunity to be a Peace Corps Volunteer, my life would have been dramatically different. In all likelihood, I would not have attended college. I would have just found a "good paying job" in any one of many manufacturing facilities located in central Ohio.

Growing up in Ohio, I thought I was poor. At times, the home I lived in was not "modern" i.e., no indoor plumbing, our drinking water came from a long handled pump in the back yard. Bathing was stripping down in the kitchen and washing from a small basin of warmed water. When I got to El Carmen, most people didn't have shoes, fresh potable drinking water, toilets, electricity, fresh food, health care, beds to sleep in, etc., etc. I realized that I hadn't grown up poor...in comparison, I was rich!

As a PCV, I soon recognized that I was a de facto grass roots ambassador from the USA. Everything I did was a reflection on the United States. I was often referred to as "El Mister." I was proud of my unexpected responsibility! I was proud to represent my country. That new-found pride lasted a lifetime. Although prompted by my draft board, that is why I had no problem wearing the uniform of our country, and subsequently, carrying the badge of the FBI.

My day to day work in the Peace Corps was that of a teacher, not a leader. I tried to set things into motion that would last after I left. Without the opportunity to see what became of my students, I can only hope that my efforts had some effect on their lives and their opinion of the United States.

I believe this was answered clearly by the current President of Colombia. In his letter of February 19, 2009 he stated, "I had the privilege to award to Friends of Colombia the "*Orden Nacional al Merito*" recognizing their important contribution to the development of our country...We are honored to formally invite the Peace Corps to return to Colombia." [37]

Carolyn Hawkins (Denton)

After traveling around South America for two months with Betsy, I returned to my home in Kentucky where I was hired by the Department of Economic Security as a social worker in the Public Assistance sector. Two plus years of that was enough.

Before getting started in another job, I made a return trip to Colombia in 1969, visiting both sites in Caloto, Cauca and Ventaquemada, Boyacá. Not much change had taken place in that short period.

Given my ability to converse in Spanish,

---

[36] Ron Halter, personal email, Dec. 7, 2008.

[37] Ron Halter, personal email, Jan. 18, 2010.

I decided to go back to college to do something with it and graduated from Western Kentucky University with a Master of Arts in College Teaching. It was there I met my husband, Dave, in a Spanish literature class. We both took jobs in different directions having gone through a placement agency.

My job took me to Martin, Tennessee teaching the reading of Spanish to majors in the medical field, and Dave's took him to Mexico, Missouri teaching English and Spanish at Missouri Military Academy. During spring break 1973, we decided to tie the knot, but we continued our jobs in the different locations until the semester ended.

In June of that year, we, along with 2 other couples were chaperones for a group of 92 high school students who did a study/travel trip to Spain, with stops in London, France and Italy.

After a hiatus to have 3 girls (from 1974 to 1977), I returned to teaching elementary Spanish at the University of Missouri in 1981 as an "other teaching staff" position for three years.

After much pleading from my husband, I finally took the real estate licensing course and to this day continue to sell real estate, along with my husband. We have sold houses to many families from Colombia. Also, we have been family liaisons for families from Mexico who purchase Habitat for Humanity homes.

Through the church, we have made various trips to Mexico and Nicaragua. Two different times we have had students from Spain and Colombia live with us during the school year.

The Peace Corps gave me a broader horizon and a love for another country and its people and language. And it has given me a continual desire to reach out to others and especially those of Spanish speaking origin. Because of the time in Colombia I am more tolerant and accepting of people from different cultures who live in our community.

I still correspond with Lilia who is from Ventaquemada, Boyacá. It was her niece, Carolina Munoz, who lived with us the school year of 2005-2006. Who knows what great things will come from her as she has a lot of ambition and is an intelligent girl. Both her parents are lawyers.[38]

Sharon and David Howell

Like so many others in the group, the Howells have continued to be involved in service work and have kept up their Spanish after returning to the United States.

We are in State College, Pa. Shari is working at PSU while I continue to find mission trips to keep me traveling. In March I helped take a group of PSU students to the Czech Republic where our group helped paint a home for men with drug and alcohol problems. Many of them could speak English so as we worked together we had a great time getting to know them.

In June I am off to Nicaragua again where we will be building a health clinic in a rural area. It is a way to work on my Spanish while helping others.[39]

---

[38] Carolyn Hawkins Denton, personal email, Feb. 1, 2010.
[39] David Howell, personal email, Apr. 30, 2009.

Elizabeth Hufnagel (Metzler)

Until January 2010 Elizabeth was our mystery lady. As hard as we tried, we had been unable to locate her, the last member on our unaccounted for list. There were hints, Bob Bezdek had talked to her shortly after his return and Tom Gallaher had run across some one who taught school with her in New York State, but only those traces hinted as to her whereabouts, until the following email surfaced:

What a surprise to receive the email from Syracuse alumni....It goes without saying that I have lived a very private life...not quite a Howard Hughes, but almost. 43 years! yikes!

Would love to recapture the faces (scratch my memory) of all the members of the group. Don't know if you have done that.

After the Peace Corps I went on to get two masters, one from Hunter College (NYC) and one from Stanford (Palo Alto). I have spent 40 of those years since the Peace Corps in education, teaching math at the Yorktown High School, Yorktown Heights, NY and am now living mostly in Florida, although I still have a home in NY. I have a wonderful daughter who has also chosen education as a profession.

Pretty normal stuff. Outside of a camping trip in the Serenghetti, not terribly eventful.

Liza (that was the Spanish name I got during the project language prep and it stuck!)[40]

Louis Jarussi

I will say that as far as how Peace Corp has changed my life, it gave me motivation to return to the states and go back to college. After seeing so much poverty and seeing how many more opportunities we have in the U.S.A, I turned down a couple of job opportunities in Bogotá and returned to old Montana to finish my degree.

Every time I think I have something to complain about, I just remember the barrios and the country people who have no electricity, medical facilities, running water and a host of other dismal circumstances of those living in the Colombian campo. It brings me back to reality and I recognize how wonderful we Americans have it.

I had intended to return to Colombia to find work after graduation, but the draft nailed me and I never did return.[41]

Louie teaches in Anchorage, Alaska. He plans on retiring in 2011.

---

[40] Elizabeth Hufnagel Metzler, personal email, Jan. 26, 2010.
[41] Louie Jarussi, personal email, Feb. 1, 2010.

Melody and Charles Lenkner

After veterinarian school at the University of Washington, this California couple wound up in Twin Falls, Idaho.

Oddly enuf we still have some links to Cali (Colombia) here in Twin Falls. The Univ. of Idaho has a research facility here in Magic (irrigated) Valley. When we came here in '72, diseases had pushed out spuds in the older farmed areas and one of the main cash crops was dry beans, both for consumption and for seed. Things have changed but the research goes on in beans. There is a PhD agronomo that works for Asgrow who worked on beans in a facility near Cali. And there is an East Indian, of Sikh origin PhD, at the research station who has a Colombian grad student that we have gotten to meet and have dinner with - nice folks.

Another project was our attempted outreach using Rotary. There was a Colombian Priest here in Twin Falls who we came to know. Apparently he was here because he had gotten crosswise of the Cartel. It seems things settled down and he was headed back to Colombia.

Melody was big into Rotary, so we hatched a plan to set up some grants for Colombians working with Father Paz as our instigator and watch dog. We did finally get the local Rotarians moving on this, but the Cali club didn't get their end lined up and the time line on the grant funding passed.

However, we did get to know Father Paz who runs a school on his folk's finca in the hills above Cali. A lady friend who works at the research station here in Twin Falls goes to Colombia to help. She has had us over for dinner with some of her grad students.

Melody has been doing a fundraiser recently for the nonprofit organization she has headed up for 17 years. They are going to start a "charter school" next fall so she is pushing enrollment.[42]

Betsy Long (Bucks)

After returning from Peace Corps, I obtained a Masters Degree in Spanish without any undergraduate courses in Spanish. I then worked as a Spanish speaking Home Economist. I also taught Spanish in middle school and high school. I taught young adults, seniors, and Hispanics at local community colleges in Phoenix, Arizona.

Later, I had a long-term career working to find employment for people with disabilities for the State of Maryland, including Spanish speakers.

---

[42] Charlie Lenkner, personal email, Mar 31, 2009.

Communicating in Spanish will always be with me. I have used it as an educator, disability advocate, volunteer, and in my family.[43]

First Lieutenant Dale Bucks and I were married in 1968 just before he left for Vietnam. While he was in Vietnam, I earned my MA degree in Spanish Education from Appalachian State University.

Upon his return, we moved to Tempe, Arizona, where we had our two children, Christa, born 1971, and David, born 1974. We camped, gardened, swam, traveled, and participated in church and community activities for the next 40 years. I taught Spanish part time at community colleges while I was a stay at home Mom. During this time I collected Spanish nursery rhymes and translated them into English with the help of three friends. These have now been published under the title *TORTILLITAS PARA MAMA.*

In 1988, we moved to Ellicott City, Maryland, where I worked in human services as a vocational counselor assisting people with disabilities to become employed; sometimes I worked with Spanish speaking clients. My daughter, who is a wheelchair user due to having muscular dystrophy, joined the Peace Corps and served in Paraguay, SA. In 1999, she married Jose Camacho who was working at her assigned site the day she arrived. She and Jose live 15 minutes from us and are the proud parents of our two grandchildren, Antonio, 5, and Ariela, 18 months.

I volunteered to lead mission teams in Puerto Rico and the underdeveloped islands in the Bahamas where we rehabbed houses and taught vacation Bible school and did basic health care with the families. I have served on the board of an agency who gives support to immigrant families as they adjust to life in the US. I have also tutored families in English. Yes, volunteerism is in my blood as I continue reading to children at the library in Spanish and English, working at the Senior Center and being part of the caring ministry at our church.[44]

Because of the lack of bilingual books, I wrote the collection of children's nursery rhymes, *TORTILLITAS PARA MAMA,* illustrated by Barbara Cooney and published by Holt Rinehart and Winston in 1981. This book has now sold over 80,000 copies and is still available in paperback. Sharing the rhymes with children, especially my grandchildren, is one of my loves in life.[45]

Si, fuimos el febrero pasado. Era fantastico regresar. Tambien visite mi sitio de Altagracia. No conoci a nadie, pero la escuela estaba alli pero con programas mas grandes.

En enero de 2009, fuimos a Cartegena con un cruise a Panama. Tambien lleve un grupo de 10 personas a conocer cartegena Viejo y la comida con la ayuda de una guia magnifica. Soy un poco active en Friends de Colombia. Abrazos, Rosita [46]

[43] Betsy Long Bucks, personal mail, Mar. 24, 2009.
[44] Betsy Long Bucks, Jan. 26, 2010.
[45] Betsy Long Bucks, "A Southern Gringa Goes to Colombia and South America," Jun. 24, 2009.
[46] Betsy Long Bucks, personal mail, Mar. 24, 2009.

Donald Lydic

Whispers, as he was known by the group, returned to Nebraska to become the Custer County Agricultural Extension Agent. Later, he helped enlarge the family ranch located in central Nebraska. It was there Don was involved in one of those nasty wind storms that occasionally kick up in the Midwest.

Lydic and long-time friend, Peg Hirsch, were at the family homestead about 10 miles northeast of Farnam the night of April 20, 2007.

The Lydic family runs a large cattle operation centered at the 1920s home and it was calving season.

"We had about 75% of our calves on the ground," Lydic said.

The couple had been looking at the ominous clouds that Friday evening and decided to put Hirsch's car in the garage and settle in the house for the night, keeping an eye on the sky.

"The first we heard about a tornado was on KRVN," Lydic remembers. "They said it was about seven miles east of Moorefield.

Lydic knew they didn't have much time to get from the house to the cellar, which has an outdoor entrance about 10 feet from the house's enclosed front porch.

"I wasn't debating," he said. "I was moving."

It's difficult to describe the sounds they heard, Lydic said.

"Imagine tree trunks snapping and cars crashing," he said. "We could hear the debris coming from a quarter-mile away. It's 100 times louder than big, big hail.

Lydic was running for the door with Hirsch six feet or so behind him when glass from the porch started flying everywhere.

"I heard her yell, 'What do we do?'" Lydic said. "I hit the floor and put my arms up over my head.

"It's hard to judge time inside a tornado."

"I remember looking up and seeing the ceiling disappear," Lydic said. "The roof was literally sucked off."

He recalls seeing the ground below him.

"I was hovering, I guess. There wasn't anything to hold onto.

And he remembers lifting himself off the ground and looking to the east where several farm buildings once stood.

"There was nothing left," he said. "It couldn't have been more than a minute, but who knows?"

Neighbor Dan Louthan arrived just as the tornado passed.

The two men found Hirsch unconscious, straddling a tree with her back over a 50-gallon barrel.[47]

---

[47] "Inside Looking Out," *Gothenburg Times*.

Don was able to walk out though he was bleeding from glass cuts all over his body and would bobble for some time from a leg injury. Peg Hirsch was not so lucky. She had to be air lifted to the hospital in Kearney, Nebraska and required weeks of rehabilitation.

The homestead buildings were totally destroyed including the main house where one of the early Colombia '64 reunions had been held. Don had hosted that get-togather which drew Volunteers from as far away as Maryland. Now it is all gone.

Brian McMahon

Jerry Schaefer, Brian's old partner in Guateque (see Chap. 8), did stay in contact with Brian off and on through the years. "After our Peace Corps tour, he stayed in Colombia and worked for an artificial insemination company and married a girl from Cali. We lost touch for a few years and then by coincidence he sent a letter that arrived on the day of our first Peace Corps reunion in Rochester, NY. He was then working for Otis Elevator and living in England at that time."[48]

The next news Jerry received was a shock.

On Dec 22, 1995, Brian was flying to Cali to join his family, wife and 2 children, for Christmas. He was on AA Flight 965 that, through pilot and instrument error, crashed into the mountains near Cali. There were 4 survivors. I did not know of his death until a few years later when his sister Maureen kindly sent us a letter.[49]

Brian's obituary published in the Hartford Current tells the story.

A former executive for a subsidiary of United Technologies Corp. apparently was among the victims of an American Airlines plane crash in Colombia last week. The Boeing 757 flight out of Miami crashed into a mountain 50 miles from Cali, and the crash site is accessible only by foot or by rope from a helicopter, making efforts to recover victims' bodies difficult, The Times reported. Only four of 164 passengers aboard the flight are reported to have survived.

"We do know that he was on that plane," McMahon's aunt Marie Willis said. "His wife, Marta was already in Cali. His wife had relatives there. Every year, they have gone back to Cali for Christmas."

"Marta McMahon had already been joined in Cali by one of the couple's twin sons, Michael," Willis said. "The other twin, Patrick, lives in Australia." Marta McMahon had formed a search team with another woman, whose son was missing in the crash, to find the bodies of their relatives, The New York Times reported Saturday.

"My husband was coming from London to join us for Christmas," McMahon told the Times in an article published Saturday. "I can't find anything to remind

---

[48] Jerold Schaefer, personal email, June 15, 2009.
[49] Ibid.

me of him, not even his briefcase. I have spent a whole night here, hoping that the rescue teams can find something. But now, I cannot wait. I have spent seven hours on horseback looking for him - nothing. It is as if the forest had swallowed everything up."[50]

Brian was appointed president of Carrier Corp.'s European and transcontinental operations in October 1989. He left Carrier in 1992 to join the Sibee Group, a London based company, as president. He had also served as president of Otis Elevator's Latin American operations and had been a vice president at Otis and held vice president and general manager positions in Europe and Latin America in Inmont Corp. Brian had a bachelor's degree from Dartmouth College and an MBA in industrial management from Valle University in Colombia.

The members of Colombia '64 were saddened to hear of Brian's passing. He added much to the group during training and at the various gatherings in Colombia. He will be missed.

Margaret Mohler

I spent the first 32 years after Colombia teaching, one year 5th grade, 5 years at the junior high level and 26 in a high school. All my teaching has been in math. I also earned a masters degree in math education. Since then I have taken assorted graduate courses of interest.

I've traveled some in Europe, Mexico, the Caribbean on a couple of cruises, Cuba, Costa Rica and once to the Philippines and on to Hong Kong.

I returned to Colombia for a couple of weeks in the 90's with 11 other RCPVs. We visited Cartagena, Bogotá and Pereira. This trip was set up by the group "Friends of Colombia," the Colombian government and the Cafeteros. The trip was very interesting, but I discovered just how rusty my Spanish is. I'm really glad I was able to take the 2 weeks off from teaching. Guess having a school superintendent who was a Volunteer helped.[51]

At our stop in Cartagena, I found my old apartment, walked the walls and discovered that the prison cell area is now quite a tourist area. Our hotel was out on Boca Grande, the ritzy section of Cartagena, and we were treated to a wonderful dinner at Club de Pesca, traveling to and from the hotel by boat.[52]

Carol Oakes (Ford)

Like so many others of Colombia '64, Carol went back to school after her tour in the Peace Corps.

---

[50] "Brian D. McMahon," *Hartford Courant.*
[51] Margaret Mohler, personal email, Jan. 8, 2010.
[52] Margaret Mohler, personal email, May 22, 2009.

I attended the University of Oregon at Eugene and received a BA in Spanish. I returned home and continued studying at SUNY, Albany, NY and received an MA in Spanish Education. I married, had two children and moved to Florida where banking seemed to be the place for me.

I moved up the chain and became a Vice President for Nations Bank which is now Bank America. I retired from there in 1995 and we moved to South Carolina to "retire." My husband passed away in 2003.

I toured the United States with my mother and made a 6 week visit to rural Mexico (I actually drove my own vehicle) with my grandson who was 6 at the time. I must say that rural Mexico was just like Colombia in the 60's.

I am now working as a secretary at the First Baptist Church of Chester, South Carolina and raising the same grandson, now 13. I guess I'll keep working through braces (expensive).

Peace Corps was the defining moment in my life. I also did the NO NO – I married a Colombian and put him through school and then it was adios.

I have remained friends with the reunion group and that has always been important to me. I do see the world differently and can see why some of those who make surface visits are considered "ugly Americans." There is an appreciation for the rest of the world that I would not have except for my stint in Colombia.

Spanish has always been important to me. I used it all during the banking years in South Florida, and still run into people who need help in our community who are of Latin decent.

The area where Don Lydic and I were stationed was left with a school and lots of rabbits due to his work with the rabbit project. The 4-H club members learned how to cut out clothing without much of a pattern, making rope knotted purses and knitting. I also left behind friends who still write to me.

I would not have traded the experience for anything and am glad for the continued support for the program.[53]

Gary Peterson

As was the case with others, my draft board was waiting for me when I set foot on U.S. soil. In order to get back into college, I had to enroll in ROTC. I graduated with a degree in mechanical engineering, but was obliged to serve my time in the Air Force. The government sent me to the University of Utah in Salt Lake City for a degree in meteorology and there I met my wife, Pauline.

After five years as a weather forecaster in Massachusets where I picked up an MBA, I left the Air

---

[53] Carol Oakes Ford, personal email, Jan. 11, 2010.

Force at the end of the Vietnam War and went to work for Ford Motor Company in Dearborn, Michigan, then for a power equipment manufacturer in, of all places, Nebraska.

In 1984, with three daughters and lots of furniture, we moved to Utah where I took a job with the Air Force. Our fourth daughter was born here in Utah. My last assignment was as a radar engineer, which provided for some interesting trips to Hawaii, Puerto Rico, and the Arctic, from Point Barrow, Alaska, across Canada to Iceland. I retired from the government in 2007.

Pauline and I live just north of Salt Lake City, but make regular trips to the ranch in Montana and to visit children and our nine grandchildren. Two daughters and their families live here in Utah. We have one daughter in Texas and another in Louisiana.

I began writing magazine articles while still working for the government. This led to my first book, *Warrior Kings of Sweden,* published by McFarland in 2007. Much of the success of that book must be attributed to my wife, Pauline, who was my chief critic and editor. In assembling this book, Pauline has again spent hours reading and editing. I have also had the help of two daughters, Amanda did the cover design and Emily has helped with editing and proof reading.

Fortuitously, 2007 was also the year of our reunion in Nevada which gave me the idea to put this book together. The stories provided by the members of our group have been entertaining and enlightening. I have gained a real appreciation for the people that made up Colombia '64. This was one time the government got it right.

Arlene Ratliff (Rorapauph)

Arlene and her husband (and fellow Volunteer), Martin Rorapaugh, returned to the United States to raise a family. Our group lost track of her until a couple of years ago I was able to reach her son, Eric. Eric wrote, "I am sad to say that she passed away on March 11th, 1999. In 1996 she found out that she had colon cancer, and fought it well for 3 years. In growing up, I heard many stories of her life in the Peace Corp."[54]

For the second time we learned of the passing of a member of Colombia '64. This news was especially heartbreaking because Arlene was so well thought of by those in our group who knew her well. She was quietly self-effacing and inevitably cheerful, a sad loss for her family and our group.

Through Eric, I was able to reach Arlene's husband, Martin, who has generously contributed stories of their life in Bogotá for this book.

Jeanette Reeser (Cannon)

Jaunita (her Colombian name) returned to the United States to serve as Associate Director of a five year program at Wilmington College that involved recruiting students to serve in the Peace Corps as part of a studies curriculum to obtain an advanced degree.

Attending graduate school Jeannette met and married Bob Cannon, also attending graduate school. After completing their studies, Jeannette took her husband on a trip to Colombia where they stayed in Caloto with Celia's family. While there, she had a chance to renew old acquaintances.

Jeannette relates that Bill Higgins, the Community Action Volunteer in Santander that was a good friend of Jeannette and me, died some time ago of cancer.

---

[54] Eric Rorapaugh, personal email, Mar. 18, 2009.

Eugene Roberts

Eugene returned to Fairwood Farm in Glenn Dale, Maryland, and the family farm operation. He will be one of the hosts for our reunion that will coincide with the Peace Corps anniversary festivities in Washington D.C. the fall of 2011.

Jerold Schaefer

After his two years in the Peace Corps, Jerry headed back to Wisconsin, but returned to Colombia some years later.

> Vincent, the Colombian I mentioned earlier, was a life long friend, staying with my family in Wisconsin for six months. But I lost contact with him in about 1985. Then after 15 years, I was able to reach him when I went to Colombia in 2000. While there, I met his family. His daughter was married last weekend but unfortunately we were unable to attend the wedding.[55]

Carol Scharmer (Tobash)

Carol returned to Maryland and married Tom Tobash. She has been instrumental in organizing several of the reunions that have been the key in keeping our group in contact with one another. The last get together (2009) in Maryland for instance, "Carol Tobash did a great job of making the arrangements and making sure everyone was taken care of. Her husband Tom has become a mentor for several of us with our golf games."[56]

Milton Scott

Milt is working for the National Fatherhood Initiative as a Program Specialist for Community-Based Programming. He is married and has four children. After returning to the USA, he received his MBA from Harvard. Milty, as he was affectionately called in Peace Corps, passes on an observation most of us would agree with, "My theory is that the best job description (at least in our family) is that of the grandfather. Our kids are located in St. Louis, MO, Durham, NC, Baltimore, and Pittsburgh."[57]

> I'm in Western Pennsylvania, near Pittsburgh where I've lived most of the time since Peace Corps. My wife Christie (who visited me and the Fenimores in Colombia) and I have four adult married children, four grandchildren, and a fifth grandchild on the way.
> Probably the most interesting thing Christie and I have done over the past 3 years is to take 5 trips to Africa—mostly related to Lutheran Missions projects,

[55] Jerold Schaefer, personal email, June 15, 2009.
[56] Jerry Brelage, personal email, Sep. 29, 2009.
[57] Milton Scott, personal email, Feb. 18, 2009.

Habitat for Humanity construction projects, etc. We're expecting to go to South Africa again in May to help build housing for AIDS orphans, many of whom have lost both parents to AIDS.[58]

Rodney Spokely

After Peace Corps, it was back to the Red River Valley of the north for Rod where he took over the family farm. Besides joining Steve Burgess in horse trading some fine examples of Colombia's Paso Fino breed, he has battled the farmer's constant nemesis, the weather.

Rodney's house was completely surrounded with water. He moved his horses a few days early to a neighbor's place and moved his vehicles up on high ground. He had to rowboat from the house to higher ground for several days. No water got in his house. It was ok but had to rowboat to his vehicles which he had put on higher ground about one quarter mile away. [59]

Gerald Vogenau

Gerald has retired from his editor position at the Detroit Free Press. He has written two books, *Islands: Great Lakes' Stories* and *Shipwreck Hunter: Deep, Dark & Deadly in the Great Lakes*. Finally, he has time to pursue his passion, kayaking and do some mountain climbing. His latest adventure was a trip to Florida for some kayaking.

The Everglades were great [Gerald relates] -- mostly good weather, camping on white sand beaches with waving palms and -- this is big -- no mosquitoes.
As they say, a little slice of heaven.[60]

Kenneth Waissman

Talented and audacious, Ken was the showman of our group. He returned to New York and moved into show business seriously, apprenticing with veteran producer/director George Abbott. His first production was *Fortunes and Men's Eyes* followed by *Miss Reardon Drinks a Little*. He then discovered, promoted and produced *Grease* which ran for 3,882 performances, making it the longest running Broadway show up to that time. The Broadway show was also made into

---

[58] Milton Scott, personal email, Feb. 17, 2009.
[59] Steve Burgess, personal email to Jerry Brelage, Apr. 7, 2009.
[60] Gerald Volgenau, personal email, Apr. 6, 2009.

323

a movie. Among his other productions are, *Agnes of God* (a Tony Awards® winner) also made into a movie, *Torch Song Trilogy* (another Tony Awards® winner), *Street Corner Symphony, The Octette Bridge Club, Today I Was a Fountain Pen, Asinamali, New York Salutes Congress, V.I.P. Night on Broadway, Over Here!,* and the stage production of *The Days of Wine and Roses.* Ken is currently working on a new musical, *Josephine.*

Louie Jarussi tells of a visit he made to Ken's place in the Big Apple.

I went back to visit Tom Gallaher in New York in the late 70's and we went to visit Ken at his penthouse in down town New York. Ken had had a big hit by then, being the producer of *Grease*. It was fun visiting him and remembering old times.[61]

Michael Weber

I had two good years of pre-engineering studies under my belt at Southern Illinois University when Sargent Shriver came to campus and stimulated me to give Peace Corps a try.

The Shriver speech, the training in Nebraska and Puerto Rico, and the following 3 years really turned my world upside down – and clearly it seems it was for the better. I was also changed fundamentally much more than those I sought to help. You really come to understand better your own culture when you are able to see it through the eyes and expression of those looking at it from afar.

Thinking back to Colombia, there are likely a few farmers around Zuluaga, where I worked for 2 of the 3 years in-country who were helped with improved chickens, rabbits, and gardens, giving them at least a short-term boost.

But when I look back, I also think the more important contribution during this time was that I was fortunate to have a good Colombian counterpart extension agent, and our collaboration helped him make a spurt in his training and work. Even while in Colombia, his knowledge and contributions to small farmers grew to be much greater and more lasting than were mine.

Following the 3 years in Colombia, I returned to SIU to finish my undergraduate work, but turned back to my roots, taking up agricultural economics instead of continuing in engineering. Then I headed off to Michigan State University to work on an MS and PhD degree in agricultural economics.

I married in 1971 and we have two wonderful daughters.

Soon after finishing my PhD in 1976, I was hired by MSU to teach and help with research projects at the Federal University of Ceara, in Fortaleza, Northeast Brazil where I had to learn Portuguese.

After 2 years in the classroom I was pretty fluent, and have kept it so, along with Spanish. Yet today speaking in either Spanish or Portuguese, I still mix the two confusing myself, my wife and others.

---

[61] Louie Jarussi, personal email, Jul. 11, 2008.

Following that work, I returned to MSU to work on research, outreach and teaching in the international agricultural development and agricultural marketing area. I have been here ever since.

I was able to work on short-term assignments for a few years in locations in the Eastern Caribbean, Bolivia and Ecuador. I also got involved with four great PhD students doing field work in Thailand, which was my first exposure to Asia and to 12 hour time zone changes – a hefty price to pay to get there. This work was great and yet another eye opener for me.

Then more changing winds swept in. Most Latin American countries were considered to have "graduated" from US foreign development assistance while funding for similar work became available for Africa. I helped build and direct a food security in Africa program, here at MSU from 1986 to 2006. Among other things during that time I went off to Quebec for total immersion training in French and later took a sabbatical leave in Montpellier, France, working with an international agricultural research institute and studying more French.

In 1996, my first wife decided it was time to move on from our marriage. I recovered from that change and remarried in 2000 to Francisca, whom I met in East Lansing, but is originally from Guayaquil, Ecuador. So Spanish is now dominant over the Portuguese!

Over these years of working in Africa my focus was with students, and setting up and backstopping field-level applied research, outreach and in-service training in many countries. Through repeated short-term trips of 2-3 weeks, I got to know reasonably well rural life in Senegal, Rwanda, Mali, Zimbabwe, Zambia and Mozambique(where I used my Portuguese).

In 2006, I stepped down from being Co-Director of this work, and my wife and I decided to take up an MSU assignment back in the field, this time focusing on food security in Zambia, (in Southern Africa) for some 2.5 years, living in the capital city of Lusaka. One of the things we do in these projects is to work with host country partners to carry-out national-level social-economic surveys of small farm households. So I really got to know a lot about the reality of smallholders over the entire country, and to work with a great group of Zambians. We truly enjoyed the Zambia experience but funds for keeping me involved in-country ran out, and in the summer of 2009, we moved back to our house in East Lansing. I am now back at MSU, working mostly to backstop campus on-going work in Zambia. If we can keep the grant funding coming, I will continue to make 3-4 short-term trips there each year. I will also be 66 this coming June, and my wife says it's time to think about retiring. Maybe then we will have time to attend more of the great PINA '64 reunions.[62]

---

[62] Michael Weber, personal email, Feb. 1, 2010.

21

COLOMBIA – A RETURN TO TURBULENCE

The Volunteers of Colombia '64 left Colombia, but they were only 41 of some 600 Volunteers in the country at that time and they would be replaced by new Volunteers. So the Peace Corps remained a factor in the country. The country the members of Colombia '64 left behind was a nation that once again seemed to be righting itself after the disastrous Violencia of the 1950s. Most of the bandit groups had been tracked down and eliminated or reduced to ineffective pillaging and occasional kidnappings, a nuisance, but not a serious threat to national stability. The government was gaining control thanks to the Liberal-Conservative cooperation in establishing the National Front. Once again, a talented people and resource rich country seemed to be on the path to prosperity. Sadly, it was not to be. As Bob Bezdeck points out, "Since we left in 1966, some critical themes are the rise of drug dealers and the dramatic increase in political violence." [1] Because of the increased danger inherent in these trends, the number of Volunteers was reduced and their movements restricted.

> I made contact with a RPCV from Colombia named Tom. He and his wife, or the PVC nurse who became his wife, were in Colombian in '78-'80 [reports Charlie Lenkner]. He was in Antioquia circa Medellín and worked for the "coffee growers," the Cafeteros (who along with the big breweries funded about everything as I recall). He said that while he was there, the Peace Corps Program had about 200 Volunteers and that a third of Colombia was considered off limits due to the kidnapping of a Volunteer in Santa Marta. Seems the Volunteer was recovered intact. [2]

As the violence increased, the number of Volunteers in country was reduced until in 1984, the last Volunteers were removed from the country all together.

The descent into near anarchy was not immediate however. In May 1966, Carlos Lleras Restrepo, a Liberal, was elected president as the National Front candidate, replacing Conservative Guillermo León Valencia, the president while Colombia '64 was in the country for most of their tour. During the Lleras administration, some of the old bandit groups, those with communist leanings, began to revive aided by outside money. They turned to aggressive guerrilla warfare. Among these were the Fuerzas Armados Revolucianarios de Colombia (FARC) and the Ejeraito de Liberacion Nacional (ELN).

In the 1970 election, the National Front candidate, Misael Pastrana Borrero, was challenged by former dictator General Gustav Rojas Pinilla. Four recounts were required to determine the outcome, in Pastrana's favor. Following their defeat, many of the Rojas supporters joined another guerrilla organization, the *Movimiento 19 de Abril* (M-19) which grew rapidly and vowed to topple the government.

For the 1972 election, the National Front was dissolved in accordance with its charter (there was a 16 year sunset provision) and the two party system was reinstated for presidential and congressional elections. The next two elections were narrowly won by

---

[1] Robert Bezdek, personal email, Jul. 15, 2008.
[2] Charlie Lenkner, personal email, Apr. 6, 2009.

Liberal candidates, Alfonso López Mechelsen (1974) and Julio Cécar Turbay Ayala (1978). Because of the close election and the rising guerrilla violence, both presidents continued the practice of including the out-of-power party in their cabinets and other government posts.

But political violence continued to grow with two new elements being added. Drug refining and trafficking in Colombia began to infect the country during the decade. To make matters worse, the multitude of small independent drug operators became organized, first as the Medellín Cartel and later as the rival and eventual winner, the Cali Cartel. Therefore, more violence was added to the country's woes by the competing drug lords. Finally, right-wing paramilitary groups began to take the law into their own hands creating still more chaos and violence to the point that both presidents were forced to declare a state of siege at times, assuming special powers to try and deal with the terrorism.

A Conservative, Belisario Betancur Cuartas, was elected in 1982. Again, he included the opposing party (Liberals) in his administration and he began a policy of trying to negotiate with the various guerrilla groups. He was able to secure a truce and cease fire with FARC, but made little progress with the other organizations. The end of his term was punctuated by the seizure of the Palace of Justice by members of M-19 on November 6-7, 1985. During the military's storming of the building, it was destroyed by fire and 115 people were killed including 11 Supreme Court Justices. "Many citizens were furious with the government."[3]

Liberals won the next three presidential elections, Virgilio Barco Vargasa (1986), Cesar Gaviria (1990) and Ernesto Samper (1994). Political violence continued unabated with escalating conflict between right-wing paramilitary groups, drug lords, leftist guerrillas and government military and security forces. In September 1989, M-19 formerly gave up its armed struggle and committed itself to pursuing its ends through political means. But FARC, in 1990, broke its truce with the government and resumed its campaign of murder and kidnappings.

Beginning with the death of Medellín Cartel leader Pablo Escobar in a police shootout in December 1993, some success was achieved in cracking down on the powerful drug cartels. Eventually, these large organizations were broken up, but that has only resulted in many smaller drug groups competing and killing each other. However, this fragmentation has reduced the political influence once wielded by the drug lords.

Meanwhile, FARC, estimated at 15,000 members, negotiated a deal with the government by which the government agreed to remove all security forces from an area south of Bogotá effectively turning over a quarter of the country to FARC control. By this time the drug traffickers and leftist guerrillas had formed symbiotic relationships increasing the power and resources of both.

The election of 1998 returned the Conservatives to power with Andrés Pastrana winning a 50.5% majority. He turned to the United States for help in combating the violence in his country, negotiating the "Plan Colombia" with America, a one billion dollar initiative to root out the drugs and leftists. Emphasis was on military action over the economic programs preferred by the people. Pastrana also attempted to negotiate settlements with the guerrillas which went nowhere and his popularity declined. His

---

[3] Robert Bezdek, personal email, Jul. 15, 2008.

administration was hampered by high unemployment, increasing guerrilla attacks by FARC and ELN, widespread drug trafficking and the expansion of paramilitary groups.

Alvaro Uribe, a Harvard and Oxford educated lawyer and former Liberal Party leader, ran as an independent in the 2002 election on a platform of getting tough with the guerrillas and drug traffickers. He won with 53.1% of the vote, a veritable landslide in Colombia. Uribe built a coalition of Liberal and Conservative legislators allowing him to push through laws and programs to deal with the drugs and violence.

FARC, which had lost its "liberated zone" in 2001, fought back launching several attacks on major cities, including a rocket attack on the presidential palace, killing 19 people. The war between Uribe and the guerrillas was on. For the first time, American Special Forces were directly engaged in Colombia on an operation in Arauca, a department on the Venezuelan border.

Uribe also pushed through legislation expanding international trade (though a free trade agreement with the U.S. presently languishes without Senate approval), providing for new means of industrial development and initiating reforms in the judicial system. By 2004, his aggressive prosecution of the war against guerrilla factions had reduced homicides, kidnappings and terrorist attacks by 50%, to the lowest levels in 20 years.

As to the drug war, Uribe arrested and extradited more traffickers to the U.S. and other countries than all other presidents combined. The paramilitary organizations began to demobilize *en masse* cutting violence from that source.

Supporters of Uribe arranged to have the Colombian constitution amended to allow him to run for a second term. He was reelected in 2006 by a 62% vote becoming the first Colombian president to be re-elected in over a century.

Uribe maintained good relations with other Latin American countries even those with leftist leaders including Cuba. He was on good terms with Venezuelan president Hugo Chávez until 2007 when relations began to sour.

On March 1, 2008 Colombian troops killed FARC top officer Raúl Reyes in a camp inside Ecuador. This incursion caused some tension between the two countries and the condemnation of the Organization of American States (OAS). FARC was dealt another blow when its commander, Pedro Antonio Marín (known by his *nom de guerre*, Manuel Marulanda Vélez or his nick name, Tiro Fijo – Sureshot) died of a heart attack on March 26th of the same year. This was the same Tiro Fijo that was roaming the mountains with his bandit group when Colombia '64 was in country. And finally, in July 2008, a rescue operation conducted by Colombian Special Forces disguised as FARC guerrillas freed Senator and former presidential candidate Ingrid Betancraft, Americans, Marc Gonsalves, Thomas Howes and Keith Stansell, and 11 Colombian soldiers and police officers. The once formidable communist organization that had had its own territorial state was reduced to running and hiding.

Given the descent into chaos and what seems to now be a recovery, did the work of Colombia '64 make any difference to the country? Did any of the 4,600 Volunteers that served there between 1961 and 1984 make a difference?

This is a hard question to answer definitively. We know that the country as a whole made progress in spite of the anarchy. We have the testimonies of Volunteers who have returned to see for themselves. Betsy "Rosita" Long Bucks was there in 2007.

Our trip to Colombia in February was awesome. Cartegena was the site for the reunion of 175 Colombian Volunteers planned by Friends of Colombia and the Colombian Embassy. It was terrific with so many stories and tales to share. Dale (Betsy's husband) loved Bogotá which now has mass transit, bike lanes on Sunday for 6 hours of R & R, of course there were vendors to fix your bike and nourish you.

Another highlight was visiting my site, Altagracia, which now has paved roads; teachers commute from Pereira for their classes; the vocational school is huge with high school students coming from Pereira to learn about agriculture, coffee, cashews, fish farming, etc. Paneca, near Armenia, would be a great site for a reunion. Carolyn Denton put us in touch with the general manager. Everything went so well. *Hasta pronto!*[4]

Margaret Mohler told of returning to Cartagena to find it beautiful and much more modern than when she was there forty years ago. Jeff Andrews tells much the same story.

"Cartagena was not like it is today," Jeff says. "When I was there the largest hotel in the city was El Caribe, a two story complex. The boom in high rise condominiums has

Cartagena today

occurred in the last few years. Much of the old section in Cartagena has been restored. Houses, schools and convents have been turned into 5 star hotels and B&Bs. The Hotel Santa Teresa used to be a convent."[5]

---

[4] Betsy Long Bucks, personal email, Jul. 9, 2008.
[5] Jeff Andrews, personal email, Feb. 26, 2009.

Tom Galleher took his family to Colombia and discovered the good and the bad of modernization.

To celebrate our 30th anniversary [Tom writes] we took our children to Colombia in 1996 (our first visit since leaving in 1967) and revisited our old Peace Corps sites. Change was everywhere: high rise buildings in Villavicenco; Barranquilla had doubled in size, and the once pristine beaches of Santa Marta were grimy with the residue of coal slurry.

One of the most noticeable changes was the amount of trash littering the countryside. After three weeks traveling around Columbia, I was beginning to think, the plastic trash bags which we encountered almost everywhere festooning bushes and trees should be nominated as Colombia's national flower – the downside of progress and development.[6]

The Fenimores have heard from their old site of Silvia.

"We are told that the mayor of Silvia and governor of Cauca are both Guambianos. (We have not verified this). The Guambianos now have their own market buses, roads to the villages, etc. so they can do their own deliveries and not be captive of the town market."[7]

And through all this, Colombia continued to produce important literature. "G.G.Marquez received the Noble Prize for Literature in 1982, two big books for him were/are *LOVE IN THE TIME OF CHOLERA* and *100 YEARS OF SOLITUDE*."[8]

So, in spite of the political turmoil, Colombia has made progress in modernizing. But did Peace Corps contribute anything to advancing these improvements? Again, it is not possible to quantify or even find grounds for a solid argument either way.

However, on a personal basis, on the local scale, in terms of the village, the vereda, the community, the family and the individual, a little more may be determined. Probably the first to investigate the effects of their service was Doug Dunn who actually did a study, thanks to his academic pursuits. Doug's study showed that the families that had participated and followed through with his chicken project had increased family incomes an average of 25%. So, here is real evidence of meaningful improvement from work done by a Volunteer.

The Fenimores returned to Silvia to find the chicken improvement breeding program they started was still going ten years later. The other practice they initiated that caught on was contour farming, replacing the old method of cultivating up and down the hills.

Steve Burgess visited his site with Rodney Spokely and their wives.

On our return visit ten years later I was really pleased with the progress. The 4th and 5th grade class room that I had started, but did not complete, was now finished. The water line bringing running water from the mountain to the community was now finished. The commercial tomato farm was

---

[6] Tom Gallaher, personal email, Feb. 2, 2010.
[7] Bob Fenimore, personal email, Mar. 26, 2009.
[8] Charlie Lenkner, personal email, Feb. 22, 2009.

still operating. The chicken farm was going again. The community now had electricity and every one had a TV.[9]

Bruce Borrud returned with his wife in 1976 to find many of the fish ponds still in operation and old friends that still remembered him.

Carolyn Hawkins Denton (Bruce's partner) also returned to Boyacá, and Cauca. Visiting in 1969, she found things unchanged, for the most parting, in the three years since serving there.

However, of equal importance may be the long lasting personal relationships that some Volunteers developed with Colombians. Bruce kept in contact with Luis Eduardo Moreno and visited him in 1976. He also kept in contact with the Munoz family as did Carolyn. In 2005-06, Carolyn hosted Carolina Munoz as an exchange student. Perhaps it is these kinds of people to people relationships that are the most important.

For many of us who did not stay in contact with Colombians, I think Jerry Brelage expresses our sentiments:

> I may have had an effect on the Nucleo in general, but I don't think I changed many individual lives. For anyone working in an educational setting it is difficult to see short term accomplishments.
>
> It may be possible to attribute to Peace Corps some element in Colombia's recovery from the anarchy of the 80's and 90's. Obviously many Colombians feel there was an impact because President Uribe has requested that Peace Corps return.[10]

In the letter of invitation President Uribe describes the special relationship between our two countries epitomized by Peace Corps involvement:

> When we review the history of Colombia it is very clear that with the arrival of the first Peace Corps Volunteers in 1961, under President John F. Kennedy's initiative and Colombia's President Alberto Lleras' vision, a wide door opened to an enriching and enduring relationship for both our countries. The benefits were immeasurable and when the Peace Corps decided to withdraw from Colombia all the Volunteers came back home with a feeling of leaving a second family and an unfinished job in villages and in remote communities.
>
> I want to once again extend an invitation so that new generations of Peace Corps Volunteers unite with us and that with all our institutional support both countries can design and plan new programs that can help us better the conditions of our underprivileged population and strengthen and enrich new ties of friendship between our countries.
>
> We know what a valuable contribution the Peace Corps makes to both our countries.[11]

---

[9] Steve Burgess, personal email, Jan. 9, 2010.

[10] Jerry Brelage, personal email, Jan. 8, 2010.

[11] Alvara Uribe Vélex, *Presendante de la Republico de Colombia*, to Ms. Jody K. Olson, Acting Director, Peace Corps, Feb. 18, 2009.

And in just the last few months two important events have occurred. On April 7, 2010, Juan Manuel Santos Calderón was inaugurated President of the Republic of Colombia. Santos has an impressive résumé in Colombian government including former Minister of Foreign Trade, Minister of Finance and Minister of National Defense. Originally from Bogotá, his education credentials include degrees from the Escuela Naval de Cartagena, an MBA from the University of Kansas and a master degree from the London School of Economics, and degrees from Harvard and Tuffs University. As RPCVs of Colombia, we certainly wish President Santos success with his administration and prosperity for Colombia.

The second item is the return of Peace Corps Volunteers to Colombia. On May 11, 2010, Colombia's Foreign Minister signed an accord with Director of the Peace Corps, Aaron S. Williams, agreeing to the return of Volunteers after an absence of almost three decades.

> The first group of about 20 Volunteers will arrive in Colombia in the fall or last quarter of this year (2010), and they will work as English teachers in primary and secondary schools and at institutions for teacher training.
>
> They will also work on community development initiatives along Colombia's northern coast.[12]

It is indeed heartening to see the progress Colombia has made in the last few years and the return of Peace Corps Volunteers is just icing on the cake. Perhaps, this time, Colombia is truly on the road to a prosperous future. No country has suffered more or endured more hardships in its quest for a bright future. As former Volunteers in Colombia and with a love for this, our adopted country, we can only wish the people of Colombia all the best.

---

[12] "Peace Corps to Return to Colombia After 3 Decades," *Latin American Herald Tribune*, January 7, 2011, p.1.

EPILOGUE
PEACE CORPS SINCE

Some reminders of the early days – Colombia '64 days - of the Peace Crops have cropped up recently. An obituary in a newspaper recalls the memory of a few of the people who helped build the Peace Corps.

CSU professor, architect of Peace Corps dies.
FORT COLLINS, Colo. — Maurice Albertson, a Colorado State University researcher and an architect of the Peace Corps, has died after a brief illness. He was 90.

Albertson and fellow CSU researchers Andrew Rice and Pauline Birky-Kreutzer responded to a request for a proposal in 1960 from the federal government for a model to encourage the nation's youths to serve in Third World countries. The three wrote a book that set up the basic design of the Peace Corp.

The program was officially launched in 1961 by President John F. Kennedy. It now has more than 190,000 Volunteers serving in 139 developing countries.
"Maury was an extraordinary man who truly embodied the best of America," Peace Corps Director Ronald A. Tschetter said in a statement. "The many people whose lives Maury touched will always remember him, and for those of us in the Peace Corps family, we will remain forever indebted to him for his vision and commitment to volunteerism and international fellowship."[1]

And Ron Halter ran across a bit of news that stirred his memory of an earlier time.

I heard Maria Shriver's testimony before Congress the other day. I had no idea that R. Sargent Shriver was still alive. He was our director and the first Director of the Peace Corps. Now, he is 93 and suffering with severe Alzheimer's. What a pity that he is in such a state. He must have had numerous experiences setting up the Peace Corps that no subsequent director could have had. It appears that all of his stories may be lost.[2]

As this book goes to press, we learned of Sargent Shriver's passing on January 18, 2011, just three days short of the 50th anniversary of President Kennedy's request of Robert Sargent Shriver, "to report how the Peace Corps could be organized and then to organize it."[3]

The Peace Corps has changed significantly since those early days of 1964-67. Tom Gallaher reports on the changes in the training program he experienced as "resident shrink" for a group bound for Samoa in 1971.

---

[1] *CSU professor, architect of Peace Corps dies,* http://www.coloradoan.com, (Jan. 12, 2009).
[2] Ron Halter, personal email, Mar. 26, 2009
[3] Gerard T. Rice, *The Bold Experiment,* (Notre Dame, Indiana: University of Notre Dame Press, 1985), p. 35.

This was one of the first Peace Corps training projects where the training was done in country. It was a rather small group, about twenty Volunteers. By that time Peace Corps' MO had moved from accepting the BA generalist with no specific skill set, sticking a pin in the map, and dropping them off with the hope he or she would do more good than harm, to a more professional approach. The new paradigm was to recruit Volunteers with specific skills to fill specific jobs.

In the training program we had accountants, engineers, physical therapists, two experts in aquaculture, nurses, horticulturists, attorneys and architects. A Peace Corps architect helped design and build the Samoan Parliament Building. The training program emphasized language training, cultural studies and cultural sensitivity and adaptability.

Their selection process became one of self selection. My job was to help the trainees determine if they really wanted to commit two years of their lives to living and working in Samoa.[4]

Tom's description of the program is corroborated by books I have read, written by recent Volunteers. The Peace Corps seems to have reverted to the emphasis on highly skilled Volunteers trained for specific positions, the approach used in the first two groups that went to Ghana and Tanzania in 1961 (see Chapter 2). It was the first group to go to Colombia where the Peace Corps experimented with generalists, the practice used through our group's selection and many that followed, the emphasis being on person to person relationships and a belief in the ability of motivated young Americans to improvise and develop programs on their own initiative.

Besides the change in emphasis on skills, the training and selection is obviously different. The new method of training "in country" may be more efficient and perhaps less expensive, but I certainly believe our time spent at the University of Nebraska was an integral part of the whole Peace Corps experience and I would not have missed it for the world.

And the selection process has been revamped; I suppose to make it less stressful. Perhaps a good idea though it takes some of the toughness out of the program.

Changes in the organization are, of course, inevitable; revisions must be made to accommodate the changing world environment. There is no longer a Cold War, the impetus for the creation of the Peace Corps in the first place. In our day, service was as much about blunting the advancement of communism (Castro, Che and the like) as it was about improving the lives of those we served. Though the two were inexorably entwined, I hope, we certainly believed, and apparently the U.S. government assumed.

Today the Peace Corps must stand on its own as a means of improving conditions or providing a needed service to the peoples and nations it serves. Maybe the Peace Corps has become more professional, there certainly is more emphasis on Volunteers with specialized backgrounds, educations and technical skills, engineers, medical people, trained school teachers, etc. Perhaps this is all to the good. But it was the belief, in the early days of the Peace Corps, that young, idealists without specific skills could make a difference that gave us the opportunity to serve in Colombia, an opportunity for which I will be forever grateful.

---

[4] Tom Gallaher, personal email, Feb. 2, 2010.

Appendix I
ANCIENT COLOMBIA

Rich Bennett's site, San Agustín, coincided with an area renowned for stone monuments, artifacts and subterranean structures, a legacy left by an ancient people who had occupied that region thousands of years earlier. Ron and Steve, in Tolima, traversed ground where flint tools and weapons were commonly found and to the west of their site was an area known for the quantity of gold that had been extracted from burial mounds, another reminder that a pre-Colombian populous had existed in this country long before the European conquest.

To comprehend Colombia today, it is necessary to have an understanding of the indigenous inhabitance that is the base of the nation's population. All the other races were newcomers, intruders that added their customs and traditions to the civilizations and societies already there, like the building blocks of a pyramid set on a foundation layer of stones, the Amerindian substructure. The Conquistadors discovered a native civilization already established when they first set foot on Colombia's beaches. What they found was a complex patchwork of societies, tribes and empires that had been forming and reforming over millenniums, a native system of governments, traditions and religions, constructed on an economy of domesticated plants and animals adapted to this diverse geography.

So who were the first Colombians? What kind of people initially traversed the mountains and valleys of this north-western part of South America?

We know that humans had reached the southern tip of South America by 10,000 BC.[1] The arrival of these people to this southern continent almost certainly was via Colombia and the Isthmus of Panama as navigation and boat building skills sufficient for an over-water route did not exist until later.

Stone artifacts, scrapers and knives, found on the Pacific Coast and in the interior suggest an early occupation by hunter-gatherers preceding the later hunters of the Late Pleistocene mammals (mastodons, amerhippus, mylodons, etc.). These giant animals may have persisted in South America longer than in North America. By 7000 BC, however, the climate had modified with dryer, cooler conditions contributing to the extinction of the maga-fauna. The humans of Colombia in that distant past were forced to adapt. They had to turn to hunting small game supplemented by fishing and the gathering of wild plants.

By 3000 BC a distinctive culture had developed along the Colombian Caribbean coast. The so called Shell-mound Dwellers were semi-nomadic people who subsisted on small-game, fishing and foraging. They left behind large mounds of their refuse composed mainly of sea shells. Sometimes these mounds were partially leveled to make a site for a later occupation. Over the next 2000 years this culture spread along the coast, into lagoons and river estuaries. This first identifiable culture in Colombia is especially significant because it produced the earliest pottery anywhere in the Western Hemisphere.[2] At first there were only crude and simple bowls, but later there are variations in construction and decorations are added.

---

[1] Reichel-Dolmatoff, G., *Colombia* (London: Thames and Hudson, 1965), p.41.
[2] Reichel-Dolmatoff, G., *Colombia* (London: Thames and Hudson, 1965), p.54.

Gradually, offshoots of this culture migrated up the Magdalena, Cauca, Sinú and San Jorge River valleys. As the culture moved, either by population migration or by people already established along these rivers adopting the culture, agricultural practices changed. Gathering gave way to cultivation of root crops, principally, varieties of manioc which probably came from Venezuela by way of the sea coast.

The several species of manioc, called yuca in Colombia, may be divided into two categories, sweet yuca, and bitter yuca. Bitter yuca contains prussic acid (a cyanogen) which gives the tuber its bitter taste and makes it unpalatable. In sweet yuca, the acid content is so low that it can be eaten raw or cooked and eaten without processing. The bitter yuca, however, must be ground, soaked and then squeezed dry to remove the poisonous acid. Over time, the sweet manioc came to be the primary source of dietary starch in Colombia's western lowlands while cultivation of bitter manioc spread into the eastern plains and southern jungles where it is abundant today. In addition, this rich food source has been disseminated to all parts of the tropical world and is now one of mankind's major staples. In the United States, it is used as the basis for tapioca.

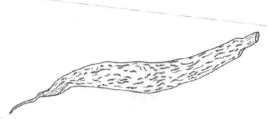

Yuca root-tuber (manioc or cassava)

Along with root crop cultivation came more permanent settlements and a refinement of pottery making and decorating. Again, the new pottery traditions may have come from Venezuela along with the manioc.

About 700 BC the climate of the coastal plains and associated interior lowlands changed from semi-arid to a more humid environment with greater rainfall. Shortly after the weather modification, implements associated with maize cultivation and use began to appear in artifacts. Corn had been cultivated in Mexico since 3500 BC, but only showed up in South America at the close of the pre-Christian era.

Moreover, along with the maize tools, new pottery designs and other implements appear such as bird shaped whistles. This suggests a migration, possibly from Central America, was involved rather than an assimilation of ideas only. This lowland culture, called Momil II, also saw the introduction of ritual cannibalism, the first use of gold to make jewelry in Colombia, and clay figurines probably of religious significance.

Corn farming allowed the culture and population density to spread from the tropical lowlands and deep valleys into the mountain sides and hill tops. Where there had been only the occasional hunter passing through, there were now permanent settlements in groups of three or four families. This migration up into the mountains caused a diversification of culture. No longer connected by a river, lagoon or sea coast, these new settlements, over time, developed their own traditions, tools, clothing, agricultural practices and probably religions.

Some of the Colombian '64 Volunteers found themselves in communities where distinct clothing was worn and social customs were at variance with mainstream Colombia. These "Indians" and their cultures are a result of this mountain isolation and their origins often date back to this invasion of the cordilleras by these early corn growing farmers. Later migrations, the coming of the Spanish and modern infrastructure sometimes sealed off these communities in the high mountains preserving a way of life

Likeness of a San Agustín stone statue.
Height of these statues range up to 17 feet.

developed over thousands of years. The distinctive Guambianos of Silvia, the Paez of Cauca and the Kogi of the Sierra Nevada de Santa Marta, all people Colombia '64 Volunteers came into contact with, fit this category.

By the beginning of the Christian era the mountains of Colombia were populated with small communities of maize growing farmers while the tropical lowlands and coastal areas maintained their manioc-maize cultures.

Beginning about 500 BC a new outside influence appears along the Pacific coast of Colombia. This is an advanced culture of a Mesoamerican type with characteristics related to Gulf of Mexico traditions. These invaders apparently arrived by sea-going canoe or raft, and planted colonies in the estuaries and islands mainly between the mouth of the San Juan River, in the Buenaventura area, and Tumaco Island near the Ecuadorian border. The early colonies were reinforced by waves of immigrants of these maize growing farmers and they began to move inland crossing the Western Cordilleras into the Cauca Valley. This outside culture brought with it an advanced pottery tradition, thin-walled bowls with hollow mammiform supports, bridged double spouts, red and brown-slipped ware with incised geometric designs and anthropomorphic figures.

Influenced by these new Mesoamerican settlers along the west coast, several advanced cultures or civilizations arose in the southern part of the Western and Central Cordilleras. Here population densities reached a level that craft specialization and social stratification occurred. The most well known of these is the archeological site of San Agustín along the head waters of the Magdalena River where the Central and Eastern Cordilleras split - Rich Bennet's site.

The first visitor to the site that has left us a record was Friar Juan de Santa Gertudis who met a priest there from Popayán in 1757. The priest was digging for gold in the graves and mounds of the area. It is due to these treasure hunters that the monuments and artifacts were discovered and became known to the outside world. In 1935, the Colombian government established an Archaeological Park in the area containing the principle ruins of this culture.

Strewn across the area are earthen mounds, stone lined shelters or galleries and a variety of graves. The earthen mounds, some as large as 120 feet in diameter and 15 feet high, cover temple-like rooms, measuring 15 by 20 feet made of large stone slabs. These subterranean structures often bear traces of geometric designs painted in dull colors. The chambers usually contain carved stone statues or stone sarcophagi.

There are stone shelters that protect stone statues scattered about the area. Other statues and reliefs carved in rock are in the open, some as large as twelve feet in height. They are of humans, frogs, lizards and mammals. But the classic statues are of human or demonic figures with large heads, short squat bodies and thick limbs. Often the faces have feline sharp pointed canines reminiscent of the Mesoamerican jaguar culture.

The graves range from simple pits and stone lined structures to deep shaft graves and there are large multiple burial pits.

Pottery found in the graves is colored brown, red or orange and decorated with incised geometric designs. Also, found in the more elaborate grave sites are gold objects, nose ornaments, ear pendants and small necklace beads. This is the gold for which the priest was searching.

The San Agustín "civilization" began about 555 BC building wooden structures, then turning to stone as a building material later. It flourished into the 13th Century AD, a time span of over 1,700 years. This was a civilization with staying power.

Just north of San Agustín is another and possibly related archaeological site. It has similarities to its southern neighbor in pottery, cists, shaft graves, carved boulders and statues, but is most notable for the large underground rooms chiseled out of the soft rock that underlays the area. Entry is by steep spiral staircases, the tops of which are covered by rock slabs. The oval or round subterranean rooms have square columns supporting flat, slanted or vaulted ceilings. The interiors of these rooms are painted with black, white, red and yellow abstract designs of parallel lines, concentric rhomboids and circles along with large human faces. On the floors are urns and shallow pits with human skeletal remains.

To the west along the headwaters of the Calima River in the Western Cordillera, due east of Buenaventura, another archaeological area has been exposed, mostly by treasure hunters. Here are found terraced house sites petroglyphs and ancient fields laid out in large squares. Most interesting are the human effigies, discovered among the pottery, figurines and anthropomorphic containers, with facial features of almond-shaped eyes, thick lips of a Negroid character and deep vertical furrows on either side of the mouths accenting full cheeks. Of interest to the Spanish, and even modern

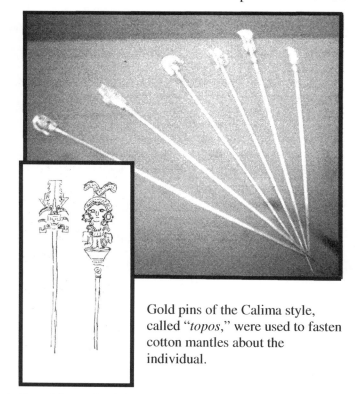

Gold pins of the Calima style, called "*topos*," were used to fasten cotton mantles about the individual.

treasure hunters, are the graves, shafts with vaulted lateral chambers containing pottery and objects of gold, masks, breast-plates, diadems, bracelets, necklaces, nose and ear rings, spoons and more. The goldsmithing is often complex combining cast elements with hammered parts.

To the east and a little north of the Calima sites, in the Central Cordillera and extending into the Cauca Valley is a rich archaeological area known as Quimbaya. When the Spanish arrived here in about 1540, the region was occupied by a tribe called the Quimbaya who resisted the Spanish fiercely under their chieftain Tacurumbi.

The Spanish were dogged in their conquest of these people because of the tribe's fame as goldsmiths. The Conquistadors won the war and took the gold from the Quimbaya. The Quimbaya, as it turns out, had only been in the area a short time having moved in from the north. After looting the Quimbaya, the Spanish discovered that beneath the ground were the graves of a more ancient people. Shaft graves, some with side chambers, slab-lined graves, single pit and multiple burials, and even the large underground Tierradentro-style chambers were found. In these graves have been discovered a treasure trove of ceramics, containers in the shapes of birds, toads, mammals and other animals. Unusual square containers, and beautifully decorated vases and jars are hidden in these graves. Gold in its pure form was cast, forged and hammered into nose pieces, breast plates, masks and jewelry. *Tumbaga*, an alloy of gold and copper, was used as well as pure copper to make bells, disks and wire. The whole region is still one of the richest in Colombia for grave looters who supply private and even public antiquity collections.

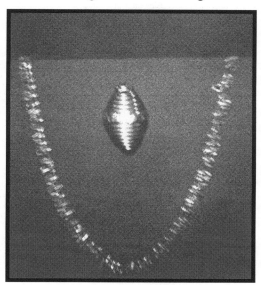

Gold necklace and pendant of the Quimbaya style.

Finally, there is the Tumaco culture, near the Ecuadorian border, which includes, not just the island, but the coastal area to the north and south. Here are found pottery of a very high quality. Ceramics characteristic of this culture are the anthropomorphic figurines. These are of animals, jaguars, reptiles, owls, snakes and imaginary creatures like a dragon-type monster with fangs and a tongue sticking out. Human figurines showing women with infants, masked people, warriors and chieftains in elaborate feather headdresses. The details show period hair styles, skirts, aprons and loin-cloths, jewelry and head ornaments. This pottery indicates there was continuing contact with both Peru and sea coasts to the north. Chavín from Peru, Mayan and Mexican influences are clearly indicated.

While areas of the cordilleras were developing socially, economically, and culturally, regions of the lowlands were making progress also. In part this was due to the spread of intensive maize farming and partly because the sea coast and river systems were being used more and more as trade routes. Salt, gold, cotton, cloth, certain valuable feathers and seashells were being traded over long distances. More advanced pottery and anthropomorphic figurines show up along the Caribbean coast particularly in the area of the Ranchería River and the Sierra Nevada mountains off the northern end of the Eastern

Cordilleras. Even the Guajira Peninsula has produced artifacts indicating craft specialization, a product of dense population. At times the peninsula must have been much more fertile than the dry desert it is today.

Even more advanced, however, was a culture identified by the large burial mounds they built along the Sinú and San Jorge rivers. The pottery associated with this culture is very advanced with human figures molded and then attached to containers in some cases. Gold objects include nose pendants and earrings, wrist and neck jewelry, hollow-cast figurines of birds, reptiles, mammals and fantastic creatures. Known as the Betancí-Viloria complex, the culture was probably derived from mountain traditions moving back into the lowlands and was still flourishing when the Spanish arrived in the Sinú Valley about 1530. They describe three federations of tribes each ruled by a chieftain or *cacique,* Fincenú (along the Sinú), Pancenú (on the San Jorge drainage), and Cenúfana (in the Nechí River Valley). The Spanish reported finding a large temple, apparently of wood, that could hold up to 1,000 people. It contained 24 large wooden idles covered in gold. Needless to say, the Conquistadors made short work of the three federations, their temples and absconded with the gold. Then they burrowed into the burial mounds for more treasure.

Other cultural artifacts have surfaced in the Chocó region of the northern Pacific coast though less advanced than the Betancí-Viloria.

There is one other report of ruins worth mentioning. Juan Bautista Sardela, writing in the Sixteenth Century about Captain Jorge Robledo's conquest of Antioquia, passes on a discovery made by Spanish troops. In the valley of Arbi scouts came across ancient large buildings, roads of dressed stone and store houses. Unfortunately, no one knows where this valley of Aribi is today.

As Colombian cultures flourished then faded into obscurity, two events of particular significance occurred prior to the European intrusion. The first, beginning about 1000 AD, was the wide spread use of urn burials. Though practiced from time to time earlier in one place or another, this custom came into vogue everywhere, eventually spreading across the whole country, even into the eastern plains and Amazon Basin.

The second, and perhaps related, event was the invasion of the Caribbean coastal areas by the Caribs. Emanating from the Guiana and Venezuelan coasts, these fierce warriors spread by sea into the Caribbean and attacked along inland waterways. By the time the Spanish arrived these Indians had subdued much of the Colombian north coast and penetrated into the northern extremities of the cordilleras.

While nearly all the indigenous peoples the Spanish encountered upon their arrival in Colombia were either nomadic, as in the eastern plains, semi-nomadic as in the jungle areas or sedentary, principally in the mountains and coastal areas, none were organized politically above the village or tribal level with the exception of the Betancí-Viloria already discussed, the Tairona of the Sierra Nevada de Santa Marta and the Chibcha of the Eastern Cordilleran high plateau in the vicinity of Bogotá and Tunja. Though these units could not be termed empires, as central control was not that well developed, there was central leadership in the form of a chieftain or *cacique* who "ruled" a federation of villages.

These federations were substantial enough to allow for armies to be raised for the protection of the inhabitance. The Spanish said Pocigueica, one of the two capitals of the Tairona was defended by a standing army of twenty thousand warriors. Pocigueica was built in the Sierra Nevada Mountains while the other capital, Bonda was situated near today's Santa Marta. Each had a population of thousand, maybe tens of thousands. Each was ruled by a casique who controlled all the villages in the surrounding area. This chieftain was both military and political leader and at times, the high priest.

Maize farming was the basis of the economy and allowed for the creation of a dense population in the area. Pottery was complex and elaborate featuring red and black ware, vessels decorated with human faces as well as abstract geometric designs. Anthropomorphic ceramics were shaped in the form of jaguars, foxes, bats, snakes, turtles and crocodiles. Jewelry was made of carnelian, agate, quartz, gold, copper and emeralds imported from the interior. Stone was worked into masks, ceremonial batons and monolithic axes among other items. Homes and temples were constructed of wood situated on raised mounds. A single village might have a few houses or several hundred arranged around one or more ceremonial structures. Stone was used to build bridges, retaining walls, reservoirs, stairways and amphitheater type structures used for religious ceremonies.

Religion was based on the jaguar culture and organized well enough to create the historically ubiquitous struggle between the military-political leaders and the priesthood class, a division the Spanish exploited all too well in their conquest. Authority of the two casiques was never absolute and these war-like peoples would often fight each other, village against village, similar to the feudalism of Medieval Europe. In spite of these internal divisions, military organization was sufficient to battle the Spanish to a standstill. It took almost a hundred years for the Spanish to complete their conquest of the Tairona.

The third federation of villages to be considered was the Chibcha or Muiscas as they called themselves. Like the Tairona, they were divided into two factions, one, ruled by the Zipa, was centered in the area around Muequetá (today's Bogotá). The other, with a chieftain called the Zaque, occupied the region around Hunza (present day Tunja) to the north. Also like the Tairona, the political structure was feudal-like, with local chieftains battling each other to expand, or defend, their domination over villages and land areas. The Zipa and

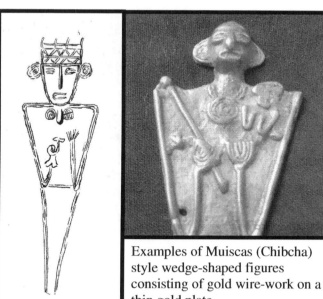

Examples of Muiscas (Chibcha) style wedge-shaped figures consisting of gold wire-work on a thin gold plate.

Zaque did, however, have enough control to be able to maintain special troops, called *guechas*, along their western borders where they fought the Pance, Colimas and Muzos, Carib tribes from the Magdalena Valley. In addition to protecting their territory, the *guechas'* task was the capture of prisoners to be used as human sacrifices to the sun god.

The Chibcha religion was centered on worship of the sun as the primary deity and the moon secondarily with temples to each. The most famous of these structures was the "Temple to the Sun," at Sogamoso. Child sacrifices were offered here using children purchased or captured from the tribes of the Llanos.

Unlike the Tairona, the Chibcha were not settled in large towns, but were scattered in the mountains in single homes or communities of a few houses. Villages were, for the most part, small and infrequent much as is characteristic of the area today.

While Chibcha political cohesion, social structure, agriculture, commerce, economic efficiency and religious complexity were advanced over any other people in their region, their pottery and metallurgy lagged behind many of the lowland tribes. The farmers grew at least two types of potatoes, as well as *guino, ulluco, oca* and *topinambur*. (While the cultivation of maize was imported from the north, potatoes arrived later from the south and spread rapidly among the high Andean agriculturalists). They traded locally obtained emeralds, salt and cotton goods for gold, shells and decorative feathers.

Farmers lived in adequate single family dwellings, but the nobility luxuriated in large, well-built houses the Spanish referred to as palaces. The noble leaders were carried across the mountain trails, and into battle, by bearers in litters encrusted with gold. The social and religious structure was well developed enough to require a special training period for both chieftains and priests. For several years candidates-in-training were secluded in a temple where they fasted, abstained from sexual contact, and studied the religious and cultural practices of the society.

The Chibcha or Muiscas were not indigenous to the area where the Spanish found them. They had moved into the region in fairly recent times, but were able to conquer the natives militarily and stay organized enough politically to maintain control.

Of perennial interest to the Spanish was the legend of El Dorado and this fable may very well have originated with the Chibcha. High in the mountains behind Bogotá lays Buatgavita, a small lake considered sacred by the Chibcha. Before a new cacique could take his place as ruler of the nation, he had to be consecrated at this lake. Thousands of people ringed the small body of water as the new chieftain was rowed to the center of the lake on a raft. He had been painted with a resin, and then covered from head to foot with gold dust. He was, for a time, the gilded man. The people threw offerings, ceramics, jewelry and other precious objects into the water as offerings to the gods while the golden one dove into the lake and washed away the glittering, metallic dust. Regaining the raft, he was proclaimed the new cacique by his people and very possibly El Dorado by legend.

As to actual historical events, we know only what the Spanish chroniclers wrote down about occurrences immediately preceding their arrival. About 1470 Zipa Saguanmachica marched north with his army in response to the capture of his fortress Pueblovieho (the later Spanish name) by Zapue Michua of Hunza (Tunja). In the ensuing battle both caciques were killed ending hostilities. Nemequene succeeded his uncle Saguanmachica as ruler at Muequetá (Bogotá) and began a systematic conquest of the immediate region, incorporating Guatavita, Ubaqua, Simijaca, Susa, Ubaté and other areas. He then launched a new war against the northern domain, where Quemenchatocha ruled, successor to Michna. The Zaque and the Zipa again met in battle and Nemequene should have won easily with his veteran warriors uniting the Chibcha Empire, but he was killed by an arrow while moving about the battle field in his litter. His army withdrew to Muequetá. The new Zipa, Tisquesuza, arranged a fifteen year truce between the two rulers, leaving the Muiscas divided and vulnerable to a new invasion force for which they were totally unprepared. The collision of the American and European peoples would demonstrate in dramatic fashion the outcome of the intersection of two cultures one of which was technologically vastly superior to the other (see Append. II).[3]

Many Volunteers of Colombia '64 would take the opportunity to visit some of the archeological sites and museums featuring artifacts left by these pre-Columbian civilizations. Even those who didn't would be exposed, at one time or another, to the influence of these ancient Colombians. Almost everywhere in Colombia there are artifacts, petroglyphs or ruins from the pre-Columbian people. On the street corners of every major city there were street venders, even children, selling artifacts, ceramic vessels and statuary, stone and gold figurines looted from the graves of these ancient peoples.

Many of the mountain villages, customs, crops, trails and roads used and experienced by the Volunteers were features of Colombia long before the Spanish arrived. The indigenous peoples of Colombia, unlike their cousins in what would become the United States, were, in many cases, already settled with substantial populations. Foreigners invaded their territory, indigenous (the Caribs), European (as conquerors) and African (as slaves), but the majority of the population would remain Amerindian.

---

[3] Fals-Borda, *Peasant Society* (Gainseville: University of Florida Press, 1962), p. 5-11.

Appendix II
CONQUEST AND THE COLONIAL PERIOD

At the close of the 16th Century, Colombia was populated by an Amerindian population divided into various tribes and family units. In some instances, particularly in the mountainous western portion and coastal regions, these groups had risen to the level of villages, primitive states and even kingdoms or confederations. The indigenous peoples of the northwest were battling a foreign invader, the Caribs, from the eastern Caribbean coast, but the civilizations and tribes of Colombia were about to collide with a culture much more threatening than even these ferocious interlopers. This new menace would prove to be much more advanced technologically and organizationally than anything even the Chibchas could imagine.

The Spanish Conquistadors who had crossed the Atlantic and were now invading the Americas had been trained and toughened over the last two hundred years in the wars of the *Reconquista*, the campaign to recover the Iberian Peninsula from the Moors. The final expulsion of the last Moslems in 1492, freed a whole class of soldiers and officers for the conquest of this new world discovered by Columbus. With the Conquistadors would come priests, miners, merchants, farmers and slaves, and all would leave their mark on Colombia. To understand the social, religious, racial and particularly the political structure of this country, it is necessary to explore the immigration of the European and African peoples.

The first European to sight Colombia was Alonso de Ojeda. He had been with Columbus on his second voyage, the one that discovered Puerto Rico, and upon his return to Spain he was able to mount his own expedition. In 1499, he sailed to the Gulf of Maracaibo naming the coast Venezuela (little Venice) because the Indian houses built on pilings reminded him of the Italian city. With him were Amerigo Vespucci, for whom the Americas would be named, and Juan de la Cosa. Ojeda rounded Cape de la Vela, thus reaching Colombia before he turned back due to lack of provisions.

In 1509, Ojeda set out again with the intention of founding a colony on the Colombian coast. He tried the harbor of Cartagena, but was driven off by Indians with poison arrows, about the only native weapon truly effective against the Spaniards. Ojeda moved on to the Gulf of Urabá where he did plant his colony. Again, hostile natives kept the company pinned inside their palisade.

Ojeda eventually left the colony in charge of Francisco Pizarro and headed for Santa Domingo for supplies, but was shipwrecked on Cuba, finally making it to Jamaica to die in obscurity.

Meanwhile, Ojeda's partner, Martin Fernandez de Enciso, set sail from Santo Domingo with reinforcements. He stopped in the Gulf of Urabá, picked up Pizarro and his survivors and went on to the Darien River in Panama where he conquered a large Indian village and established his colony.

Enciso was displaced as governor of the colony by one Vasco Nunez de Balboa who had been a stowaway on one of Enciso's ships leaving Santa Domingo. This was the Balboa, of course, who then crossed the Isthmas of Darien in 1513, and discovered the Pacific Ocean opening up a whole new vista for Spanish exploration.

Still a new leader emerged in Panama, one Pascual de Andagoya, who founded the capital of Panama and then set out to explore the Colombian west coast. He sailed as far south as Buenaventura where he established a colony making himself governor. But it was Francisco Pizarro, the same Pizarro left at Darien by Ojeda, who captured the real prize. After a couple of exploring expeditions down the South American coast trying to locate the seat of the fabled Inca Empire, Pizarro disembarked near Tumbez, Peru in 1532 and began a march inland with only 180 men. At Cajamarca he captured the Inca, Atahuallpa, who was caught at a distinct disadvantage having just fought and won a civil war, and mistaking the new arrivals for the creator god Viracocha with his entourage of demi-gods.

Following his conquest of Peru, Pizarro sent Sebastián de Belalcázar north to take Ecuador, the northern district of the old Inca Empire. After conquering Ecuador and establishing Quito, the former northern capital of the Inca Empire, as his capital, Belalcázar marched north fighting his way into Pasto and the Cauca Valley in 1535. He founded the cities of Cali and Popayán to anchor this northern Spanish territory.

Meanwhile on the north coast of South America, the Spanish had established footholds at Santa Marta (1525) and Cartagena (1533) in Colombia, and Maracaibo plus Coro in Venezuela, though the Venezuelan territory was soon ceded to the Welsers (German merchant princes) by Charles V, the Holy Roman Empiror and King of Spain.

Fired by the success of Cortez in Mexico and Pizarro in Peru, and by stories of El Dorado rumored to be located in the interior mountains of Colombia, three expeditions were mounted almost simultaneously to find the legendary riches. And why not, Colombia was situated between the fabulous riches of Peru and the treasures of Mexico. Surely there must be untold wealth to be had in those endless mountains and jungles of this still unexplored (by Europeans) land.

Gonzalo Jiménez de Quesada advanced overland from Santa Marta with six hundred men supported by six ships that were to sail up the Magdalena. But when he reached the great river, he found only two ships had made it. The rest were lost or turned back because of the treacherous shoals and swamps at the mouth of the river. The soldiers slashed their way up the Magdalena Valley fighting off Indians armed with the dreaded poison arrows.

In December of the same year, the German Nicolás Federman left Coro, Venezuela with 300 Europeans soldiers, 130 horses and a company of native bearers. He would spend two years crossing the Venezuelan and Colombian Llanos losing 70 soldiers, 40 horses, and an unknown number of native barriers before reaching the foothills of the Eastern Cordillera just east of Bogotá.

Far to the south, Belalcázar learned he was in trouble with Pizarro who suspected him of trying to arrange his own *encomienda* in Ecuador. To escape agents sent by Pizarro and probably to do just what he was being accused of doing, Belalcázar left Quito with 200 soldiers and many times that number in barriers heading for Popayán. From there he turned east crossing the Central Cordillera in search of the fabled El Dorado. This crossing proved to be difficult with cold, hostile Indians and little food available. In four months Belalcázar lost most of his horses and a good share of his bearers. Finally, gaining the upper valley of the Magdalena River and Antoquia in 1539, the Spaniards found relief, less hostile Indians, food and even some gold.

Meanwhile, Quesada and his men had fought their way three hundred miles up the Magdalena to today's Barrancabermeja where they found the river too swift for their boats and no natives to supply them with provisions or bearers. A scouting party did find a storehouse up a tributary, the Opón River, which contained some provisions, a canoe, painted cotton cloth and salt cakes. Encouraged by these signs of civilization, Quesada and his men proceeded up the Opón, then hacked their way up the west slope of the Eastern Cordillera. In early March 1537, Quesada with 170 men and 30 horses broke out onto the high plateau in the area of Hunza (Tunja). The Muiscas knew they were coming, but as so often happened in the Americas, mistook them for "children of the sun," and greeted the Conquistadors with gifts and tribute.

The respect and aw were short lived, however, and quickly a defense of their land was offered by the Muiscas. Two battles were fought, the final one right at Muequetá (Bogotá) itself. The Chibcha overlords were vanquished and replaced by the Spanish who introduced new things, some of which benefited the mountain farmers – iron hoes, plows, wheat and barley, pigs, sheep, cattle and horses.

Quesada established his headquarters, to be called Nuevo Reino de Granada (New Kingdom of Granada), at the old site of Muequetá naming it Santa Fe de Bogotá (a slight corruption of the Chibcha name for their capital). He had nearly completed his conquest of the Muiscas when Federman appeared from the east having climbed the steep and rugged trails out of the Llanos onto the high plateau with his 160 remaining men.

Next Quesada received word of Spaniards to the southwest and he sent scouts to investigate. They found Belalcázar and his company from Ecuador floundering around in the upper Magdalena region. The third contingent of Conquistadors was guided to Bogotá.

What ensued might have been a three way war, considering the determination and greed of these tenacious captains, but instead they managed to settle things amicably. Federman and his men agreed to compensation in the form of goods and land. Quesada and Belalcázar agreed to let the Spanish crown decide who would rule in New Granada.

As first arrival, Quesada was awarded governorship of the mountain province which was tied to the north coast for administrative purposes. Popayán, the Cauca Valley and west coast were to be ruled from Quito (Belalcázar's domain), a situation not changed until 1549, when rule from Bogotá was extended to that area.

More Conquistadors (and some Germans from Venezuela) invaded Colombia, Robledo, Cesar, Badillo, van Hutten, Pedro de Ursua and others, each with harrowing tales of adventure and conquest, until the general geography of the country was known. Though real domination was limited to the immediate areas of the many settlements the Spanish established - control was sufficient for Spain to claim the county.

Colombia had, at this point, fallen into four natural divisions, 1) the eastern Llanos and Amazon Basin, 2) the Eastern Cordilleras and upper Magdalena Valley, 3) the Caribbean Coast and Lower Magdalena Valley, and 4) Western Cordilleras, Cauca Valley and West Coast, The four distinct regions of Colombia began the colonial period as individual entities, separate and divided, but gradually the lines of demarcation would blur, though the process was impeded by geography, economics and politics. The western and eastern mountain areas were separated geographically by the Central Cordillera, difficult to navigate even on foot and by hostile Indians, some of the last to be subdued. Further, the Western Cordillera, west coast and Cauca Valley remained, for much of the period, ruled from Quito.

The economy of the western area, with its capital at Popayán, was based on gold. From here gold mining spread to Antioquia (1541), Tocaimo (1545), Ibagué(1550),

Marquita (1551), Lo Victoria (1557), and la Palma (1560). In the 1600s, Caloto, north of Popayán, became an important gold producer. Entrepreneurs from Antioquia discovered deposits in Rionegro and the Osos Valley. These enterprising Antioquanos spread out along the Atrato and San Juan rivers in the Chocó and established mines at Remedios and Zaragosa. Meanwhile, Spaniards from Popayá were invading the coastal region of Barbacoas south of Buenaventura where they had to battle indigenous tribes in order to exploit the gold deposits.

Most, perhaps two-thirds, of the gold production was from placer mining accomplished by panning. Sometimes individuals or small groups of free agents would work a stream or river, but gangs of slaves were also used in panning. However, slave gangs were more commonly used in sluice mining and underground shaft mining where veins of ore were found.

Indigenous slave labor was used in the early phases of the gold mining, but the mortality rate was high and desertions common place. Imported African slaves were more reliable, but expensive. So a mixture of the two was used. However, pressure from the Catholic Church and the Spanish Crown gradually curtailed the use of Indian slave labor by the 1800s.

Never-the-less, New Granada was Spain's largest producer of gold even though its output in terms of absolute value was dwarfed by the silver from Mexico. Still Colombia's gold was important to the Spanish Empire and established the western region as Spanish America's gold producer.

To feed the mining labor force, food was produced using Indian workers. Wheat, imported from Quito, was grown in Pasto, then its cultivation spread to Papayán. This supplemented native cassava and maize. In the mountains, potatoes were available and later, sugar cane was grown around Cali and Buga.

In contrast to the west's gold economy, the Eastern Cordillera region depended primarily on the production of grains and woven textiles. The only significant gold production came from the area between Pamplona and Bucaramunga, with some silver from the mines of Mariquita and a smattering of emeralds. All the mining was done using indigenous labor so there was never an African component to the population here as there was in the west.

Instead of precious metals, the eastern mountains exported flour, hardtack, cheese, hams, canvas cloth, and rough woolens, all of which were traded for imported luxury goods delivered from the coast. Internally, the east produced its own coca, cotton, textiles, maize, potatoes, wheat, barley, pork and chickens. Cattle were raised in the upper Magdalena plains, and plantains, cassava and sugar cane became readily available as farmers moved into the Guanentá basin north of Vélez. From the cane came a liquor to augment *chicha* (corn beer), molasses and *panela* (unrefined sugar). The eastern mountain region was quite self-sufficient.

To better control and Christianize the indigenous population, the conquerors concentrated the Indians in towns designed along Spanish lines with a central plaza dominated by the parish church. The local people, residing on individual plots or in small villages were induced to move to these towns most of which exist to this day. These are the towns many of the Volunteers of Colombia '64 lived and worked in.

So the west had gold, the eastern mountainous region thrived on agriculture, while the Caribbean coast and lower Magdalena River Valley area depended on commerce.

Cartagena was the authorized Spanish seaport for external trade of New Granada. This monopoly meant that European oils and wine, along with African slaves and manufactured goods had to pass through the port to reach the interior. Gold flowed from the west, while textiles and agricultural products arrived from the Eastern Cordillera. A lucrative contraband trade sprang up all along the north coast. Finally, Cartagena's primary mission was to supply, support and protect the Spanish treasure fleet when it stopped to pick up New Granada's precious metals and jewels bound for Spain.

Thus, Cartagena became the focus of New Granada's overseas commerce. By the late 1700s, it was the largest coastal city, boasting a population of over 12,000. It had the strongest fortifications in the Caribbean and the largest contingent of troops in Colombia. The city was the ecclesiastic center of the Catholic Church with four monasteries, two convents and an office of the Inquisition.

Still sectionalism was a problem and stunted the city's growth. Trade with the interior was difficult and expensive. Food stuffs that supplied the city and passing ships were mostly grown on the coastal plain, beans, cassava, plantains, maize, even cattle and pigs for the production of salt beef and salt pork.

The main artery into the interior was the Magdalena River, but the mouth of the great river was a swampy morass, difficult and dangerous to navigate. Access to the river from Cartagena was, therefore, overland by mule train. To alleviate this expensive mode of transportation, the city built the Canal de Dique between Cartagena and the navigable river south of the swamps in 1650. This was a big boost to commerce, but the canal was allowed to deteriorate and was unusable for years at a time during the 1700s.

All this wealth concentrated in one city made Cartagena the focus of repeated attacks by the pirates and privateers of the Spanish Main. Sir Frances Drake sacked and burned the city in 1586. Cartagena was captured again in 1697 by French buccaneers under Pointis.

In 1741, the English took a turn at conquering the richest of Caribbean prizes. Admiral Edward Vernon arrived off shore with a fleet of 180 ships and an army of 23,600 men under General Wentworth. But after several weeks of attacks and maneuvering the English gave up and retired.

Not just Cartagena was raided of course. All the cities, ports and towns along the coast were subjected to attacks, plundering and looting culminating in the expedition of Sir Henry Morgan across the isthmus to capture Panama City in 1688. Riches there were in Colombia's northern coastal region, but with the wealth came marauders, danger, destruction and death.

Racially, the coast had a large European population and as the indigenous peoples declined in number, African slaves were brought in as labor for the agricultural estates. A mixing of the three races occurred with only the Spanish upper classes maintaining any kind of purity.

The eastern half of Colombia (the Llanos and Amazon Basin) was mostly neglected by colonial Spain except for the cattle ranches established along the Eastern Cordillera foothills and western plains by Jesuit missionaries. After an initial burst of exploration, the eastern Llanos and Amazon *selva* (jungle) were left alone. Cattle were herded by the tough *llanaros* on the eastern plains and sold in markets in the Eastern Cordillera. Other than that, only the Jesuits and a few other missionaries ventured out onto the Llanos to stay.

In 1662, the Jesuits began building missions in the Llanos, first in the foothills and then out on the lower plains along the Rio Meta and beyond. The priests converted Indians who then worked at the reductions. These missions were self-sufficient. On the higher ground, next to the mountains, they raised maize, cotton and grains to trade in Bogotá, Sogamoso, and other markets of the Eastern Cordillera. But out on the plains they turned to cattle. In 1767, the Jesuits left South America by order of the Pope. The missions, established at such a great cost in hard work and sacrifice were sold to cattle interests or turned over to other orders, the Franciscans, Dominicans and, along the Meta, the Recoletos. Except for the scattered missions and the cattle herded by llaneros, the eastern half of New Granada remained the domain of indigenous peoples.

Throughout the 16th and 17th Centuries Spanish control over New Granada was tenuous at best. As long as the gold arrived to fight the European wars, little effort was expended in gaining absolute authority over the territory. Each region operated independently for the most part, though in theory all were under the jurisdiction of Bogotá.

With the Bourbon's takeover of Spain from the Hapsburgs in the early 1700s, an attempt was made to consolidate control. Spain created the Viceroyalty of el Nuevo Reino de Granada (the New Kingdom of Granada) in 1717, with the capital at Bogotá. Included in this viceroyalty were Colombia, Panama, Ecuador, most of Venezuela, Trinidad and Margarita. After a few decades of struggling to make this giant amalgamation work, Spain gave up in 1777, removing coastal Venezuela from the kingdom and allowing authority in Ecuador to slip back to Quito.

In the viceroyalty, all top positions were held by European born Spanish administrators with second and third tier positions going to American-born Spaniards (*Creoles*). While the production and even increase in output of gold bullion was a priority, an attempt was made to develop other exports as well, emeralds, copper, dyewoods, balsams and fine hardwoods. This diversification met with only limited success due to the lack of available transportation. Where there was a question, the movement of the precious metals prevailed. Also, the almost constant wars among the European nations of the period made legal sea commerce difficult. Avoiding enemy ships was easier for small fast moving contraband boats. So smuggling remained a significant factor in the Caribbean trade.

Attempts to increase production did spark an enlightenment in New Granada. Mining engineers were imported to improve gold output. Botanists worked on improving cotton yields. José Celestino Mutis came to Bogotá in 1761 as the Viceroy's physician. Mutis was also a botanist and mathematician. He taught at the Colegio del Rosario and stirred up a controversy by instructing classes on Copernican cosmology. Creoles of the upper classes took notice and began applying scientific methods to social and economic problems. And, of course, this enlightenment eventually led to a questioning of the country's political situation. A smoldering undercurrent of resentment toward Spanish rule developed, though it might have died still-born had it not been for the crown's levy of, what else, new taxes.

In the mid 1700s the government established a monopoly on the sale of cane liquor (aguardiente) and tobacco products. The revenues were used to build fortifications and patrol the Caribbean coast. But the increased income came at a price. Intermittent rioting broke out in Quito in 1765 and spread to the Cauca Valley, Popayán, Cali and Cartago, then to the Chocó and upper Magdalena Valley. By the 1780s periodic riots had spread to the Eastern Cordilleras in response to, not only the tobacco and aguardiente monopolies, but the destruction of the tobacco plots (to preserve the monopoly) vital to the Guanentá lowland farmer's survival. With a renewed war against England in 1779, taxes on cotton were added hitting the eastern mountain region especially hard.

In May 1781, 20,000 *Comuneros* (Colombian born revolutionaries) camped just north of Bogotá threatening to take the city if their demands were not met. Though the Comuneros were led by mostly aristocratic Creoles, the grievances were primarily those affecting the lower classes: government monopoly of tobacco and playing cards, the high prices of aguardiente, wartime head tax and the high regular sales taxes. Participation by high-born Creoles was motivated by their being excluded from the very highest government positions, those reserved for Spanish-born administrators.

The government in Bogotá found itself essentially defenseless. Spanish forces were stationed in Cartagena and along the coast, but there were few troops inland. The government officials fled and negotiations were conducted by the archbishop in the city who acceded to the demands that included, lowering the taxes, removal of the tobacco monopoly and preference be made for Creoles over Spanish-born in all government administration positions.

The rebellion was defused and the Comuneros demobilized. Soldiers arrived from Cartagena and the government officials returned to Bogotá. Once order was restored, a limited crack down followed. Four of the peasant Comuneros were hanged. Some of the landless were sent to colonies in Panama and a few received public lashings. Some of the high-born leaders were imprisoned in Cartagena for a while. The rest of the participants were granted amnesty. At the same time, all of the agreed to conditions called for by the Comuneros' list of grievances were retracted. Though subdued, a burning resentment toward Spain smoldered just beneath the surface. It would take only a spark to ignite the flame of rebellion and that spark was about to be struck on the other side of the Atlantic.

In 1789, revolution erupted in France. Ten years later Napoleon Bonaparte came to power. In 1807, Napoleon badgered the weak Charles IV of Spain into letting him cross his country to invade Portugal. However, once in Iberia, his army never left. Charles abdicated in favor of his son Ferdinand VII who was then pressed by Napoleon to turn over the crown to him. The Spanish objected, but Napoleon, with 100,000 troops to back him up, quickly put down any organized resistance and then installed his brother Joseph as king. The once greatest power in all of Europe (thanks to the gold and silver of the Americas) had been completely humiliated.

Spain was not entirely cowed yet, however. Juntas sprang into existence in all the Spanish provinces and they sponsored guerilla bands that harassed the French troops and government officials.

The Viceroy of New Granada, Antonio Amar y Borbón, called the Spanish and Creole leaders together and asked them to support the junta of Seville and pledge loyalty to Ferdinand VII. This they did, even pledging 500,000 pesos to fight the French.

Napoleon, meanwhile, reinforced his army in Spain to 300,000 men and began to systematically dismantle the juntas and their associated guerilla units. The Creoles in Colombia started to ask, "If the government in Spain had devolved from the monarchy to local juntas, why should not juntas be set up in the Americas as well?"

The first overt action was taken in Quito in 1809, when the Spanish administrators were removed and replaced by an elected junta. Forces from Popayán, Pasto and Bogotá converged on Quito and put down the rebellion.

An abortive attempt, led by Antonio Nariño among others, to establish a junta in Bogotá was crushed in its formative stage. Nariño, who had also participated in the 1798 crisis, was imprisoned in Cartagena.

In Spain the Council of Regency was created to coordinate the activities of the various juntas, but by February 1810 the only part of Spain not under French control was the port of Cádiz. This collapse of any form of an indigenous Spanish government spurred independence activities in South America.

Led by military commanders of American-born troops, the citizens of Cartagena displaced the Spanish governor with a junta on June 14, 1810. Caracas, Venezuela was next to establish a junta followed by Pamplona on July 4th, Socorro on July 10th and Bogotá on July 20th. Several other provincial capitals followed suit.

The junta in Bogotá attempted to organize a congress to write a constitution for a new independent nation, but these efforts were resisted by the Cartagena junta which saw itself as a potential capital. Likewise Popayán objected on the grounds it led the richest of the provinces. It also harbored strong pro-Spanish sentiments. Any effort to organize a general movement toward nationalism was further frustrated because many provinces had declared themselves free and independent states not subject to Spain or Bogotá. And some important towns broke away from their provinces in an attempt to become capitals of their own provinces.

Cali declared itself separated from Popayán where a Spanish governor still ruled and royalist sentiment dominated. A Cauca federation was formed that included Cali, Auserma, Toro, Cartago, Buga and Caloto.

Antonio Nariño, released from prison during the uprising in Cartagena, moved to Bogotá where he gained control of the junta there. He attempted to create a new state called Cundinamarca (a Muisca name) that would include all of present day Colombia east of the Magdalena River. He was opposed by a new Federation of provinces that included Cartagena, Antioquia, Tunja, Pomplona and Neiva.

Meanwhile, royalist forces had recovered somewhat from the initial wave of rebellion and were mounting an offensive. Royalists controlled Riohacha, Santa Marta, the Panama Isthmus and Popayán. In Venezuela, royalists had defeated the rebel forces under Simón Bolívar who fled to Cartagena. There he took command of rebel forces in the Magdalena Valley and defeated a Spanish army in Pamplona. In May 1813, he invaded his native Venezuela once more. After taking Caracus and all of the western provinces, he was defeated in 1814 and fled once more, this time to Jamaica.

In the west, Spanish general Juan Sámano drove north from Peru and captured Quito. Moving on, he picked up support from the Pastó Indians and Afro-Colombians of the Patía Valley. He was welcomed in Popayán, where he received supplies and additional troops. Reinforced, he marched on the northern Cauca Valley rebels and conquered all the insurgent towns.

Sámano's success alarmed the Creole juntas to the point Cuncinamarca and the Federation built an army naming Nariño general. Nariño led this army into the Cauca Valley and succeeded in freeing the northern towns. He was finally defeated in Pastó by royalists in 1814.

Now the rebel juntas were in a panic. And to make matters worse, they learned that Napoleon had been defeated in Europe and Ferdinand VII was back on the Spanish throne. The Spanish monarch would now be in a position to send a regular European army to conquer the renegade provinces.

In desperation, the juntas of the Federation attempted to create a united front by force. Bolívar, back from sojourns in Jamaica and Haiti, led an army of Federation troops against Cundinamarca to force an alliance. He took Bogotá, then descended the Magdalena River to attack Santa Marta. In the heat and humidity his troops began to die and desert. His army disintegrated leaving the lower Magdalena open to conquest by Santa Marta royalists.

Meanwhile, Spanish General Pablo Morillo landed in Venezuela with 10,000 men. After securing Venezuela, he attacked Cartagena, laying siege to the city. One hundred and eighty days later the fortress fell after a third of the population had died. The rest of New Granada succumbed rapidly and Colombia's first attempt at independence (1810 – 1816) came to an end.

Executions followed and New Granada, including Ecuador and Venezuela were subjected to occupational rule by the Spanish army. The only area not subjugated was the Llanos. Here, the tough, independent llaneros plus the rain, heat, humidity, insects and swamps combined to defeat any forays by loyalist or Spanish troops into the eastern plains. At Casanare, refugees from the defeated rebel forces collected including Simón Bolívar.

Bolívar was from a Venezuelan aristocratic Creole family. Well educated in Venezuela and Spain, he had espoused independence from Spain since his teenage years. Having been defeated by the Spanish three times now, he set about once more building an army to drive the Spanish from his country. Hold up out on the Casanare Llanos with access to both Colombia and Venezuela, Bolívar began collecting men from whatever source he could find. There were refugees from the Colombian rebel provinces, old comrades from Venezuela, and the tough, independent llanero horsemen. With the defeat of Napoleon, Britain had cut the size of its military releasing large numbers of trained soldiers. Some of these made their way to Bolívar's camp along with a number of Irish volunteers.

At the height of the rainy season Bolívar left his camp in Casanare with about 3,000 men and crossed the flooded, swampy Llanos, a feat the Spanish considered impossible. His little army climbed the steep mountain trails of the Eastern Cordillera.

As his troops gained the high plateau, they suffered terribly, especially his llanero cavalry. Unaccustomed to the high altitude and cold, many sickened and some died. Their horses, never shod in the Llanos, bruised their feet on the sharp rocks of the mountain trails. In spite of these hardships, Bolívar was able to surprise Spanish forces at Gámeza on July 12, 1819 and win a quick victory.

Now alerted, Spanish General José Maria Barreiro with about 3,800 troops began to retreat toward Bogotá but was intercepted at Vargas swamp near Paipa, just north of Tunja, on July 25th. Bolívar was down to about 2,600 men, but they were committed. Even though the rebel army had to climb the Páramo (high plain) of Pisba and cross the swamp, their attack was successful, killing or wounding some 600 of the Spanish troops. Bolívar's losses were 140 men.

Barreiro and his remaining army withdrew to Paipa where he picked up munitions and reinforcements including three artillery pieces. Bolívar recrossed the Chicamocha River returning to his old camp in Corrales de Bonza where he refitted his llaneros with shod mountain horses and allowed his men time to recuperate. Barreiro, meanwhile, having been harassed by partisans in Paipa, left the town.

With his troops somewhat rested and refitted, Bolívar marched toward Paipa camping at El Salite, then on to La Toma del Molino. Barreiro, afraid Bolívar was making a move on Bogotá, determined to intercept him at Tunja, but he arrived too late. Bolívar beat him to the town in a 21 mile forced march taking a short cut unknown to the Spaniard. Having lost the race to Tunja, Barreiro bivouacked in Molavia.

In Tunja, Bolívar found food, medicines, ammunition and other supplies intended for Barreiro and his Spanish soldiers. Bolívar was quick to appropriate the much needed supplies. He allowed his troops 40 hours of rest and then set out for Bogotá. Barreiro was forced to move. He had the only royalist military force standing between the rebels and the capital city which lay virtually undefended. The two armies met at El Puente de Boyacá on August 7, 1819.

Spanish forces numbered about 3,000 while Bolívar had some 3,200, but 800 of those, militia from Tunja and Socorro, were held in reserve and never entered the fight.

First to make contact was Brigade General Francisco de Paula Santander, leading the vanguard of about 1,000 men. He came upon the Spanish forces split into two divisions. The lead division of 1,000 men commanded by Colonel Jiminez was just crossing the bridge at El Puente de Boyacá with the main body a mile behind under General Barreiro.

Santander immediately attacked the lead division while Brigade General José Antonio Anzoátegui with another 1,000 troops moved in between the two Spanish divisions preventing a reuniting of forces. Bolívar then arrived with 1,200 men and ordered an attack on the main Spanish division. He sent Battalion Barcelona (300 men) and the Battalion Bravos de Paez (300 men) into the right flank, and the Battalion of Rifles (220 men) and the British Legion (120 men) into the left flank.

Barreiro had his troops drawn up to receive the attack with the three guns and the infantry in the center, and his cavalry on the wings. Bolívar ordered his own cavalry the 2nd Squadron Guides of Apure (100 horses) and the 3rd Squadron Dragoons (the Carabineros - 90 horses) against the wings and the Spanish cavalry collapsed. With their flanks exposed, the Spanish infantry began to give ground and at that point, Bolívar sent his regiment of lancers, the Llano de Arriba (300 horses) into the middle. Barreiro tried to rally his troops, but was over whelmed and finally forced to surrender.

Meanwhile, at the bridge, Santander had routed the lead division taking its commander and most of his men. In all, 250 Spanish were killed or wounded and 1,600 were captured including Barreiro and Jiminez. Bolívar suffered 66 men dead and wounded. The main royal army was crushed and the road to Bogotá lay entirely open. On August 10th, Bolívar entered the capital in triumph as the viceroy and other Spanish authorities fled.

Patriots rose up in most of the provinces, drove out the Spanish and restored the local juntas. Royalists remained in power in Ecuador, Venezuela, the Colombian north coast and lower Magdalena Valley, the Cauca Valley and Pasto.

Despite the unsettled state of the revolution, Bolívar and other constitution-makers met at Augostura in 1819 and called for the creation of a Republic of Colombia to include

New Granada, Venezuela and Ecuador. But such long ranging visions would have to wait. For the moment, Bolívar was elected president and Santander was elected vice-president of Cundinamarca (Colombia).

By 1820, patriots had secured the Lower Magdalena Valley and were laying siege to Cartagena. A year later most of the coast was cleared except for scattered resistance which drug on until 1823, especially around Santa Marta. The balance of power in the Cauca Valley see-sawed back and forth until 1821 when patriots finally gained the upper hand. Only Pasto continued to be a problem.

In 1821, Bolívar led an army back into Venezuela defeating the Spanish at Carabalo ending Spanish rule in that country. Antonio José de Sucre, one of Bolívar's generals, took Quito in 1822, liberating Ecuador. In 1824, Bolívar and Sucre defeated a Spanish army at the Battle of Juniu freeing Peru and later that year Sucre destroyed the last remnant of Spanish authority in northern South America at the Battle of Ayacucho.

The Spanish had been vanquished. Now it was a question of whether these newly independent states could build viable, functioning countries without their European overlords. The answer to that question was certainly not a foregone conclusion and as to what form the governments would take, or even the geographic shape of the nations, there was no obvious answer.

Appendix III
WELDING TOGETHER A LAND DIVIDED

When the Colombia '64 Volunteers arrived in country, Colombia was recovering from a period of chaos called the Violencia in which the two rival political parties were literally at war with each other causing the deaths of tens of thousands, perhaps hundreds of thousands, of Colombians. To understand how this kind of violence between political parties could have come about, it is necessary to look into the history of the country beginning with formation of an independent Colombia.

While the war of liberation continued, a constitutional convention met at Rosario de Cúcuta in 1821. The delegates pursued the creation of a republic large enough to stand up to the European powers. The desire was to include Ecuador, Colombia and Venezuela in a single Grand Colombia. The constitution they constructed at the convention was patterned after the U.S. Constitution, but with important differences. Like the U.S. Constitution, it provided for a bicameral legislative branch, a judiciary and executive branch, but was much more centralist than our constitution. Provincial governors were appointed by the president with no regional legislatures. Control of the government would remain in the hands of the educated elite through restricted suffrage. It did abolish the Inquisition and proclaimed freedom of the press. It declared children born to slave mothers would hence forth be free and citizens of the republic. Indians would be called "indigenes" from then on and were also to be citizens. The capital would be Bogotá which rankled Venezuelans and some in Cartagena, Popayán and Quito.

No sooner had the new republic been organized than problems developed. Communication with Ecuador was difficult because of the war with the Pasto royalists. While Bolívar was in Peru exterminating the last of the Spanish army, Santander, as Vice-President and acting head of state made decision on his own in several matters of national importance without consulting Bolívar and a rift began to develop between the two leaders. One of these matters was a division growing between Colombia and Venezuela.

Besides the normal jealousies and competition, there was a split in the new Republic's style of management. Most of the military officers were Venezuelan while the doctors and lawyers tended to be Colombian. The two factions disagreed on how the government should be run.

Exacerbating these fractures was Bolívar's continued absence. After the war had been won, he stayed in Peru to guide the creation of a new country named after him. Once Peruvian independence had been gained, Upper Peru decided to secede from greater Peru and become the new state of Bolivia. Bolívar assisted this new republic in setting up its government.

Meanwhile, General José Antonio Páez, one of Bolívar's senior officers and a Venezuelan, led a revolt in Venezuela against the government in Bogotá. Instead of putting down the rebellion, Bolívar, who had come north finally with a contingent of Peruvian troops, granted Páez *de facto* rule of Venezuela. This recognition of Venezuela as an autonomous region of the Republic defied the constitution itself and the rule of law under it.

This crisis of state led to the development of two parties in the Republic of Colombia. On one side were the Bolívarians, who promoted a dictatorship of Bolívar.

355

Leaders of this movement were the military officers, mostly Venezuelan, but also some Colombians and even a few British officers who had joined Bolívar's army. Opposing this party were the Constitutionalists who supported the Republic of Colombia government and saw Santander as their leader.

A new constitutional convention was called to meet at Ocaña, March of 1828. The Bolívarians proposed a new constitution with a strong executive of unlimited tenure. The Constitutionalists fought for a more balanced sharing of powers with a legislature and a limited executive. The Constitutionalists had done a better job of getting their representatives elected to the convention and were on the verge of winning when the Bolívarians simply pulled out. Leaving Ocaña, they moved to Bogotá where they declared Bolívar dictator and ruler of the Republic of Colombia.

The Constitutionalists countered by devising a plot to capture Bolívar and reinstate the old constitution with Santander as president. But the plot was discovered before it could be carried out. Fourteen conspirators were summarily executed. Among those was José Padilla, one of the few black generals in Colombia. Santander was imprisoned in Cartagena and then exiled. Bolívar became, in effect, dictator of Greater Colombia and was seen as the only person capable of holding the country together.

However, even Bolívar, the Great Liberator, could not pacify everyone. There was a threat of war by Peru over Ecuador. The Cauca region smoldered with rebellion and sentiments of joining Ecuador as a separate state. A project was considered to save Greater Colombia by making it a constitutional monarchy patterned after the British government. But this movement died after Bolívar finally rejected the idea.

In January 1830, General Páez announced Venezuela's independence from Greater Colombia. A new constitutional convention was called in Bogotá in one last attempt to save the union. It was dominated by Bolívarians, but produced nothing that would prevent the departure of Venezuela from the Republic of Colombia.

Bolívar was still seen as the only savior of the union, but he was now visibly ill and wanted to give up the presidency. He pressed Congress to replace him. Two moderate generals were finally elected as president and vice-president. Bolívar departed for Cartagena.

The new presidency began appointing old Constitutionalists to high posts as a means of mollifying the country's liberals. The military objected to these appointments and a Venezuelan battalion in Bogotá threatened to act against the Colombian battalion that supported the government which forced a division of the military along party lines. The Venezuelan battalion defeated government forces at the battle of Santuario leaving the Bolívarian general Rafael Urbaneta in charge of the government as president which he said he would turn over to Bolívar upon the Liberator's return to Bogotá. But the Great Liberator died in a hacienda near Santa Marta in December of 1830.

With the death of Símon Bolívar, and the outbreak of rebellion in several parts of the country, Urbaneta turned the government over to the constitutional Vice-President, General Domingo Caicedo. It would fall upon his shoulders to lead the country in this post-Bolívar era.

A new constitutional convention was called in 1831 to create the basis for a government of a Colombia much as it is today geographically. The Casanare llanos department had declared itself ready to be annexed by Venezuela, but Caracus showed little interest in this wild frontier area and the wayward region returned to the Colombian fold. The Cauca Valley and Pasto were nominally under control of Quito from 1831 to 1832, but finally opted for reconciliation with Bogotá thanks to the high handed tactics of the Ecuadorian dictator and a Colombian garrison being stationed in Popayán. The Isthmus of Panama decided in favor of Colombia due to an attempt by Venezuelan military officers from Peru to take the region for themselves. Thus Colombia began to take shape stripped of the appendages of Ecuador and Venezuela.

As the new Colombia emerged, two parties began to materialize. The old Constitutionalists had secured dominance in the country and government as most of the military elite left Colombia for their native Venezuela. The Bolívarians were now powerless. However, the Constitutionalists began to split over how to deal with the old Bolívarians that remained. The purists who took the name Liberals wanted to exclude the Bolívarians from any participation in the government in the hopes of their eventual extinction. But the Conservative wing felt the Bolívarians could be used to broaden their base by incorporating at least the more moderate elements into the party.

Party division became evident in the constitutional convention of 1831-32. The liberal wing, called *Exaltados* (Extremists), though they called themselves "Patriots" or *Progresistas* had been in the ascendance up to that time having instituted a purge of the military. They saw to it that 35 Venezuelan and 25 British officers were ejected from military service. This got rid of some Bolívarians in the army and reduced the size of the military saving a significant amount of money.

At the convention the Liberals pushed for New Granada as the name of the new country reserving "Colombia" as the term for a greater Colombia confederation to include Venezuela and Ecuador. The moderates or Conservatives voted for the name Colombia hoping to prevent any possibility of a reunification. The Liberals won again and New Granada it would be. As the convention closed, it elected José Ignacio de Márquez, a moderate (Conservative) over General José María Obano, a leader of the Liberals, as the country's Vice-President. The president would be elected in a national election in accordance with the new constitution. Santander received 80 percent of the vote for president in the national election and returned from exile in Europe to lead the country.

Santander restored some of the old Bolívarians to positions in his government, but when a group of them made an abortive attempt to seize control of the Bogotá garrison in 1833, he executed 18 of the plotters after their conviction and imprisoned 34 others, thus gaining the enmity of some of the aristocracy of Bogotá and Cartagena. Santander walked a fine line between the two parties, for the most part successfully.

Prevented from a second term by the constitution, Santander threw his support behind General José María Obando, a Liberal, for President. Many Liberals were worried about electing a military man and they turned to a civilian Vicente Azuero. Moderates (Conservatives) coalesced around José Ignacio de Márquez though there were some who feared the army would not support a civilian and for those Conservatives there was General Domingo Caicedo.

Márquez won a clear plurality, but not a majority and by Constitutional law Congress would decide the issue. Márquez was elected easily. Obando, meanwhile slipped out of the capital moving to the area south of Popayán where he would be in close proximity to people on the verge of rebellion. These were the inhabitance of Pasto, an ultra-religious region concerned about Márquez's move toward a more secular society.

Obando declared he was in rebellion against the Márquez administration and Pasto followed his lead. Groups in other provinces and cities joined the rebellion, Vélez, Casanare, Tunja, el Socorro, Antioquia, Santa Marta, Cartagena, Mompox and Panama.

Though significant in number and even size, the secessionist had little in common. There was no overriding cause except for resistance to the Márquez administration. In Pasto it was religion, on the coast it was trade restrictions, etc. Some rebels supported Obando, others favored Vicente Azuero.

The war lasted from January 1840 through May 1842. Santander died in May 1840 which only released his followers from his restraining hand. Ecuador sent troops to help quell Pasto and defeat Obando. Government forces eventually prevailed in all areas, but at a fearful cost in money and the devastation of the countryside. The economy of New Granada was left in tatters. The war accomplished little except to delineate the two political parties of Colombia more clearly.

Understanding the political parties of Colombia at this stage in the country's development is difficult. Generally, in Latin America, conservatives have been associated with landowners, clergy and the military elite. Liberals have been identified with lawyers and merchants. But this generalization does not seem to hold in the case of Colombia where both parties had a range of occupations represented in their constituencies.

Another approach is to see conservatives as the descendants of colonial administrators, social and political elitists defending centralized and more authoritarian government. While liberals tend to be outsiders agitating for better positions, economically, politically and socially. But, again, there are so many exceptions to this scheme, as far as Colombia is concerned, that it breaks down for this country.

The two parties seemed to be most consistent in their division over church affairs. Liberals, though Catholic in practice, believed the Church influence tended to hurt the economy and dampen public enlightenment and therefore needed to be restrained. Conservatives, on the other hand, believed the Church was vital in maintaining social and moral order and therefore should be encouraged.

During and immediately after the wars for independence, the regions of Colombia maintained their sectionalism. Except for textiles, gold, cattle, and imports, there was little commerce between the regions. Trade within each area was extensive and the self-sufficiency of the colonial period was maintained.

Eastern Colombia remained neglected, the Amazon jungles particularly so, with cattle being the only product of the Llanos. The western mountain region stagnated with declining gold production and extensive devastation from both the wars of independence and the 1840-42 civil war.

The Eastern Cordillera staggered along with its exports of textiles and wool, and the attention this region received was because it contained the capital, Bogotá.

The Caribbean coast had its trade with the outside world. With the clogging of the Canal del Dique, Cartagena yielded its trade supremacy to Santa Marta. Panama became particularly active as the main transit point from the Atlantic to the Pacific. This activity became even more pronounced with the discovery of gold in California. The isthmus swarmed with U.S. citizens and Europeans bound for the gold fields of California and other points west.

The one really bright spot in the New Granda economy was Anioquia. As the Cauca region's gold production declined, Antioquia's exports of the precious metal increased.

There were three contributing factors, the easy transition from slave labor to free after independence, the introduction of ore mills and better vein mining methods and the aggressive business practices of the Antioqueños.

Antioquia had never had a high slave population, only 2.2% in 1835. Slave labor was quickly replaced by the free black, malatoe and mestizo workers already doing most of the mining and refining work.

French, British and Swedish mining engineers were hired to improve mining and production methods. This development was possible because the free-enterprise atmosphere of the area produced the capital for reinvestment in the mining business. Gold panning was done, to a large extent, by self-employed free laborers who also grew crops or had other jobs.

Antioquia's gold industry fueled an economy which produced a bourgeoisie with accumulated capital. This class of businessmen turned to investing and trade, importing Socorro textiles from Bogotá and foreign manufactured goods from Cartagena and Mompox. Medellín and Rionegro became the merchant capitalist centers of the country loaning to even the government in Bogotá.

Though all this wealth did lead to some ostentatiousnous, the successful Antioqueño was often seen, and liked to think of himself, as a self-made man who had risen from poverty through entrepreneurial skills, hard work, self-discipline and honesty. Indeed, writers of the day often scorned the new rich of Anioquia, as opposed to the refined elite of the Bogotá upper classes, as uncultured dolts. This idea of hard work, austerity and honesty added to a business sense combined with a scorn for poetry, music and the other trappings of culture. These attitudes were passed on to the youths of wealthy and middle class families, so that the entrepreneurial, merchant-capitalist character of the Antioqueño did not die out in a generation or two, but persists to this day.

The free market practices of the Antioqueños were furthered by the new president General Tomás Cipriano de Mosquera (1845-49). He pushed for increasing exports and the obvious commodity to work with was tobacco. Since colonial days tobacco had been a government monopoly providing revenue to Bogotá second only to customs duties. Production was limited to a few small areas that could be controlled. The price was thus kept high, so high that Colombian tobacco could not compete on the world market.

Under Mosquera, the government made a contract for tobacco production with an Antioqueño firm, Montoya Sácuz. Additional contracts were let and tobacco production spread from the lower Magdalena Valley to the upper Magdalena. Production increased by 30%. New Granada tobacco became competitive in the world markets finding a niche between the fine leaf of Cuba and the cheap tobacco of the United States. Annual exports doubled even as domestic consumption declined. When free cultivation was finally permitted, exports tripled. Tobacco became New Granada's first really successful export after gold.

Other exports were promoted, but the only one that showed any promise was cinchona bark used for making quinine. It became a major export for the country though considered inferior to the Bolivian and Peruvian product.

Mosquera also promoted an improved infrastructure, again with an eye to exports. A U.S. construction company was hired to build a railroad across the Panama isthmus. Roads were initiated to connect the Cauca Valley with the Pacific port of Buenaventura. Army units were put to work on improving cart trails between Bogotá and the Magdalena

River. But the most effective project was to replace the pole-boats plying the Magdalena with steam boats thus expanding exports, particularly tobacco.

Government revenues lost from giving up the tobacco monopoly were offset by money from increased custom duties because of the growth in trade. Mosquera lowered even these duties to free up trade even more which resulted in a backlash from Bogotá craftsmen and Eastern Cordillera textile manufacturers who now had to compete with imports.

Meanwhile, the upper-classes of New Granada began to consume European luxury imports, silks, clothing, leather goods and wine. Even commoners started buying the softer, though less durable, European finished clothing, women first and eventually men.

The presidential election of 1848 once again brought the political parties into serious conflict. The Conservatives were split between several candidates while the Liberals united behind General José Hilario López who won a plurality, but not a majority. By the constitution, this meant Congress would decide the issue. Conservatives outnumbered Liberals in the Congress, yet López won the vote. There were accusations of voter fraud and even intimidation methods used by Liberals.

The two parties agreed on the expansion of foreign trade and strengthening the power of the provinces versus the central government. They disagreed on the roll of the Catholic Church in society.

Pressed by imports, the craftsmen of Bogotá formed an artisan's society which became the Democratic Society of Bogotá. After the election of López it joined the Liberal movement.

In Cali, where Conservatives dominated, small farmers took up the Liberal cause forming bands that attacked the haciendas of Conservatives and even assaulted individuals. These attacks spread to Buga, Tuluá, Cartago and eventually throughout the Cauca Valley. Conservatives complained. Liberals in the government dismissed the accusations.

Jesuits, originally expelled by the Spanish in 1767, returned at the behest of the New Granada government in February 1844, to instruct the youth and provide proper discipline. The Society of Jesus was again ejected in 1850 by the Liberals of the López government.

After the 1848 election, the Conservatives tried to define their party as committed to religion, order, and morality. The party leaders also tried to appeal to the lower classes as the Liberals had done with the Democratic Society of Bogotá and the small farmers of the Cauca Valley. Societies and fraternities were formed all over Colombia under a variety of names. Soon these Conservative groups were clashing violently with Liberal organizations in Bogotá and in the Cauca Valley. The number of newspapers proliferated and took up the cause of one party or the other.

Conservatives had been reluctant participants in abolishing the tobacco monopoly where Liberals had taken the lead. But after the López election, their positions reversed.

In 1851, Liberals won a large majority in both houses of congress for the first time. The Liberal controlled government moved quickly to completely abolish slavery, important by then only in the Cauca Valley. Of more consequence was legislation affecting the Church. Priests would be tried in civil courts for civil and criminal matters instead of ecclesiastical courts and municipal councils would have a voice in choosing parish priests.

Actual rebellion and hostilities broke out in the Cauca Valley first, probably based on dissatisfaction over the abolition of slavery. Insurrection spread to Pasto where the Jesuit expulsion was of overriding concern. In late 1857, violence infected Antioquia and then Bogotá. By year's end the rebellion was crushed leaving the Liberals in unrestrained control.

The Conservatives didn't even enter a candidate in the 1852 election which General José María Obando won overwhelmingly. Obando was an old time traditional Liberal, but under his administration Congress came to be dominated by Conservatives who partnered with a new radical wing of the Liberal party known as Draconian Liberals. These two groups united to change the constitution to increases the autonomy of the provinces. Governors would be elected. Power was steadily shifted from the central government to the departments until New Granada became a country of mini-states.

The Draconians also pushed through measures that reduced the size of the military from 3,400 men to 2,500 and then 1,500, cutting the officer corps in half and weakening its political influence. Other innovations included the recognition of civil marriages, divorce, the separation of church and state, and the end of the death penalty.

Reacting to the threat to careers of many military officers, General José María Melo, head of the Bogotá garrison led a move to unite the military, politically, with the artisans of Bogotá in an attempt to retake the Liberal party from the Draconians. Congress reacted by passing a bill that would reduce the standing army to just 800 men commanded by a colonel (no generals at all) and eliminate the Bogotá garrison altogether. Obando vetoed the bill.

But the damage was done. Melo led a *coup d'estate* backed by the artisans of Bogotá. Melo took over the government as dictator reversing all those laws passed by the Conservatives and Draconians. He found support in the provinces among old non-radical Liberals thus splitting the party. Leaders of both parties united in opposition to Melo and, backed by the National Guard, defeated Melo in December 1851.

The split in the Liberal party allowed the Conservatives to gain power in the provinces, sometimes by violent means, using suppression of the revolution as an excuse. In the elections of 1855, the Conservatives gained control of both houses of congress and a Conservative, Mariano Ospina Rodríguez, was elected President in 1856.

Under the Conservatives decentralization of the central government continued. The laws passed by the Draconians were reinstated, civil marriage, election of provincial and local officials, etc. Further, Panama was given special status as a "sovereign federal state." Soon other provinces were pushing for the same privilege and by 1857, Congress had created the states of Santander, Cauca, Cundinamarca, Boyacá, Bolívar and Magdalena. The constitution had to be rewritten to accommodate the new states and in 1858 the Confederation of Granadina was created out of the old New Granada.

Panama's status as a sovereign state was part of an ongoing problem with the isthmus. As a transit point from one ocean to the other, Panama had been a hot issue since Balboa's trek across its jungles in 1513. First the Spanish and then the French and British had invaded its precincts. But with the discovery of gold in California, U.S. citizens had come to dominate the movement of people and goods across the isthmus. The port cities on either side of the isthmus were virtually taken over by North Americans who created local governments disregarding Panamanian and Colombian sovereignty over the area.

Ospin, worried about a total U.S. takeover of Panama, tried to entice either the French or British into guaranteeing Colombian rights over the area, but neither country was interested in sticking their neck out. Next he offered to allow annexation of both Panama and Colombia to the United States, but Washington had no interest. The situation was brought to a head by the "Melon Crisis" of 1856.

In April of that year, a North American killed a melon vendor in Panama. Nationalists stormed a railroad station where the Yankees were hold up for protection. The rioters broke in and the North Americans opened up with rifle fire. Two Panamanians were killed along with several North Americans.

The United States responded with a claim for a $400,000 indemnity and a demand that the two railroad terminus points, Colón and Panama be made independent municipalities joined by a 20 mile wide corridor along the tracks ceded to the U.S. along with two islands in Panama Bay to be used as U.S. Naval stations. Ospina lodged a counter claim for a $150,000 indemnity. Eventually, the crisis was settled without resolving any of the major issues.

As the Melon Crisis in Panama faded, Ospina faced a much more serious situation in the very core of his country. The decentralization of the central government and reduction of the standing army, now down to 500 men, left a power vacuum that was filled by the new states. Each was essentially autonomous and several created their own armies. The decentralization was meant to defuse the struggle between the two parties and eliminate the associated violence, but it only moved the scene of conflict from Bogotá to the individual states. Conservatives in Santander revolted against the Liberal state government. Liberals in Bolívar overthrew the Conservative government. Liberals in southern Santander invaded Conservative Boyacá. And so it went.

Ospina, to gain some control, instituted a new office, Inspector of Public Matters in each state.

This attempt to reassert some dominance by the Bogotá government was met by rebellion, particularly in Cauca. Here General Mosquera had been elected governor and he championed the cause of the independent minded states. Leading a Liberal army he set out for Bogotá. Ospina mobilized the puny Confederation army, but was outmaneuvered by Mosquera and his Liberals who took Bogotá in July 1861. That should have ended the war, but it dragged on in the various states until 1863.

With the war finally concluded in February of 1863, a new constitutional convention was called in Rionegro. Here Liberal representatives gathered from the nine states (Tolima had been added under Mosquera). Conservatives were completely excluded.

However, the Liberals were divided between the Radicals and the Mosquera moderates. The Radicals feared Mosquera's dictatorial tendencies. Having a slight majority, they were able to incorporate a presidential term limit of two years into a constitution designed to deal with the new sovereign states more effectively. The central government would benefit from customs duties, but most other taxes would go to the states. Thus the central government and the president in particular were rendered nearly impotent.

Radical Liberals ruled from 1864 to 1880. Presidents came and went in rapid succession, some removed by force, Mosquera in 1867. Yet under this weak government improvements were made. Entrepreneurial efforts not just in Antioquia, but in other areas as well increased exports, tobacco, cinchona bark, dye-woods, medicinals, sarsaparilla and ipecac. Colombian coffee began to make its mark in the world markets and rose to be the country's third largest export.

Roads were improved and the first inter-state railroads were built. Bogotá's first commercial bank was chartered. Note-issuing banks soon appeared in all commercial centers in the country. During this period some regional barriers were lowered and more of the country gained access to overseas commerce.

The closing decades of the Nineteenth Century saw the gradual emergence of the Colombia we know today. Symbolically, a national anthem was adopted and a coat of arms to go with the national tricolor flag used since colonial days.

Two civil wars were fought. The first, in 1876, was a rebellion in Cauca over voting irregularities perpetuated by Radical Liberals and over the teaching of religion in the schools. The Caucano Conservatives were handily defeated.

A second civil war in 1885 began in the state of Santander, where a disputed presidential election had been won by a coalition candidate. The Radical Liberals rebelled and the insurrection spread to the coastal region. Rafael Núñez of Cartagena, as president of the Confederation, put down the revolt and then called for a constitutional convention. Colombia needed a legal foundation that worked.

The constitution written in 1886, though often amended, would last until 1991. The Council of Delegates was made up of eighteen members, two from each state, one Liberal and one Conservative, appointed by the state's presidents. This new constitution strengthened the central government. The president's term was lengthened to six years. The states were reduced to departments to be run by governors appointed by the president. The death penalty was reinstated and laws restricting firearms, freedom of the press and public assembly were included. Most tax revenues reverted to the national government. Many of the privileges enjoyed by the Catholic Church stripped during the Radical Liberal era were restored. A monopoly on marriage, the responsibility for educating the youth and recognition as the state religion characterized the new alliance between church and state.

At the conclusion of the convention the Council unanimously elected Núñes as president. The period known as the Regeneration had begun. This era that was to last through the end of the century would affect events well into the Twentieth Century. It was a time of nationalism with an anti-liberal, anti-Yankee, anti-capitalist tenor.

The government of the Regeneration period became progressively more conservative, especially with the death of Núñez in 1894, alienating the Liberals. Finally, in October of 1899, the Liberals rebelled beginning the War of a Thousand Days. The conflict began as a conventional war, but the government with its new army of 6,500 men defeated the Liberals at which point the Liberals turned to guerilla tactics. Over the next two and a half years, Liberal insurgents were crushed in department after department until the last vestiges of rebellion were confined to Panama.

This civil war had two serious consequences for the nation. The end of the Regeneration occurred when the Vice-President, José Manuel Marroquín, ousted the president in a coup d'estat in 1900. The second was the loss of Panama.

Flooded by foreigners and tangled in construction, Panama had been on the verge of secession for some time. The final stage of the War of a Thousand Days, being played out in that department only served to exacerbate the situation.

In 1879, the Frenchman Ferdinand de Lesseps, already famous for the construction of the Suez Canal, formed the New French Company and contracted with the Colombian government to build a canal across the isthmus. Construction began in 1882, but Lesseps was defeated in his attempt by a bad design concept, malaria and the worst political scandal of the Third French Republic.

After the collapse of the French effort, the United States took up the challenge. The U.S. acquired the rights from the New French Company and signed a treaty with Colombia in 1903. Unfortunately, the Colombian senate rejected the treaty. Liberal rebels, Panamanian separatists and foreigners, backed by the U.S. Navy declared Panama's independence. The United States recognized the new republic in November of 1903.

During the Regeneration Era migration from the high mountains into the lower altitudes had accelerated, particularly in Antioquia. By the turn of the century, Colombia had a total population of about 5.5 million people, still a land vastly under populated. Though the nation had expanses of land between the cordilleras, not to mention the eastern Llanos, selva and west coast, to be settled, these were at lower altitudes where yellow fever, malaria and parasites were a major problem. Still the migration continued fueled by people hungry for land.

Coffee continued to grow in importance as an export. First produced by small farmers of the Eastern Cordillera, its cultivation spread and large haciendas began to participate in its production and marketing. The expansion of the coffee industry also facilitated the growth of the railroad system and helped break down regional barriers. But railroad construction was slowed because of the lack of capital and the difficulty of building rail lines in the mountainous terrain.

The loss of Panama certainly brought into sharp focus Colombia's need to deal with the colossus of the north. Up to that point Europeans had played the major roll in Colombian external affairs. Explored by Spaniards and Germans, colonized by Spain from whom independence had been won with the help of British citizens, and then there was the French canal contract. Colombia had been able to select its associations between several European countries, in some cases even playing them off against each other. But in the future, the nation would be, negotiating primarily with this new power in its own hemisphere, a relationship that would run hot and cold, and end, at least for forty-one Peace Corps Volunteers, with very direct person-to-person contact. How friendly or adversarial that contact might be would depend on the events and dealings between these two countries in the Twentieth Century leading up to their arrival.

The association had not gotten off to an auspicious start with the forced loss of a section of Colombia's territory. This was mitigated somewhat by the payment of an indemnity of $25 million between 1922 and 1926. But even this money was tied to negotiations over the exploration for oil in Colombia. Because of the money, U.S. companies gained an advantage over British petroleum interests. Colombia's position was dealt a blow, however, when it was determined the major oil reserves in northern South America were in Venezuela, and weakened still further with the huge middle eastern oil field discoveries. Oil would not become a major Colombian export, at least not in the immediate future.

Not a mineral, but an agricultural product, coffee, would become Colombia's chief export, replacing the country's perennial and dependable asset, gold. Haiti had been the

364

world's leading coffee producer in the 1700s, but in the Nineteenth Century cultivation spread to Jamaica, Cuba and Puerto Rico, then to Mexico, Central America, Brazil and Venezuela. From Venezuela coffee production migrated into the Eastern Cordillera. At the same time, world consumption of coffee expanded and the United States emerged as the major consumer.

Though Brazil came to dominate the coffee trade in terms of quantity, Colombia was the second largest producer by 1920 and its mild coffee was highly valued. Cultivation spread from the Eastern Cordillera to the central mountains. With the opening of the Panama Canal in 1914, the Western Cordillera increased production. Exports could now reach Atlantic markets from the port of Buenaventura via a Canal. Cali became the terminus of transportation lines where the prized bean was collected and shipped to the Pacific port. In the 1920s coffee represented 70% of Colombian exports; by the 1980s it had achieved 80%.

Increasingly, the primary consumer was the United States. In the 1800s half of Colombia's coffee went to the U.S. and half to European markets. By the mid 1950s, 90% was being shipped to the United States.

Colombian coffee markets were controlled by Medellín exporters early on, but they went broke at the beginning of the Great Depression. The vacuum was readily filled by U.S. companies who dominated until the 1930s when they were squeezed out by a Colombian organization that came to control the country's coffee industry.

The Federation of Coffee Growers (the *Cafeteros*) was founded in 1927 as a private concern interested in resting control of the Colombian coffee market away from the U.S. companies. The Federation organized the coffee growers, fixed prices, classified and certified the grades and quality of coffee and established repositories to store excess beans enabling the organization to control prices.

The Federation became even more powerful with the establishment of the National Coffee Fund. As a result of the First Inter-American Quota Pact which required all coffee producing countries to hold back a portion of their harvest to control the world price, the Colombian government created the National Coffee Fund in 1940 to purchase the country's harvest. It was a government program funded by two taxes on coffee, but administration was turned over to the Federation of Coffee Growers. The Federation, now a semi-government agency, had a complete monopoly on the country's number one export. But this also gave it tremendous leverage in negotiating international contracts.

Through the 1950s the Federation financed, insured, stored, transported and marketed Colombian coffee. It dealt with the large haciendas and the small grower who could still compete because the labor intensive nature of coffee production limits the advantages of scale.

The growers of the coffee industry also led to the change of emphasis in the method of transportation. In the early 1930s, the priority switched from railroads to highways, an infrastructure much more compatible with Colombia's mountainous terrain. In the 1940s, automotive transportation passed rail as the primary means of moving cargo within the country.

Though coffee had replaced gold as Colombia's principle export, there were other agricultural products important to the country's economy. Bananas, grown by large and small sized farmers, were marketed abroad by the United Fruit Company of Boston, Massachusetts. United Fruit, with holdings in Central America, arrived in the Santa

Marta area just before the turn of the century and monopolized the export market of Colombian bananas. Tension between United Fruit and Colombian laborers come to a head in 1928, when the workers went on strike for higher wages and better working conditions. The strike was put down by soldiers firing into a mass of strikers killing thirteen.

While the United Fruit monopoly did survive the strike, it did not fair as well against another adversary. Sigatoka disease devastated the Santa Marta region in 1943 and United Fruit moved its operation to Urabá. But its monopoly was broken and by 1960 much of the industry was in the hands of Colombian companies.

Besides bananas, dye wood and other valuable woods were being reaped from the forests of the Chocó and Urabá. A good share of these products was being plundered illegally.

But the real pillaging was being done in the Amazon jungles of Colombia. Here the prize was a product known by the Incas and Aztects, and used by the Indians of the jungles for a millennium. They painted it on their feet and ankles to make water proof "boots." The prize was wild rubber – Amazon gold. The rise of the automobile created a demand for the elastic substance and the wild rubber industry of the Amazon Basin boomed. The *caudillos* (chiefs) who invaded Colombia to profit from this bonanza were ruthless and unprincipled.

Tomás Funes established an empire, based in the upper Orinoco, that included much of Colombia's Vichada Territory between 1913 and 1921. Julio César Arana, headquartered in Peru controlled vast areas of the Colombian Caquetá and Putumayo.

With little government oversight in these areas, both men ran organizations that exploited and abused the llaneros, Indians and migrant laborers. Violence, political corruption, murder, slavery and sexual abuses were the common *modus apperandi.*

Seizure of Leticia, Colombia's port town on the Amazon River, even ignited a short war between Colombia and Peru. Colombia recovered its outlet to the great river by sending a commandeered United Fruit ship loaded with troops from the Caribbean down the coast and up the Amazon – there are no roads between the Cordilleras and Leticia. The incident did provoke wide spread patriotism throughout Colombia.

As suddenly as the rubber boom of the Amazon had blossomed, it died. Seeds from Brazil were used to start plantations in Malaya and Ceylon. Soon rubber was being grown on plantations in Indonesia, Thailand, Indochina, and the Philippines. The demand for the wild rubber of South America dried up.

The Great Depression did not have as serious an effect on Colombia as it did on the more industrialized nations. But it did usher in a period of Liberal rule and a move toward more government centralization. Presidents were Liberal radicals or moderates. The period from 1930 to 1946 is known as the "Liberal Republic" era.

At the same time there was growth in the cities. Urban growth began to accelerate in the 1930s and reached a maximum in the 1950s. In 1938, Bogotá had less than a half million people. By 1958, it had over 2 million. Medellín, Cali and other cities experienced growth, but at a slower rate.

This period, during and after the Depression, also saw a policy of promoting industrialization. Tariff barriers were raised against imported manufactured goods and favorable loans were made available to start up enterprises. Light industry did develop in Bogotá, Cali, Medellín, and Barranquia principally and even some limited heavy industry. But internal markets proved inadequate to foster the kind of industrial expansion seen in the U.S. and European countries. The importation of automobiles, manufacturing equipment and parts for assembly, though expensive, remained important aspects of the Colombian economy.

The Liberal Republic era came to an end with the election of 1946. As before, the Liberal candidate, Gabriel Turbay, appeared to be on the path to continue his party's dominance when a dissident interfered. This was Jorge Eliécer Gaitán, a rising populist who appealed to the new urban populations. He and Turbay split the Liberal vote allowing the Conservative, Mariano Opina Pérez to win the election.

Liberal losses were not confined to the presidency. In the Congressional elections of 1946-47, the Liberal majority was dramatically reduced and many city councils across the country became Conservative dominated.

As the shock of the political turn around began to register, the number of killings in urban areas rose significantly. It has been estimated that 14,000 people died violent deaths in 1947.

To protest this violence, Gaitán organized a gathering of his supporters in the Plaza de Bolívar in Bogotá in February 1948. 100,000 people assembled dressed in morning black. Though suppressed by the Liberal party leaders, Gaitán had demonstrated he was the people's choice and would be the Liberal candidate to restore Liberal control of the government in the next election.

However, on April 9, 1948, Gaitán was assassinated as he left his office in central Bogotá for lunch. The perpetrator was never apprehended, but Gaitán's supporters believed his murder was the result of a plot. Mass rioting broke out in Bogotá and across the country. This violent outburst became known as the *Bogotázo* because of the concentration of violence in the capital, but it is also called *El Nueva de Abril,* indicating there were riots in the other cities and even in small municipalities especially where Liberals were a majority. In such places Conservative government officials were often killed, their bodies mutilated.

La Violencia which began with the election of 1946 and its violent aftermath reached a fever pitch. President Ospina tried to build a coalition government, but it fell apart in less than a year and the chasm between the two parties widened. At the local level, killings and reprisal killings continued unabated.

The election of 1949 merely served to exacerbate the situation. The Conservative candidate, Laureano Gómez, won an uncontested election as the Liberal party abstained from entering a candidate and from voting in order to delegitimize the election.

Gómez stepped up pacification programs and was successful, for the most part, in the departments of Nariño, the Santanders, Boyacá and the upper Cauca Valley. Liberal resistance shifted to the eastern side of the Eastern Cordillera, to the llanos of Casanare and Meta, to the Urrao region of Antioquia, the Lower Cauca, Middle Magdalena and Tolima. In these areas, the Liberal resistance began to organize into guerrilla bands. On the Llanos the units were particularly well organized to the point they were able to tax the local cattle operations. In northern Cauca and southern Tolima, these bands were tainted with Communist affiliations.

To counter the Liberal guerrilla bands, Conservatives organized pro-government paramilitary groups that committed the same kinds of atrocities, murder, rape, looting, pillaging, that the Liberal bands were guilty of. With the creation of these bands and groups, however, the violence took on more of a civil war character, less family oriented less personal revenge and more political, Liberal versus Conservative. The guerillas operated in rural areas, the plains and mountains. They were led by *cadillos* with picturesque nicknames like Songruenegro (Blackblood), Terofejo (Sureshot) and Desquite (Revenge). Farmers, small towns and rural committees suffered. Something like 100,000 to 400,000 people died in this violence.

Amazingly, the country, in general, prospered during the early stages of La Violencia. Coffee prices were up and the economy grew steadily. Gómez even sent an army battalion and one naval vassal to the Korean Conflict. Colombia was the only Latin American country to participate it the war and their units performed admirably according to U.S. commanders that worked with them.

Violence in Colombia abated somewhat in late 1951 and early 1952, but spiked again in late 1952, after Conservative mobs sacked the offices of the two leading Liberal newspapers, *El Tiempo* and *El Espectador*.

Because of La Violencia, Gómez was able to declare a state of siege and rule with almost dictatorial powers. He even suspended Congress from the end of 1949 through 1951. But it was this same La Violencia that was his undoing.

As the gulf between the two parties widened and the bitterness grew, public confidence in Goméz descended to new depths. He seemed to be unable to cope with La Violencia and was under increasing pressure from the Liberal majority in Congress.

Finally, on June 13, 1953, General Rojas Pinilla, head of Colombian armed forces, dismissed Gómez and took control of the government in a *coup e'stat*. Pinilla offered amnesty to any guerillas willing to surrender. Many of the guerilla bands, particularly in the Llanos and Tolima, demobilized and the worst of the partisan violence came to an end.

Though the remaining bands nominally claimed linkage with one political party or the other, after 1954 they became progressively more like criminal bandits. Around Caldas, the Quindío and in northeastern Tolima, these armed gangs could devastate coffee growers by driving off the labor at critical times, like harvest. Murder and raids on opposition haciendas was all to frequent. Violence might be politically motivated or done for pay. If one could generalize at all, it could be said that the Conservative bandits concentrated on the coffee growers where as the Liberal gangs leaned toward rustling cattle.

At the end of the 1950s and early 1960s, there was the very real problem of bandits roaming the mountains as Jerry Brelage and Arlene Ratliff could testify. But these guerilla groups were left over from the Violencia. They had not become involved in the illicit drug industry. That was yet to come.

It is during this period the revolutionary and Communist organizations began to emerge. Fuerzas Armados Revolucionarias de Colombia (FARC) had its roots in this era. Headed by Manual Marulanda of Génova, Quindío, nicknamed Tiro Fijo (Sureshoot), this group began as a champion of peasant causes, but later incorporated a Marxist ideology. Unlike FARC, which was wholly home grown, Ejército de Leberacíon Nacional (ELN) was inspired by the Cuban Revolution and the doctrines of Che Guevara – revolution to begin in the countryside among the peasants then blossom into urban civil war. Another Cuban influenced band was the 19th of April Movement (M-19) and there were other smaller groups.

Pinilla had changed the character of La Violencia, but had not been able to end it. This combined with a decline in Coffee prices after 1955, helped to produce a stagnate economy. The people of Colombia were ready for a change.

The groundwork for a new approach was laid by Liberal ex-president Alberto Lleras Camargo and Laureano Gómez who was in exile. They concocted a new scheme to put down La Violencia once and for all. Under their plan, refined by leaders of both parties, all aspects of the government would be shared equally. The presidency would alternate between the two parties, each one serving one term before turning the office over to the other party. Congress would be split 50/50. The same rules of parity applied in departmental assemblies, municipal councils, governors, mayors, etc. This bipartisan arrangement was known as the National Front. It was the system of government in effect when the Colombian 64 Peace Corps Volunteers arrived and would continue throughout their stay.

In May 1957 the country's businesses and professionals staged a general strike against the Pinilla regime. Workers, who were locked out, made no protest to show support for the president and Rojas Pinilla quietly exited the country. The military ruled during a plebiscite that allowed voters to approve the new constitutional rules. Then elections were carried out under the new electoral system of the National Front.

Though an observer might expect the election to be sterile, similar to one party rule, it was not. Lively campaigns were conducted with Liberals running against Liberals and Conservatives vying for their assigned offices. The first president elected under the new system was the Liberal, Alberto Lleras Camargo. The second National Front president (1962 to 1966) was Guillermo León Valencia an old style, but well meaning, politician who was chief of state while the Colombia '64 group was in country.

The election held while we were in Colombia was anything but dull. I wrote about it at the time:

> Carlos Lleras R. is the Liberal candidate and therefore the candidate of both parties. The papers are full of the campaigning for him and of the head of the other party, Mariano Opina P.
>
> But today in the paper at the bottom of the front page there is an article about Gustavo Rojas Pinilla, one time dictator of Colombia, and his disastrous attempt at a campaign speech in Popayán, at least that is the way the paper put it. There are posters around promoting everyone and his brother, but that doesn't seem to mean much. Actually, I am told, that there are three other candidates besides Lleras, Rojas, a Communist, and another candidate who I never heard of.[1]

The National Front put an end to the confrontational election process that had led to so much violence. The central government then went after the bandit groups capturing or killing nearly all their leaders and forcing them to disband. Violent crime dropped sharply. Army units were stationed in the most notorious areas and a special mounted division of the national police, the Carabineros, was stationed at strategic points in rural areas to maintain control.

Efforts were made to improve the rural educational system. Nucleos, national government sponsored grade schools, were located in the areas of the worst violence and

---

[1] Gary Peterson, *Colombian Diary,* Jan. 29, 1966.

a nationwide educational television network for municipal and rural schools was constructed.

This was the government and political situation while the Colombia '64 Volunteers were in Colombia. It was a time of relative peace in between La Violencia and the drug wars that had not yet taken root, a window of opportunity to move this country forward and make things better for an industrious and talented people.

Made in the USA
Lexington, KY
18 October 2013